SIXTH EDITION 6

Technical Communication

商务沟通与写作（上）

（第6版）

Rebecca E. Burnett

IOWA STATE UNIVERSITY

北京大学出版社
PEKING UNIVERSITY PRESS

北京市版权局著作权合同登记号 图字 [01-2010-4301] 号

图书在版编目 (CIP) 数据

商务沟通与写作 · 上 = Technical Communication (Sixth Edition) /（美）伯奈特 (Burnett R. E.) 著. —北京：北京大学出版社，2011.1

（商务英语写作系列丛书）

ISBN 978-7-301-18347-2

Ⅰ. 商… Ⅱ. 伯… Ⅲ. ①商业管理—公共关系学—教材—英文 ②商务—英语—应用文—写作—教材 Ⅳ. ①F715 ②H315

中国版本图书馆 CIP 数据核字（2010）第 260412 号

Technical Communication (Sixth Edition)

Rebecca E. Burnett

Cengage Learning Asia Pte. Ltd.

5 Shenton Way, # 01-01 UIC Building, Singapore 068808

书　　名：**Technical Communication (Sixth Edition)**

商务沟通与写作（第 6 版）（上）

著作责任者：［美］Rebecca E. Burnett 著

责 任 编 辑：黄瑞明

标 准 书 号：ISBN 978-7-301-18347-2/H · 2729

出 版 发 行：北京大学出版社

地　　址：北京市海淀区成府路 205 号　100871

网　　址：http://www.pup.cn

电　　话：邮购部 62752015　发行部 62750672　编辑部 62754382　出版部 62754962

电 子 邮 箱：zbing@pup.pku.edu.cn

印　刷　者：山东省高唐印刷有限责任公司

发　行　者：新华书店

787 毫米 ×960 毫米　16 开本　23.25 印张　300 千字

2011 年 1 月第 1 版　2011 年 1 月第 1 次印刷

定　　价：48.00 元

专家委员会

总 序

北京大学出版社继《英语写作原版引印系列丛书》之后，2010年，又专题引进商务英语写作原版系列教材。这套教材体系完整，应用性强，商务内容丰富，十分贴近英语教学改革的需要和广大学生提升未来就业能力的需求，填补了我国商务英语写作领域内没有高质量商务英语写作教材的空白，并得到15所商务英语专业院校教学协作组和中国英语写作教学专业委员会相关专家的联合推荐。

随着我国对外开放的不断深入，高水平的商务英语写作人才一将难求，能用地道规范的英文起草法律合同、撰写咨询报告的专业写作人才更是凤毛麟角，部分国际咨询机构提供的一份英文公司咨询报告价格高达百万美元，如此激烈的竞争值得我们认真反思现有的写作教学。即将出台的高等学校商务英语专业本科教学要求（试行）明确指出，商务英语写作是学生的核心能力，商务英语专业应加大毕业设计的比重，鼓励学生采用商务报告（如市场调研报告、商业计划书、营销方案等）多种形式。而全面提升商务英语写作能力，按照过去传统的写作教学模式，已无法适应，必须要有新的改革思路，要改变“费时低效”的困境，就必须做到以下几个转变：(1）从重写作技能转向技能与内容并重；(2）从传统写作教学转向机辅写作教学模式；(3）从开设单一写作课转向开设写作课程群；(4）从大班课堂写作教学转向个性化写作教学中心。通过对美国普林斯顿大学、英国华威大学等世界名校的考察，我们建议，可分阶段分层次为不同水平的学生开设商务英语写作课程群（Writing Portfolio)，具体可包括：基础英语写作、国际贸易写作、国际营销写作、金融英语写作、法律英语写作、学术英语写作、财经新闻写作、商务函电写作、商务报告写作、职业应用文写作等，全面提升学生的写作能力。

本套系列教材在国外畅销经久不衰，多次再版或重印，此次由北京大学出版社首批引进出版10本：《商务沟通：以读者为中心的方法》（上、下册）、《商务沟通与写作》（上、下册）、《最新商务报告写作》（上、下册）、《职场英语写作》（上、下册）、《成功商务英语写作》（上、下册），由对外经济贸易大学商务英语写作教学团队的教师魏明博士、冯海颖博士、杨颖莉博士、李玉霞博士、尹珏林博士分别撰写导读。

本套丛书既是职场英语写作的优质教材，又是商务写作的经典教材，教材深入浅出，语言简明，可帮助学生理解、记忆和应对多种国际商务场合下的写作需求。通过本丛书的学习和训练，学生可提高写作水平，为踏入职场做好准备。本套丛书可用作全国大专院校的商务英语学生和教师的写作课教材和参考书，还可供经管类学生学习商务英语写作之用，同时也可供爱好商务英语写作的广大社会读者和各类公司企业人员提高英语写作使用。

中国英语写作教学专业委员会主任

对外经济贸易大学英语学院院长

教授、博士生导师

王立非

2010 年国庆节于北京

导 读

一、本书的特色

1. 作者简介

Rebecca Burnett 现为佐治亚理工学院教授。2007 年自依阿华州立大学退休，曾任该大学修辞与专业交流高级教授，获“杰出教师”之美誉。Burnett 为《商务与专业交流》杂志前主编。她同时在多家美国大型公司担任专家鉴定人与交流顾问等职。她的研究领域包括专业交流、团队合作、交流评估、跨文化交流和风险沟通等。

2. 本书特色

《商务沟通与写作》自 1986 年以来已再版五次。本书内容覆盖面广，涉及从商务领域到学术领域各行各业的专业交流；交流的形式也不仅限于文本，而把口头报告、视图设计、网络交流也考虑在内；不仅详细介绍了交流的过程与步骤，还具体分析了职场常见的各种体裁。

作者提出评估专业交流的标准是可读性、可理解性与可用性，并以此标准贯穿全书。此书自身其实就是可读性、可理解性与可用性的典范。全书设计精致，插图丰富，结构清晰；有来自不同领域的新鲜实例，示例文本有边际注解以鼓励读者批判性的评估；每章有边栏讨论相关的一个职业道德问题；本书还有配套网站，每章附有众多网络链接，学习者因而可以了解更多相关内容；每章后的个体与协作任务也极具实用价值。

3. 使用对象与方法

鉴于其可读性和实用性，无论是在校学生还是职场人士，阅读此书都将获益匪浅。对于开设商务交流或高级写作的大学教师来说，此书也是难得的好教材；配套的教师专用网站可为教师提供丰富的教学资料。

二、本书内容

本书共有十六章，分为四部分。

第一部分 职场中的交流

第一章 职场交流特点

定义了职场交流为各行各业之话语活动，如撰写与制作专业文件、口头报告，以及视图等。讨论了职场交流的重要性，引导读者思考体裁、科技与职业道德在职场交流中的角色；以具体的例证说明如何使职场交流更具可读性、更易懂、更可用，以及影响交流的各种限制性因素。

第二章 理解文化与职场的关系

定义并解析了国家文化、机构文化以及身处文化中的个体。文化影响着工作场所的交流，因此无论机构 / 公司采取全球化或本地化策略，都应增强文化意识，了解并尊重不同文化。

第三章 阅读技术信息

专业人士需阅读文件、聆听口头报告和观看视图文件来了解背景信息，评估并做出决定，学习并最终完成某项任务。该章讨论了读与写之间的相互影响，以及有效的阅读策略。

第四章　满足交流对象需求

职场交流服务于两大目的：传递信息并说服读者 / 听众关注此项信息。因此了解读者 / 听众，分析他们的教育背景、工作经历、阅读能力、工作环境与职务都至关重要。该章讨论了如何针对读者 / 听众不同水平的专业技能调整材料的复杂度，针对他们不同的职务调整内容的选择。

第五章　职场中的合作

讨论了合作在职场中的重要性，合作中可能出现的问题，以及合作者应有的行为与技巧。良好的合作须避免情感（人际）冲突，协调潜在的程序冲突，鼓励关于实质问题的冲突。

第二部分　掌握信息筛选过程

第六章　搜集与使用信息

讨论了在交流前如何搜索与使用各类电子资源；如何采用其他手段如访谈、调查等收集资料；在采用信息资源的同时如何避免踏入剽窃的误区。

第七章　设计与起草

介绍了在交流前勘察、设计以及起草的技巧。勘察阶段可采用头脑风暴法、因果或综合分析法等技巧。设计阶段采用项目管理工具，思考所需交流的内容、目的、对象、结构和设计等因素，评估交流的内在逻辑。起草阶段则需考虑如何选择恰当的人称和动词语气，使用平实的语言，采用“已知—新信息”的组句结构等。

第八章　修改与编辑

修改侧重于整体，而编辑侧重于具体与局部。该章介绍了修改与编辑的过程、技巧以及需要注意的问题，并以一可行性报告为例分析了修改与编辑的重要性。

第九章　确保可用性

专业交流需确保可用性，即把使用者放在首位，满足不同目的与技巧的人们在各种复杂情境下的需求。该章介绍了三类可用性测试（基于文本的、基于专家的和基于使用者的），以及可用性测试的全过程（从建立可用性测试计划，到分析使用者与任务，到实施测试，到最后报告测试结果）。

第三部分　信息梳理

第十章　组织信息

介绍了如何利用大纲、故事板和表格来组织信息，如何利用主题句和过渡词 / 句来标志结构，如何利用六种传统结构形式——整体 / 部分、时间顺序、空间顺序、升 / 降序、比较 / 对比、因果——来展示信息。

第十一章　设计信息

为了有效地结合视图和文字来组织和展示信息以增加可读性、可理解性和可用性，该章介绍了一些利用页面空白、对齐方式、行间距和行长、标题、字体等来设计信息的技巧。

第十二章　使用视觉形式

介绍了各种视觉形式——图表、绘画、地图、照片等——在现代职场交流中的重要性及功能，并建议了如何正确、妥当地使用颜色。

第十三章　设计电子交流

基于网络的电子信息交流，是互动而非线性的，虚拟而开放的，复杂而动态的。为满足可读性和可用性，该章介绍了设计网站所需注意的几个因素：信息架构、网页设计和内容；具体讲解了如何组织、标识以及导航信息，如何设计界面，包括留白、滚屏、导航、颜色和图片，如何使内容更适应屏幕阅读的特点等。

第四部分　理解交流者采用的策略

第十四章　创建定义

在职场沟通中，情境化的定义是必不可少的。针对多变的词义及读者不同的理解能力，该章介绍了正式定义、非正式定义、归纳步骤的操作性定义以及扩充性定义。非正式定义包括同义、反义、否定、限定、类比、例释六类；而扩充性定义包括介绍词源、历史及举例。

第十五章　创建技术描述

技术描述概括物质特性，解答读者关于某一物体、物质、机制、有机组织、系统或位置的外观及组成的疑问。写一篇好的技术描述，我们需要了解读者的需求和目的，确定物质的结构和功能组成，选择精确而生动的措辞，设计直观而有效的视图，以空间顺序来安排说明文的结构。

第十六章　创建过程解释

过程解释不同于操作指南（后者见第二十一章）；过程解释提供足够的信息让读者了解某一行为或过程，而非引导读者完成这一行为或过程。写过程解释，我们同样需要了解读者需求，确定具体步骤，使用各种视图（如流程图），选择恰当措辞（如根据具体情况选择主动或被动语态），以时间顺序来组织文章结构。

三、推荐相关参考书

1. 常玉田，2010，《商务报告写作》，高等教育出版社。

2. 段平等编，2010，《专业信息交流英语教程》，中国人民大学出版社。

3. Jean Wyrick, 2008，《成功写作入门》（英文版）（第 10 版），北京大学出版社。

4. Bonnie L. Tensen, 2008，《数字时代写作研究策略》（英文版）（第 2 版），北京大学出版社。

5. Steven H. Gale, 2008，《公司管理写作策略》（英文版），北京大学出版社。

6. David Rosrnwasser, 2008，《分析性写作》（英文版）（第 5 版），北京大学出版社。

7. Edward P. Bailey, 2010，《实用写作》（英文版）（第 9 版），北京大学出版社。

8. Cheng, W. & Kong, K. (2009). *Professional communication: Collaboration between academics and practitioners*. Hong Kong: Hong Kong University Press.

9. Guffey, M. E. & Du-Babcock, B. (2008). *Essentials of business communication*. Singapore: Thomsom.

10. Lannon, J. M. (2008). Technical communication. Longman.

11. Pfeiffer, W. S. (2006). Technical communication: A practical approach. Beijing: Publishing House of Electronics Industry.

对外经济贸易大学

冯海颖

译 者 序

《商务沟通与写作（第 6 版）》的主要目的是帮助学生和在职人员面对各种读者（客户）需求时能进行有效的书面、口头和视觉上的信息交流。本书依据最新理论、研究和实践成果，用简明直白的语言解释了进行有效信息交流的方式和方法。设计精巧实用，提供了很多文本、数据和表格实例。本书设计的讨论和课堂练习可以帮助使用者成为更好的交流者。本书易读易教，强调创作有效书面和电子文档的过程是反复综合的过程，鼓励学生把创作和修改看成是不断发展的过程，把视觉方式看成是展现信息的手段，并重视语言在影响读者对信息内容评判中的重要作用。

本书使用者在进行信息交流的过程中将学会对修辞相关因素如语境、内容、目的、对象、组织、视觉手段及设计等的使用做出决断，并且了解做出各种交流方式决定的原因。本书不仅涉及信息交流中与修辞技巧相关的传统内容，即技巧（如定义、描述及过程）和形式（如信件、指南、提案和报告），而且详细描述了关于合作、职业道德、视觉手段及设计方面的内容以及扩展了国际交流、可用度测试和技术方面的讨论。与以前的版本相比，本书有以下变化：

- 增加了评估标准。第一章介绍了本书采用的可访性、理解性及可用性等标准来分析和评估书面、口头和视觉交流的效果。
- 增加了新例子。这些例子多与国际热点相关，如科技革新、药学发展、疾病控制、食品生产、生态平衡。
- 国际流行重点。许多国家的国际性企业的业务交流强调使用文本和视觉例子。
- 增加了关于文化的章节。第二章“理解文化与职场的关系”阐释了国际和企业文化及其对本企业员工的影响。
- 增加了关于可用性的章节。第九章“确保可用性”描述了可用性和可用性测试的特点，介绍了进行各种测试的指导原则，区分了可访性和可用性。
- 增加了关于技术的章节。技术内容贯穿全书。第十三章“设计电子交流”突出了各种新媒体的特点。
- 更多注释。本书样例配有更多的注释。
- 增加了职业道德注释栏。每个章节都有一个职业规范注释栏，讨论专业人士可能遇到的职业道德方面的冲突。
- 增加了网址链接。本书每个章节列举的网址可以通过本书的网址链接。这些网址提供了很多相关例子和文章，供进一步讨论。
- 增加了图片。本书新增图片阐释了工作中如何创作和使用技术文件、口头展示和视觉手段。

本书共分四部分十六章。第一部分包括五章，介绍了职场交流的主要内容。第二部分包括四章，讨论了信息筛选的主要过程。第三部分包括四章，讨论了如何整理收集到的信息。第四部分包括三章，讨论了交流者在信息交流准备中采用的策略。

北京外国语大学英语学院

杨鲁新

CONTENTS IN BRIEF
简要目录

CONTENTS
目 录

9. Ensuring Usability 确保可用性 305

PART III Shaping Information 信息梳理 343

10. Organizing Information 组织信息 345

PREFACE
前言

Technical Communication, Sixth Edition, has a clear goal: to help students and workplace professionals communicate technical information — written, oral, and visual — to audiences in a variety of complex workplace contexts.

Technical Communication, Sixth Edition, presents straightforward explanations and guidelines based on current theory, research, and practice. The elegant, usable design of this edition enables students to use many of the text's pages, figures, and tables as models. The discussions and the classroom-tested exercises and assignments, both individual and collaborative, help users become better communicators. This highly readable and teachable edition stresses the integrated, recursive nature of producing effective print and electronic documents, encouraging students to think of invention and revision as ongoing processes, to think of visuals as ways to present information, and to think of language as having the power to shape and influence users' perceptions.

What's the approach? This edition emphasizes a rhetorical, problem-solving approach. Users of this text will learn to make decisions about rhetorical elements such as context, content, purpose, audience, organization, visuals, and design as they engage in the process of communicating technical information. In addition, they will learn the *reasons* behind their communication decisions.

Users of this text — both traditional and nontraditional students as well as workplace professionals — will learn that effective technical communication contains both creativity and craft, a point I make by the continued use of Leonardo da Vinci's technical drawings on all the chapters openers throughout the book. Like Leonardo da Vinci's technical drawings, technical communication should be precise, detailed, functional, and focused. That's not all it should be; it's the least it should be.

Creativity and craft play out in another way with this edition's new cover featuring a photograph of wind turbines. The image is not only aesthetically pleasing, but it also represents the leading edge of a centuries' old technology that captures many of the challenges that technical professionals and technical communicators face. Traditions exist, but to endure they must adapt to a dramatically changing world.

Throughout the text, the traditional concerns of technical communication — techniques such as definitions, descriptions, and processes; and forms such as correspondence, instructions, proposals, and reports — are always related to rhetorical elements. Beyond these concerns, the text continues to include detailed information about collaboration, ethics, visuals, and design and has significantly expanded its discussion of international communication, usability testing, and technology.

What's new in this edition? This sixth edition of *Technical Communication* maintains the strengths of the previous editions while incorporating important new information. The changes in this edition are drawn from current theory and research, leading-edge practices from the workplace, and helpful tools and strategies from practitioners. Twelve of the changes are particularly important:

- *Evaluation criteria.* Chapter 1 introduces easy-to-use evaluation criteria — *accessibility, comprehensibility,* and *usability* — which are used as a heuristic throughout the book to analyze and assess written, oral, and visual communication.
- *New examples.* New examples come from a variety of disciplines and professions. Many relate to global themes — scientific/technological innovation, medical advances/disease control, food production, and ecological/environmental balance — which demonstrate that scientific and technological concerns are global.
- *International emphasis.* The international workplace is emphasized with textual and visual examples from many countries and in many languages.
- *Special features.* Two-page spreads highlight interesting situations where technical documents, oral presentations, and visuals are created and used.
- *New chapter about culture.* Chapter 2, "Understanding Culture and the Workplace," addresses international and organizational cultures as well as characteristics that influence individuals in those cultures.
- *New chapter about usability.* Chapter 9, "Ensuring Usability," characterizes usability and usability testing, introduces guidelines for conducting various types of tests, and differentiates usability from accessibility.
- *New chapter about technology.* Throughout the new edition, you will find increased information about technology, including Chapter 13, "Designing Electronic Communication," which highlights critical features of new media, ranging from e-mail and PowerPoint® to animated Web sites.
- *More annotations.* More extensive marginal annotations for the sample documents include questions and comments to encourage critical evaluation.
- *New Ethics Sidebars.* Each chapter includes an Ethics Sidebar that focuses on a complex ethical issue considered by workplace professionals. Several of these sidebars are new to this edition.
- *WEBLINKS.* Numerous WEBLINKS in each chapter are accessible through the book's Companion Web site, which also has a wide array of relevant examples and articles for discussion.

- *Photographs throughout.* New photographs throughout the text illustrate workplaces where technical documents, oral presentations, and visuals are created and used.
- *Improved design.* The sophisticated, usable design features full-color pages that demonstrate ways in which color can be functional and contribute to interpreting and using technical information.

What critical concerns are addressed? While accuracy is arguably the most critical aspect of any technical document, oral presentation, or visual, technical accuracy is not enough. This text balances theory and research, pedagogy and practice, and classroom and workplace needs. The balance is demonstrated in ten critical concerns:

- *Rhetorical base.* Most problems communicating technical information occur in complex workplace environments. In addressing this challenge, *Technical Communication,* Sixth Edition, uses rhetorical elements — for example, the context of the communication; the constraints of the situation; needs of the audience(s); purposes of the writers, speakers, and designers; conventions of the genres; strategies for organizing and designing information — which influence the process of creating documents, oral presentations, and visuals.
- *Communicating with audiences, including international audiences.* The text provides early and ongoing in-depth coverage of audience analysis, focusing on practical suggestions for evaluating audiences and developing strategies for adjusting material to different audiences, including those in a variety of international and organizational cultures.
- *Visuals and document design.* The text emphasizes the rhetorical nature of visuals and establishes parallels between visual and verbal information. The text also explores the role of color and emphasizes the impact of information design, both in print and electronic documents. The design of this text models ways to make information accessible, comprehensible, and usable.
- *Collaboration.* The text not only presents a chapter about collaboration, but the end of each chapter includes collaborative assignments. Throughout the text, students are reminded that the workplace is a collaborative environment and that written, oral, and visual information is seldom produced or used in isolation. Students not only learn the importance of collaboration and teamwork, but they also learn how to be productive collaborators.
- *Testing.* Creating effective documents, oral presentations, and visuals should include text-based, expert-based, and user-based testing. The results of testing can be used as the basis for revising and editing.
- *Process and product.* This edition shows how technical professionals are involved in a complex process to create as well as interpret technical

documents, presentations, and visuals. The text discusses ways to approach communication problems; explains options available to writers, speakers, and designers; offers suggestions about logical organization; and illustrates appropriate language use.

- *Technology.* Because technical communication takes place in a rapidly changing electronic environment, this text discusses the impact of technology on creating and interpreting documents, oral presentations, and visuals. Users learn ways to make informed decisions about technology as well as ways that enable them to take advantage of the power of new media.
- *Examples.* Throughout the text, annotated examples from students and workplace professionals around the world illustrate the key points and serve as models.
- *Style. Technical Communication* is a reader-based text; it directly addresses students and workplace professionals in a straightforward manner that is both appealing and accessible.
- *Apparatus and computer support.* The extensive marginal annotations prompt critical thinking and offer opportunities to discuss ideas and apply the practices presented in *Technical Communication.* The Individual and Collaborative Assignments at the end of each chapter encourage planning and developing a wide array of documents, oral presentations, and visuals.

What support materials are available? This new edition of *Technical Communication* has a greatly expanded *Instructor's Manual* and a Book Companion Web Site.

- The *Instructor's Manual (IM)* is a valuable resource both for highly experienced and for new instructors. It offers strategies for teaching each chapter successfully, including the use of a new convenient heuristic: RADAR (Read, Act, Discuss, Assess, and Reflect). The *IM* also includes suggestions for planning and preparing course material, additional activities and assignments, strategies for managing different classroom formats (traditional, computer lab, and online), PowerPoint® presentations for introducing or reviewing concepts, and tools and strategies for assessing student work (written, oral, and visual; individual and collaborative; print and electronic). In addition, the *IM* includes essays by nationally recognized researchers and educators; written specifically to accompany *Technical Communication,* Sixth Edition, these essays discuss innovative approaches and practices being used in technical communication classrooms. Many of the articles are new to this edition's manual. The *IM* is available free to all adopters of this new edition of *Technical Communication.* (You may request a copy of the *IM* from your Thomson representative or download the PDF version from the instructor side of the Book Companion Web Site, available at **www.english.wadsworth.com/burnett6e.**)

- *Student side of the Book Companion Web Site.* The student side of the Web site includes for each chapter an overview, tools and tips, "Workplace Realities" (videotapes with workplace professionals), annotated interactive examples, a variety of classroom and Internet activities, key terms, Web links to chapter-related content, and a tutorial quiz. Additionally, the student side of the Web site includes many cases, new assignments, a complete handbook, and career resources. To access the Book Companion Web Site, go to **www.english.wadsworth.com/burnett6e**.
- *Instructor side of the Book Companion Web Site.* The instructor side of the Web site includes for each chapter an instructor overview, chapter teaching tips, PowerPoint® lecture slides, and answers to chapter quizzes as well as suggestions for integrating the additional examples and assignments into the course. The instructor side of the Web site also includes course management tools, sample syllabi, rubrics for assessing student work, and suggestions for using the Web site's cases and career resources. To access the Book Companion Web Site, go to **www.english.wadsworth.com/burnett6e**.

I have made changes in each edition based on the recommendations of colleagues from colleges, universities, agencies, businesses, and companies around the world. If you have suggestions about changes I should consider, please contact me. If you have examples that would work well for the next edition, please contact me as well. I value your feedback.

Rebecca E. Burnett, PhD
University Professor of Rhetoric & Professional Communication
Iowa State University
c/o Thomson Higher Education
25 Thomson Place
Boston, MA 02210

Acknowledgments 致谢

Technical Communication would not exist without the personal and professional support of family, friends, and colleagues.

Researchers. In preparing this edition, I have been thankful for the skillful and thorough researchers from Iowa State University who assisted me in preparing this revision: Brian Hentz, Katherine Miles, and Rebecca Pope-Ruark. They posed alternative approaches, updated information, located examples, suggested two-page spreads, provided valuable editing, and drafted new activities, glossary lists, PowerPoint presentations, and quizzes. Their assistance has been essential.

Co-author. Donna Kain, at East Carolina University, has been my trusted and expert co-author for Chapters 9 and 13, my co-author for the expanded and updated *Instructor's Manual,* and the creative and insightful developer of the content on the Book Companion Web Site. She has been invaluable in this revision.

Personal thanks. As always, Dorothea Burnett, Margaret Burnett, Christopher Burnett, and Paula Thompson provide me with the confidence and support to make the revision possible. William Jeffries continues in his unwavering support and serves as a voice of reason.

Friends and colleagues. I appreciate the support and contributions provided by friends and colleagues around the world: Philippa Benson, Mort Boyd, Shelly Boyd, Linda Driskill, Marcia Greenman Lebeau, Muriel McGrann, Susie Poague, Bev Sauer, Don Stanford, Judith Stanford, Anette van der Mescht, and Ben Xu. They have helped to shape my thinking as I went about this revision.

I want to thank my friends and colleagues at Iowa State University who see wisdom in balancing theory, research, workplace practice, and pedagogy. Their curiosity, dedication, and insight are an inspiration to me. My undergraduate and graduate students at Iowa State University and technical professionals in university seminars have also been important to this edition. I want to acknowledge the valuable discussions and contributions of various kinds provided by ISU friends and colleagues, most especially Gloria Betcher, Daniel Coffey, Dan Douglas, Laura Hannasch, Carl Herndl, Lee Honeycutt, Denny Howe, Robert Martin, Linta Meetz, Michael Mendelson, Neil Nakadate, Elizabeth Orcutt-Kroeger, Lorrie Pellack, Lee Poague, Diane Prince-Herndl, David Roberts, Caskey Russell, Geoff Sauer, Sarah Stambaugh, Lana Voga, and Loren Zachary. And in this revision, I also want to thank my friends and colleagues at Rice University who provided many opportunities that have enabled me to select useful new examples.

Contributors. I especially appreciate the colleagues and workplace professionals who contributed examples for this edition: Paul Boyd from the US Army Corps of Engineers; Maria Cochran, Marisa Corzanego, Mark Gleason, Oskana Hlyva, Ken Jolls, and Arvid Osterberg — all from Iowa State University; Sarah Helland from Pioneer; Zachary Lavicky from Emporia State University; Melissa Poague from University of Washington; Lee Tesdell from Minnesota State University–Mankato; and Tara Barrett Tarnowski from University of Georgia.

Previous editions. The contributions by the following people to the fifth edition have been substantially retained: Jill Bigley, Arricka Brouwer, Christopher Burnett, Larry Chan, David Clark, Irene Faass, Patty Harms, Elizabeth Herman, William Jeffries, Ken Jolls, Kari Krumpel, Muriel McGrann, Walden Miller, Kate Molitor, Matt Turner, Peggy Pollock, Janet Renze, Daryl Seay, Doug Schaapveld, Clay Spinuzzi, Don Stanford, Judith Stanford, Melissa Waltman, and Julie Zeleznik as well as friends, colleagues, and students at Iowa State University.

The contributions by the following people to the fourth edition have been substantially retained: Susan Booker, Kaelin Chappelle, David Clark, Andrea Breemer Frantz, Woody Hart, William Jeffries, Lee-Ann Kastman, Elenor Long, Muriel McGrann, Ron Myers, Tom Myers, Mike Peery, Clay Spinuzzi, Don Stanford, Judith Stanford, Gary Tarcy, Lee Tesdell, Christianna White, Dorothy Winchester, Mark Zachry, and Stephanie Zeluck as well as friends, colleagues, and students at Iowa State University.

The contributions by the following people to the third edition have been substantially retained: Reva Daniel, Michael Hassett, William Jeffries, Muriel McGrann, Cindy Myers, and Christianna White as well as colleagues and students at Iowa State University.

The contributions by the following people to the second edition have been substantially retained: Philippa Benson, William Jeffries, and Barbara Sitko as well as my friends, colleagues, and students at Carnegie Mellon University.

The contributions by the following people to the first edition have been substantially retained: Geraldine Branca, Christopher Burnett, Robert Carosso, Bernard DiNatale, Arline Dupras, Elizabeth Foster, Nancy Irish, Elizabeth Carros Keroack, Marcia Greenman Lebeau, Muriel McGrann, Stephen Meidell, Leon Sommers, and Judith Dupras Stanford as well as students at Northern Essex Community College, Merrimack College, and the University of Massachusetts at Lowell.

Reviewers. I appreciate the helpful feedback from colleagues around the country who suggested revisions, sometimes in a quick e-mail message, sometimes in a short conversation at a conference. The official reviewers' practical and often insightful suggestions were, of course, instrumental in revisions for this edition. Detailed reviews were provided by

Scott Chadwick	*Creighton University*
Dave Clark	*University of Wisconsin–Milwaukee*
Lee Ann Kastman Breuch	*University of Minnesota*
Cezar Ornatowski	*San Diego State University*
Penny Sansbury	*Florence-Darlington Technical College*
Geoffrey Sauer	*Iowa State University*
Karen Schnackenberg	*Carnegie Mellon University*
Stuart Selber	*Pennsylvania State University*
Clay Spinuzzi	*University of Texas–Austin*
Cindy Raisor	*Texas A&M University*

The Thomson Wadsworth team for *Technical Communication* has been extraordinary. Dickson Musslewhite, my trusted and supportive Acquisitions Editor, provided excellent editorial direction. Michell Phifer, Senior Development Editor, kept me on track in this complex revision with intelligence, patience, expertise, and humor — for which I am immensely grateful. Linda Beaupre redesigned the book, creating a design that is elegant and usable (a remarkable and wonderful combination); her design reflects the spirit of the text. Joe Gallagher and Cara Douglas-Graff supported the development of the Web site for the book. Janet McCartney copyedited the manuscript and the endnotes, saving me from embarrassing errors. Sally Cogliano, Senior Production Editor, began the production process with efficiency and good humor. Lianne Ames, Senior Production Editor, saw the book through the production process with remarkable energy, insight, flexibility, patience, and grace. Christina Micek was invaluable as the photo researcher for this edition. Karyn Morrison handled the complex task of permissions with thoroughness. Joy Westberg wrote wonderful marketing materials. Beth Callaway from Graphic World supervised and coordinated the composition process with care and deliberation. For all, I am immensely thankful.

PART I

Communicating in the Workplace
职场中的交流

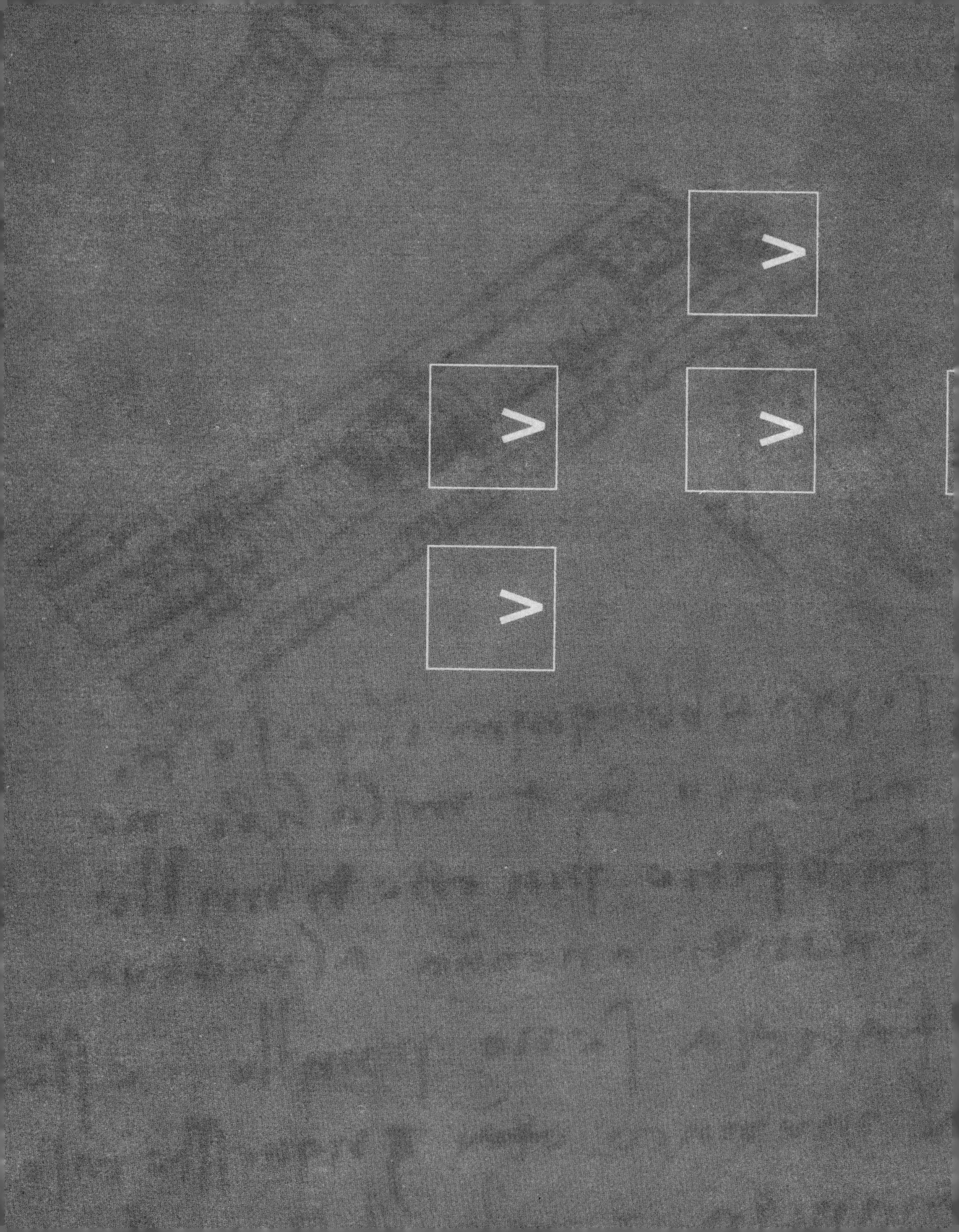

CHAPTER 1

Characterizing Workplace Communication 职场交流特点

本章首先指出了职场上有效交流的重要性以及如何定义技术交流。任何一种技术交流的有效性需考虑交流的内容、背景、目的、对象（读者、听众或观众），机构、视觉手段、信息设计、信息可用性及语言规范等修辞内容。同时，本章还说明了文体、技术、职业规范在技术交流中的重要作用。最后，本章指出了技术交流中可能遇到的问题。

Objectives and Outcomes 学习目标

This chapter will help you accomplish these outcomes:

- Define technical communication, its criticality in the workplace, and its relation to job success
- Understand the role of genre, technology, and ethics in technical communication
- Describe rhetorical elements that experienced communicators consider, including context, purpose, audience, organization, and document design
- Identify factors that contribute to accessibility, comprehensibility, and usability
- Identify constraints that affect workplace communication

What do astrophysicists, obstetricians, electrical engineers, ecologists, farmers, musicians, and veterinarians have in common? All create and interpret technical documents, oral presentations, and technical visuals. What do the moons of Jupiter, in vitro fertilization, silicon chips, wetlands conservation, soybean crops, flutes, and foals have in common? All are subjects of technical communication, a broad field that touches nearly every profession because it connects ideas, people, and their activities. Technical communication defines, describes, and directs activities in business and industry, government and research institutions, hospitals and farms.

Although certain professions such as engineering have traditionally been associated with technical communication, virtually all disciplines and professions have technical documents, oral presentations, and visuals. For example, detailed information about sound formation is important for speech pathologists, computer engineers, and human factors experts designing voice-activated computer systems. Knowledge about muscle conditioning is equally relevant to physical therapists, ballet dancers, and veterinarians. Data about weather changes are crucial to meteorologists, airline pilots, and commercial fishers.

Importance of Effective Communication

有效交流的重要性

Two broad categories of professionals are responsible for virtually all the technical documents, oral presentations, and visuals in any organization: technical communicators and technical experts. Technical communicators have evolved as specialists whose primary responsibility is to design, develop, and produce a wide range of documents, oral presentations, and visuals. As essential members of project teams, technical communicators support the products and services of an organization. Equally important are technical experts who communicate as a regular part of their job. These scientists, engineers, technicians, and managers regularly plan and prepare a wide range of technical communication.

How much do you anticipate communicating when you're in the workplace? Examine your profession's journals, trade magazines, and Web sites to see if you can determine the role of reading, writing, and speaking in your field.

Professionals who communicate effectively, whether technical communicators or technical experts, usually achieve more career success and have greater job satisfaction than those without the skills to communicate their technical knowledge. Successful professionals see reading and writing, listening and speaking, and viewing and designing visuals as integral parts of their job, not as something extra that they have to fit in. They assume responsibility for their own communication — from organizing ideas to final proofreading of documents.

For more than 20 years, surveys have touted the importance of communication skills in the workplace: More than 90 percent of technical professionals have reported that speaking and writing skills are important to their success. They have also reported that the amount of time they spend writing increases as their responsibilities increase: Nearly half spend up to 40 percent of their time writing and more than one-quarter spend between 40 percent and 100 percent of their time writing.[1]

Results from a variety of recent surveys, four of which are summarized here, support these long-accepted views and illustrate the importance that successful professionals place on effective communication:

- A survey by Robert Half International of 1,400 chief financial officers identified interpersonal skills such as communication and listening as critical for professional success.[2]
- A survey by the American Management Association of nearly 300 U.S. administrators identified written and oral communication skills as the highest ranked performance skills for professional success.[3]
- A survey by American Express of nearly 800 small business owners reported that 86 percent believe oral communication skills are very important, 77 percent believe that interpersonal skills are very important, and 60 percent believe that written skills are very important.[4]
- A survey of more than 200 Canadian technical professionals who are members of L'association canadienne de l'informatique (Canadian Information Processing Society) and a survey of more than 100 technology-based Canadian organizations identified critical job skills. Technical professionals identified top skills as the ability to conduct analyses and make recommendations; use project management tools; and write, speak, and listen well. Employers identified top skills as project management, communication skills, teamwork, and leadership.[5]

These representative surveys show that you will gain tremendous professional advantages if you write and speak well, work on teams and manage projects effectively, and listen carefully. Your communication needs to be technically complete and accurate, logically organized for the audience, visually appealing, and interesting; it also needs to be mechanically and grammatically conventional, and it must say something worthwhile.

As customer satisfaction with products and services becomes more important, companies increase the attention they give to paper and electronic documents, which are now seen as essential parts of the product by most companies. Since operations increasingly depend on rapid, accurate communication, companies expect all employees to be good communicators. In fact, a poll by the National Association of Manufacturers stated that poor reading or writing skills prevent 32 percent of entry-level applicants from being hired; poor oral skills prevent 18 percent from being hired.[6]

Defining Technical Communication

定义技术交流

Although technical communication has existed as long as people have recorded information, technical communication as a profession evolved exponentially during the second half of the twentieth century. Recent definitions of technical communication consider it rhetorical.

Why the term *rhetorical? Rhetoric,* the art and craft of communicating appropriately and persuasively, is concerned with the ways in which written, oral, and visual information is planned, conveyed, and interpreted in particular contexts, for particular audiences, for particular purposes. Technical communication is rhetorical because it is the art and craft of communicating technical information appropriately and persuasively to intended audiences, in complex contexts, for particular purposes. The rhetorical elements identified in Figure 1.1, considered collectively, provide a broad and useful way to characterize technical communication. These elements apply to all modes of technical communication, whether paper or electronic texts, oral presentations, or visuals.

> *Can you find an example of a technical document that fulfills most of the characteristics in Figure 1.1?*

FIGURE 1.1 **Rhetorical Elements Characterizing Technical Communication**

Rhetorical Elements	Effective Technical Documents, Oral Presentations, and Visuals
Content	▪ Present accurate, appropriate technical information adjusted to the audience(s) ▪ Provide appropriate source citations and documentation as necessary
Context	▪ Respond to the organizational situation ▪ Fulfill the identified task ▪ Are revised frequently for currency
Purpose(s)	▪ Inform and persuade the intended audience(s) ▪ Identify the position being taken
Audience(s)	▪ Address identified audience(s) — readers, listeners, or viewers — who often have different needs and constraints ▪ Recognize that multiple interpretations of documents, oral presentations, and visuals occur
Organization	▪ Organize information so that it is logical, accessible, and retrievable, and so that it is easy to comprehend, navigate, and recall
Visuals	▪ Convey content through various kinds of visuals that aid audience understanding and decision making
Document design	▪ Design information so that it is accessible, comprehensible, and usable
Usability	▪ Provide functional and usable information for the audience(s)
Language conventions	▪ Provide straightforward information that differentiates opinions from verifiable information ▪ Use clear and direct language without unnecessary complexity; often use short- to medium-length sentences and subject-verb-object word order; provide simple but stylistically varied information

These rhetorical elements also are important because they are the very factors that experienced communicators typically consider when planning, drafting, and revising documents, oral presentations, and visuals. For example, experienced communicators consider far more than the content. They ask themselves about the context in which they're working and in which the information will be used. They identify the purpose and audience and then determine ways to adapt, organize, and support the information appropriately. They design effective visuals and create an appealing, usable design. And they conform to the conventions of their organization and their profession. However, they can take an effective shortcut and use these evaluation criteria: Is the information *accessible, comprehensible,* and *usable*? The following scenario about Jon Baliene, an experienced manufacturing supervisor and skillful communicator, illustrates these rhetorical elements and evaluation criteria in a typical workplace situation.

As a reader, listener, or viewer, what criteria do you use to determine if a document, oral presentation, or visual you use is effective? As a writer, speaker, or designer, what criteria do you typically use to determine if a document, oral presentation, or visual you prepare is effective?

Context
Jon thinks about his company — the corporate culture as well as the particular circumstance that he's responding to.

Division manager Sandy Schaeffer asks her manufacturing supervisor, Jon Baliene, to recommend solutions to production problems in his department. During his initial planning, Jon considers the immediate situation as well as expectations and constraints that could influence what he might say and how Sandy might interpret it.

Context
He understands the specific task he is asked to do and thinks about what's involved in completing it.

Purposes
1. *Provide information*
2. *Offer persuasive recommendations*
3. *Meet deadline*

As Jon plans his recommendation report, he identifies his purposes: provide and analyze verifiable information; recommend credible solutions that persuade Sandy to accept his analysis of the situation and, thus, his recommendations; and submit a report by the deadline.

Context
Jon selects information appropriate to the task.

Because Jon selects his information in response to Sandy's request, he knows he cannot use a boilerplate report format and simply fill in the blanks; the dynamic nature of the situation requires that he adapt the form and content to meet his manager's specific needs and expectations. And he knows he'll submit the report as an electronic attachment that will probably be read on-screen (though it could also be printed), so he chooses a font appropriate for on-screen reading and plans to hyperlink the section headings in the table of contents to the headings in the report.

Audience
Jon adapts material to Sandy, the decision maker.

Document Degisn
He adapts the design for the place the report will most likely be read — on a computer screen.

Accessibility
He ensures that Sandy will be able to easily access the information in an electronic format.

Because the company has a strong corporate identity program for internal and external communication, Jon knows he needs to use the report

Document Design
Jon uses a standard report format appropriate for the workplace culture of his company.

conventions detailed in the company's style guide, easily available on the company's intranet.

Jon organizes an audience-based report — that is, one geared specifically to Sandy's needs, experience, and capabilities. Because her background is in business, Jon adjusts the technical material by adding explanations of highly specialized information. In addition, he includes an appendix with calculations and specifications appropriate for secondary readers who have more technical experience than his manager.

Beyond identifying and analyzing the problems, Jon includes recommendations, which, he emphasizes, are based on current projections and costs; in six months, he would have to write a different report. He hopes the background information along with his carefully selected support and persuasive arguments convince Sandy to accept his recommendations. However, even though Jon has worked hard to prepare an effective report, he can't guarantee the way that Sandy Schaeffer will interpret the information and his argument. Jon checks the text as well as the visuals to make sure nothing seems ambiguous or confusing.

Because Jon knows that Sandy likes well-designed tables and graphs to support a narrative, he organizes numerical data into a table and creates a graph that shows the trends he has identified from the tabular data. He places these visuals in the text immediately following his discussion of the key points.

Despite Jon's enthusiasm for his recommendations, he explicitly explains the problems and proposes his recommended solution. He checks that all the headings signal the following text correctly and double-checks that the hyperlinks in the table of contents take readers to the appropriate sections.

Jon realizes that his primary reader (Sandy Schaeffer) and secondary readers (others in management and manufacturing) are intelligent, well educated, and well informed; however, they have little time to read an unnecessarily complex report. He checks that his text and visuals are understandable and that his recommendations are easy to find and well supported in a clear timeline for implementation.

Comprehensibility
He ensures that Sandy will be able to understand information needed for decisions.

Audience
Jon consider more than the primary reader.

Organization
Jon uses a conventional sequence of information to present and argue for his recommendations.

Audience
Jon recognizes the report is open to interpretation.

Visuals
Jon conveys data in a table and graph that are integrated into the text.

Language Conventions
He uses clear, direct, and accessible style.

Content
Jon presents accurate technical content adjusted to the decision maker.

Content
He provides current information that will become rapidly outdated.

Usability
He ensures that readers will be able to locate information needed for decision making.

Document Design
Jon provides headings and subheadings to signal main sections and ease reading.

Accessibility, Comprehensibility, and Usability
He ensures that all intended readers will be able to access, understand, and use the information.

Contexts for Constructing Meaning
构建意义的环境

Meaning does not reside in any of the documents, presentations, or visuals that you create or use. Instead, meaning is constructed from your interpretation of the information. Each individual's construction of meaning helps account for intelligent, well-informed readers, listeners, and viewers sometimes having different interpretations of the same information. Attitudes, education, experience, and contexts shape interpretations. Understanding some of the factors that affect people's interpretations and uses of technical information will help you become a more skillful communicator.

Genre in Technical Communication

As the situation with Jon shows, technical information does not occur in isolation. A document, oral presentation, or visual *and* the rhetorical situation in which it is created and used combine to constitute the *genre.* Researchers Carol Berkenkotter and Thomas Huckin explain that genres (information and situations) are *dynamic:* they change synergistically in response to particular circumstances — that is, each affects the other. They are also situated in a particular community's workplace tasks or activities.[7]

In these workplace communities, technical professionals use and reproduce genres as part of their regular work; that is, they regularly prepare information and modify it for particular situations and purposes. This book as a whole is about genres in technical communication — the ways documents, oral presentations, and visuals are created and used for particular purposes, in particular situations and cultures, at particular points in time.

What other factors can you think of that could affect the way members of an audience respond to documents, oral presentations, and visuals? What might affect their comprehension? What might affect their recall of information?

Like Jon, you can have the goal of creating audience-based documents, oral presentations, and visuals that consider audiences' needs and reactions and that organize information for audiences' understanding. Creating audience-based materials requires awareness of the rhetorical situation in which they are generated and used. Audiences are, of course, influenced by the actual words or images, but these words and images may carry different meanings for each member of the audience. And, whether written, spoken or visually presented, they are only part of what contribute to understanding. Audience comprehension of and response to information are influenced by a range of factors, including attitudes, cultural perspectives, values, education, job function, political position, personality, and experiences.

Because meaning is constructed by your audiences, you need to be especially careful to select words and visuals and then organize information so the meaning your audience constructs will be similar to the one you intend. No document, oral presentation, or visual fully conveys your intended meaning, nor does any reader, listener, or viewer ever understand everything you intend. As a communicator, you both add and omit things that were part of the original rhetorical situation. As a reader, listener, or viewer, your interpretation is affected by what linguists call *exuberance* (that is, your interpretation always adds something not intended) and *deficiency* (that is, your interpretation always ignores things you could have noticed).

Communities 社 团

As the brief discussion about genre shows, one of the important characteristics of workplace professionals is that they belong to communities that influence their understanding and their activities. Although people belong to multiple communities simultaneously, two types of community are particularly important to think about in a work context.

Workplace professionals belong to various *discourse communities,* identifiable groups with a common, often specialized, language. They can be members of discourse communities without working together or even seeing each other. For example, optical engineers, organic chemists, horticulturalists, and athletic trainers each have a specialized and shared vocabulary, whether or not they know each other personally. Thus, an optical engineer in Tuscaloosa can understand an article written by an optical engineer in Toronto, even if they are strangers. Their discipline and profession share concepts, practices, and vocabulary.

Do you think communities of practice are formed as permanent groups, or do you think that they go through stages of development — coalescing into a community, actively working together, and eventually dispersing?

Workplace professionals also belong to various *communities of practice.* Etienne Wenger, internationally recognized researcher and consultant, defines a community of practice as a group of people who have a joint enterprise, mutual engagement, and a shared repertoire of resources.[8] With his collaborator, Jean Lave, Wenger explains that people in a community of practice establish a relationship that over time enables them to work together doing things that matter to them. They not only share concepts and language, but they also share commitment and resources. They develop a history — the way they do things in their community of practice. Their common experiences bind them together and enable them to undertake even more challenging activities.[9]

As a workplace professional, you will belong to several discourse communities and communities of practice. You will also regularly communicate with people outside your own discourse communities and communities of practice, so you need to consider what will make information accessible, comprehensible, and usable to those in your own communities as well as those outside your communities.

WWW

WEBLINK

To learn more about communities of practice in the workplace, go to **www.english.wadsworth.com/burnett6e** for a link to a more detailed article.
CLICK ON WEBLINK
CLICK on Chapter 1/communities of practice

Technology in Technical Communication 技术交流中的技术运用

Interpretation is not only influenced by genres and communities, it is also influenced by the technology you use. What is broadly called *computer-mediated communication* (CMC) is a process of human communication via computers. CMC provides a way for people to communicate, interact with, retrieve, and interpret information in a variety of contexts and to shape communication for a variety of purposes. Media influences the shape of the information and its interpretation. For example, print and oral information are necessarily linear — that is, one sentence follows the next sentence, one paragraph follows the next paragraph. In contrast, electronic and visual information are not necessarily linear; for example, hypertext allows users to sequence information in multiple ways.

How does technology affect people's interaction with and interpretation of information? In general, it is based on their familiarity and comfort with the technology. More specifically, technology influences several factors:

- Sustaining reading of lengthy text or reading for extended periods
- Keeping track of your place in the text
- Managing and maintaining multiple, active on-screen windows
- Locating and reviewing difficult or confusing information
- Taking notes, highlighting relevant text, adding personal comments and questions
- Checking other places in the text and returning to your original place

Technology further influences what you say and how you say it, affecting privacy, immediacy, and permanency.

- *Privacy.* Virtually all electronic communication in the workplace can be monitored. It is simply not private — ever. Knowing that someone other than the intended audience might read your e-mail should promote some caution in what you choose to write and send. For example, e-mail messages and online chats are not necessarily protected by privacy laws. As much as you may object, some legal experts argue that "the writer of an e-mail message is implicitly consenting to its recording."[10]

To learn more about the lack of privacy in electronic communication — especially e-mail and online chats — go to **www.english.wadsworth.com/burnett6e** for a link to an article about cyberlaw.
CLICK ON WEBLINK
CLICK on Chapter 1/cyberlaw

WWW
WEBLINK

- *Immediacy.* You can decide when to communicate by participating in synchronous or asynchronous communication. *Synchronous communication* is concurrent or simultaneous (real-time) digital communication such as computer conferencing, chat rooms, or white board environments. Such environments often promote comments that are not carefully thought through. *Asynchronous communication* is digital communication that takes place independently in time; accessing and responding to communication exchanges such as voice mail, e-mail, or online newsgroups can be delayed by minutes, hours, or days. While asynchronous communication allows more time for reflection, the informal nature often promotes casual, hurried responses.

What factors besides privacy, immediacy, and permanency are influenced by computer-mediated communication?

- *Permanency.* Information on a computer — especially on corporate and institutional servers — is frequently backed up and archived. You can record and then delete information on your computer; however, that information can often still be retrieved. Just because you can no longer see or access a file does not mean that no one else can access it. Furthermore, information you think of as yours (such as e-mail) resides on a server and can be accessed, even if you have deleted that information on your own computer. In fact, some companies' primary business is retrieving supposedly inaccessible information.

Ethics in Technical Communication 技术交流中的职业道德规范

Preparing documents, oral presentations, and visuals that are accessible, comprehensible, and usable is not enough for workplace professionals. Certainly, to meet the needs of your audience, you must initially decide about your purposes to inform and persuade. Beyond these considerations, you must also respond to the context and culture, define and focus the content, analyze the task and audience, organize the information, and design the specific document. But you still need more.

To be an effective communicator, you must also consider factors that influence you and your audience as you and they construct meaning. What's one of the most important factors that influences everyone involved in writing, reading, and responding to technical documents? Ethics. In this textbook, ethics are a focus of every chapter, presented prominently in sidebars.

ETHICS 职业道德规范知识吧 SIDEBAR

Public vs. Private: Ethics and the Technical Professional
公共与隐私：职业规范和专业技术人员

Imagine the following workplace situation:

You are working on your first major report, a technical description of the company's latest product. You know your technical description should highlight the product's state-of-the-art features. Those features are a key selling point. However, some field tests indicate those features are unreliable under adverse weather conditions—conditions common in the intended market for this product. Other tests, though, are planned. You are faced with a decision: Do you include the current test results in your technical description? You know what your company would prefer, but you feel an obligation to let customers know about the possibility of problems. The description is due by the end of the day. What do you do?

How can you decide what information to include in a document and what information to exclude?

Writing situations like this one require technical professionals to make ethical decisions. Ethics determine what we are willing to communicate and how we are willing to communicate. Ethics come from many different perspectives: personal beliefs, professional guidelines, organizational practices, cultural expectations, and legal or judicial requirements.

Communication researcher Cezar Ornatowski[11] believes ethical dilemmas for technical professionals occur because of two "incompatible" goals: serving the interests of employers while attempting to write technical documents that are "objective, plain, factual." Due to these conflicting pressures, technical professionals are at increased risk for ethical violations — either producing a document that does not meet the employer's goals or producing a document that may not be verifiable.

Dealing with these ethical dilemmas is not always easy: Sometimes, technical professionals must make difficult decisions. However, many ethical dilemmas can be addressed by knowing that these dilemmas exist and understanding various ways to resolve them. Even if you don't find ethical violations that challenge your personal beliefs, you should be aware of ways they might affect your standing among your colleagues and in your profession. Ethical violations affect a document's credibility, which, in turn, affects how you will be professionally perceived.

Reread the scenario at the beginning of this sidebar. Upon consideration, how would you deal with this conflict? Would you include the questionable test results? Would excluding them be an ethical violation?

Accessibility, Comprehensibility, and Usability

可访性，理解性及可用性

Regardless of the genre, communities, technology, or ethics involved, a document, oral presentation, or visual must meet three essential criteria, ones that are central to this book. Each document, presentation, or visual must meet these criteria:

1. Be physically accessible, so a reader, listener, or viewer can see or hear it
2. Be comprehensible, so a reader, listener, or viewer can understand it
3. Be usable, so a reader, listener, or viewer can use it easily and productively

If you take one thing from this introductory chapter, remember that effective communicators need to make information accessible, understandable, and usable. Figure 1.2 shows how these three important criteria are affected by rhetorical elements that experienced communicators consider. Each cell in Figure 1.2 identifies

FIGURE 1.2 **Factors Affecting Accessibility, Comprehensibility, and Usability**

Although the table identifies the factors that affect accessibility, comprehensibility, and usability of information, it does not explicitly convey the interactive nature of writing/reading, speaking/listening, designing/viewing. These factors all presume that effective communication — whether written, oral, or visual — is accurate, purposeful, appropriate to the context, adapted to the audience, organized, well designed, and responsive to the conventions of its medium.

		ACCESSIBILITY How easily can the audience see, hear, and/or touch the information?	COMPREHENSIBILITY How easily can the audience understand the information?	USABILITY How easily can the audience use the information?
Audience		**What physical factors of the audience affect their ability to access information?** Visual acuity? Aural acuity? Tactility? Coordination? Cognitive ability?	**What social and cultural factors affect the audience's understanding of information?** Language? Prior knowledge? Cultural presumptions? Reaction to gestures? Genre knowledge?	**What pragmatic factors affect the audience's use of the information?** User representation of task? User role? User attitude and experience?
Context		**What physical factors in the environment affect the audience's ability to access information?** Technology? Lighting? Temperature? Noise? Distractions? Interruptions?	**What situational factors affect the audience's understanding of information?** Stated or implied purpose of information? Perceived value of information?	**What situational factors affect the audience's use of the information?** Benefits to user? Sufficiency of time and/or support? Division of labor? Organizational structure?
Information	Text	**What physical characteristics of text affect the accessibility of information?** Headings? Typography? White space? Resolution?	**How does the text affect the audience's understanding of information?** Terminology? Organization? Coherence?	**How does the text affect the audience's use of the information?** Navigability? Credibility of sources?
Information	Oral	**What physical characteristics of an oral presentation affect the accessibility of information?** Volume? Clarity? Articulation? Pace? Gesticulation? Speaker movement?	**How does delivery of an oral presentation affect the audience's understanding of information?** Arrangement? Coherence? Dialect/accent? Modulation?	**How does the delivery of the oral presentation affect the usability of the information?** Repetition and emphasis? Forecasting? Signposting?
Information	Visuals	**What physical characteristics of visuals affect the accessibility of information?** Image quality? White space? Paper type/quality? Color? Screen size/resolution? Figure-ground contrast?	**How do the visuals affect the audience's understanding of information?** Recognizable images? Scale? Coherence? Nature of argument?	**How do the visuals affect the audience's use of the information?** Sequencing of images? Coordination with text?

a key question that you can ask yourself and minimal factors you need to consider when planning or evaluating technical communication. Throughout the book, you'll learn more about these factors and others that you need to consider.

What additional factors could you add to any of the cells?

In applying the factors identified in Figure 1.2, you can draw on the work of Herbert Paul Grice, a philosopher of language who taught at Oxford University and at the University of California, Berkeley.[12] Although Grice's work dealt specifically with conversation, it also applies to written communication.[13] Grice's overarching principle suggests that your communication should be timely and purposeful, which can happen if you follow four maxims:

- ***Quality.*** What you say should be accurate and verifiable.
- ***Quantity.*** What you say should be as informative as necessary — not too much information or too little information.
- ***Relevance.*** What you say should be relevant.
- ***Manner.*** What you say should be "perspicuous"; thus, you need to avoid obscurity and ambiguity and also be brief and well organized.

Can you think of situations in which H. P. Grice's cooperative principle and/or the four maxims are contradictory if you try to apply them at the same time?

Communication in the Workplace
职场中的交流

What are the most common types of technical documents, presentations, and visuals in your career area? When are they used? What are their purposes? Who are their audiences? How much does it matter that you be able to create and use them?

If you identified every workplace situation that requires some type of technical document, oral presentation, or visual, the list would extend for pages, both because so many types exist and because the terminology is not standardized. Several easy ways exist to differentiate technical documents, presentations, and visuals: by the workplace situation necessitating them, by genre, by the audience, or by the purpose.

In the next section, you will read excerpts from five common types of workplace documents. They are similar to the ones you are likely to prepare and use: a technical brochure, a PowerPoint presentation, a technical report, a Web site, and a set of instructions. The examples are annotated to identify ways in which each is accessible, comprehensible, and usable. As you read the examples and their annotations, note that they incorporate elements that you can use in your own communication:

- Preview what's to come.
- Define critical terms.
- Use headings to call attention to key points.
- Select details appropriate for the audience's level of understanding.
- Use a design that contributes to accessibility, comprehensibility, and usability.
- Use an accessible font appropriate for print or on-screen use.
- Select typographic devices (such as bullets, italics, and boldfacing) to call attention to information.
- Use visuals (such as a table) to reinforce, illustrate, or explain the text.

One common function of technical documents, oral presentations, and visuals is providing information, sometimes for background, sometimes for decision making. What genres provide information? Sales, marketing, and promotional materials sent to customers. Product and process specifications sent to purchasing agents. Brochures for patients in medical and dental offices.

Figure 1.3 presents an excerpt from ***Allergy Relief Guide,*** a booklet for people suffering from respiratory problems. The booklet has been prepared by the American Academy of Allergy and Immunology, a group of physicians "who specialize in the diagnosis and management of asthma and allergy disorders of adults and children." The introduction explains that information in the booklet helps readers know more about their own health and, thus, take better care of themselves and their families.

This excerpt is from a section that begins with a simple definition of asthma (an allergy that occurs in the lungs) and its triggers: allergens (such as pollen, mold), viral infections, irritants (such as tobacco smoke, air pollutants), distance running, sensitivity to drugs, and emotional anxiety. Thus, the information in this excerpt is presented after readers have some general background.

What other genre (information and situations) can help with background and decision making?

Following this excerpt, the booklet includes a two-column list of "industrial materials known to cause occupational asthma." For example, flour can cause occupational asthma for bakers as well as for farmers and grain handlers. Similarly, phenylglycine acid chloride and sulphone chloramides can cause occupational asthma for workers in the pharmaceutical industry.

Accessibility

- *Sufficiently large serif font is easy to read.*
- *Related information is chunked into short paragraphs.*
- *Individual topics are separated by white space.*
- *Bulleted items draw attention and make reading easier.*

Comprehensibility

- *Questions as headings make key points easy to understand.*
- *Sequence of information is logical: what before how.*
- *Limited use of technical information; necessary terms are defined and explained.*

Usability

- *Bold headings and italics make text easy to scan to locate information.*
- *The question-and-answer format makes information usable because it is easy to locate.*
- *Each cause is discussed in a separate paragraph.*
- *Examples have sufficient details for readers to relate to their own experiences.*
- *Cause-effect explanations help readers understand symptoms.*

OCCUPATIONAL ASTHMA

What is Occupational Asthma?

Occupational asthma is generally defined as a respiratory disorder directly related to inhaling fumes, gases, or dust while on the job. Symptoms include wheezing, chest tightness, coughing, and may also include runny nose, nasal congestion, and eye irritation. The cause may be allergic or nonallergic in nature. The disease may persist for lengthy periods in some workers even if they are no longer exposed. Many workers with symptoms have been incorrectly diagnosed as having bronchitis.

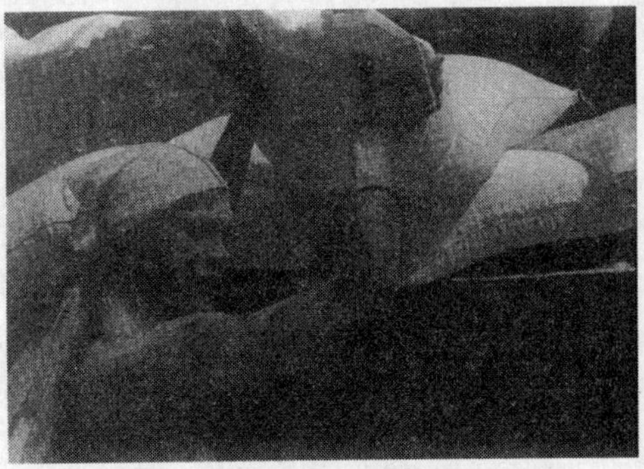

AP Photo/John Moore

Covered in flour, an employee working for a flour wholesaler unloads a shipment in Haiti.

It's important to remember that persons living in residential areas near factories are also exposed to fumes and may suffer symptoms as well.

In many cases, a previous family history of allergy will make a person more likely to suffer from occupational asthma. Yet many individuals who have no such history still develop this disease. Studies show that the length of exposure varies and can range from 4 to 36 months before symptoms occur.

How Prevalent is Occupational Asthma?

The exact prevalence of occupational asthma is not known. Researchers have found, however, that at least 15% of all male cases of asthma in Japan result from exposure to industrial vapors, dust, gases, or fumes. In the U.S., 5–10% of all cases of asthma are thought to have job-related origins.

What are the Causes of Occupational Asthma?

Occupational asthma may be caused by one of three mechanisms: irritants, allergic, or environmental factors:

- Examples of ***irritants*** that provoke cases of occupational asthma include exposure to hydrochloric acid, sulfur dioxide, or ammonia found in the petroleum or chemical industries. People who may already have asthma or some other respiratory disorder are particularly affected when exposure occurs. In instances where irritants are responsible for causing the asthma, allergic mechanisms are not actively involved. (An allergic mechanism refers to the body's immune system responding adversely to an offending substance.)
- *Allergic factors* do play a role, however, in the following instances: exposures to the enzymes of Bacillus subtilis in the washing powder industry, exposure to castor and green coffee beans, and contact with papain in the food processing industry. Other examples include complex salts of platinum in metal refining and other agents such as ethylene diamine, phthalic anhydride, toluene diisocyanate (TDI), and trimellitic anhydride (TMA) in the plastics, rubber, and resin industries.
- *Environmental factors* include the inhalation of dust or liquid extracts of dust from cotton, flax, or hemp. In these cases, tissue cells in the lung directly release chemicals, such as histamine, which can cause bronchial smooth muscle to contract and, thus, block airways. Yet this reaction can occur in subjects who are not allergic to any of these substances. The exact role that these factors play in producing this drug-like effect is not yet completely known.

FIGURE 1.3 **Excerpt from an Extended Definition from a Medical Booklet for Nonexperts**[14]

IDENTIFYING PROBLEMS
发现问题

Technical communicators use a variety of strategies to identify problems before they propose feasible solutions. The following example shows five slides from a PowerPoint presentation in which a student team argued that dependency on external energy sources is environmentally and economically unsound for their state. They argued instead that their state has the resources to become largely energy self-sufficient using wind turbines. As part of a class project, they formed a fictitious company that sought funding for an alternative energy project. The five-slide excerpt in Figure 1.4 is from their PowerPoint presentation to persuade an agency to provide funds for research about and expansion of the wind turbines in their state. The light tan bubbles present excerpts from their oral comments. During your classes as well as during your career, you'll need to create effective PowerPoint presentations for a variety of purposes and audiences.

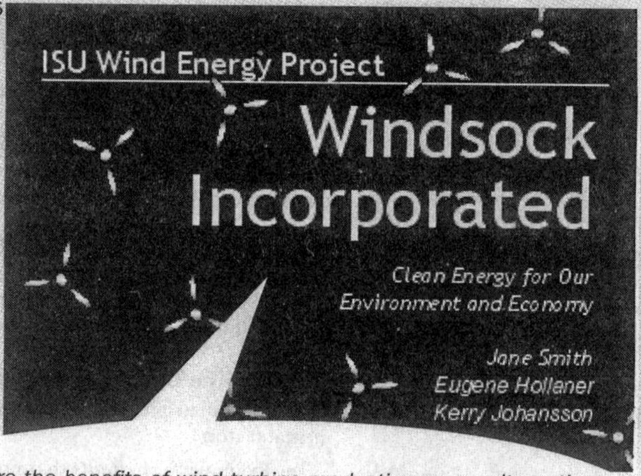

FIGURE 1.4A **Title Slide**[15]

Accessibility

- *The sans serif font, Trebuchet MS, is used on all the slides. It is a font especially designed for easy screen readability.*
- *The font of the title is large enough — 80 point — to visually signal it as the title.*
- *The header that appears on all the slides provides a visually coherent reminder of the topic.*

Comprehensibility

- *The slide identifies the topic, title, goal, and presenters*

"To explore the benefits of wind turbine production as an alternative energy source, Windsock Incorporated looks forward to showing you our proposal for creating viable, cost-efficient turbines over the next five to seven years. Our presentation explains the impact this clean energy can have on our environment and economy."

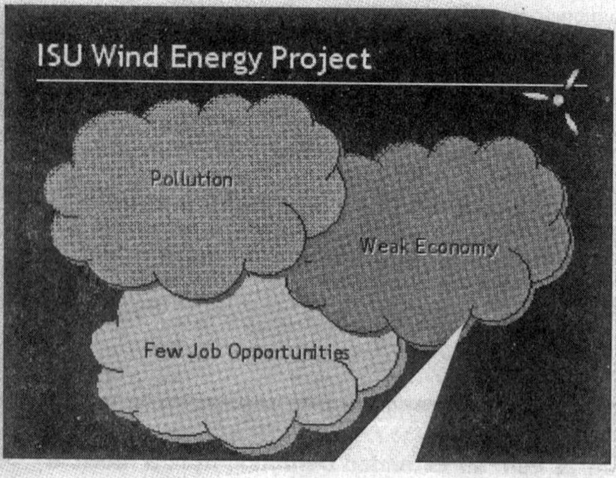

FIGURE 1.4B **Overview Slide**

Accessibility

- *The main text is easy to see because of the figure-ground contrast: dark text on the light background.*

Comprehensibility

- *The slide introduces the three key topics in the presentation.*
- *The windmill icon is repeated on each slide for visual coherence — and whimsy.*

Usability

- *The pollution clouds help the audience connect the critical concepts to a visual image that is used throughout the presentation.*

Many factors currently contribute to the state's financial and energy crisis. Not only are pollution rates alarmingly high, but fewer job opportunities and a stagnant economy have dissuaded many struggling citizens from pursuing postsecondary education.

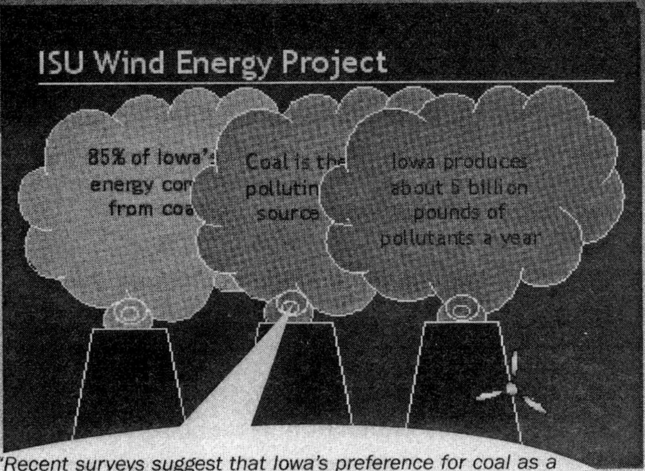

FIGURE 1.4C **Slide Introducing Pollution Problem**

Accessibility

- *The text is easy to read because the 24-point sans serif font is large enough to see when projected on a screen.*

Comprehensibility

- *Each key point is easy to distinguish (in its own pollution cloud).*
- *The sentences are short and easy to understand.*

Usability

- *When the presentation is animated, each point is projected individually.*
- *The slide presents only three main points, easy for the audience to hold in short-term memory.*

"Recent surveys suggest that Iowa's preference for coal as a primary energy source remains strong. In fact, coal continues to be the most popular energy source in the state. Specifically, state officials estimate that Iowans produce about five billion pounds of coal-based pollutants every year. . . ."

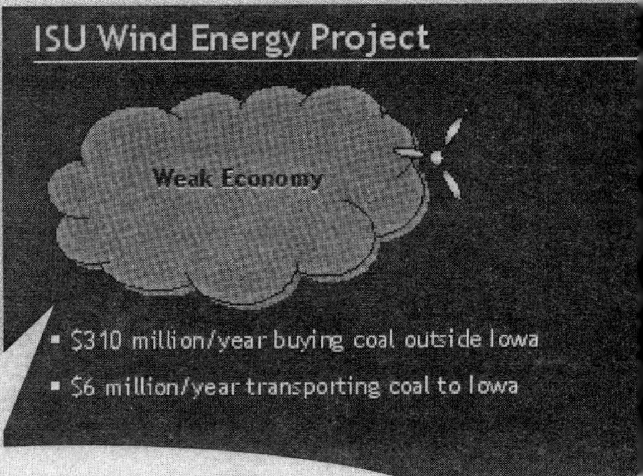

FIGURE 1.4D **Slide Introducing Economic Problem**

Accessibility

- *The text under the cloud is easy to see because of the high figure-ground contrast: light text on a dark background.*
- *Bullets distinguish the key points.*

Comprehensibility

- *Two key points are in easy-to-read phrases, with the most important information first.*

Usability

- *For fast recognition, the main topic is in the same visual form as when it was initially introduced — the same size and color of pollution cloud.*

"However, Iowans' dependence on coal has contributed significantly to the weakened economy. More than $300 million was spent last year purchasing and transporting coal from neighboring states to regional energy centers throughout Iowa. While our proposed wind turbine system would require significant start-up costs, the annual expenditures for coal would eventually be phased out of the state budget."

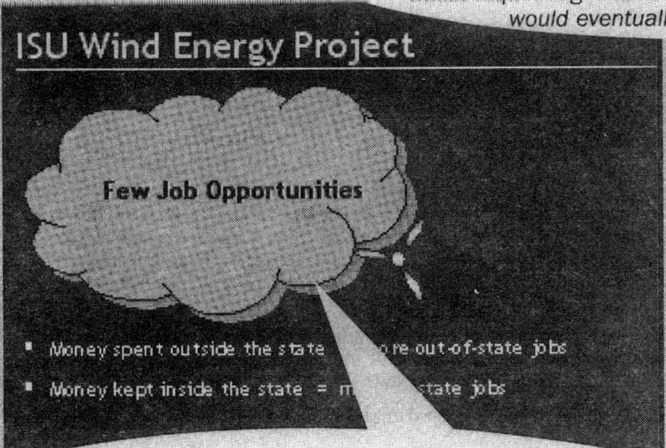

FIGURE 1.4E **Slide Introducing Job Opportunity Problem**

Accessibility

- *A shadow font in the cloud distinguishes it from the primary text.*

Comprehensibility

- *An equation with the = sign rather than words is faster to understand than the word "equals."*

Usability

- *Slides with the same general purpose use the same general design — such as this slide and the preceding one.*
- *The color of the heading identifying the project and the color of the key text are identical, creating a topical connection.*

"More important, reducing our dependence on neighboring states for energy sources will generate jobs for Iowans. Our proposal addresses a fundamental aspect of the state's energy budget — that we spend an inordinate amount of our annual energy budget on out-of-state expenses — and seeks a turbine system to create jobs and ultimately give Iowa's economy a much-needed boost."

REPORTING PROGRESS
报告进展

Much of the technical communication you do will be reporting progress on a project. Sometimes the report will be a brief, informal, oral presentation at a small meeting; at other times, it will be a lengthy formal report with a large distribution.

The example in Figure 1.5 is an excerpt from a long internal company report presenting an assessment of the capabilities of one of several battery manufacturers being considered as a supplier for the company. The readers are company employees — engineers, industrial buyers, managers — who are members of a committee to review the capabilities of ten major battery manufacturers. (The names of all the companies have been changed.) This committee will recommend which manufacturers the company should select as primary and secondary suppliers. A major portion of the committee's decision rests on the capability of the battery manufacturer and the quality of the batteries. And that quality depends on the production processes — that is, the way the batteries are manufactured. Based on information obtained from site visits to each manufacturing facility, one of the engineers on the committee produced a separate, detailed, and lengthy report for each manufacturer being considered.

The engineer/writer decided that each of the ten reports — completed over a six-month period, coinciding with the site visits — would include the same eight sections so that comparisons among the various manufacturers could be made easily. The excerpt in Figure 1.5, from the report about the site visit to Dalton Battery Company, is a subsection of the third main division of the report about chemical processes.

Paul A. Souders/CORBIS

The quality of paste production is critical in the manufacture of aluminum.

Accessibility

- *Sufficiently large font is easy to read.*
- *A boldface section heading matches the table of contents (and has a parallel heading in all ten reports assessing the other battery companies).*
- *Related information is chunked into short paragraphs.*
- *Each parameter is discussed in a separate paragraph so that it is easy to identify.*

Comprehensibility

- *Important information is effectively signaled and organized. For example, two kinds of paste are clearly distinguished.*
- *Definitions and explanations enable the less technical members of the committee to follow the discussion but do not annoy technical readers who don't need as much explanation.*
- *Critical definitions and explanations help members of the committee who do not have an engineering background.*
- *Technical details are important to the engineers on the committee.*
- *Words such as* only *and* instead *help readers interpret the information.*

Usability

- *Information in the table reinforces and illustrates the text.*
- *Foregrounding of critical parameters prepares readers for the next three paragraphs.*
- *Effective use of standard comparisons helps readers assess the information made over a six-month period.*

PASTE PRODUCTION

Paste production involves mixing lead oxide with water, sulfuric acid, organic fibers, and red lead to produce a dough-like substance called *paste*. In this section, I discuss Dalton's general paste formula and control parameters but not the exact formula. No comparison with other vendors can be made because these formulas are closely guarded secrets. However, I do provide a comparison of Dalton's control parameters both to industry standards and to optimum conditions for known parameters.

Formulations for the positive and negative paste differ primarily because red lead is added to the positive paste and not to the negative, while expander is added to the negative paste and not to the positive. In the battery industry, red lead is usually 10–30% of the total lead oxide: the higher the percentage of red lead the better. Dalton uses only 10% red lead. The expander, a mixture of lignin, carbon black, and barium sulfate, is usually added at about the 1% level. The best expander is Anzon-Kx. Instead, Dalton uses HL-120, from Harrington Lead Company. Harrington has the reputation for occasionally producing erratic quality expanders. Dalton's paste formulation — rounded off to 1% — is given in the table below.

	Positive Formula	Negative Formula
Oxide	72%	82%
Red Lead	8%	None
Water	11%	10%
Acid	9%	7%
Expander	None	2%

The quality of the paste is determined by three parameters: peak temperature, dump temperature, and cube weight. The temperatures are monitored continuously but are controlled by the rate of reaction between the lead oxide and sulfuric acid. The other two parameters are manually measured with each batch of paste prior to dumping into the pasting machine. Usually only one measurement is taken per batch.

Peak temperature is probably the most important of the control parameters because it sets the amount of nuclei of tetrabasic lead sulfate, the phase necessary for long life in the battery. The hotter the peak temperature the better. The industry standard for this critical parameter is 160°F; in contrast, Dalton's control point is 140°F ± 10°F. (Note: I would prefer to see peak temperatures of 190°F.)

Unlike peak temperatures, ***dump temperatures*** should be kept as low as possible to prevent premature curing of the paste. The industry standard is 110–115°F, which is considerably cooler than Dalton's 125°F. Perhaps Dalton Battery is partially compensating for the low peak temperatures with high dump temperatures to increase their tetrabasic lead sulfate nucleation count.

Cube weights, which measure the density of the paste, are best if kept between 72–75 g/in³ for the positive in order to achieve long battery life. The negative is less critical but traditionally has cube weights of 68–78 g/in³. In comparison, Dalton uses cube weights of 66–68 g/in³ and 72–74 g/in³ for the positive and negative, respectively.

FIGURE 1.5 **Excerpt from a Technical Report**[16]

How big is the Internet? Worldwide in 2002, the host count (a *host* has an active and permanent IP address that is directly connected to the Internet) was nearly 175 million. While the United States has more Internet hosts that any other country, with an annual growth rate of about 10 percent, the growth rate of Internet hosts in many other countries is much higher. For example, Belgium, Denmark, Estonia, and Turkey have annual growth rates exceeding 50 percent, while China, the Czech Republic, Italy, and Ukraine exceed 65 percent.[17]

What does this mean in practical terms for individuals and businesses in the United States? The Stanford Institute for the Quantitative Study of Society (SIQSS) reports that 65 percent of American households have at least one computer, and 43 percent are connected to the Internet.[18] On the business side, the Internet is a $200 billion industry in the United States,[19] with at least two-thirds of small U.S. businesses using the Internet.[20]

Figure 1.6 contains three excerpts from Science@NASA, identified as best science site on the Internet and recognized for excellence in science communication and "the spread of science culture" using the Internet.[21] NASA representatives summarize the goal of the site: "The communication of newly acquired knowledge and understanding [are placed] on an equal footing with the generation of that knowledge and understanding."

The annotations identify some of the more than 100 critical features for Web site accessibility, comprehensibility, and usability that Jakob Nielson and Marie Tahir discuss and illustrate in their book, *Homepage Usability.*[22]

The first excerpt, from the top of Science@NASA's home page, provides quick descriptions for the general public of a range of discoveries, with links to more detailed information. The information focuses on detecting earthquakes before they strike.

FIGURE 1.6A Science@NASA Home Page[23]

Accessibility
- *Users can easily see NASA's logo and site categories.*

Comprehensibility
- *The terminology and level of concepts are understandable to most nonexperts.*

Usability
- *The homepage is distinctive from other pages on the site.*
- *Users have a clear starting point.*
- *Users can easily follow links to learn more about any topic.*

The second excerpt drills down one level into the Web site to an article intended for knowledgeable, interested nonexperts.

Accessibility

- *This page gives users the option of accessing streaming audio and animated photos.*

Comprehensibility

- *The text is written at about the level of the weekly science page in the* New York Times.

Usability

- *Critical identifying information is available on the initial screen*
- *The bottom of this page has direct links to more technical information.*

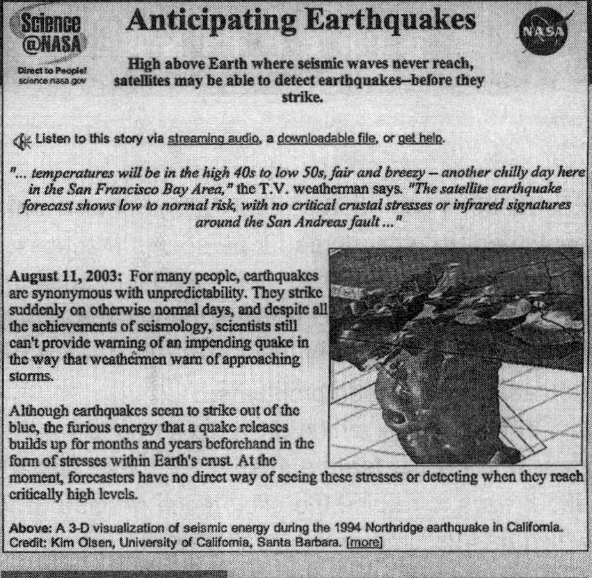

Science @NASA

Direct to People! science.nasa.gov

Anticipating Earthquakes

NASA

High above Earth where seismic waves never reach, satellites may be able to detect earthquakes--before they strike.

Listen to this story via streaming audio, a downloadable file, or get help.

"... temperatures will be in the high 40s to low 50s, fair and breezy – another chilly day here in the San Francisco Bay Area," the T.V. weatherman says. *"The satellite earthquake forecast shows low to normal risk, with no critical crustal stresses or infrared signatures around the San Andreas fault ..."*

August 11, 2003: For many people, earthquakes are synonymous with unpredictability. They strike suddenly on otherwise normal days, and despite all the achievements of seismology, scientists still can't provide warning of an impending quake in the way that weathermen warn of approaching storms.

Although earthquakes seem to strike out of the blue, the furious energy that a quake releases builds up for months and years beforehand in the form of stresses within Earth's crust. At the moment, forecasters have no direct way of seeing these stresses or detecting when they reach critically high levels.

Above: A 3-D visualization of seismic energy during the 1994 Northridge earthquake in California. Credit: Kim Olsen, University of California, Santa Barbara. [more]

FIGURE 1.6B **Excerpt of Article for Interested Nonexperts[24]**

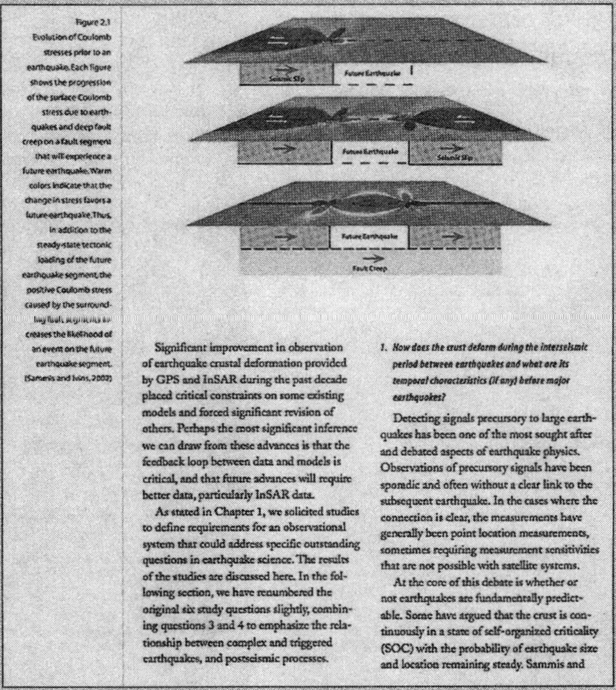

Figure 2.1 Evolution of Coulomb stresses prior to an earthquake. Each figure shows the progression of the surface Coulomb stress due to earthquakes and deep fault creep on a fault segment that will experience a future earthquake. Warm colors indicate that the change in stress favors a future earthquake. Thus, in addition to the steady-state tectonic loading of the future earthquake segment, the positive Coulomb stress caused by the surrounding fault segments increases the likelihood of an event on the future earthquake segment. (Sammis and Ivins, 2002)

Significant improvement in observation of earthquake crustal deformation provided by GPS and InSAR during the past decade placed critical constraints on some existing models and forced significant revision of others. Perhaps the most significant inference we can draw from these advances is that the feedback loop between data and models is critical, and that future advances will require better data, particularly InSAR data.

As stated in Chapter 1, we solicited studies to define requirements for an observational system that could address specific outstanding questions in earthquake science. The results of the studies are discussed here. In the following section, we have renumbered the original six study questions slightly, combining questions 3 and 4 to emphasize the relationship between complex and triggered earthquakes, and postseismic processes.

1. *How does the crust deform during the interseismic period between earthquakes and what are its temporal characteristics (if any) before major earthquakes?*

Detecting signals precursory to large earthquakes has been one of the most sought after and debated aspects of earthquake physics. Observations of precursory signals have been sporadic and often without a clear link to the subsequent earthquake. In the cases where the connection is clear, the measurements have generally been point location measurements, sometimes requiring measurement sensitivities that are not possible with satellite systems.

At the core of this debate is whether or not earthquakes are fundamentally predictable. Some have argued that the crust is continuously in a state of self-organized criticality (SOC) with the probability of earthquake size and location remaining steady. Sammis and

The third excerpt drills down another level to a technical article intended for experts.

Accessibility

- *The sans serif font makes long reports easy to read.*
- *Two column text is easy to read.*

Comprehensibility

- *The final GESS report is a 104-page technical discussion that is understandable by a broad scientific audience*
- *This report incorporates an executive summary as well as a large number of visuals.*
- *Appropriate use of color makes the figures easier to understand and interpret.*

Usability

- *The captions are placed next to the relevant figure and provide clear, complete explanations and citations.*

FIGURE 1.6C **Excerpt of Article for Experts[25]**

DIRECTING ACTION
指导行动

Instructions can address everything from the operation of manufacturing equipment to procedures for personnel practices. Every product and process — whether for the commercial or consumer market — can be accompanied by paper or online manuals to direct assembly, guide operation, recommend maintenance, specify steps, caution about safety, and troubleshoot common problems.

Virtually every airline provides its passengers with an in-flight magazine. One regular feature in some of these magazines is instructions about ways to reduce the occurrence of deep venous thrombosis (DVT), which has become an increasing health concern due in part to cramped seating and extended trips. The example in Figure 1.7, originally published in *Royal Wings*, the in-flight magazine for Royal Jordanian Airline, presents six illustrated steps to reduce the likelihood of DVT.

What causes DVT? Seated immobility for extended periods is a big factor. Who's at risk? People at risk include those who smoke, are obese, have a history of malignancy, or have had recent surgery. Women are more at risk more than men, especially those taking oral contraceptives or hormone replacements. People over 40 are usually more at risk; however, young people with hereditary incidents are at risk as well.[26] Many airlines actively educate passengers in order to reduce the likelihood of DVT.

Accessibility

- *Both the English and Arabic texts are large enough for most people to see easily.*
- *The size and quality of the images are sufficient.*

Comprehensibility

- *Many passengers on Royal Jordanian Airline read Arabic as their first language; many also read English.*
- *The introduction defines DVT but doesn't explain the criticality—that is, that a blood clot in one of the large veins can block the flow of blood back to the heart. The most serious risk of DVT is a pulmonary embolus, which can cause death. More typically, DVT causes chronic pain and swelling.*
- *Except for the name of each exercise, the terminology is adjusted to nonexperts.*
- *The scale in the visuals realistically shows the cramped space in which these exercises are done.*
- *Most of the visuals are sufficiently accurate and detailed to enable people to do some of the exercises even if they can't read Arabic or English.*

Usability

- *The numbered steps follow the English text by moving from left to right. If the sequence followed the Arabic text, it would move from right to left.*
- *The instructions do not make clear that seated immobility for extended periods is a major cause of DVT and, therefore, that doing the exercises is very important.*
- *The visuals include clearly marked directions for movement.*
- *The visuals are coordinated with the relevant text.*

ECONOMY CLASS SYNDROME: FICTION OR FACT?

ظاهرة الدرجة السياحية حقيقة أم وهم

Clotting of blood, usually occurring in the lower legs is known as deep venous thrombosis 'DVT'. This has become known in the press as 'Economy Class Syndrome', but the term is misleading. Individuals seated in cars, buses and trains may all be at risk, and cases of DVT occurring in flight have been reported in premium cabins as well as economy. The term 'traveller's thrombosis' is much more accurate.

Certain people are at increased risk of developing DVT, such as those who have previously been affected by this condition in the past, cancer patients, smokers, elderly people and those who are obese. Women who are taking oral contraceptive pills may also have a higher risk.

RECOMMENDATIONS

1. Wear loose-fitting comfortable clothes
2. Avoid knee-length stockings
3. Avoid alcohol and caffeine
4. Drink plenty of water
5. While seated, avoid crossing legs, and do simple physical exercises for feet and knees for two to three minutes every 30 minutes as shown in the pictures below.

يحدث تخثر الدم عادة في الساقين و هو ما يدعى تخثر الأوردة العميق و هو ما اصبح يسمى بالصحافة ظاهرة الدرجة السياحية لكن هذا المصطلح فيه بعض التضليل.

إن الأشخاص الذين يستقلون السيارات الصغيرة ، الحافلات و القطارات يتعرضون لحدوث هذا الاضطراب ، و هذه الحالة تحدث في الطيران أيضا لدى مسافري الدرجة الأولى كما هو الأمر لمسافري الدرجة السياحية ، و ربما كان مصطلح تخثر الأوردة لدى المسافرين اكثر دقة. يحدث هذا الأمر عند أشخاص لديهم التاهب و القابلية لذلك كالذين أصيبوا به سابقا، المدخنين، كبار السن، و المصابون بالسمنة . إن النساء اللواتي يتناولن حبوب منع الحمل لديهن قابلية وخطورة اكبر.

التوصيات:

١- ارتداء الملابس الفضفاضة

٢- تجنب ارتداء الجرابات الطويلة التي تصل إلى الركبتين

٣- تجنب شرب الكحول و السوائل التي تحتوي مادة الكافئين

٤- اكثر من تناول الماء و العصائر

٥- بينما أنت جالس على مقعدك تجنب وضعية تقاطع الساقين و قم بإجراء التمارين البسيطة للقدمين و الركبتين لمدة (٢-٣) دقائق كل حوالي ٣٠ دقيقة كما هو موضح بالصورة .

1 **(Knee flex):** Lift knee towards chest, decreasing the amount of joint space at the back of the knee. Repeat with other leg.

١ **عطف الركبة:** قم برفع الركبة نحو الصدر، مقلصا مساحة المفصل من الناحية الخلفية للركبة.
- كرر ذلك للساق الأخرى.

2 **(Knee Extension):** Straighten knee, increasing the amount of joint space at the back of the knee to its full range. Repeat with other leg.

٢ **بسط الركبة:** قم بمد الركبة بحيث تزيد مساحة المفصل من الناحية الخلفية للركبة.
- كرر ذلك للساق الأخرى.

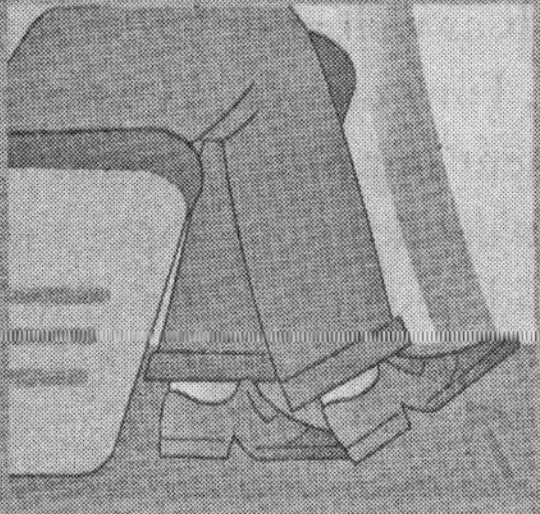

3 **(Dorsiflexion):** With heel on floor, point toes upwards, decreasing the angle between the foot and front of the leg. Repeat with other foot.

٣ **عطف ظهر القدم:** بينما العقب على الأرض، ارفع أصابع القدم للأعلى مقلصا الزاوية بين القدم و مقدمة الساق.
- كرر ذلك للقدم الأخرى

4 **(Plantar flex):** Stretch the foot and toes down and back, increasing the angle between top of the foot and front of the leg. Repeat with other foot.

٤ **عطف أخمص القدم:** ابسط القدم بينما أصابع القدم للأسفل و الخلف بحيث تزيد الزاوية بين مقدمة القدم و مقدمة الساق.
- كرر ذلك للقدم الأخرى

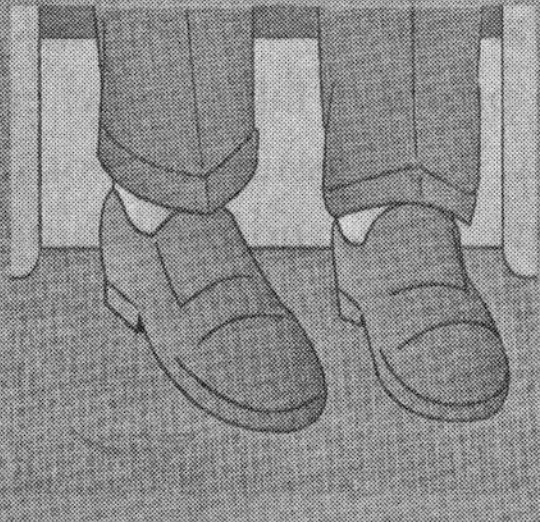

5 **(Inversion):** With foot on floor, gently roll the sole of the foot inward. Repeat with other foot.

٥ **دوران داخلي:** بينما القدم على الأرض، أسحب بلطف أخمص القدم للداخل.
- كرر ذلك للقدم الأخرى.

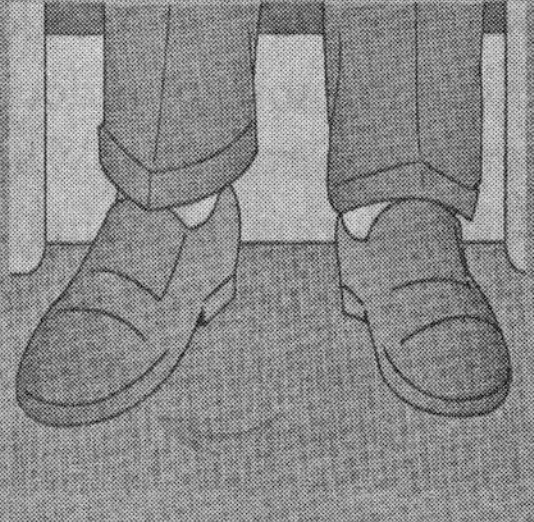

6 **(Enversion):** With foot on floor, gently roll the sole of the foot outward. Repeat with other foot.

٦ **دوران خارجي:** بينما القدم على الأرض، اسحب بلطف أخمص القدم للخارج.
- كرر ذلك للقدم الأخرى

FIGURE 1.7 **Instructions to Reduce Occurrence of Deep Venous Thrombosis**[27]

Constraints that Communicators Encounter

交流中可能遇到的局限

> *What kinds of constraints have you already faced in the workplace? How did you manage these constraints so they did not cause major problems?*

Regardless of the kinds of technical documents, oral presentations, and visuals you create and use (such as those in Figures 1.3–1.7), you'll need to manage constraints that affect the entire process of creating and interpreting technical information.

Time Constraints 时间局限

You'll often work within time limits that seem unreasonable; for example, the schedule may have been set by someone unaware of the demands of documenting technical projects. In practice, time considerations and deadlines limit every stage of preparing technical information. One of your responsibilities is deciding how much time you can devote to each project.

Subject and Format Constraints 主题与格式局限

The subject for a technical document, oral presentation, or visual is usually predetermined. However, you'll face the challenge of focusing on details appropriate for the intended audience and presenting them in an interesting and useful manner. You will seldom be given a specific approach. Rather, you'll need to be able to narrow your subject, select and organize content, and then determine the limitations. To do this, you'll need to assess the audience's needs and identify its purposes.

Audience Constraints 读者（或客户）局限

Sometimes you'll prepare technical information for an audience in which everyone has similar education, experience, and expectations. Frequently, however, the members of the audience will have varied backgrounds as well as different reasons for reading a document or listening to a presentation. For example, a business manager might have an advanced degree in management but little expertise in the company's technical field. As a result, you'll need to make decisions about the level of technical complexity, organization, diction, and design to respond to the needs of a variety of readers or listeners. (See Chapter 4 for a more detailed discussion about audience.)

Collaboration as a Constraint 合作带来的局限

Sometimes you'll work independently, sometimes collaboratively. Your actual role in preparing any given document or presentation will probably fall somewhere between two extremes. When you work independently, you'll assume responsibility for exploring, planning, drafting, and perhaps even editing and publishing a document. When you work collaboratively, you'll share the responsibility for one or more stages of the process. (See Chapter 5 for a more detailed discussion about community and collaboration.)

Constraints in Data Collection 数据收集的局限

The information you need won't always be easily or quickly accessible. To collect information, you must confidently approach new equipment and unfamiliar processes. As you learn to operate the equipment or complete the process, you'll often discover what your audience needs to know. Don't be surprised, however, when you are hampered by limited access to the necessary equipment or when the available information seems skimpy. Sometimes the deadlines will be too tight to learn everything you need to know. In these situations, you must depend on others for the information you need. Develop persuasive skills so that people who have busy schedules agree to make time to talk with you. Once you've located the people who have the information and have made an appointment with them, you need strong interviewing skills to collect the data. (Chapters 7 and 19 and the Companion Web site [**www.english.wadsworth.com/burnett6e**] provide guidelines for conducting or participating in various kinds of interviews.)

WWW

WEBLINK

Constraints in Technology 技术中的局限

Technology is part of communication in every workplace, from agribusiness to nanoscale physics laboratories, from endangered species breeding programs to software engineering departments. You face several potential constraints. First, you will need access to appropriate technology as well as the capability and training to use it. You will be at a tremendous disadvantage if you aren't familiar with and don't have the training to use a wide range of appropriate electronic tools. Other constraints you might encounter include limited access to electronic tools, lack of technical support for the hardware and software, and users' unfamiliarity with the technology if they need to access information electronically.

Constraints Caused by Noise 噪音引起的局限

Interference, or what is sometimes called *noise,* can come from the context or environment, from any of the communicators, or from the document, oral presentation, or visual itself.

- *Noise from the context or environment.* One kind of environmental interference occurs because the physical reception is garbled or masked. Physical interference may be as simple as a noisy air conditioner in a meeting room or static on a phone line. Another kind of environmental interference occurs because the social or political environment influences the way in which people interpret information. Social or political interference may be caused by organizational policies and practices. For example, if safety updates are typically given only cursory attention in a particular company, a writer has a more difficult time than if these updates are carefully read and implemented. No environment is neutral; some form of interference always exists.

What constraints do you anticipate you might have in the future when preparing a technical document or presentation? How do you plan to deal with these constraints?

- *Noise from any of the communicators.* Writers, speakers, and designers as well as readers, listeners, and viewers can generate noise. The experiences and attitudes of the writers, speakers, or designers (factors such as vested interests, emotional biases, perceptions) affect their selection and slant of information. This interference may also come from problems that the writers, speakers, or designers have in formulating the information (for example, ambiguity or failure to consider audience needs). The experiences and attitudes of readers, listeners, and viewers (factors such as boredom, doubt, disagreement, anger, or indifference) affect their interpretation of information. No communicator is neutral; interference of some type is always part of those who generate the information as well as those who interpret it.
- *Noise embedded in information and in its delivery.* Information can be incomplete, inaccurate, illogical, unsupported, or inflammatory, thus causing interference in understanding. Beyond that, interference can occur because of confusing design, low-quality reproduction, or problems with electronic transmission. Interference can occur in oral presentations due to inadequate amplification or inappropriate visuals for the room size. No delivery is neutral; some form of interference always affects the information and its reception.

Being aware of the constraints that communicators face — time, subject and format, audience, collaboration, data collection, technology, and various kinds of noise — should help you anticipate and manage some of the problems that these constraints generate.

Individual and Collaborative Assignments
个人作业和小组作业

1. **Define technical communication.** Create a definition of technical communication for colleagues in your profession that accurately reflects the complexity of creating and interpreting technical information so that it is accessible, comprehensible, and usable. Use information in this chapter, information from two organizations, the Society for Technical Communication in the U.S. (**www.stc.org**) and the Institute of Scientific and Technical Communicators in the UK (**www.istc.org.uk; www.istc.org.uk/site/news.asp**), and information from the Web sites of the organizations in your own profession. Compare your definition to those created by others in the class.
2. **Identify general audiences.** Read the following list of subjects. Identify at least two realistic technical audiences for any five of these subjects. Explain what technical information each audience might need to learn or use.

   Example: Renaissance paint might be of interest to any of these technical professionals: a museum curator for authenticating a painting; an art historian for characterizing materials in a particular period; a chemist for conducting a spectrographic analysis.

arrows	ethanol	magnifying glass	running shoes
ballet	fax machine	modem	soybeans
butter	frisbees	motor oil	steroids
CDs	furniture stripper	peanuts	styrofoam
cell phone	golf balls	perfume	tires
coffee	hot dogs	plastic film	tricycles
condors	jogging	poetry	trout
eggs	legumes	rainbows	ZIP code

3. **Identify accessibility, comprehensibility, and usability.** Work in a small group to visit any three of the following Web home pages, which represent a range of national and multinational corporations as well as nonprofit organizations. Consider these questions:

   - **Who's the sponsor?** Can users easily identify a name, logo, and tag line on the home page describing what the organization does?
   - ***Who are the intended audiences?*** Who are the probable users? What are their purposes for using the site?
   - ***How accessible is the site?*** How is the site accessible? To users reading other languages? To users with visual disabilities? To users with limited or old computer resources? Does the home page have distracting or competing elements?
   - ***How easy is the site to understand?*** Can users easily determine what's most important on the home page? What prior knowledge is assumed? What conventions does the home page use? What is the technical level of definitions and explanations?
   - ***How easy is the site to use?*** How easily can users determine the site's organization from the home page? Can users find a clear place to start? How are links to other parts of the site indicated? How easy is the site to navigate?

www.admworld.com	www.fedex.com	www.dupont.com
www.bayerus.com	www.nestle.com	www.oracle.com
www.birdseye.com	www.lucent.com	www.ups.com
www.cocacola.com	www.merck.com	www.whymilk.com

4. **Assess a short memo.** The following memo was submitted as a weekly progress report about project activities. It is typical in several ways — amount of information, tone, length, and attention to detail — of the memos and reports produced by Wayne Jackson, an associate engineer. Because Mr. Jackson has always been extremely careful to double-check his content for accuracy, he is surprised that his semiannual review identifies his writing as a block to rapid advancement. Examine the memo and use the factors for assessing documents presented in this chapter to help explain

whether you agree with the assessment by Mr. Jackson's supervisor. What advice would you give Mr. Jackson to help him become a more effective communicator? Revise the memo.

> **Memo**
>
> September 26, 20——
>
> **To** Mark Hager
> **From** Wayne Jackson *WJ*
> **Subject** Project Update
>
> We're on schedule except for setting up the grinding wheels because they haven't been recieved yet and calibrating the tools because new master blocks haven't been uncrated. Joe Simons has been out all week with the flu.
>
> Everything should be done next week.
>
> The electrician is scheduled Tuesday to install new lines and wire equipment.

5. Assess a technical explanation. Read the following text, "Understanding and Avoiding the Leading Cause of Death among Pilots," written by an experienced pilot for beginning student pilots. In the partially completed rubric on page 32, read the abbreviated criteria for *excellent* for each feature listed. While managers and supervisors (and teachers) use rubrics to help assess various kinds of communication, rubrics can provide the most help to writers, presenters, and designers as they revise their work to meet the criteria.

Using the information in this chapter and the generic rubrics on this textbook's Companion Web site, **www.english.wadsworth.com/burnett6e**, expand each criteria to provide more detailed help to writers as to what will make the document to pilots excellent. Then complete the rubric's cells for *unacceptable, weak,* and *acceptable* in relation to the document for student pilots. The *weak* and *unacceptable* columns will help you identify elements to avoid. Based on your completed rubric, explain whether the writer has created an effective technical document.

Note: Throughout this text, you will be asked to create and use rubrics as tools to help you assess documents, oral presentations, and visuals. This textbook's Companion Web site, **www.english.wadsworth.com/burnett6e**, presents generic rubrics that you can modify as needed for specific print documents, oral presentations, and visuals.

Understanding and Avoiding the Leading Cause of Death among Pilots[28]

More pilots are killed in ***stall-spin accidents*** than in any other type of incident. The next cause of fatalities is inadvertent flight into bad weather by pilots not trained in instrument flight, which usually leads to a stall-spin scenario. At the end of this discussion, you should be able to answer these questions:

- What holds the airplane up?
- What is a stall?
- What is a spin?
- How can you recover from a stall?

The engine doesn't hold the airplane up in the air, the wing doesn't hold it up in the air, and (although we're reluctant to admit it) the pilot's skill doesn't hold it up in the air. Airplanes are held aloft by a physical force called lift. ***Lift*** is an upward force generated by the smooth flow of air over the wing's surfaces.

The illustration below uses tiny balloons to represent paired air molecules passing above and below a wing. In 1738, a Swiss physicist named Daniel Bernoulli suggested that the air mass remains undisturbed by the wing and that each pair of balloons would join again at the back of the wing. Wings have a certain shape: the top is convex; the bottom is flat. Slats at the leading edge of the wing and flaps at the trailing edge of the wing exaggerate the difference. As the illustration shows, the curved line traveled by the balloons above the wing is a greater distance than the straight line traveled by balloons below the wing.

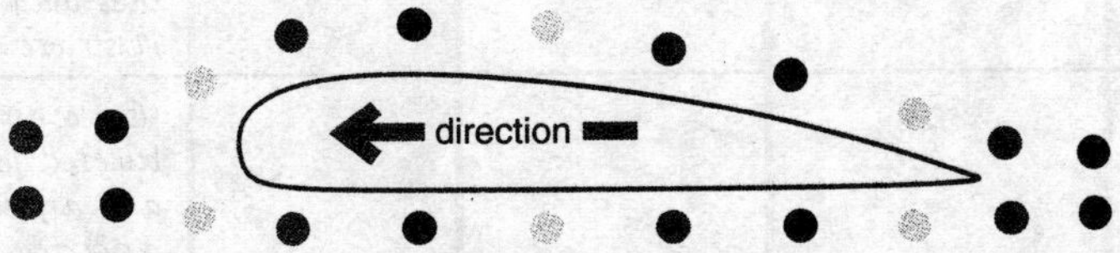

In order for the balloons to rejoin, the speed and spacing of the upper balloons must be greater than the speed and spacing of the lower balloons; the difference in speed and distance causes a relatively lower *air pressure* along the top of the wing. This relative suction translates into a force called lift. Lift increases as the flow of air increases over the wings. When the speed of the airflow over the wings generates a lifting force stronger than gravity, the plane flies. The engine does not thrust the plane into the sky; the engine moves the plane forward at a speed permitting the wings to generate sufficient lift.

What happens when this goes wrong? When the airflow is disturbed, the subtle relative suction disappears, and gravity re-asserts itself over the mass of the aircraft. The airflow can be disturbed by ice or by an extremely nose-high attitude. The loss of lift is called a ***stall***, a phrase that has nothing to do with the way a jalopy quits on the highway. One warning: Never attempt to takeoff with ice or frost on the wings. Keep the wings clean of dirt and bugs. Lift requires clean wings.

When one wing stalls before the other, the aircraft becomes asymmetrical, resulting in a disorienting rotation dive called a ***spin***. Low-time pilots can be overwhelmed by the physical forces of a sustained spin and may be unable to regain controlled flight.

Recovery from the stall is straightforward: Level the wings to avoid a spin, drop the nose to increase airflow over the wings and restore lift, increase to full engine power to climb to safety, and reflect on the audacity of flight.

Your experienced flight instructor will show you how to intentionally stall and spin your aircraft to practice recovering from these situations. When you start these maneuvers at a safe altitude and with your instructor's guidance, you will learn how to avoid, recognize, and resolve the situations that put novice pilots at risk. Remember: Level the wings, drop the nose, and apply full power.

Rubric for Assessing the Explanation about Spin and Stall

Document Features	Unacceptable	Weak	Acceptable	Excellent
Accurate information	Includes many errors	Includes several errors	Includes few errors	Includes accurate and sufficient information
Accessible information				Makes information completely accessible to the intended audience
Response to context				Responds to major concern of beginning pilots
Understandable information				Defines/explains information at a level appropriate for beginning pilots
Clear purpose				Announces purpose/goal up front
Adapted to audience				Uses appropriate vocabulary and level of explanation
Effective organization				Identifies and develops key topics in order
Appropriate visuals				Uses diagram to clearly illustrate textual discussion
Effective design				Uses coherent paragraphs, bulleted list, boldface terms, and an embedded diagram appropriate for nonexperts
Usable information				Enables beginning pilots to answer key questions
Conventional language				Uses conventional language with no errors

Chapter 1 Endnotes

1 Barnum, C., & Fischer, R. (1984). Engineering technologists as writers: Results of a survey. *Technical Communication, 31*(2), 9–11.

2 "The [2003] survey was developed by Robert Half Finance & Accounting. . . . Conducted by an independent research firm, the survey includes responses from 1,400 CFOs from a stratified random sample of U.S. companies with more than 20 employees." Various Web sites about the survey are listed below:

- Retrieved August 16, 2003, from http://www.roberthalfmr.com/PressRoom;jessionid=AEBifnjywmB1ecw5VvgtYj2KokMNGTx2C0Yo3G1fyKq1BvYLCX!-221591521!NONE
- Retrieved August 16, 2003, from http://www.roberthalffinance.com/PressRoom?LOBName=RH&releaseid=357
- Retrieved August 16, 2003, from http://www.ivc.ca/studies/us.html

3 *AMA 2003 Views on Administrative Professionals' Tasks and Competencies.* Retrieved January 13, 2004, from http://www.amanet.org/research/pdf.htm

4 The National Institute for Literacy (NIFL) was created by a bipartisan congressional coalition and currently authorized under the Workforce Investment Act of 1998. NIFL, which supports the development of high quality regional, state, and national literacy services, is administered by the Secretaries of Education, Labor, and Health and Human Services with the help of a ten-member advisory board. Data are from the survey of Workforce Skill Requirements. Retrieved August 16, 2003, from http://www.nifl.gov/nifl/facts/workforce.html

5 The 2000 survey of 204 members of L'association canadienne de l'informatique were compared with results from the Information & Advanced Technology Survey 2000, which surveyed over 100 technology-based organizations in Canada. Retrieved August 16, 2003, from http://www.wynfordgroup.com/cips/CIPS_2000_Results.htm

6 Data are from the survey of Corporate Concerns. Retrieved August 16, 2003, from http://www.nifl.gov/nifl/facts/workforce.html

7 Berkenkotter, C., & Huckin, T. N. (1995). *Genre knowledge in disciplinary communication: Cognition/culture/power.* Hillsdale, NJ: Lawrence Erlbaum. (See especially pages 1–25.)

8 Wenger, E. (1998). *Communities of practice: Learning as a social system.* Retrieved January 13, 2004, from http://www.co-i-l.com/coil/knowledge-garden/cop/lss.shtml

9 Smith, M. K. (2003). Communities of practice. *The encyclopedia of informal education.* Retrieved September 7, 2003, from http://www.infed.org/biblio/communities_of_practice.htm

10 Kaplan, C. S. (2000, 14 January). Judge says recording of electronic chats is legal. *New York Times.* Retrieved October 1, 2003, from http://www.nytimes.comibrary/tech/00/01/cyber/cyberlaw/14law.html

11 Ornatowski, C. (1992). Between efficiency and politics: Rhetoric and ethics in technical writing. *Technical Communication Quarterly, 1*(1), 91–103.

[12] For biographical details about H. P. Grice, check this Web site: http://www.artsci.wustl.edu/-philos/MindDict/grice.html

[13] For interesting discussions about Grice's cooperative principle and related maxims, refer to these two articles:

- Davies, B. (2000). Grice's cooperative principle: Getting the meaning across [Electronic version]. In D. Nelson & P. Foulkes (Eds.), *Leeds Working Papers in Linguistics, 8,* 1–26.
- White, R. (2000). Adapting Grice's maxims in the teaching of writing [Electronic version]. *ELT Journal, 55*(1), 62–69.

[14] American Academy of Allergy and Immunology. *Allergy relief guide.* [Brochure]. Reprinted by permission of the Academy.

[15] The slides are reproduced here with the permission of the students who prepared them in a technical communication class at Iowa State University, Summer, 2003.

[16] Gary Tarcy, "Site Visit to Dalton Battery." Reprinted by permission of the author.

[17] "Data on internet activity worldwide." Updated March 16, 2003. Retrieved August 18, 2003 from http://www.gandalf.it/data/data1.htm

[18] Nie, N. H., & Erbring, L. (February 2000). *Internet and society: A preliminary report.* Retrieved August 17, 2003, from Stanford University, Stanford Institute for the Quantitative Study of Society Web site.

[19] In Stat MDR. (2001, January 16). *Internet infrastructure continues to grow: U.S. businesses to spend nearly $200 billion in 2004.* Retrieved August 18, 2003, from http://www.instat.com/pr/2001/ec0008ms_pr.htm

[20] Intellisites. (2002, March 29). *Two thirds of small businesses using the Internet.* Retrieved August 18, 2003, from http://www.intellisitedesign.com/articles/art-Two-Thirds-of-Small-Businesses-Using-the-Internet.htm

[21] See press releases:

- NASA Space Science News. (1999, January 19). *The Oscars of the Internet.* Retrieved August 23, 2003, from http://www.southpole.com/newhome/headlines/sc19jan99_1.htm
- Science@NASA. (2001, April 4). *Tireless Science Communication Pays Off for Science@NASA.* Retrieved August 23, 2003, from http://science.nasa.gov/headlines/y2001/ast04apr_1.htm

[22] Nielson, J., & Tahir, M. (2002). *Homepage usability: 50 Websites deconstructed.* Indianapolis, IN: New Riders Publishing.

[23] Retrieved August 17, 2003, from http://science.nasa.gov/

[24] Retrieved August 17, 2003, from http://science.nasa.gov/headlines/y2003/11aug_earthquakes.htm

[25] *Global Earthquake Satellite System: A 20-year plan to enable earthquake prediction.* Displayed is an excerpt from page 18. Retrieved August 17, 2003, from http://solidearth.jpl.nasa.gov/gess2.html

26 Information compiled from these sources:

- Cleveland, M. (n.d.). Deep venous thrombosis. In *Diseases and conditions encyclopedia.* Retrieved August 17, 2003, from http://health.discovery.com/diseasesandcond/encyclopedia/590.html
- *Deep venous thrombosis (DVT) and air travel.* (n.d.). Retrieved August 17, 2003, from http://www.caa.co.za/resource%20center/av.%20medicine/docs/thrombosis.html
- National Air and Space Administration, Occupational Health. (2001, July 1). *Flight-related deep vein thrombosis (DVT) — "Economy class syndrome."* Retrieved August 17, 2003, from http://ohp.ksc.nasa.gov/alerts/dvt.html

27 "Economy class syndrome: Fiction or fact?" (2003). *Royal Wings,* (July-August), 51.

28 Quigley, E. (nd.) Understanding and avoiding the leading cause of death. School of Communication and Information Systems. Robert Morris College. Pittsburgh, PA. Reprinted by permission of the author.

CHAPTER 2

Understanding Culture and the Workplace
理解文化与职场的关系

本章首先阐释了文化的内涵及其在职场上的关键作用，然后分析了民族文化以及企业文化差异。本章还指出了个体对民族文化和企业文化的理解直接影响其在职场中的交流。本章最后提供了一些理解不同文化的练习，尝试与不同文化背景的同事有效合作。

Objectives and Outcomes 学习目标

This chapter will help you accomplish these outcomes:

- Define culture and recognize the critical role that it plays in the workplace
- Understand factors that contribute to various cultures
- Analyze and understand the ways in which culture affects workplace communication
- Work more productively and respectfully with colleagues from various cultures

What are negative words or phrases that people sometimes use to describe attitudes, actions, tools, and artifacts that are unfamiliar? Weird. Funny. Stupid. What else? Why do people label the unfamiliar negatively?

Professionals who understand workplace cultures have a remarkable advantage. This chapter encourages you to think about culture — both your own culture (which may be strange to others) and the cultures of others (which may be strange to you). A culture seems strange when it is unfamiliar, uncomfortable, and sometimes even inaccessible. Learning how to make sense of and function productively with unfamiliar cultures in the workplace increases your value as an employee and improves your performance as a professional.

This chapter encourages you to think about culture in a new way: not just as nationality and ethnicity but also as workplace and community organizations, as a factor that influences our way of living, and as a factor that comprises our demographic identity and personal way of life. While we can discuss these aspects of culture separately, in practice they are synergistically integrated.

Noticing Culture in the Workplace
关注职场中的文化

A recent survey of more than 1,000 CEOs around the world showed these findings:[1]

	Companies with customers in six or more countries	Companies with suppliers in six or more countries	Companies with employees in six or more countries
Europe	83%	76%	67%
Australia/New Zealand	75%	75%	64%
Asia	68%	69%	56%
North America	62%	55%	43%
Latin America	57%	50%	33%

Given findings such as these, your chances are better than average of working for a company that has international customers, suppliers, and/or employees.

You don't even have to leave the United States or work for a multinational corporation to find cultural differences. The U.S. workplace itself is multicultural and multiracial. For example, the U.S. Census for 2000 shows the following demographics:[2]

- Nearly 18% of people in the United States speak a language other than English at home.
- Racial minorities own nearly 15% of U.S. companies.
- Slightly less than 70% of people counted by the U.S. census are white. Slightly more than 12% are black. Another 12% are of Hispanic or Latino origin. Nearly 4% are Asian. About 1% are American Indian or Alaska Native.
- Slightly more than 11% of people counted by the U.S. census were born in another country.

And this multicultural and multiracial workforce exports goods and services to more than 200 countries around the world[3] and imports goods and services from nearly 250 other countries.[4]

How do the gender and racial descriptions of the workforce in your community and state differ from the national percentages? Go to **www.english.wadsworth.com/burnett6e** for links to search for this information.
CLICK ON WEBLINK
CLICK on Chapter 2/census

WWW
WEBLINK

Your ability to communicate successfully in the workplace includes your ability to recognize and positively respond to culture-specific attitudes, actions, tools (processes and procedures as well as physical tools), and artifacts such as documents, oral presentations, and visuals. You can start by thinking about cultures as being societies that have structures, purposes, and group-specific meanings.

Culture can be associated with nationality, race, ethnicity, or religion. For example, South Africa, a country with black, Indian, multiracial, and white citizens who speak many different languages, has both a national culture striving for post-apartheid unity and a role in the world economic community as well as many subcultures defined by race, religion, and tribal heritage. Similarly, the United States has a national culture that includes Native Americans as well as people from many other countries, who in turn form subcultures defined by race, ethnicity, religion, and many other factors such as economics, sexual orientation, gender, and education.

Culture, however, is not just about these factors. You can also accurately talk about a culture of disability — that is, people whose physical or mental disabilities, whether visible or not, shape their lives. Or you can talk about the culture of specific types of companies. While Apple, Dell, Gateway, IBM, and Microsoft each has a distinctive corporate culture, collectively these computer companies differ from the corporate culture of Ford, General Motors, Nissan, Saturn, and Toyota.

Teams, which are the norm in many workplaces, typically include people from different cultures. Taking advantage of multiple perspectives usually increases the quality of the work the team does.

© Ryan McVay/Photodisc/Getty Images

What's Normal? 什么是常规?

> What other factors besides clothing, speech, and meeting conventions signal differences that affect workplace attitudes, interactions, and performance?

Whether you can understand a culture sometimes depends on its visibility to you. Parts of other cultures tend to be visible to us; our own culture tends to be invisible because we see it as "normal." We notice, for example, when others wear clothing at work that attracts or distracts us; we tend not to notice our own clothing because we see it as "normal." We notice when people at work speak with a different accent, volume, inflection, or pace than we're accustomed to; we tend not to notice our own speech because we hear it as "normal." We notice when people at meetings change the order or focus of business, such as taking time at the beginning of a meeting to discuss personal concerns or share stories; we tend not to notice our own meeting conventions because we consider them "normal." Part of becoming culturally aware is looking at what we do through someone else's eyes, through someone else's experiences. When we encounter something outside our own experience, we can ask ourselves if it is, perhaps, normal or familiar to someone else.

Cultural Blindness 文化盲点

This notion of "normal" can also make us blind to certain aspects of other cultures. Just as we don't give a second thought to what we believe is normal, we also don't usually realize that a comparable event, circumstance, or accommodation may exist in another culture.

Try this quick question: "What do July 5, August 24, December 6, and December 12 mean to you?" The question would perhaps be easier if the question were changed slightly: "What do July 4, July 5, August 24, December 6, and December 12 mean to you?" Then you would have one clue that they are all national holidays celebrating independence. When you are working with people from other cultures, their holidays are likely to be meaningful to them the same way that your holidays are meaningful to you.

> What other cultural differences besides holidays and building accommodations surround us but are often invisible? How can these differences affect workplace attitudes, interactions, and performance?

Maybe you're thinking to yourself that knowing these dates is unrealistic (and unfair), so let's test your cultural sensitivity closer to home. Think of five buildings that are regularly used by the majority of people at your college (e.g., library, medical center, computer facilities, theater/auditorium, police department, post office, offices of institutional officials, gymnasium/sports facilities). Try this quick question: "Where, exactly, is the wheelchair access to each building, where is the elevator once you're inside, and where are the wheelchair-accessible restrooms?" If you have a disability that requires a wheelchair (or have a close friend who does), you probably know the answers. If you are not using a wheelchair, you may have to think about, or not even know, the locations.

Defining Culture 文化定义

What is culture? A number of researchers have spent a great deal of time investigating culture and trying to create a workable definition. Most see culture as a system of learned beliefs and values that influences attitudes and actions. In completing these actions, people in a particular group use common tools to create artifacts. In technical communication, these artifacts range from documents, oral presentations, and visuals to meeting behaviors, team interactions, and organization hierarchies. According to anthropologist John Bodley, "Culture involves . . . what people think, what they do [along with the tools they use], and the material products they produce."[5]

These learned attitudes, actions, tools, and the resulting artifacts comprise a culture — whether defined by nation or race or disability or organization or any number of other factors. Clearly then, culture is sometimes more easily identified in other people than in ourselves. Raymond Williams provides an explanation for this: "Culture is ordinary."[6] Simply put, what we do in our communities and our corporations seems ordinary to us, so we don't identify it as "culture"; it's just the way things are. For example, U.S. culture includes predictable workdays — typically Monday through Friday from 8:00 a.m. to 5:00 p.m. But your vendors in Israel may want to reach you on a Sunday, which is a normal workday for them. And some of your vendors in Mexico may not be in their offices Monday through Friday from 1:00 to 3:00 p.m. Each of these cultures has a different sense of what constitutes a "normal" workday and workweek.

When a multinational corporation opens offices in another country, should the corporation adhere to the workday practices of the corporation's home country or adapt to those of the new country? For example, should IBM offices in Mexico have a siesta like many other Mexican businesses, or follow U.S. business practices and have no siesta?

Understanding the Importance of Culture
理解文化的重要性

More and more companies are paying attention to culture as part of making their organization a good place to work. Many organizations are addressing cultural differences by encouraging diversity and including forthright statements about culture, diversity, and human rights for its employees, contractors, and suppliers. Figure 2.1 presents an example from GlaxoSmithKline, a major pharmaceutical company headquartered in the UK with operations in the United States. This part of GlaxoSmithKline's Web site demonstrates the ways in which cultural differences are valued and respected in the corporation and the ways its human rights position are enforced.

What are the pros and cons of making an organization's diversity statement explicit? How does naming or omitting particular groups affect the inclusiveness of the statement?

Every year *Fortune* magazine publishes a list of the 100 best companies to work for in America. In what ways does workplace culture contribute to a company being named as a "best company"? Go to **www.english.wadsworth.com/burnett6e** for links to the "best companies" lists published by the Great Place to Work Institute. You can check the Web site to view the companies by year, by location, or by type of organization.

CLICK ON WEBLINK

CLICK on Chapter 2/best companies

WWW

WEBLINK

FIGURE 2.1 **GlaxoSmithKline Web Site Statement about Corporate Culture, Diversity, and Human Rights**[7]

gsk GlaxoSmithKline

The Impact of Medicines
Corporate and Social Responsibility Report 2002

→ REPORTING FRONT PAGE → DOWNLOADS

- CSR 2002 home
- A global challenge
- The scope of our business
- Our contribution to society
- Medicines for the developing world
- Community investment
- Research and development
- Valuing people
  - Case study
- Environment, health and safety
- Business ethics and integrity
- Management of CSR
- Web references
- Corporate Social Responsibility Committee

People are the greatest single source of competitive advantage for any company.

At GlaxoSmithKline, we believe that attracting, retaining and motivating the very best people is the foundation for our future success.

Valuing people

GSK employs over **100,000** people and operates in more than **150** countries.

PREVIOUS
NEXT

We are committed to providing the opportunity for our employees to do meaningful and challenging work in pursuit of our goal to improve the quality of human life by enabling people to do more, feel better and live longer.

Last year we reported on the principles that underpin our approach to people management, and a range of programmes which were designed to deliver our global human resources strategy. We are now pleased to report the progress we have made and set out, where we are able, how we intend in future to measure our performance on issues such as diversity.

THE GSK CULTURE
At GSK, great emphasis is placed not only on what we must achieve as a company, but also on how we deliver our achievements. Our culture is summed up in the GSK Spirit which defines the qualities we expect all our employees to embrace:

- performance with integrity
- entrepreneurial spirit
- focus on innovation
- a sense of urgency
- passion for achievement

Globalization and Localization 全球化与本地化

Why should this concern with culture matter to you? You are likely to work in situations that put you in contact with other cultures. When that occurs, you'll be more successful if you understand and respect other cultures, whether those cultural differences are based on nationality, race, ethnicity, religion, economics, sexual orientation, gender, education, or disability.

FIGURE 2.1 **GlaxoSmithKline Web Site Statement about Corporate Culture, Diversity, and Human Rights[7], continued**

ETHNICITY OF US EMPLOYEE POPULATION, 2002

Total US employees 24,000

DIVERSITY

Diversity is a business imperative for GSK; we are committed to the principles of equality of opportunity and equal treatment. We aim to have a workforce and working environment that reflects the diversity of background, culture, beliefs and characteristics of the communities in which we operate.

We are therefore embedding the values of diversity and equal treatment into our key business processes. For employees, this means that diversity measures are included in manager and employee training, external recruitment and internal appointment processes, performance assessments and pay reviews, succession planning and developmental assignments.

For customers and stakeholders, it includes the development of measures to reach targeted customers, outreach programmes for specific patient groups and advertising that reflects the many communities we serve.

HUMAN RIGHTS

GSK believes that on human rights issues, we can lead by example and thereby influence the behaviours and practices of others through clear demonstration of our own values. Our most effective contribution can be made through pursuing policies in our own operations that respect the rights and interests of all those affected by and involved in our business. GSK supports and is committed to upholding the United Nations Universal Declaration of Human Rights[26] and the core labour standards set out by the International Labour Organization[27].

During 2002, we carried out an internal review which demonstrated that, wherever we operate as an employer, we believe we are complying with the Universal Declaration of Human Rights and the core conventions of the International Labour Organization, and according to the Guidelines for Multinational Enterprises set by the OECD[28]. Conducted through the Head of Human Resources for each country, the review was also used to build awareness and understanding of human rights issues.

Also during the year, we began to put in place binding requirements to ensure that our major contractors and suppliers adopt GSK's standards on human rights and core labour standards.

Web references	
26	www.un.org/Overview/rights.html
27	www.ilo.org/public/english/standards/decl/declaration/text/index.htm
28	www.oecd.org/pdf/M000015000/M00015419.pdf

What's the focus in GlaxoSmithKline's position on workplace culture?

- *Opportunity for improved quality of life*
- *Equality of opportunity and treatment*
- *Diverse workforce*
- *Recruitment and training*
- *Active commitment to United Nations' Universal Declaration of Human Rights and International Labour Organization standards for their company as well as for contractors and suppliers*

Let's look at the statistics for some organizations where you might work, even if you never leave your own community. The nearly 40,000 organizations that are often called "global" or "multinational" account for approximately four-fifths of world trade.[8] Many of the organizations are for-profit companies, but others are organizations such as the United Nations or non-government organizations (NGOs) such as the Red Cross.

According to the Financial Times–Stock Exchange (FTSE) and Standard & Poor's (S&P) World Index, a company is a "multinational" if 30 percent or more of its sales are outside its own region of the world. For example, a German company is considered multinational if 30 percent of its sales are outside Europe. Of the 2,218 companies listed on the FTSE/S&P World Index, 506 are multinationals.[9]

ETHICS 职业道德规范知识吧 SIDEBAR

Minimizing Cultural Bias in International Web Sites[10]

减少国际网站的文化偏见

Although you can find Web sites in Chinese, Japanese, Portugese, and Ukrainian (and hundreds of other languages), English dominates the Web in international business, industry, government, and science, which necessitates new ways of working across national boundaries and presents cross-cultural challenges in creating bilingual and multilingual Web sites. These challenges mean that Web developers must accommodate various technical and linguistic differences, which can be difficult, not only from a technical standpoint, but also from an ethical one. Current practice suggests three possible strategies, each of which has ethical implications.

> *Why may bias that privileges a dominant culture be unethical? Why may cultural insensitivity be unethical? What are some other advantages and disadvantages of globalization, localization, and collaboration beyond those discussed in the sidebar?*

One communication strategy that many companies have implemented is *globalization*, which often includes standardization of writing styles in several ways:

- terminology guidelines — using consistent nomenclature and avoiding words with multiple common meanings
- cultural guidelines — avoiding humor and culture-specific examples in text, photos, and symbols
- readability guidelines — using short sentences and keeping subjects and verbs close together to make writing unambiguous and predictable

Unfortunately, standardization often ignores culture differences because the standards may resemble the "dominant" culture and marginalize or even ignore the local culture.

A second strategy is *localization*. This attends to cultural differences by incorporating verbal and visual colloquialisms as well as the history and culture of the audience into the Web site. While this strategy is increasingly viable, few companies have adopted it because it is time consuming and expensive. Localization can also backfire because not everyone is receptive to outsiders' attempts to blend into the local culture. If a translation is naive, incomplete, or haphazard, the result reflects insensitivity to the local culture — the opposite of the intended effect.

A third strategy is collaboration by people working on *multicultural/multilinguistic teams*. This strategy shows the most promise for companies looking for creative ways to address cultural differences. Technical communicator Steve Chu compares the collaborative process to the dilemma of which utensils to offer at a Chinese restaurant outside a Chinese-speaking country:

> The last time you dined at a Chinese restaurant . . . were forks, a pair of chopsticks, or both on your table? Did it seem odd that you had to request a pair of chopsticks because, after all, you were in a Chinese restaurant? Or did it seem odd that you had to request a fork because, after all, you were in a Western European country? (206)

According to Chu, one solution — the combined availability of chopsticks and a fork — is an appropriate metaphor for a bilingual Web site. The combination is a cultural hybrid that neither ignores cultural differences nor naively attempts to localize. In practical terms, this means Web sites that have features such as these:

- Parallel hypertext, or versions of the same page in different languages
- Similar layout and color schemes of the pages to create cohesion
- Links for visitors to switch from one language version to another
- Simple design that avoids cultural icons to minimize misinterpretation by international users

As markets continue to expand on a global scale, technical professionals will face decisions about creating Web sites that efficiently, accurately, and fairly communicate across many cultures and languages.

As a Web developer or a manager for an organization, which of the three communication strategies would you advocate? How might you defend your chosen strategy as a sound workplace practice, as a matter concerning both economics and ethics?

Globalization. Defining a global organization is more difficult because the definitions of "global" vary. Social theorist Anthony Giddens explains that globalization links local and distant cultures in ways that affect both.[11] In practice, *globalization* is the unrestricted movement of ideas and people, services and systems, goods and money across national borders around the world, made possible because of cooperative global economics, politics, and technologies.

One example of global impact of text and visuals is the series of warnings on cigarette packages in Canada. These new warnings provide dramatic, full-color images that in Canada must cover the top 50 percent of the front and back of the cigarette package along with explicit text warnings about the dangers of smoking. Do the warnings work? A study of more than 2,000 Canadians by the Société canadienne du cancer reports that 58 percent of the smokers interviewed said that the full-color pictures made them think more about the health effects of smoking. The new warnings increased the motivation of 44 percent of the smokers to quit smoking.[12] Figure 2.2 shows three of the 16 images and warnings that cigarette manufacturers are legally obligated to put on their Canadian packaging.

To see all 16 of the images and warnings in the Canadian series and the Société canadienne du cancer report about the impact of the warnings, go to **www.english.wadsworth.com/burnett6e**.

CLICK ON WEBLINK

CLICK on Chapter 2/warning images

CLICK on Chapter 2/Société canadienne du cancer evaluation

WEBLINK

FIGURE 2.2 **Visuals and Text of Three of the Sixteen Warnings on Canadian Cigarette Packs**[13]

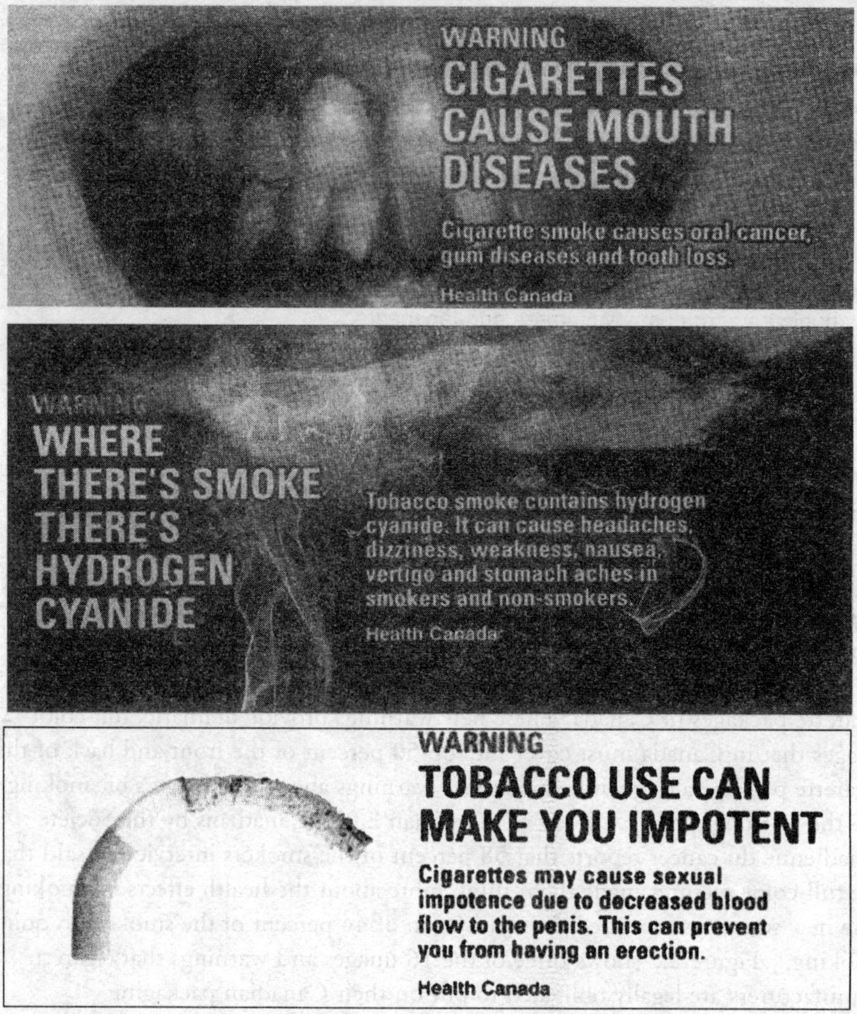

The effectiveness of these warnings has been noticed beyond Canada's borders, sparking global interest in similar graphic, explicit warnings. Others interested in this approach include the World Health Organization (WHO) and the United Nations, a number of countries in Africa and the European Union, Brazil, New Zealand, Thailand, and the United States.[14] A national warning may become a global warning.

While the warnings used on Canadian cigarette packs are a highly visible side of global interest in public health, such warnings are supported by a less visible and more technical side: the ongoing research reported in technical reports. Figure 2.3 shows the first page of a WHO press release summarizing a major technical report about global cancer rates.

FIGURE 2.3 **Page 1 of Press Release about World Health Organization Technical Report**[15]

World Health Organization

English | Español | Français

Search

OK

Media centre

- Home
- Countries
- Health topics
- Publications
- Research tools
- WHO sites
- Media centre
- Press releases
- Events
- Fact sheets
- Background information
- Notes for the press
- Statements
- Multimedia

Location: WHO > WHO sites > Media centre > Press releases 2003

printable version

Global cancer rates could increase by 50% to 15 million by 2020

World Cancer Report provides clear evidence that action on smoking, diet and infections can prevent one third of cancers, another third can be cured

3 April 2003 | GENEVA -- Cancer rates could further increase by 50% to 15 million new cases in the year 2020, according to the World Cancer Report, the most comprehensive global examination of the disease to date. However, the report also provides clear evidence that healthy lifestyles and public health action by governments and health practitioners could stem this trend, and prevent as many as one third of cancers worldwide.

In the year 2000, malignant tumours were responsible for 12 per cent of the nearly 56 million deaths worldwide from all causes. In many countries, more than a quarter of deaths are attributable to cancer. In 2000, 5.3 million men and 4.7 million women developed a malignant tumour and altogether 6.2 million died from the disease. The report also reveals that cancer has emerged as a major public health problem in developing countries, matching its effect in industrialized nations.

"The World Cancer Report tells us that cancer rates are set to increase at an alarming rate globally. We can make a difference by taking action today. We have the opportunity to stem this increase. This report calls on Governments, health practitioners and the general public to take urgent action. Action now can prevent one third of cancers, cure another third, and provide good, palliative care to the remaining third who need it, "said Dr. Paul Kleihues, Director of the International Agency for Research on Cancer (IARC) and co-editor of the World Cancer Report.

The World Cancer Report is a concise manual describing the global burden, the causes of cancer, major types of malignancies, early detection and treatment. The 351-page global report is issued by IARC, which is part of the World Health Organization (WHO).

Dr Gro Harlem Brundtland, Director-General of WHO, states: "The report provides a basis for public health action and assists us in our goal to reduce the morbidity and mortality from cancer, and to improve the quality of life of cancer patients and their families, everywhere in the world,"

Examples of areas where action can make a difference to stemming the increase of cancer rates and preventing a third of cases are:

- Reduction of tobacco consumption. It remains the most important avoidable cancer risk. In the 20th century, approximately 100 million people died world-wide from tobacco-associated diseases
- A healthy lifestyle and diet can help. Frequent consumption of fruit and vegetables and physical activity can make a difference.
- Early detection through screening, particularly for cervical and breast cancers, allow for prevention and successful cure.

The predicted sharp increase in new cases – from 10 million new cases globally in 2000, to 15 million in 2020 - will mainly be due to steadily ageing populations in both developed and developing countries and also to current trends in smoking prevalence and the growing adoption of unhealthy lifestyles.

"Governments, physicians, and health educators at all levels could do much more to help people change their behaviour to avoid preventable cancers," says Bernard W. Stewart, Ph.D., co-editor of the report, Director of Cancer Services, and Professor, Faculty of Medicine, University of New South Wales, Australia. "If the knowledge, technology and control strategies outlined in the World Cancer Report were applied globally, we would make major advances in preventing and treating cancers over the next twenty years and beyond."

From a global perspective, there is strong justification for focusing cancer prevention activities particularly on two main cancer-causing factors - tobacco and diet. We also need to continue efforts to curb infections which cause cancers," said Dr Rafael Bengoa, Director, Management of Non-communicable disease at WHO. "These factors were responsible for 43 per cent of all cancer deaths in 2000, that is 2.7 million fatalities, and 40 per cent of all new cases, that is four million new cancer cases."

ACCESSIBILITY

- *The document can be read in English, Spanish, or French.*
- *The document can be read online in a sans serif font, which is easy for reading on a monitor.*
- *Users can select a printed version, which automatically converts to a serif font, which is easier for reading on paper.*

COMPREHENSIBILITY

- *This is for a nonexpert audience, so the vocabulary is accessible and the mortality statistics are simplified.*
- *A clear problem-solution is established in the opening paragraph.*

USABILITY

- *The most important information is put in the headline and repeated in the opening paragraph.*
- *Possible actions are identified in the secondary headline.*
- *Information is presented in descending order of importance.*
- *The scope of the investigation is defined.*

WWW

WEBLINK

To see the complete WHO press release in Figure 2.3 and to access the executive summary and the report, go to **www.english.wadsworth.com/burnett6e**.

CLICK ON WEBLINK

CLICK on Chapter 2/WHO press release

CLICK on Chapter 2/WHO summary and report

The health information that WHO collects around the world is interesting to an array of global readers, all of whom have common interests in world health, regardless of national boundaries. Standardization of processes of both collecting and reporting information is one of the characteristics of globalization. While such standardization reduces, modifies, or eliminates idiosyncratic, local features, it also makes more information accessible to a larger number of people around the world.

Localization. The attention given to globalization has given rise to its counterpart: *localization.* Richard Harris, an economist at Simon Fraser University, explains that localization is based on preferences for familiar goods, processes, and services that have recognizable characteristics, even if global goods and services may have a higher quality or a lower price.[16] Increasing globalization has resulted in the reduction of goods and services that are localized — that is, ones that are distinctive because they reflect local culture.

A European-based organization, Localisation Industry Standards Association (LISA) works with its members to encourage global responsibility balanced with local sensitivity and usability. Companies around the world have a responsibility to respect the cultures with which they do business. The values advocated by LISA — responsibility, entrepreneurship, leadership, and cooperation — can be used by any organization that is localizing information in order to improve communication.[17]

Sometimes you'll hear the terms *globalization* and *localization* used as if they're mutually exclusive opposites, but they don't have to be.[18] In fact, both globalization and localization have compatible advantages that technical professionals need to consider. Many products that are used all over the world (for example, agricultural seed and equipment; computer hardware and software; medical equipment and supplies) require design and development for an international market. This part of design and development involves considering what capabilities users will need, regardless of their culture. For example, word processing software needs to be able to cut, copy, and paste highlighted text, regardless of the language. Similarly, computer hardware needs to be installed in the same way, regardless of the culture; however, making the information available in multiple languages increases the likelihood that the installation will be done correctly. Figure 2.4a shows the languages available for the installation of an HP Storage-Works SDLT 220 GB internal tape drive. Figure 2.4b shows one of the steps in English and then partial images of the same step in six other languages.

Products and services for people all over the world often need to be localized so they are appropriate for specific users or small groups of users, taking into account needs that are unique to their country, customers, and/or language. Sometime this means idiomatic translation of the text and redesign of visuals, including icons. For example, word-processing software often uses an icon of a trash can as a place for users to deposit their deleted text; however, in many parts of the world, trash cans don't look like those in the United States, so the icon — selected by US designers to relate the visual to the function — is an arbitrary image for much of the world.

FIGURE 2.4A **Languages for Tape Drive Installation Instructions**[19]

invent

HP StorageWorks
SDLT 220 GB tape drive

» tape storage

Technical Documentation

- **SDLT Internal Tape Drive Installation Instructions**

  » English version (304 KB pdf - October 2002)

  » Spanish version (674 KB pdf - October 2002)

  » Dutch version (674 KB pdf - October 2002)

  » French version (674 KB pdf - October 2002)

  » German version (676 KB pdf - October 2002)

  » Italian version (673 KB pdf - October 2002)

  » Japanese version (277 KB pdf - October 2002)

FIGURE 2.4B Languages for Tape Drive Installation Instructions[19]

ACCESSIBILITY

- *Steps are clearly labeled with a number and a task.*
- *The accompanying figure is labeled and placed next to the relevant step.*

COMPREHENSIBILITY

- *The imperative verbs (e.g., "install," "slide," "remove") are unambiguous.*
- *The introductory conditional phrases ("If . . .") are short enough to not interfere with the main task.*
- *Languages: English, Spanish, Dutch, French, German, Italian, Japanese*

USABILITY

- *The two situations (with and without rails) are clearly differentiated.*
- *Illustrations are easy to use because the diagrams are simplified and important parts are shaded.*

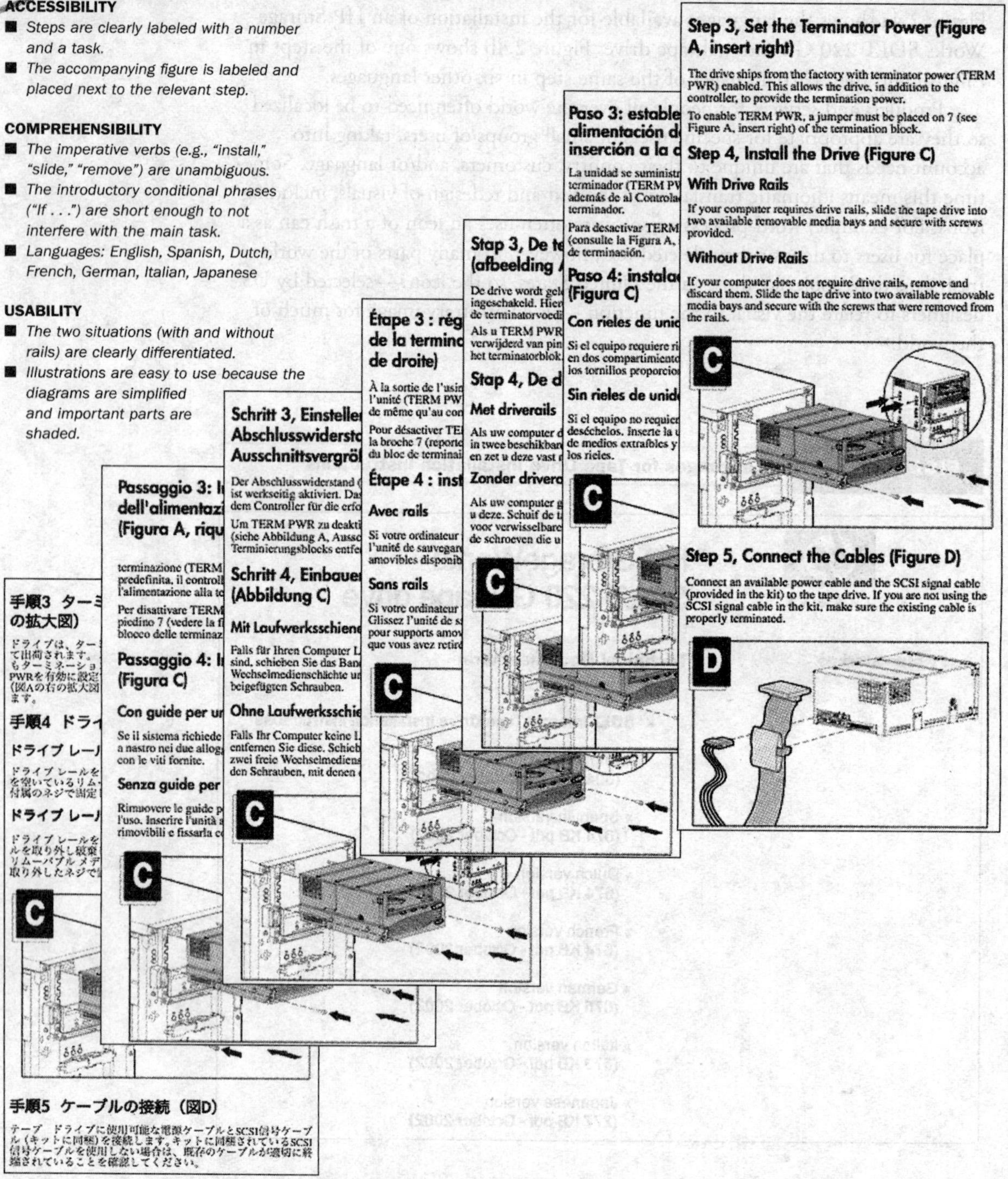

By definition, cultures are necessarily about collectives, whether characterized by nationality, race, disability, or some other defining feature, not individuals. However, no culture — even those that are remarkably consistent — is monolithic. No culture is comprised of identical individuals, and no culture is the same in different contexts and circumstances.

WEBLINK

The very term *globalization* provokes strong reactions. Go to **www.english.wadsworth.com/burnett6e** for links to different definitions, most of which reinforce territoriality and only one of which argues for a fundamental change in social geography. Then check the implications of delocalization.

CLICK ON WEBLINK

CLICK on Chapter 2/globalization

CLICK on Chapter 2/delocalization

Cultural Values 文化价值

Characterizing cultures provides information that technical professionals can use. However, technical professionals don't communicate to an entire culture; instead, they direct documents, presentations, and visuals to specific audiences. The issue is how much to localize documents — that is, how much to adapt communication to local culture in terms of language, practices, values, and so on.

While cultural awareness often involves a global perspective, in many multicultural countries (for example, Brazil, Canada, Russia, South Africa, the United States), technical professionals need such awareness to be skillful and productive *within* their own national borders. Let's consider why all of us should learn about other cultures. Understanding and respecting other cultures increases our effectiveness, so we are less likely to misinterpret attitudes, actions, and artifacts that reflect a different cultural perspective. Increased knowledge about and sensitivity to other cultures can improve performance in several ways:

- ***Response.*** Documents, presentations, and visuals that are adapted to people from other cultures are likely to get more attention and response.
- ***Productivity.*** Meetings and other interactions with people who have different cultural perspectives are often more productive and pleasant.
- ***Explanations.*** Alternative points of view can often explain attitudes, actions, tools, and artifacts that aren't immediately or obviously compatible with our own perspectives.

- ***Compliance.*** Attention to cultural perspectives is likely to increase compliance with organizational policies and procedures and thus increase consistency, safety, productivity, and compatibility within an organization.

WWW
WEBLINK

The Society of Technical Communication has a special interest group (SIG) that focuses on international technical communication. Go to **www.english.wadsworth.com/burnett6e** for a link to more information about technical communication outside the United States.
CLICK ON WEBLINK
CLICK on Chapter 2/international

Analyzing Culture
分析文化

This section focuses on ways to analyze national culture, organizational culture, and individuals in cultures. While virtually all researchers who study culture explain that culture is about groups, they also understand that culture shapes and is shaped by individuals. Individuals typically work for and with various kinds of organizations that have distinct cultures. And both individuals and organizations are located in nations with geographic, political, and cultural boundaries.

National Cultures 民族文化

Research indicates that having a long-term perspective and a focus on the individual rather than the group are both correlated with national economic growth.[21] Why do you think this may be an accurate correlation?

Cultural differences are interesting, but do they really matter? Pricewaterhouse Coopers reports that "67% of international managers blame cultural differences for the difficulties they are confronted with working internationally."[20] That's enough to get some attention — especially if understanding cultural differences can help improve productivity and cooperation.

Sometimes even understanding that differences exist doesn't prevent a cultural gap. For example, several years ago I was in Tokyo, Japan, meeting with senior managers at Fuju-Xerox. I was interested in learning how their document design and development teams functioned and how their technical manuals were produced. After lengthy and formal greetings, introductions, and refreshments, we turned to the business of the meeting: the preliminary stages of my investigation of their collaborative processes and document production. Time and again during the ensuing discussion, I had to remind myself that their smiling and nodding simply signaled that they had heard me, not that they necessarily agreed with me. In the United States, their actions would have signaled agreement with what I was saying. In Japan, their actions signaled acknowledgement and politeness, not agreement.

What's the point? Like I was in Japan, many of us are strongly influenced by our own cultural frameworks. Common sense tells us that cultures in various countries are different, but we have don't always have sufficient knowledge to function comfortably in other cultures. Figure 2.5 provides a series of binaries and questions that have been identified by anthropologists and psychologists as useful ways to distinguish national cultures. These binaries provide a way to begin discussions about culture. However, binaries tend to treat cultures as monolithic, that is, assuming that all Brazilian citizens are alike or that all Russian citizens are alike, which can lead to stereotyping extremely diverse national and organizational cultures. Despite the limitations, however, the binaries and questions in Figure 2.5 are a useful starting place.

The binaries in Figure 2.5 are not the only distinctions that characterize nations. Factors such as language, proxemics, and time, usually learned at an early age, are a few additional factors.

Languages. Language is one of the most visible aspects of national culture. English is spoken as a first or a second language on five continents by people who make up about 49 percent of the world's population.[22] This means that many of the technical documents and presentations you prepare can be in English, regardless of the geographic location of the audience. However, despite the dominant role of English in education, research, government, and business, it is often not the first language of a country; in fact, the use of English is sometimes resented and aggressively challenged. What's a reasonable professional response? Acknowledging that language is an inherent part of culture, so its use is always part of a social context and is always political.[23]

Since language is a political hot button, demanding the use of a particular language or making joking or demeaning remarks about a country's first language is a certain way to alienate colleagues. When you're trying to negotiate the complex relationships between globalization and localization, be respectful of local languages.

Unquestionably, English is the common denominator in the international workplace — but whose English? The term *world Englishes* refers to the fact that English isn't the same from country to country (or even from region to region within countries). So, even when everyone is speaking English, speakers from, for example, Australia, Canada, Hong Kong, India, Singapore, South Africa, the United Kingdom, and the United States may have remarkable distinctions. For example, some words started in a particular area but are now widely used: *bungalow,* a term from South Asia, is now used wherever English is spoken. Or a single artifact can have a number of different names — for example, *gym shoes, plimsolls, sneakers,* and *tackies* are different names for the same kind of shoes.[24]

Many people resent English being used as the primary language of the international workplace. One cause of such resentment is the belief that the use of English diminishes respect for the native language. What else might cause such resentment? How can people from English-speaking countries defuse such resentment?

A common misconception is that everyone in the United States speaks English. In fact, according to Census 2000, 28 million U.S. residents age five and over speak Spanish at home; more than half of these also report speaking

FIGURE 2.5 **A Summary of Factors Differentiating National Cultures[25]**

Factor	Continuum and question
Individualism	***Individual* - - - - - - - - - - *Group*** How much focus is on the individual, and how much focus is on the collective — that is, the group or team?
Task focus	***Tasks* - - - - - - - - - - *Relationship*** How much focus is on the tasks being completed, and how much is on the relationship of the people doing the tasks?
Forthrightness	***Indirectness* - - - - - - - - - - *Directness*** Do people tend to learn about each other indirectly, through a third party? Or do they tend to learn about each other when they speak directly to each other about their backgrounds, roles, and responsibilities?
Power distance	***Hierarchy* - - - - - - - - - - *Equality*** How is power concentrated — at the top of a hierarchy or distributed equitably? What's the distance between people who make decisions and people who do the work resulting from those decisions? Are opportunities equally available to everyone?
Interaction	***Nonverbal interaction* - - - - - - - - - - *Verbal interaction*** Do people tend to be cautious, using clichés and assuming that body language and tone of voice convey hidden messages, or do they speak openly, expressing opinions explicitly?
Source of credibility	***Formal status* - - - - - - - - - - *Achievement*** How much attention is paid to status: age, rank, title, longevity in the organization, education, and how much attention is paid to a person's actual accomplishments relevant to the task?
Perspective	***Short-term perspective* - - - - - - - - - - *Long-term perspective*** Do people have a short-term perspective, concerned with fulfilling social obligations and protecting their reputation (saving "face")? Or do they have a long-term perspective, forward thinking, valuing perseverance and thrift (work hard now and get rewarded later)?
Materiality	***Material success* - - - - - - - - - - *Quality of life*** Are the people more concerned with material success or with quality of life?
Uncertainly avoidance	***Preference for certainty* - - - - - - - - - - *Tolerance for ambiguity*** Does the culture generally prefer certainty (and thus focus on laws, rules, regulations, and controls to reduce the uncertainty)? Or does the culture have a tolerance for ambiguity (and thus more readily accepts change and takes more and greater risks)?

fluent English.[26] Few people are surprised that Arizona, California, Florida, New Mexico, and Texas have a large number of native speakers of Spanish. But English isn't necessarily the first language of workers elsewhere in the United States. For example, in Iowa, many meat processing and packing companies employ a large number of Hispanic employees. Communication in these workplaces is often bilingual.

Recently I was in Durban, South Africa, conducting a seminar for about 30 professors in various areas of science and technology. We were all speaking English, but I was only one of four other people in the room for whom English was a native language. South Africa is home to 31 languages,[27] 11 of which are the official languages of the country: Sepedi, Sesotho, Setswana, siSwati, Tshivenda, Xitsonga, Afrikaans, English, isiNdebele, isiXhosa, and isiZulu.[28] That meant that more than 90 percent of the people in the seminar were speaking and writing in their second or third (and, in some cases, their fourth) language. And while everyone conceded that English was necessary, not everyone was happy about the concession, because of ethnic loyalties.

Cultural differences are often conveyed with specific vocabulary. For example, what is called the *trunk* of a car in the United States is called the *boot* in countries including Australia, the UK, and South Africa. In the United States, a colleague on a business trip who wants to make sure you awake for an early-morning meeting might say, "Would you like me to give you a wake-up call?" while a colleague from the UK might say, "Would you like me to knock you up?"

Once you're on the highway driving to a meeting in Durban, South Africa, you might see a warning vehicle like the one in this photo: "Abnormal Load Ahead." And just ahead is a large truck (also called a *lorry*) with a large sign, "Abnormal," mounted on the front and rear, like the one in the next photo. In the United States, the signs would probably read, "Wide Load Ahead" on the warning vehicle and "Wide Load" on the truck itself.

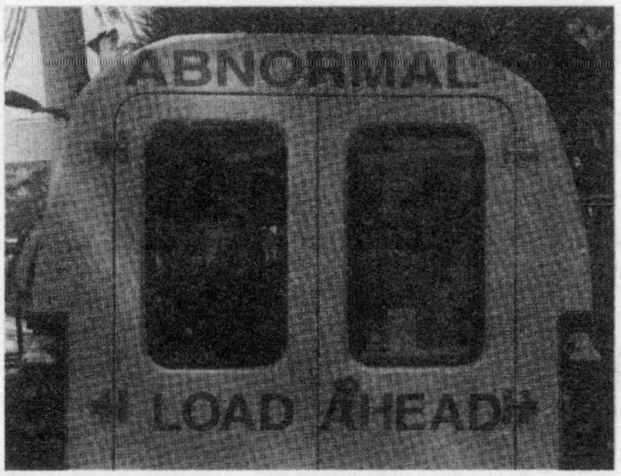

A warning vehicle in South Africa signals an extra-wide load ahead

A truck in South Africa carries a sign signaling an extra-wide load

Simply put, people who immediately understand "Abnormal Load Ahead" or "Abnormal" on a truck belong to a different *discourse community* than people who immediately understand "Wide Load Ahead" and "Wide Load." Thus, a discourse community is comprised of people who share a number of common cultural characteristics. For example, they may belong to the same gender, race, nationality, or profession. Or they may belong to the same political party, religion, athletic team, residential community, or corporation. However, their most important shared characteristic is their common use of a specific language to accomplish something and to get work done.

What discourse communities do you belong to? What are beliefs and behaviors from different discourse communities that might conflict with each other? How do you decide which beliefs and behaviors to follow in a given situation?

Clearly, everyone belongs to multiple discourse communities and usually shifts seamlessly between them. Discourse communities can be layered; you can be a member of a discourse community comprised of people who work for the same organization, while also being a member of various discourse communities within the organization. For example, you might work in research and development, accounting, manufacturing, QC/QA, training, or marketing. And within each department, you may belong to the group of people who use PCs (or Macs), participate in flextime (or telecommuting), prefer e-mail (or face-to-face) conversations, or coach the organization's softball team (or run 5k charity events).

Proxemics. The study of the physical distance between people, called *proxemics,* shows that distance means different things in different cultures. We have layers of an invisible bubble around us. We allow family members, lovers, and very close friends into our *intimate space,* which in the United States is up to about 18 inches. We allow friends and close colleagues into our *personal space,* which for most people in the United States ranges from about 18 inches to about four feet. We allow colleagues and business acquaintances into our *social space,* which in the United States is typically 4 feet to about 10–12 feet. And our *public space,* in the United States beyond 10–12 feet, is for public events: business meetings, oral presentations, lectures, performances. Different cultures vary in what is considered acceptable for intimate, personal, social, and public distance.

Generally, people from North America expect larger intimate and personal space than people from many other countries, which sometimes leads to problems. For example, North American workers expect other workers to stay outside their intimate space, that is, to stay more than 18 inches away. They can misunderstand the closeness of coworkers who regularly move inside the 18-inch invisible boundary. The following photos illustrate differences in cultural practice.

Time. Time means different things in different cultures. How late can someone be and still be "on time"? What is a "long" meeting? What does "right away" mean? What does "multitasking" mean?

© Reza Estakhrian/Getty Images

© VCL/Chris Ryan/Getty Images

Professionals from different parts of the world have different perspectives about the acceptable distance between people in a discussion. What role does gender play in acceptable distances for workplace discussions?

Some of the early work about people's sense of time was done more than 50 years ago by Edward and Mildred Hall. In a recent book, they extend their early work, which explains that cultures tend to treat time as *monochronic* or *polychronic,* as these two lists show.[29]

Monochronic people	**Polychronic people**
■ Tend to do one thing at a time	■ Tend to do many things at once
■ Concentrate on the specific job	■ Respond to interruptions
■ Take commitments seriously; set and comply with deadlines	■ Consider time commitments as desirable, not absolute
■ Are committed to the job	■ Are committed to human relationships
■ Adhere to established plans	■ Change plans often and easily
■ Are concerned about not disturbing others; follow rules of privacy and consideration	■ Are more concerned with family, friends, close business associates than with privacy
■ Emphasize promptness	■ Base promptness on the relationship
■ Build short-term relationships	■ Build lifetime relationships

Of course, general lists like this don't apply to specific individuals but, instead, characterize many people. For example, monochronic people tend to see time as inflexible and tangible, so work is often done in isolation, and it may take priority over people. In contrast, polychronic people tend to see time as flexible and fluid, so, for example, appointments are shifted around at the last minute and changes are made to accommodate more important people. Because work time is not clearly separable from personal time, relationships may be more important than tasks.

WWW

WEBLINK

If you're interested in learning a lot more about concepts and practices time, go to **www.english.wadsworth.com/burnett6e** for a link to a detailed site devoted to the study of time.

CLICK ON WEBLINK

CLICK on Chapter 2/time

Organizational Cultures 机构文化

When you're working in a multinational or global organization (whether a large corporation, small business, government agency, NGO, or nonprofit organization), you need to be concerned both with national culture and with organizational culture. When the national cultures are remarkably different, the organizational culture can provide a common bond that crosses national boundaries.

The shared beliefs and behaviors of people in an organization comprise the organizational culture. One way to describe organizational culture is to analyze dimensions that can be expressed as binaries — that is, contrasting practices that characterize activities in the organization, as shown in Figure 2.6. These are similar to the binaries for national cultures, but they apply specifically to organizations. As with nations, no single factor is sufficient to determine whether a particular practice is productive or effective, as shown in the photos on page 62. While the binaries in Figure 2.6 do not reflect all the factors that characterize an organization, they can be compiled to create a remarkably full portrait.

Sometimes organizational culture is conveyed in formal ways: policy statements, organizational charts, performance criteria. These formal procedures and policies need to be consistent with the actual policies. And sometimes organizational culture is conveyed in informal ways: common practices, lore, gossip, e-mail.

FIGURE 2.6 Factors and Questions about Organizational Cultures[30]

Factor	Continuum and question
Focus on people	***Performance oriented*** - - - ***People oriented*** Does the organization seem more interested in tasks or in the employees completing those tasks?
Approach to processes	***Results oriented*** - - - ***Process oriented*** Are employees and managers more concerned with getting the job done or with problem-solving processes that might be generalized to other tasks?
Attitude toward cooperation	***Competitive*** - - - ***Cooperative*** Is the relationship between managers and employees competitive or cooperative? Are employees competitive or cooperative with each other?
Adherence to standards	***Parochial*** - - - ***Professional*** Does the organization follow idiosyncratic local practices or professional standards?
Receptivity to change	***Closed to change*** - - - ***Open to change*** Does the organization have a closed system that follows existing rules carefully and is resistant to change, regardless of the benefits or an open system that is receptive to new ideas and activities?
Access to resources	***Restricted*** - - - ***Available*** Do employees have ready access to sufficient supplies, tools, and equipment including computer resources necessary for doing their jobs well?
Motivation to work	***Required work*** - - - ***Pride in work*** Do employees see their work as a necessary but not integral or enjoyable part of life? Or do employees see their work as interesting, important, and fulfilling?
Relation to life outside the organization	***Insular*** - - - ***Engaged*** Do managers and employees see work as part of a balanced life along with family and community commitments? Does the organization insulate itself from the activities or the community and the lives of its employees? Does the organization support people's lives outside the organization?
Respect toward employees	***Cogs in the machinery*** - - - ***Valued members*** Are employees valued for their contributions? Are their opinions valued and taken seriously?
Management style	***Tightly controlled*** - - - ***Loosely controlled*** Is the management tight and controlling, typical of hierarchical organizations, or loose and flexible? Do employees have assigned projects, set work hours, and dress codes?
Communication channels	***One-way*** - - - ***Two-way*** Is communication always top-down? Or are employees encouraged to communicate with their managers, participate in quality-control projects, and voice their opinions?
Rules and regulations	***Normative*** - - - ***Pragmatic*** Are the rules and regulations prescriptive and applied without regard to individual circumstances, or are they adapted and modified to fit specific situations?

GANSU PROVINCE PROJECT IN THE PEOPLE'S REPUBLIC OF CHINA
中国甘肃省项目

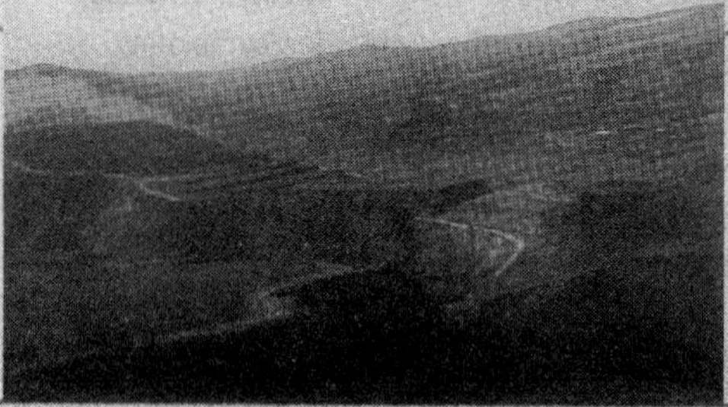

Iowa has a unique connection to Gansu Province. The Loess Hills in western Iowa contain the same type of soil as that found in Gansu. Deposited during the Glacier Age, these highly erosive, wind-blown soils are not very stable for building roadways. US experience in developing roadways on this soil meant that we could offer assistance to the Chinese in developing effective roadways.

Duane Smith, a civil engineer and trainer for Iowa State University's Center for Transportation Research and Education (CTRE), traveled to the Gansu province of China to negotiate an agreement to improve highway development in this struggling area.

For the Gansu Province Project, the American and Chinese engineers developed a Memorandum of Understanding (MOU) that identified specific individual and group tasks. Because of cultural expectations in the People's Republic of China, Duane took special care to include particular officials and groups. An excerpt from the 4-page MOU is shown below.

> The purpose of the Coordinating Council will be to facilitate research, education, extension and training services for the Government agencies of the Gansu Province, for government agencies of other Provinces of China as well as the Central Government of China and for domestic and foreign private firms that are participating in the development of improved transportation systems within the Gansu Province and throughout China.

> ……府机构、为中国
> 其它省份及中央的政府机构，以及参与发展、改善甘肃及全国
> 公路系统状况的中国及外国公司提供研究、教育和延伸服务。

Duane commented on the process: "As we discussed different aspects of the second document, the Training Agreement, I needed to have visuals and graphics to help me express my points. When we were all drawing on the board, we really started to communicate. When we could create an engineering drawing and put numbers on it, things clicked."

To make this cross-cultural experience successful, both parties needed individual preparations, specified in a Training Agreement. Party A (Gansu) agreed to provide additional English training to its engineers as well as obtain necessary visas to travel to the United States. Party B (the US hosts) agreed to provide a detailed training program that would allow the engineers to use a series of technical skills upon returning to China. An excerpt from the 4-page Training Agreement is shown below.

Parties Obligations and Responsibilities:

Party A:

1. Select and send trainees to ISU/CTRE.
2. Provide English training prior to the departure to ISU/CTRE.
3. Pay the ISU/CTRE billings within 30 days after receipt.
4. Prepare all the necessary trainee travel documents to travel to ISU/CTRE.

Party B:

1. Develop a detailed training program.
2. Provide the coordination and instruction for trainees to implement and practice the techniques provided in the training program.
3. Complete trainee evaluations for the English training, techniques training, field practice, and the training summary report.
4. Provide the necessary documentation to assist Party A in preparing all necessary trainee travel documents to travel to ISU/CTRE.

四、双方的责任和义务

甲方：

1、负责选派培训对象；
2、负责选派对象出国前的英语培训；
3、在接到培训费用通知的 30 天内，支付 ISU/CTRE 培训费用；
4、负责办理培训人员的出国手续；
5、负责审查培训计划并在 15 日内将审查意见反馈给乙方。

乙方：

1、负责制订详细的培训计划，该计划应于 2002 年 12 月 31 日前提交给甘肃省交通规划勘察设计院；
2、对理论培训组织具体的实施；
3、对每位学员作出切合实际的评价；
4、负责办理培训人员赴美的签证所需文件。
5、负责将培训费用账单寄给甘肃省交通规划勘察设计院。

五、培训时间和人数

Duane commented: "The Chinese are very serious about this project. This is one of their national initiatives. They see this project as a model that can be used for the rest of China. We plan to create a technology transfer center in Gansu, so that this initial effect will lead to future projects and ongoing training." The signatures on the Training Agreement below reflect mutual agreement.

Pan Zhengxiang Co-Chair of Gansu Center for Transportation Research Education and Extension (GP-CTREE) Director of Department of Basic Industry Development Gansu Province Ministry of Planning	Wendy Wei Co-Chair of Gansu Center for Transportation Research Education and Extension (GP-CTREE) Program Specialist-University Extension Iowa State University
Wang Jingchun President of Gansu Province Transportation Planning, Survey and Design Institute	Duane E. Smith, PE Associate Director-Outreach Center for Transportation Research and Education (CTRE)

Date: July 20,2002

甘肃交通科研教育扩展延伸中心 主席助理（签字） （甘肃省发展计划委员会基础产业处处长）	甘肃交通科研教育扩展延伸中心 主席助理（签字） （美国依阿华州立大学项目经理）
甘肃省交通规划勘察设计院 院长（签字）	美国依阿华州立大学/交通研究教育中心 副主任（签字）

© Alex Tossi/Alamy

© Patrik Giardino/CORBIS

Is formality or informality a factor in productivity? Can you tell which employees work harder, are more innovative, are more productive, or enjoy their jobs more?

Organizational culture is also conveyed by the manner of communication. For example, people who go to the Dell Computer home page at **www.dell.com** can identify their country and, within seconds, can read the entire Dell site in their native language. If Mexico is their country (as in Figure 2.7a), the site will be in Spanish (Figure 2.7b). This concern for users and respect for their own language contributes to Dell being identified as one of the top five most admired companies in the world.[31]

Individuals and Their Culture 个体与其文化

While all workplace professionals are part of a national culture as well as an organizational culture, they all have personal factors that influence the ways in which they participate in, contribute to, and react to these cultures. These personal factors also make us members of several subcultures that affect our professional opinions and, in many cases, complicate our decision making by providing contradictory information. This section helps you begin a description of yourself and the subcultures to which you belong:

> *How do you characterize yourself for each of these factors? Are any factors mutually exclusive? Which of them affect others? Do you find any of the boundaries of these factors fuzzy or ambiguous?*

- Current and ancestral nationalit(ies)
- Races and ethnicities
- Age
- Gender
- Residences: Rural, suburban, urban
- Job status: white, pink, or blue collar
- Education
- Income
- Health and disabilities
- Marital status
- Sexual orientation
- Role(s) in community
- Political views and affiliations
- Religious views and affiliations

FIGURE 2.7A **Choosing the Country and Language for Dell Computer Company Web Site from Dell's U.S. Home Page**[32]

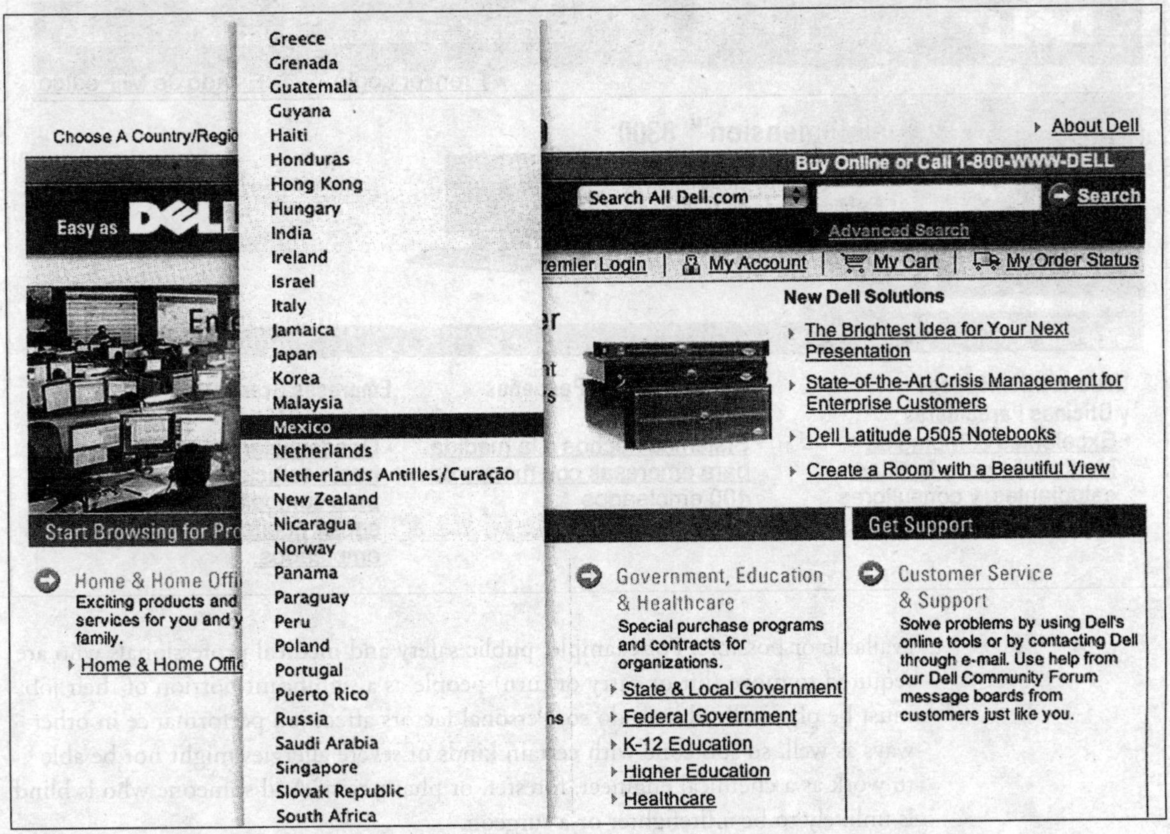

Do you want to better understand your personal cultural preferences? Go to www.english.wadsworth.com/burnett6e for a link to take a self-test that may help you see one version of ways you might react in certain organizations around the world.

CLICK ON WEBLINK

CLICK on Chapter 2/self-test

WEBLINK

Any professional must be qualified to fulfill the essential functions of a job. Sometimes personal factors prevent this, and no reasonable accommodation is

FIGURE 2.7B Dell Computer Company's Latin American Home Page[33]

available or possible. For example, public safety and medical professionals who are required to move (lift or carry or turn) people as a significant portion of their job must be physically able to do so. Personal factors affect job performance in other ways as well, so someone with certain kinds of severe allergies might not be able to work as a chemical engineer, forester, or pharmacist. And someone who is blind is unlikely to be a firefighter or a surgeon.

WEBLINK

The American with Disabilities Act (ADA), passed by the U.S. Congress in 1990, prohibits discrimination on the basis of disability. Go to **www.english.wadsworth.com/burnett6e** for a link to the text of the ADA.
CLICK ON WEBLINK
CLICK on Chapter 2/ADA

Some personal factors can indirectly affect professional performance. For example, a person's economic circumstances often affect access to education and computer technology and, thus, to workplace opportunities. And, similarly, a person's education affects job qualifications as well as job performance.

However, except for circumstances similar to those just mentioned, personal factors seldom influence professional competence. A person's success as, for exam-

© Walter Hodges/Getty Images

Workplaces benefit from the experience and expertise of professionals with a variety of abilities.

ple, an environmental engineer, physician's assistant, nanoscale physicist, or software designer typically does not depend on personal factors. For example, while race and ethnicity are powerful contributors to culture, they do not affect professional competence; our reactions (and prejudices) about race and ethnicity are learned rather than inherent. Similarly, nationality does not affect professional competence; it is often a circumstance of birth: on which side of a border a child is born or what nationality the parents claim. And a person's age, gender, sexual orientation, marital status, politics, and religion don't play any role in job performance. As the photo illustrates, doing a job well depends more on a person's professional competence than on physical abilities.

What factors affect people's access to workplace opportunities and to technology?

What are examples of personal factors that have been mistakenly correlated with job access or performance?

Increase Cultural Awareness
增强文化意识

How can you work more productively and respectfully with colleagues from various cultures? This final section of the chapter offers some suggestions that may make your cross-cultural experiences more successful whether you're working on a cross-cultural team in your own organization, moving to a new job in a different organization, or traveling halfway around the world to work in another country.

Make some initial decisions about your own behavior and attitude. How you choose to approach a new culture may be a strong influence on your success.

- Be a keen observer. Some things are often more important than words: seating arrangements, order of speaking, body language, pauses and silences, the way people dress, interactions among people. Watch what's going on. Think about what it might mean, both in order to learn and to avoid making unintended gaffes.
- Demonstrate respect for people and practices. How? Defer judgement on things that are unfamiliar. Ask questions. Presume that input from everyone involved will inprove the output. Consider all possibilities equally.
- Demonstrate genuine interest in other cultures by your actions and attitudes. Try new foods. Adopt new ways of doing things that enhance your regular practices. Be aware of local politics, events, and controversies.
- Listen carefully, which is difficult when you don't know what you might hear. Listening for new information is challenging especially when you don't have criteria for effectively differentiating very useful but unexpected information from less useful and unexpected information. Also, tune your listening to better understand unfamiliar accents and vocabulary.
- Consider alternative interpretations; things may not be the way they seem. Does a smile mean friendliness or embarassment? Does nodding mean "I agree" or "Continue your explanation"?

WWW

WEBLINK

The Society of Technical Communication publishes a bibliography on international technical communication with an extensive list of resources. Go to **www.english.wadsworth.com/burnett6e** for a link to the bibliography.

CLICK ON WEBLINK

CLICK on Chapter 2/bibliography

Before you enter a new culture, whether a new organization or a new country, do your homework. Learn some basics so that you'll be less surprised when unfamiliar things happen and more prepared to act appropriately.

- Understand the hierarchy (whether an organizational chart or the government's structure).
- Make a list of people with whom you'll be working — names, positions, areas of responsibility, history with the organization, relation to others with whom you'll work. And get photos if possible so you'll recognize the people.

- Learn some common cultural customs such as giving business cards and gifts, greetings and handshakes, behaving conventionally at meetings and meals. Learn what's typically considered rude and polite, especially in relation to time, proxemics, and social behavior.
- Understand what contributes to credibility. For example, in some cultures summarizing accomplishments relevant to the current project is seen as boasting. In some cultures skipping the personal conversation and jumping directly into the business agenda is a personal affront.
- Learn some basic language ("Hello" "Thank you" "Excuse me" "How do you say . . . ?" "Where is . . . ?" "How do I get to . . . ?" "What is the cost of. . . ?").
- Know the basic layout; try to get a site plan or geographic map before you leave.

Once you arrive, welcome new experiences. To have a productive experience, you need to be receptive and considerate, even when things don't go the way you expected. The situation may be as unfamiliar to those you're working with as it is to you.

- Expect that things you never anticipated will happen, sometimes challenging your best intentions.
- Be patient about how long things may take to accomplish and how things may be done.
- Identify absolutes that affect your daily life (e.g., dietary restrictions, severe allergies, physical limitations, need for a refrigerator for medication, and so on).
- Be flexible. You may need to do some things differently. For example, you may need to offer indirect suggestions rather than give straightforward directions, revise contractual items, or acknowledge that your plans are seen as impossible — or at least intrusive and inflexible (regardless of your intentions).
- Make every effort to meet individuals and engage in conversations. Even when you're awkward and uncomfortable using unfamiliar language, keep trying.

Global corporate trainer Sivasailam Thiagarajan, from Chennai, India, offers a list of guidelines and brief explanations that make intercultural communication easier. Go to **www.english.wadsworth.com/burnett6e** for links to his site.
CLICK ON WEBLINK
CLICK on Chapter 2/global training

WWW
WEBLINK

Individual and Collaborative Assignments

个人作业和小组作业

1. **Assess global citizenship.** HP's Web site positions the company as a responsible global citizen:

   At a minimum, "global citizenship" is a commitment made by companies striving to do business in a manner that upholds local and international standards and values everywhere the business invests and operates, in areas including the environment, ethics, labor and human rights.[34]

   Does HP meet its own high standard? According to this definition, how do the corporate cultures of Lucent Technologies and Kodak stack up? Search their Web sites and general news articles for more information to help you form an opinion. Be prepared to make a two-minute oral argument in class supporting your position.

Lucent Technologies' Culture and Diversity Statements[35]

Home | Solutions and Products | Customer Support | Bell Labs | About Lucent   Glossary   Contact us   Log in

Search

Go

Advanced search

Lucent Technologies
Bell Labs Innovations

About Lucent:
- News & Events
- Investor Relations
- Industry Analyst Relations
- Company Information
- Social Responsibility
- Work@Lucent
  - Search jobs
  - My profile
  - Life@Lucent
    - -Compensation & Benefits
    - -Workplace Diversity
    - -Frequently asked questions
  - College recruiting
- Partner Programs

Workplace Diversity

Employees are the heart of our company — and the key to our competitive success in the global marketplace. Lucent's Human Resources team provides policies, practices and tools that create a workplace capable of motivating, developing and rewarding employees to achieve success.

We have an ironclad commitment to:

- **Promote an open and supportive work environment;**
- **Value diversity in all its forms;**
- **Encourage the candid expression of ideas**
- **Allow a free exchange of points of view to make the best business decisions;**
- **Support each other in the pursuit of common goals; and**
- **Help employees strive for breakthrough performance.**

As a socially responsible employer, we also respect our employees' rights, including: a safe and supportive workplace; fair policies and procedures regarding hiring and dismissal; equal treatment for all employees; opportunities to contribute to the company's success through challenging work; and having their voices heard and acknowledged.

Kodak's Diversity Statement[36]

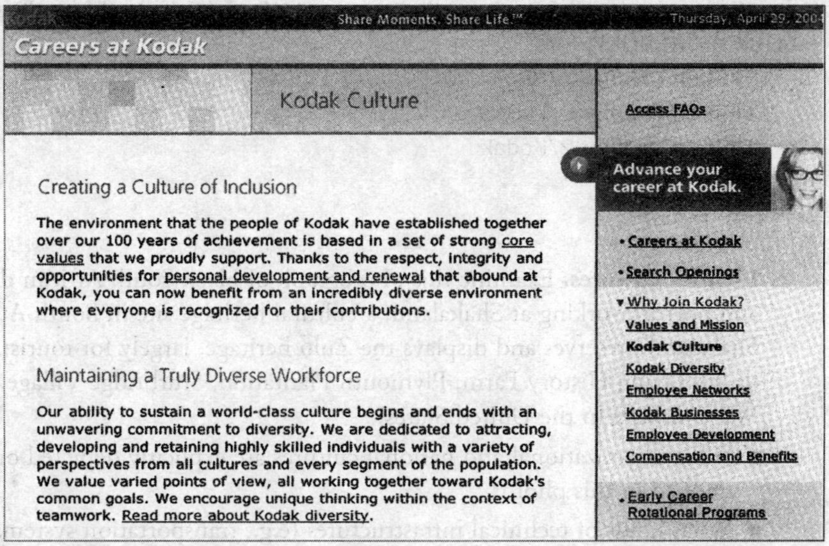

Kodak   Share Moments. Share Life.™   Thursday, April 29, 2004

Careers at Kodak

Kodak Culture

Access FAQs

Advance your career at Kodak.

Creating a Culture of Inclusion

The environment that the people of Kodak have established together over our 100 years of achievement is based in a set of strong core values that we proudly support. Thanks to the respect, integrity and opportunities for personal development and renewal that abound at Kodak, you can now benefit from an incredibly diverse environment where everyone is recognized for their contributions.

Maintaining a Truly Diverse Workforce

Our ability to sustain a world-class culture begins and ends with an unwavering commitment to diversity. We are dedicated to attracting, developing and retaining highly skilled individuals with a variety of perspectives from all cultures and every segment of the population. We value varied points of view, all working together toward Kodak's common goals. We encourage unique thinking within the context of teamwork. Read more about Kodak diversity.

- Careers at Kodak
- Search Openings
- Why Join Kodak?
  - Values and Mission
  - **Kodak Culture**
  - Kodak Diversity
  - Employee Networks
  - Kodak Businesses
  - Employee Development
  - Compensation and Benefits
- Early Career Rotational Programs

2. **Tell a story.** Study the following sketches and jot down the story of what you think is happening in each sketch. Then get together in a small group to see if your interpretation agrees with or differs from the interpretations of others in your group. Compare the interpretations in your group with those of the entire class. Discuss aspects of culture that might contribute to differences in interpretations.[37]

WWW

WEBLINK

Check out the culture, diversity, and human rights statements for HP, Lucent, and Kodak. Go to **www.english.wadsworth.com/burnett6e** for links to these sites.

CLICK ON WEBLINK

CLICK on Chapter 2/HP

CLICK on Chapter 2/Lucent

CLICK on Chapter 2/Kodak

3. **Identify cultures.** Examine this photograph of black South African dancers and porters working at Shakaland, a cultural heritage site in South Africa. Shakaland preserves and displays the Zulu heritage, largely for tourists (similar to Living History Farm, Plymouth Plantation, Sturbridge Village, or Williamsburg in the United States).
   - What organizational and national cultures are explicitly depicted or implied in this photo?
   - What kinds of technical infrastructures (e.g., transportation systems, sanitation systems) need to be in place for a cultural heritage site to function?
   - Investigate the current Zulu culture. How much does this photo reflect the lives of contemporary Zulus in South Africa?

© William L. Jeffries, 2003

South African dancers double as porters at Shakaland, a cultural heritage site in South Africa.

4. **Argue an opinion.** Read the three-article series "What is Global Language?" by Barbara Wallraff. These article about English as a global language challenge some common misperceptions about the nature of languages in international business, science, and technology. Select a country you're interested in learning more about and imagine that you are managing a project in that country. Investigate the country's culture (for example, check **www.cia.gov** for general background about the country). Write a memo to your manager in which you argue that conducting all business related to your project in English in this particular country is (or is not) a good idea.

Select a culture outside the United States and do some library or online investigation to identify the intimate, personal, social, and public distance in that culture.

5. **Characterize an organization.** Work with a partner to select an organization (government agency, nonprofit organization, small business, or large corporation) that interests both of you.
   - With your partner, create a list of questions based on the binaries presented in this chapter that you both can ask during a face-to-face or electronic interview with an employee in order to help you characterize the organization, at least from this one employee's perspective.
   - Encourage the employee to provide a general description as well as specific examples.

Access the three-article series by going to **www.english.wadsworth.com/burnett6e** for links to the site.
CLICK ON WEBLINK
CLICK on Chapter 2/ Wallraff Part 1
CLICK on Chapter 2/ Wallraff Part 2
CLICK on Chapter 2/ Wallraff Part 3

WWW
WEBLINK

   - Arrange a 20- to 30-minute interview. Take careful notes. Tape record it if you have permission.
   - Use the information from your interview notes to write a memo to potential employees that describes the culture of the organization.

   Your goal is to help potential employees decide if the organization is a good match for them. Your informant (the employee you interviewed) and your audience (potential employees) do not necessarily know the technical terms used to describe culture, so you need to explain these terms.

6. **Recommend an effective diversity statement.** Reread the three diversity statements in this chapter (GlaxoSmithKline, Lucent Technologies, Kodak) to review the key components. Do a Web search to select diversity statements from at least two other organizations. Analyze these statements to determine the focus, identify the kinds of examples provided, and assess whether the ramifications of noncompliance are identified. Select an

organization that needs to add or update statements regarding culture, diversity, and human rights. In your memo describe the range of options in composing such statements (content, tone, level of detail, compliance, and so on) and offer your recommendations for this specific organization.

7. **Identify your own cultural communication style.** Is your communication style linear, moving straight to your point? Do you circle around your subject until you get to your point? Different styles reflect different cultures, but spiral communicators might perceive linear communicators as abrupt or rude, and linear communicators might perceive spiral communicators as deceptive or indecisive. Write a one-paragraph description of yourself as a workplace communicator. Include examples to support your description, which can serve as preparation for a face-to-face job interview when you are asked questions about how you interact with others and how effective you are as a communicator.
   - **Courtesy:** How do you greet colleagues? How tactful are you in e-mail, discussions, and meetings? How do you respond to criticism? Are you an active listener?
   - **Directness and simplicity:** Do your explanations tend to be simple and direct or long and complex? Do you tend to use a linear or spiral approach?
   - **Assertiveness:** How assertive or reticent are you? How likely are you to raise issues you see as problems? Do you avoid ever presenting an opinion?
   - **Timing:** How do you decide the appropriate time to discuss a problem? How do you bring up problems or disagreements?
   - **Argument:** What's your style of argument? Confrontational? Emotional? Logical and rational? In making an argument, do you focus on immediate goals or long-term goals? How do you manage conflicts and disagreements?
8. **Identify cultural similarities.** One of the best ways to gain some understanding of another culture is to look for things that are common both in your own culture and the other culture. Identify a cultural group on your own campus that you know nothing about. It might be a group defined by ethnicity, nationality, lifestyle, athletics, or hobby. Attend at least one meeting of the group. Conduct 10-minute interviews with at least two members of the group. Prepare a three-minute oral presentation in which you identify the group and then explain three things you have in common with people from that culture.
9. **Describe the culture of your best company.** Access **www.fortune.com/fortune/bestcompanies**, one of the WEBLINKS presented earlier in the chapter. Select one of the companies that interests you. Using both print and online resources, identify the organizational culture of that company, drawing on Figure 2.9 as a starting place. Write a one-paragraph explanation that can serve as preparation for a face-to-face job interview when you are asked questions about why you think the particular organization is a good match for you.

Chapter 2 Endnotes

1 Rosen, R., Digh, P., Singer, M., & Phillips, C. (2000). *Global literacies: Lessons on business leadership and national cultures* (p. 21). New York: Simon & Schuster.

2 U.S. Census Bureau. (2003, July 15). *State and county quick facts.* Retrieved August 23, 2003, from http://quickfacts.census.gov/qfd/states/00000.html

3 U.S. Census Bureau. (2003, July 11). *U.S. exports to all countries from 1998 to 2002 by 5-digit end-use code.* Retrieved August 23, 2003, from http://www.census.gov/foreign-trade/statistics/product/enduse/exports/index.html

4 U.S. Census Bureau. (2003, July 11). *U.S. imports from all countries from 1998 to 2002 by 5-digit end-use code.* Retrieved August 23, 2003, from http://www.census.gov/foreign-trade/statistics/product/enduse/imports/index.html

5 Bodley, J. H. (1994). *An anthropological perspective.* Retrieved August 23, 2003, from www.wsu.edu:8001/vcwsu/commons/topics/culture/culture-definitions/bodley-text.html

6 Williams, R. (1958). *Moving from high culture to ordinary culture.* Retrieved August 23, 2003, from www.wsu.edu:8001/vcwsu/commons/topics/culture/culture-definitions/raymond-williams.html

7 GlaxoSmithKline. (n.d.). *The impact of medicines: Corporate and social responsibility report 2002.* Retrieved August 23, 2003, from http://www.gsk.com/financial/reps02/CSR02/GSKcsr-12.htm

8 Pitchon, P. (1997). Globalization versus localization. *Share International,* (April). Retrieved June 9, 2003, from http://www.shareintl.org/archives/economics/ec_ppglobal.htm

9 Simmons, P. (1999). *Isda forms new committee for equity deratives.* "Equity Risk Special Report." Retrieved August 23, 2003, from http://www.financewise.com/public/edit/riskm/equity/equity-news-p.htm

F.T.S.E. acronym. (n.d.). Retrieved August 23, 2003, from http://havenworks.com/acronyms/a-z/f/ftse/

10 The following sources were consulted for this ethics sidebar:

- Arnold, M. (1998). Building a truly World Wide Web: A review of the essentials of international communication. *Technical Communication,* (May), 197–207.
- Chu, S. W. (1999). Using chopsticks and a fork together: Challenges and strategies of developing a Chinese/English bilingual Web site. *Technical Communication,* (May), 206–219.
- Hoft, N. (1999). Global issues, local concerns. *Technical Communication,* (May), 145–148.
- Kohl, John R. (1999). Improving translatability and readability with syntactic cues. *Technical Communication,* (May), 149–166.

11 Smith, M. K. (2002). Globalization. In *The encyclopedia of informal education.* Retrieved August 23, 2003, from http://www.infed.org/biblio/globalization.htm

12 Canadian Cancer Society. (2003, August 29). *Evaluation of new warnings on cigarette packages—Highlights.* Retrieved August 30, 2003, from http://www.cancer.ca/ccs/internet/standard/0,2939,3172_334419_436465_langId-en,00.html

13 *Canadian health warnings.* (n.d.). Retrieved August 30, 2003, from http://home.online.no/~smpeders/ind-can6.htm

14 Summarized from these sites:

- Schneider, K. L. (2002, July 22). *Gross pics intended to help Canadian smokers.* Retrieved August 30, 2003, from http://healthfactsandfears.com/featured_articles/jul2002/pics072202.html
- *Grisly new smoking warnings.* (2002, March 6). Retrieved August 30, 2003, from http://health.iafrica.com/healthnews/905729.htm
- Canadian Cancer Society. (2002, April 1). *Canadians overwhelmingly support graphic cigarette warnings.* Retrieved August 30, 2003, from http://www.cancer.ca/ccs/internet/mediareleaselist/0,,3172_15232_356973_langId-en.html

15 World Health Organization. (n.d.). *Global cancer rates could increase by 50% to 15 million by 2020.* Retrieved August 30, 2003, from http://www.who.int/mediacentre/releases/2003/pr27/en/

16 Harris, R. G. (1998). Economic approaches to language and bilingualism. In A. Breton (Ed.), *New Canadian Perspectives.* Retrieved on 9 June 2003, from http://www.pch.gc.ca/progs/lo-ol/perspectives/english/economic/ch2_02.html

17 This information is from the LISA Web site. Retrieved September 2, 2003, from http://www.lisa.org/info/about.html

18 For a more detailed explanation that differentiates these terms, see Esselink, B. (2001). *A practical guide to localization.* Amsterdam/Philadelphia: John Benjamins. Chapter 1 of this book, which differentiates critical terms, is available at http://www.lionbridge.com/kc/ec.asp?kb=content_g11n&content=g11n_terms

19 Retrieved September 2, 2003, from http://h18000.www1.hp.com/products/storageworks/sdlt110220/documentation.html

20 ITIM Culture and Management Specialists. (n.d.). *A short introduction.* Retrieved September 7, 2003, from http://www.itim.org/3.html

21 Retrieved September 2, 2003, from http://www.itim.org/3.html /kubnw5.kub.nl/web/iric/hofstede/page3.htm

22 Oxford University Press. (n.d.). *More about world English.* Retrieved August 23, 2003, from http://www.askoxford.com/globalenglish/worldenglish/

23 Pennycook, A. (2001). *Critical applied linguistics: A critical introduction.* (pp. 59, 112) Mahwah, NJ: Lawrence Erlbaum Associates.

24 Oxford University Press. (n.d.). *More about world English: Summary.* Retrieved August 23, 2003, from http://www.askoxford.com/globalenglish/worldenglish/summary/

25 Adapted from these sources:

- Gundling, E. (2003). *Working globalsmart: 12 people skills for doing business across borders.* Palo Alto, CA: Davier-Black.
- Hall, E. T. & Hall, M. R. (1990). *Understanding cultural differences.* Yarmouth, ME: Intercultural Press.
- Hofstede, G. (1997). *Cultures and organizations: Software of the mind.* New York: McGraw-Hill.
- Hofstede, G. (2001). *Cultural consequences: Comparing values, behaviors, institutions, and organizations across nations.* Thousand Oaks, CA: Sage.

26 U.S. Census Bureau. (2002, September 3). *Hispanic heritage month 2002: Sept. 15–Oct. 15.* Retrieved August 24 2003, from http://www.census.gov/Press-Release/www/2002/cb02ff15.html

27 SIL International. (n.d.). *Languages of South Africa.* Retrieved September 7, 2003, from http://www.ethnologue.com/show_country.asp?name=South+Africa

28 Constitutional Court of South Africa. (n.d.). *Chapter 1 Founding Provisions: Languages.* Retrieved September 7, 2003, from http://www.concourt.gov.za/constitution/const01.html#6

29 Adapted from Hall, E. T. & Hall, M. R. (1990). *Understanding cultural differences.* Yarmouth, ME: Intercultural Press.

30 Retrieved September 2, 2003, from kubnw5.kub.nl/web/iric/hofstede/page4.htm
Team Dynamics. (n.d.). (n.t.). Retrieved September 2, 2003, from http://teamdynamics.org/workplac.htm
ABS Consulting. (n.d.). *Changing the workplace culture to reap the benefits of good reliability programs.* Retrieved September 2, 2003, from http://www.jbfa.com/changing-workplace-culture.html

31 *2003 global most admired companies.* (n.d.). Retrieved August 31, 2003, from http://www.fortune.com/fortune/globaladmired

32 Retrieved September 2, 2003, from http://www.dell.com

33 Retrieved September 2, 2003, from http://www.dell.com/la/mx/es/gen/default.htm

34 Hewlett-Packard Company. (n.d.). *Our commitment to global citizenship.* Retrieved August 23, 2003, from http://www.hp.com/hpinfo/globalcitizenship/commitment.html

35 Retrieved September 1, 2003, from http://www.lucent.com/work/culture.html

36 Kodak Culture. Retrieved on April 29, 2004, from http://www.kodak.com/US/en/corp/careers/why/culture.jhtml

37 Drawings done by Professor Donna Kain, Clarkson University, Potsdam, NY.

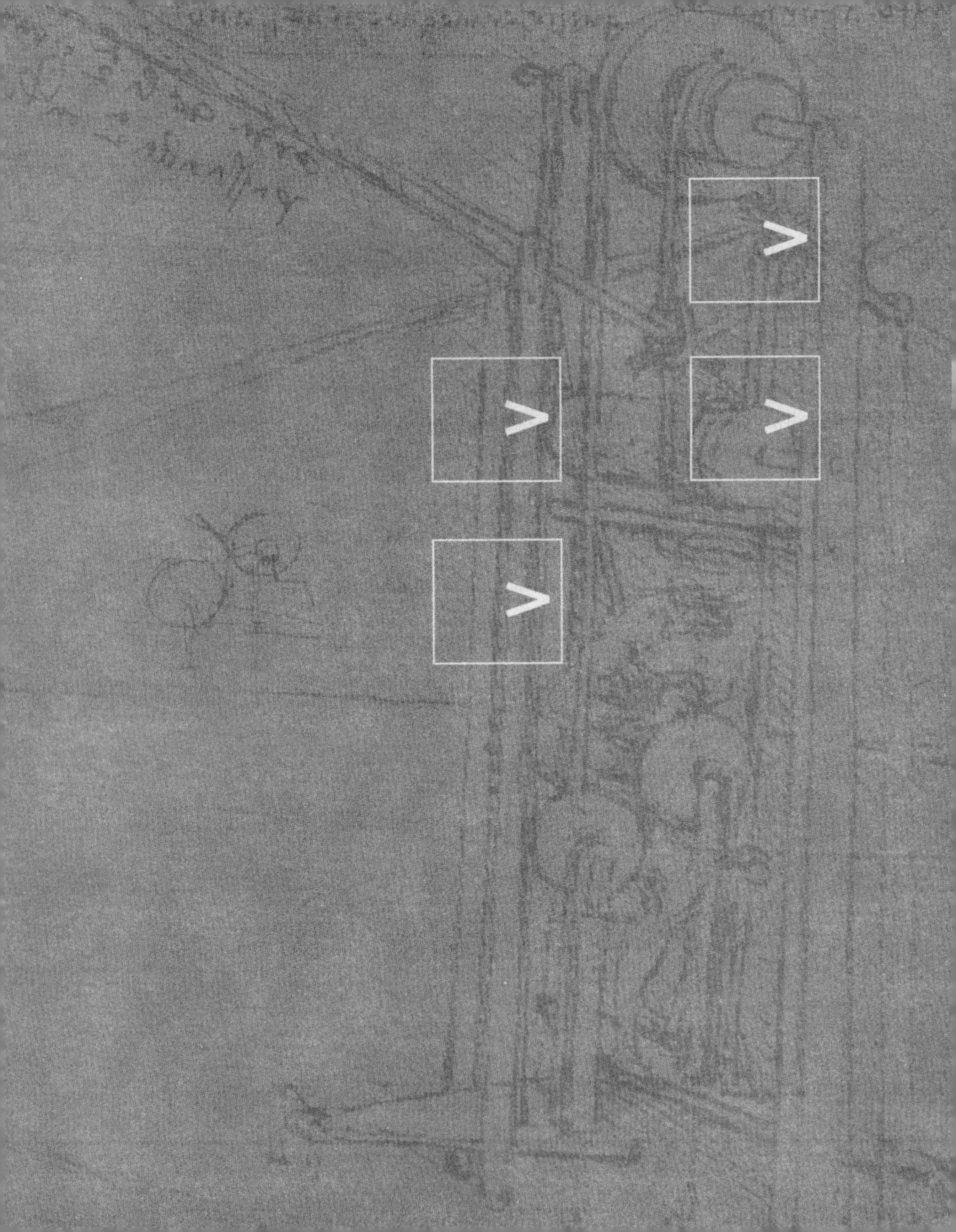

CHAPTER 3

Reading Technical Information

阅读技术信息

本章首先分析了阅读直接影响职场人士在工作中的学习以及做出的各种决策，并讨论了阅读与写作的紧密关系。最后，重点分析了职场中六类有效阅读策略（浏览预测、找出结构、确定主要内容、进行推断、提出问题、在阅读过程中调整策略）。

Objectives and Outcomes 学习目标

This chapter will help you accomplish these outcomes:

- Understand that workplace professionals read documents, listen to conversations and presentations, and view visuals for a variety of purposes: assessing and making decisions, learning background, learning to do a task, and actually doing a task.
- Recognize that reading and writing are synergistically linked activities — each affects the other.
- Use the strategies of experienced communicators:

What is reading? Some people think of reading as simply looking at a page or screen with words and decoding them — that is, figuring out their pronunciation and definitions. But the process of reading is not so simple.

Experts in reading consider it a complex activity and believe that making meaning involves interpreting rather than just decoding ideas. Meaning comes from more than simply the words on a page or screen because their interpretation is strongly influenced by an individual's prior experiences and knowledge as well as by the context in which the document is written and the purpose for which it's read. As a result, the same words can be interpreted in different ways by different readers. For example, the sentence "The cell has been examined" doesn't mean much, even when you decode the words. You need to know whether the sentence is about a cell in a spreadsheet, a cartoon animation, a Braille transcript, a biological organism, a terrorist organization, a political party, a monastery, a prison, a geographic area covered by a mobile phone, or a battery. Simply put, you need to do more than decode the words in order to make meaning from that document.

Throughout your professional life, you'll read and respond to a variety of documents. Some of these documents will require very little effort or attention; others will be exceedingly difficult to understand. This chapter suggests ways to make all of your reading easier and more productive. Your workplace literacy, your ability to both read and create paper and electronic documents, is highly correlated with your professional success.

The chapter begins by summarizing reasons that workplace professionals might have for reading and then discusses the strong relationship between reading and writing. Most of the chapter is devoted to discussing six critical strategies used by effective readers.

Identifying Purposes
确定目的

As a workplace professional, you read for a variety of purposes. Virtually all of these workplace purposes can be categorized into one of four often overlapping categories, as shown in Figure 3.1[1] — reading to assess, reading to learn, reading to learn to do, and reading to do.

> *What purposes for reading are you likely to have in your professional work?*

Regardless of the purposes that workplace professionals have for reading, they expect information in documents to be accessible, accurate, comprehensible, and usable. These expectations can usually be met if a document has a clear purpose, well-organized and appropriately developed points, and an effective balance of verbal and visual information.

Depending on the reader's needs in a particular context, a document such as a technical report will probably be read for a number of purposes. For example, an engineer might read an interim project report for any of the four purposes described in Figure 3.1. She might skim to *assess* whether she should read the report thoroughly later; she might read to *learn* how well a modification she designed for

FIGURE 3.1 **Purposes for Reading**

Purposes	Examples
Reading to assess. This reading, which is often skimming, enables you to decide whether a document will be useful for you or someone else, usually at a later time.	A forester might skim summaries of legislation about support for reforestation that he or she might need to study.
Reading to learn. This reading enables you to learn information for problem solving, decision making, and background knowledge.	A small-animal veterinarian might read an article in a professional journal to learn about new medication for feline colitis.
Reading to learn to do. This reading enables you to learn how to complete tasks.	A dental assistant might read a continuing education booklet about ways to minimize pain and anxiety for pediatric patients.
Reading to do. This reading, which serves largely as an external prompt, enables you to complete tasks.	A furniture refinisher might read the product label and information sheet to determine safety requirements for using a new paint remover.

the production line is working; she might read to *learn to do* the calibration of the new furnace controls; she might read to *do* a procedure for mechanical inspection that the report outlines.

Reading-Writing Relationships

阅读与写作的关系

Your reading and writing are closely related, whether you're working on a hard copy or electronic document. Consider these typical examples:

- A shipping manager writes instructions for sending products overseas; she rereads these instructions as she revises them following user testing. Later, her revised instructions are read by shipping clerks preparing the paperwork to accompany international orders.
- A greenhouse worker reads the package insert that came with a pesticide, specifically studying the section about application. Later he accesses the greenhouse's online database to record changes in greenhouse plants treated with this pesticide.
- A heating contractor reads the troubleshooting section of the manual for a new computer-controlled thermostat that isn't working properly. Later she completes a form she downloaded from the company's Web site to return the defective thermostat to the manufacturer.

What kinds of online documents are you likely to read? What complicating factors of online reading are likely to be the most problematic for readers?

- A hospice nurse makes notes about a patient's weekly medication; he rereads these notes before he writes a recommendation to the supervising physician for modifying the patient's care. Later, the patient's physician reads the recommendation in order to make her decision.

As a writer, imagine yourself as a member of your intended audience and then try to read the document you're preparing from that reader's perspective. For example, if you are working on a food safety Web site that discusses food irradiation, you should try to anticipate reader questions. One of the symbols that would probably appear on this site is the *radura,* an international symbol identifying foods that have been irradiated. You realize that some readers will not recognize the radura, so it will need to be defined. Other readers will recognize the symbol but will not necessarily know its purpose. The marginal questions next to Figure 3.2 show some of those questions readers might have about the radura before reading the information on this Web site.

What are your strongest strategies as a reader? Which features of electronic text do you find most influential in reducing your comprehension and/or speed in reading?

As a reader, you need to be conscious of a text's features. On a Web site, for example, this means recognizing the links that you can follow to obtain necessary information or knowing that you can conduct a search to locate additional information. As an active reader, you ask yourself questions that you hope the text answers. Of course, the questions you have are not necessarily the ones that other readers will have. Readers using a Web site like the example in Figure 3.2 will

FIGURE 3.2 **Predict Readers' Questions**[2]

Before reading, readers might ask these questions:

- *What is a radura?*
- *What are the legal requirements of using a radura?*
- *What is the history of using the radura?*
- *What protection does the use of the radura provide consumers?*
- *What links provide further information about the radura?*

As a writer, you might ask: What sequence of links could readers follow to create various understandings?

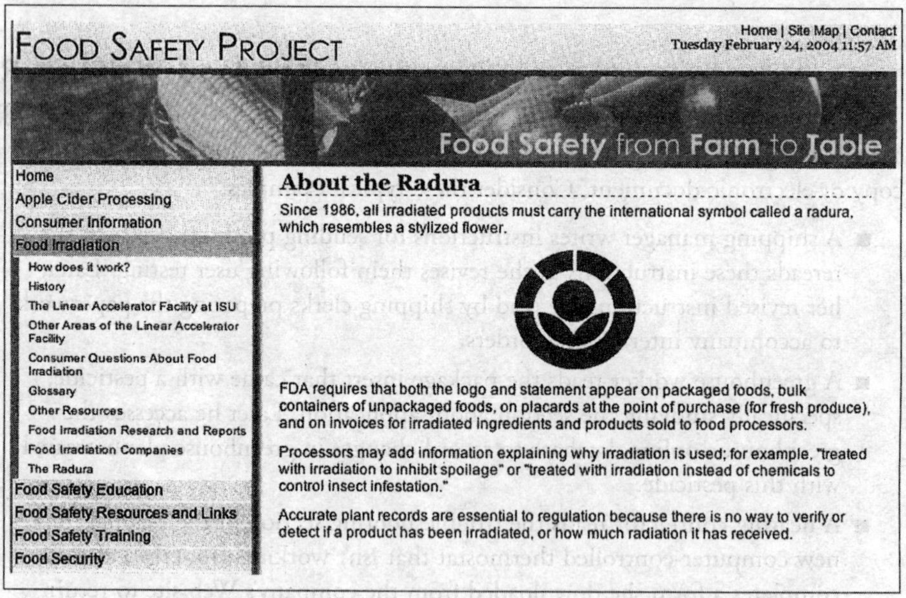

construct different meanings depending on which links they follow or what follow-up searches they do; thus, the same Web site — or print document — can be interpreted in different ways by different readers.

Readers have strong reactions to symbols as well as to words. Go to **www.english.wadsworth.com/burnett6e** for a link to review the FDA's description of *irradiation* and then two other links to review some reactions.
CLICK ON WEBLINK
CLICK on Chapter 3/radura

WEBLINK

Strategies for Effective Reading 有效阅读技巧

How do people read technical documents in the workplace? You may have started this chapter thinking of reading as decoding words. Now you know that researchers see reading as remarkably complex, having less to do with decoding than with the way readers interpret meanings in particular situations. How well people read has a great deal to do with both their prior knowledge and their reading strategies.

Experienced readers tend to see technical documents and the situation they're part of as a whole; in other words, documents cannot be separated from the situations in which they're created and used. (See the discussion of genre in Chapter 1.) Both the documents and the situations have recurring, evolving patterns that are familiar to experienced readers. These familiar patterns help experienced readers select and adapt appropriate strategies to read both print and electronic documents. This chapter is largely about these strategies.

Figure 3.3 identifies six strategies for critical reading. The first column identifies ways in which skillful writers use these strategies to make documents more accessible, understandable, and usable. If you conscientiously use these strategies as you plan, draft, and revise documents, your documents are likely to improve. The second column identifies strategies used by skillful readers to increase their comprehension and use of information. If you conscientiously use these reading strategies, you are likely to find that your reading is more productive because you'll understand, remember, and be able to use more of what you read.

Skim, Scan, and Predict 略读、速读、预测

When you need to read either a print or electronic document, you need to do three things before carefully reading the sentences and paragraphs, tables and graphs: Skim, scan, and predict.

FIGURE 3.3 **Strategies Used by Writers and Readers**[3]

Strategies	Ways for Writers to Create More Readable Documents	Ways for Readers to Increase Comprehension and Recall
Skim, scan, predict	Writers make a document easy to *skim* and *scan* so readers have an overview and can locate key information. They also know skilled readers *predict* what's coming and often ask themselves questions before reading.	Readers save time and increase their comprehension by *skimming* a document, *scanning* for key points, and then *predicting* what's coming before reading carefully.
Identify structure	Writers use familiar *document features* to help readers recognize the text's purposes, arrange *visual cues* to depict relationships, and reinforce the structure by *previewing the organization.*	Readers who relate *document features, visual cues,* and *previewed information* to a document's purpose usually remember more information than readers who don't.
Distinguish hierarchy	Writers help readers understand the *hierarchy of ideas* by using visual cues (e.g., headings), coherence devices (e.g., transitions), and textual cues (e.g., indicating relationships) that distinguish main from subordinate ideas.	Readers who understand the *hierarchy of ideas* usually recall more important information. Skillful readers often summarize the main points, which they connect to their prior knowledge.
Draw inferences	Writers anticipate readers' *purposes* for reading, which influences the information they include and the ways they imagine readers will use that information. Writers also anticipate possible *inferences* readers might make. They know readers *interpret* text.	Readers with specific *purposes* for reading are more focused. Readers who draw *inferences* usually increase understanding and recall of information. Skillful readers recognize that their understanding is an *interpretation;* they often extend ideas by applying them to new situations.
Generate questions and examples	Writers expect readers to ask *questions* and think of *examples* to increase their comprehension and recall of information.	Readers who ask themselves *questions* increase their comprehension. Skillful readers often think of examples to confirm or counter information in the document and their own prior knowledge.
Monitor and adapt reading strategies	Writers use *visual cues* (e.g., boldfacing, italics, and marginal annotations), *text support* (e.g., glossaries and checklists), and *reader appeals* (e.g., narratives, examples, and details) to increase reader engagement and comprehension.	Readers who monitor and reflect on their own reading process are aware of the ways in which *visual cues, text, support,* and *appeals* affect comprehension, and they make adjustments when their comprehension is low.

Skim. Begin reading a document by skimming — go through the entire document but do it very quickly. The idea is to get a quick, overall sense of what's in the document and where it's located. These specific strategies work well with most workplace documents:

- Determine the overall structure and organization of the document by looking through the table of contents to identify the chapter or section topics and sequence.
- Get an overview of the content and a sense of the scope and approach by examining the table of contents, the preface, and the index.
- Identify the main ideas by skimming the title, abstract or summary, headings, topic sentences, and first and final paragraphs.
- Check the bibliography or works cited to determine the authors, publishers, and currency of the references, so you can better situate the document.

Which of these skimming strategies do you currently use when reading complex documents? Which strategies would you be willing to start using?

The small amount of extra time you take to skim a document will be made up in increased comprehension when you read the document more carefully. You'll have a good sense of what you need to concentrate on carefully and what you can read fairly quickly. Skimming a print document can be easier than skimming an electronic document because readers moving through an electronic document sometimes lose their sense of place in the text.

To learn more about the difference between paper and on-screen reading, go to **www.english.wadsworth.com/burnett6e** for a link to a study comparing the two.
CLICK ON WEBLINK
CLICK on Chapter 3/comparison

WWW
WEBLINK

Scan. Before reading a document carefully, you should also scan it — run your eyes down a page or screen to look for specific information. Scanning is the kind of reading you do to locate a word in a dictionary. You scan a document to accomplish these tasks:

- Identifying key terms that are new to you
- Identifying the location of particular text features such as figures, examples, and sidebars
- Locating critical information that you must remember exactly, such as definitions, steps in a process, principles, laws, and formulas

Scanning is often aided by document design features that signal the presence of specific information. For example, italic or boldface type often signals key terms, and numbers often signal steps in a process.

WWW

WEBLINK

To learn more about reading strategies, go to **www.english.wadsworth.com/burnett6e** for a link to a Web site with more information about reading and additional links with practical suggestions.

CLICK ON WEBLINK

CLICK on Chapter 3/reading

Predict. While you're skimming and scanning a document before you begin careful reading, you can anticipate what it will contain and can formulate questions to be answered by more careful reading. You can get ideas about useful questions by thinking of key terms you'd like to know more about in relation to the document. For example, a document detailing a new product release could trigger thoughts about availability, so you might ask questions like these: "When will this new product be available?" "Is the availability of this product superior to the availability of the product I'm already using?" "What will be the availability of trained service technicians?" "What will be the availability of replacement parts?" You can predict whether the document will address your questions. The following words are a few that could trigger questions during your own reading:

- accessibility
- accuracy
- adaptability
- availability
- cost
- credibility
- development
- disadvantages
- efficiency
- long-range outlook
- maintenance
- materials
- specifications
- technical merit
- testing

Formulating questions that focus on what you want to get from your reading is a productive way to spend a few minutes before you jump into a document.

Identify Structure and Hierarchy 识别结构特点

Many technical documents have an identifiable structure and hierarchy. They use conventional document features such as headings, visual cues, and previews of what's coming up in the document.

Document Features. Standard features of a document can help readers know what to anticipate. For example, the features of abstracts, which are often described as the most important part of a technical report, are influenced by their purpose: to provide an abbreviated overview of a report.

Well-written abstracts maintain the tone and focus of the original document, presenting key points. The *Journal of the American Medical Association* (*JAMA*) recommends that articles about a clinical investigation be accompanied by an abstract with these features:

> the objective(s) or purpose, the design (e.g., randomized, double-blind, placebo-controlled, multicenter trial), the setting (e.g., university clinic, hospital), the patients or participants, the intervention(s), the measurements and main results, . . . the conclusion . . . ; [and] important outcome measures or endpoints.

JAMA recommends that review articles intended to "identify, assess, and synthesize" information be accompanied by an abstract that contains these features:

> purpose, data identification (a summary of data sources), study selection (how many studies were chosen and how they were selected), data extraction (guidelines for abstracting articles), results of data synthesis, and conclusions (which should include potential applications and research needs).[4]

You are likely to read abstracts more quickly and with greater comprehension if you anticipate their features. This is also true of other kinds of documents you read. The example in Figure 3.4 annotates the four kinds of information that most often appears in abstracts:

- objective, purpose, or rationale
- methodology
- results
- conclusions

If you look for these features every time you read an abstract, your reading time may decrease and your comprehension of key points may increase.

The example in Figure 3.4 is an abstract from the *Journal of Food Production,* a professional journal for experts interested in research about food science and technology, including food safety and quality. It is published by the International Association for Food Protection (IAFP), whose mission, according to their Web site, is "[t]o provide food safety professionals worldwide with a forum to exchange information on protecting the food supply." The journal, recognized as the leading international publication in food microbiology, is read by more than 11,000 scientists from 69 countries.[5] The abstract in Figure 3.4 accompanied an article written by researchers who were interested in finding a simple way to eliminate bacteria from alfalfa and mung bean seeds before the seeds sprouted. Most readers, even those who are not food scientists, would have an easy time identifying

FIGURE 3.4 **Online Abstract from the *Journal of Food Production* with Features That Readers Should Anticipate**[6]

AN = *accession number in the library*

AU = *authors*

PY = *year of publication*

NU = *ISSN or ISBN*

LA = *language of text*

AB = *abstract*

1. ***Purpose of study:*** *The study investigated whether ammonia fumigation is effective against selected pathogens when seeds are used for sprouting.*

2. ***Methodology:*** *Alfalfa and mung bean seeds were sealed in glass jars with ammonia. Samples were collected at regular intervals.*

DE = descriptors (all of which are links in the online version of this abstract, as are the authors and journal itself above)

AN: 2002-04-J0805

TI: Reduction of Escherichia coli O157:H7 and Salmonella Typhimurium in artificially contaminated alfalfa seeds and mung beans by fumigation with ammonia.

AU: Sakchai-Himathongkham; Suphachai-Nuanualsuwan; Riemann-H; Cliver-DO

AD: Correspondence (Reprint) address, D. O. Cliver, Dep. of Population Health & Reproduction, Sch. of Vet. Med., Univ. of California, Davis, CA 95616, USA. Tel. 530-754-9120. Fax 530-752-5845. E-mail docliver@ucdavis.edu

PY: 2001

SO: Journal-of-Food-Protection; 64 (11) 1817-1819, 17 ref.

NU: 0362-028X

DT: Journal-Article

LA: En (**English**)

SC: J Fruits-vegetables-and-nuts

AB: Sprouts eaten raw are increasingly perceived as hazardous foods because they have been vehicles in outbreaks of food-borne disease, often involving Escherichia coli O157:H7 and Salmonella Typhimurium. Although the source of these pathogens has not been established, it is known that the seeds usually are already contaminated at the time sprouting begins. Earlier studies had shown that ammonia was lethal to these same pathogens in manure, therefore this study sought to determine whether ammonia fumigation is effective against them when associated with seeds to be used for sprouting. Experimentally contaminated (10-8-10-9 cfu/g **E. coli** O157:H7 and Salmonella Typhimurium) and dried alfalfa and mung bean seeds, intended for sprouting, were sealed in glass jars in which 180 or 300 mg ammonia/l of air space was generated by the action of ammonium sulphate and sodium hydroxide. Samples were taken after intervals up to 22 h at 20 degrees C. Destruction of approx. 2–3 logs was observed with both bacteria associated with alfalfa seeds, vs. 5–6 logs with mung beans. Greater kills were apparently associated with lower initial bacterial loads. Germination of these seeds was unaffected by the treatment. It appeared that this simple treatment could contribute significantly to the safety of sprout production of alfalfa seeds and mung beans.

DE: AMMONIA-; BACTERIA-; ESCHERICHIA-; FOOD-SAFETY-PLANT-FOODS; FUMIGATION-; INHIBITION-; LEGUMES-; MUNG-BEANS; SALMONELLA-; VEGETABLES-SPECIFIC; ALFALFA-SPROUTS; ALFALFA-; ANTIBACTERIAL-ACTIVITY; BEAN-SPROUTS; ESCHERICHIA-COLI; SALMONELLA-TYPHIMURIUM

TI = *title of the article*

AD = *information for correspondence (mail, phone, fax, e-mail)*

SO = *source for bibliographic citation*

DT = *type of document*

SC = *subject code*

3. ***Results:*** *Bacteria that had contaminated the seeds were killed at various rates; seed germination was unaffected by treatment.*

4. ***Conclusions:*** *Treatment could increase safety of sprout production of alfalfa seeds and mung beans.*

what this article is about if they look for purpose, methodology, results, and conclusion in the abstract.

Whatever you are reading, you can make good use of your time by knowing the features of that particular type of document. Just as abstracts have predictable features, so do the other documents you'll read. Recognizing and then anticipating the features and their organization will help you read efficiently.

Visual Cues. Various kind of visual cues help readers distinguish the hierarchy of ideas in a document. Typically, readers have an easier time understanding and using documents that have the following features:

1. Information is chunked so that relationships are clear.
   - Related information is topically chunked.
   - Headings and subheadings signal and separate topics.
   - Leading (spacing) between lines and sections separates related information.
2. Information is arranged so that the sequence is clear.
   - The sequence of information is logical, and explicit transitions indicate the relationship between the points.
   - Numbers or letters indicate the sequence or hierarchy of the items in a list; bullets indicate equivalency of the items.
3. Information is emphasized so that important elements are signaled.
   - Placement on a page or screen can indicate hierarchy. Main ideas can be signaled with centered and left-justified text. Subordinate ideas can be signaled by indentation.
   - Type size can indicate the hierarchy of headings. A level-1 heading might be in larger type than a subordinate level-2 heading.
   - Changes in typeface can differentiate headings and text. Headings might be in a sans serif font such as **Arial Black** while the body of the text might be in a serif font such as Times New Roman.
   - Type-style variations — for example, SMALL CAPS, **bold,** or *italics* — draw readers' attention to important terms or ideas.
   - Icons can signal important categories.

Readers use visual cues to help them decide what's important in a document, but careful writers use such cues judiciously. They don't overdo their use, because when too many cues are used, they lose their effectiveness.

A well-designed table of contents demonstrates how these visual cues can be used. (See Chapters 10 and 12 for additional discussion about designing information.) The table of contents in Figure 3.5, from *NASA Tech Briefs,* gives readers multiple visual cues about chunking, arrangement, and emphasis. The annotations identify cues you might use in documents that you design.

FIGURE 3.5 **Table of Contents Showing Structure**[7]

Chunking *is signaled by increased spacing between sections of related information.* ***Arrangement*** *is clear because of section bars with reverse type as well as page numbers.* ***Emphasis*** *is indicated by design elements:*

- *Font size and style — large, boldface font for the major sections; small, plain font for the individual articles*
- *Icons — familiar to the audience and in a contrasting color to signal important categories*
- *Photos — draw attention to particularly interesting products and processes*

March 2004 • Vol. 24 No. 3

TECH BRIEFS

ENGINEERING SOLUTIONS FOR DESIGN & MANUFACTURING

You can read a remarkably informative interview with one of the country's leading experts on workplace literacy. Go to **www.english.wadsworth.com/burnett6e** for a link this interview.
CLICK ON WEBLINK
CLICK on Chapter 3/NCAL publications

WWW
WEBLINK

Previews and Reviews. Previewing and reviewing give you a chance to identify and then reinforce the structure or organization of a document. Helping readers identify the structure of a document increases the likelihood that they will understand and recall the information. Visual and verbal cues, such as numbered or bulleted lists, parallel terms, design and typography, can effectively signal the relative relationship among terms.

Figure 3.6 shows the first half of a page from a manual for farmers, *How to Grow Shiitake Mushrooms Outdoors on Natural Logs.* In this preview, readers are signaled about the purpose of the section: "Let's quickly preview the factors to consider. Then, we'll take a close look at each of them." Readers are introduced to five critical factors that are distinguished by a series of visual cues:

- **bold,** SMALL-CAP section heading (acceptable for these very short phrases)
- numbered list with hanging indents
- boldface terms
- a colon separating each term from the comment

The wording of the first item in the preview ("Tree Selection") anticipates the wording of the first subheading ("What Tree Species Should be Selected?"). Similar repetition is used throughout the section to reduce the chance of misinterpretation; the wording in the preview matches the wording in the subheadings and in the text itself. Knowing what to anticipate helps readers call on their relevant prior knowledge and begin to organize what they'll be reading.

Determine the Main Points 确定主要内容

Distinguishing between the main points and the subordinate points helps readers understand the relationships among ideas in a document, the hierarchy of information. Sometimes the main points are easy to distinguish because the writer uses typographic cues. For example, if you look again at Figure 3.6, you'll see that in the first paragraph the writer has italicized the terms *noncommercial* and *commercial,* so readers immediately know that this distinction matters.

FIGURE 3.6 **Previewed Information**[8]

Readers are clearly signaled about the purpose of this section.

The five critical factors are previewed.

These visual cues help readers:

- *numbered list with hanging indents*
- *boldface terms*
- *factors set off by colon from comment about each factor*

The language of the first item in the preview anticipates the language of the first heading.

PART 2:
BEDLOGS: SELECTING, CUTTING, AND GROWING

If you want to grow a few shiitake *noncommercially,* all you really need to know about choosing bedlogs is to get fresh, healthy logs of the proper size and species that were cut in late winter. However, if you have a *commercial* interest, a lot more is worth learning about bedlog selection.

Let's quickly preview the factors to consider. Then, we'll take a close look at each of them.

1. **Tree Selection:** You must decide which tree species to use and how to select the best individual trees to fell.
2. **Bedlog Selection:** You must know how to cut suitable logs from the trees felled.
3. **Season of Felling:** The trees must be felled at the right time of year.
4. **Bedlog Handling:** Harvested bedlogs must be carefully handled and properly stored until they are inoculated.
5. **Bedlog Silviculture:** If you plan to have an ongoing operation, you probably need to carry out some woodland management practices to ensure a future supply of bedlogs. Or, if you plan to buy logs, you have to find a logger who is willing to meet your specifications.

What Tree Species Should be Selected?

Sometimes, though, the main points are more difficult to identify, and you must be able to generate a series of questions to help you identify them. The example in Figure 3.7 is an abstract for a technical article about management architecture for wireless sensor networks. Experienced readers might begin by asking — and expecting their reading to answer — questions such as these:

- What is the main issue or problem?
- Who and what are involved in the issue or problem?
- What is the approach to the solution to the problem?
- How will the approach be addressed or the solution be implemented?

Answers to these questions will help you identify the main points of virtually any technical document.

FIGURE 3.7 **Abstract with Main Points Identified by Reader Questions**[9]

"MANNA: A management architecture for wireless sensor networks," Linnyer Beatrys Ruiz, José Marcos Nogueira and Antonio A. F. Loureiro. IEEE Communications Magazine, vol. 41, no. 2, Feb. 2003, p. 116–125.

Wireless sensor networks (WSNs) are becoming an increasingly important technology that will be used in a variety of applications such as environmental monitoring, infrastructure management, public safety, medical, home and office security, transportation, and military. WSNs will also play a key role in pervasive computing where computing devices and people are connected to the Internet. Until now, WSNs and their applications have been developed without considering a management solution. This is a critical problem since networks comprised of tens of thousands of nodes are expected to be used in some of the applications above.

This article proposes the MANNA management architecture for WSNs. In particular, it presents the functional, information, and physical management architectures that take into account specific characteristics of this type of network. Some of them are restricted physical resources such as energy and computing power, frequent reconfiguration and adaptation, and faults caused by unavailable nodes. The MANNA architecture considers three management dimensions: functional areas, management levels, and WSN functionalities. These dimensions are specified to the management of a WSN and are the basis for a list of management functions. The article also proposes WSN models to guide the management activities and the use of correlation in the WSN management. This is a first step into a largely unexplored research area.

What is the issue or problem?
The main problem is signaled by the wording: "Until now, WSNs and their applications have been developed without considering a management solution."

Who and what are involved in the issue or problem?
The breadth of the problem is clearly indicated: "This is a critical problem since networks comprised of tens of thousands of nodes are expected to be used in some of the applications above."

What is the approach to the solution to the problem?
The approach to the solution is straightforward: "This article proposes the MANNA management architecture for WSNs."

How will the approach be addressed or solution be implemented?
The details of the solution are outlined: "The MANNA architecture considers three management dimensions: functional areas, management levels, and WSN functionalities. These dimensions are specified to the management of a WSN and are the basis for a list of management functions. The article also proposes WSN models to guide the management activities and the use of correlation in the WSN management."

Draw Inferences 运用推理

Not everything that readers learn from a text is explicitly stated. Sometimes readers draw inferences: They make connections and draw conclusions beyond the words and visuals that are presented.

Most experienced readers draw inferences as they read, forming and reforming their opinions as they move through a document. Three specific strategies help you draw inferences:

- Identify the tacit assumptions on which you believe the document is based — that is, what's presumed but not articulated.

- Extend the ideas to pose reasonable but unstated implications — what's implied but not articulated.
- Speculate on the impact of the implications — what's possible but not articulated.

Drawing inferences involves identifying tacit assumptions, extending ideas, and speculating on the possible impact of what you've read in relation to what you already know. Figure 3.8 provides an example of a reader drawing inferences while reading. The excerpt is the first part of an online article about the Xanadu system, a concept for a worldwide electronic repository of documents that has received little attention. The comments are the questions and inferences drawn by Dave Clark, a cautious, perhaps even skeptical, reader who draws on his expertise to frame his questions. As you read the excerpt and Clark's comments you can consider how he identified tacit assumptions, extended the article's ideas, and speculated on the possible impact of the ideas in the article.

Figure 3.8 shows one way in which readers can be engaged with a text by articulating their own reactions as they read. Readers' reactions are shaped, in part, by prior experiences and knowledge as well as by the context in which the document is written and read.

The ethics sidebar on page 94 explains the importance of context in reading, showing how it affects our inferences and interpretations.

Generate Questions and Examples 发现问题和例子

Readers can ask questions to help themselves understand a document. Sometimes readers benefit from using a traditional taxonomy (a formal method of classification) that increases their chances of understanding important information. One widely used taxonomy uses six levels of questions:[10]

- **Knowledge questions** emphasize the recall of specifics. Such questions require recall of specialized terminology and symbols, quantifiable facts, conventions of organizing information, awareness of trends, knowledge of classification systems, evaluation criteria, methodology, principles, and theories.
- **Comprehension questions** require responses that incorporate knowledge as well as understanding. Responses to comprehension questions can involve translation, interpretation, or extrapolation.
- **Application questions** require specific applications of principles or theories.
- **Analysis questions** emphasize the separation of objects, mechanisms, systems, organisms, operations, or ideas into constituent parts, clearly establishing the relationship between these parts.
- **Synthesis questions** expect the reader to focus on organizing or structuring the parts to form a unique whole. The response may either serve as an overall plan or explain a particular phenomenon.

FIGURE 3.8 **Drawing Inferences while Reading**[11]

THE XANADU IDEAL

Theodor Holm Nelson

WHAT IS XANADU PUBLISHING?

What problems in understanding a document might occur if the writer and reader have different tacit assumptions about the subject?

The term universal electronic library has been suggested. Perhaps universal bookstore is more like it. World Publishing Repository™ is perhaps the most appropriate term.

The Xanadu system has been designed from the literary point of view, the computer point of view, the business point of view and the legal point of view.

The Xanadu publishing system will be a licensed method of online electronic publication provided by vendors throughout the world. "Publication" consists of placing a digital document somewhere in the repository network. A document may include text, pictures, audio, movies and any other form of digital information. Readers, or users, are of course at screens. Any user in the world may send for any document, or any part of a document. The publisher pays only for the storage; the user pays for delivery, including a royalty to the publisher. **Clark's Comment:** Nelson assumes that users can afford these costs and will want to pay for documents. Isn't this exclusionary, making it possible only for people with money to have access to this "World Publishing Repository"? Even if the charge is only a few cents per document, it's still more expensive than local libraries.

Clark questions one of Nelson's tacit assumptions. Clark sees economic barriers as serious and suggests that Nelson doesn't sufficiently consider cost.

The user obtains a digital copy of everything he or she sends for — to keep or discard. The user may point and click to travel among documents, obtaining only the small part needed to keep going. **Clark's Comment:** Nelson's assumption is that pointing and clicking are better, or more efficient, than shelf browsing at the library. How will users know which documents they want? Will they be paying for documents whether they "keep or discard" them? If so, every click would be an investment, and this doesn't seem like an improvement over shelf browsing.

Clark again questions one of Nelson's assumptions and speculates that Nelson's plan isn't an improvement over current practices.

Staying within the Xanadu online world, anyone may publish a connection to a document — a comment, illustration, disagreement, or link of any other type; and anyone may quote from a published Xanadu document, since the quotation is bought from the original publisher at the time of delivery. The publisher agrees to be legally responsible for the contents and agrees to interconnection by anyone. **Clark's Comment:** Again, we see "anyone"; do "anyone's" documents cost the same as famous authors' documents? This would be an interesting democratic move, but how would readers find credible and useful information if they must slog through piles of information by people they've never heard of, whose work may well not be useful or interesting?

Clark extends his concern about Nelson's tacit assumptions to include credibility of materials as a potential problem.

ETHICS 职业道德规范知识吧 SIDEBAR

"It's only a report": Ethics and Context

"只是一个报告"：职业规范与工作环境

The following is an excerpt from a technical report:

> The van's normal load is usually nine [pieces] per square yard. In Saurer vehicles, which are very spacious, maximum use of space is impossible, not because of any possible overload, but because loading to full capacity would affect the vehicle's stability. So, reduction of the load space seems necessary. It must absolutely be reduced by a yard, instead of trying to solve the problem, as hitherto, by reducing the number of pieces loaded.

How can you make sure you don't lose sight of the context for a document you are writing?

Researcher Steven Katz[12] points out that this report meets many of the formal criteria necessary for an effective document. The report addresses a concern shared by both the readers and the writer and provides answers relevant to their concerns. However, Katz also points out that we must look at this document in the context in which it was written.

This report comes from Nazi Germany in 1942. The "pieces loaded" are Jews, Poles, gypsies, and other humans who are being transported to their deaths in concentration camps.

Katz examines this report to suggest that not only the content of a document can make it unethical. How readers interpret it and use it also matters. Technical professionals must recognize the purposes behind technical documents and the effects those documents might have. Many involved in indirectly supporting the Holocaust argued that they should not be held responsible for their actions. They were "only doing their jobs." Most scholars believe that we cannot accept this argument. When individuals are not held accountable for the contexts in which they perform their jobs, when they are not held responsible for interpreting and implementing ideas, then atrocities like the Holocaust continue.

The context in which technical professionals work is not as horrific as the Holocaust of World War II. Even so, technical documents affect readers. We must be aware of those effects and be willing to examine their ethical consequences. As you write, ask yourself: Do I know who is affected by this document? Am I willing to be responsible for those effects? Perhaps, if the writer of the 1942 report had asked himself this question, fewer such documents would exist.

- **Evaluation questions** require readers to judge something's qualitative and quantitative value. Such questions examine internal elements for logic and consistency as well as examining external comparisons to establish the relationship of the subject with accepted principles, theories, and works of recognized excellence.

Figure 3.9 presents "Slowing the Progress of Aortic Regurgitation" from the *Harvard Heart Letter*, a monthly newsletter written to interpret complex medical information for general readers interested in heart-related medical issues. In addition, Figure 3.9 presents questions based on the above taxonomy that a reader asked when reading this article. You can see how the reader used the taxonomy to develop questions that could help check comprehension. Whenever you read, you should ask yourself questions about the text and the accompanying visuals. You can jot these questions in the margins of the document you're reading (if it belongs to you), or you can keep a separate paper or electronic notepad for jotting notes and recording questions.

Monitor and Adapt Reading Strategies 调整学习策略

Effective readers are aware of what they're doing when they move through a document. They're actively engaged in their reading; they're aware of their comprehension of concepts and terms. When their comprehension or speed decreases, they adjust their strategies to meet the needs of the situation.

Your goal is to develop reading strategies that work well for you. Your strategies will vary depending on your purpose. Most likely, you haven't had any instruction about how to be a better reader since elementary school. And you do just fine until the stakes are raised when the documents are more complex, the information is more important to understand and recall, and you have less time. Figure 3.10 gives you practical strategies to understand the visual and verbal information in technical documents. Effective readers usually engage in certain strategies before, during, and after reading very difficult or complex documents.

Monitoring your reading process may feel uncomfortable at first but, like reflecting on your writing processes as you plan, draft, and revise documents, monitoring your reading processes using the questions in Figure 3.10 will soon become second nature to you. Like other skillful readers, you'll learn what works well for you so that your reading is productive. Just like experienced writers, experienced readers are distinguished by their ability to adjust strategies to match the situation they're in.

To demonstrate the differences that may occur with readers of the same text, you'll have a chance to "listen in" on two different professionals as they read the opening three paragraphs from an article in *Scientific American*, "Smart Rooms."[13] The article is about the potential benefits of a project at MIT to create computer systems that recognize human faces, expressions, and gestures. Two expert readers were asked to read these paragraphs and to "interrogate" the article — to record the questions and comments they had while reading.

- Figure 3.11 presents the introductory paragraphs that embed the questions and comments made by Clay, who has a computer science degree. Clay read the article as preliminary background for work he was doing about the computer-human interface.

FIGURE 3.9 **Applying Taxonomy of Questions to Reading**[14]

SLOWING THE PROGRESS OF AORTIC REGURGITATION

A leaky aortic valve allows blood that has just been pumped out of the heart and into the aorta—the large blood vessel that distributes blood to the body—to flow backwards, or regurgitate, into the left ventricle. This problem, which is also known as aortic regurgitation or aortic insufficiency, forces the left ventricle to do extra work, since this blood must be pumped out a second time. Only by doing this additional work can the heart sustain a normal flow of blood to the body.

Over time, this added burden can take a toll on the heart. The left ventricle enlarges to accommodate the blood flowing back into it from the aorta and works less efficiently when its architecture becomes distorted. Eventually, some people with aortic regurgitation develop congestive heart failure, which may not be reversible even if the valve is replaced surgically. In heart failure, the heart is unable to pump enough blood to maintain normal circulation; the result is a buildup of fluid in the body.

***Comprehension question:** How does the extra work the heart must do because of aortic regurgitation lead to an irreversible problem?*

Until recently, aortic-valve surgery was the only way to stop this process. Although the surgery is usually successful, the patient must live thereafter with the problems associated with an artificial valve. However, scientists have been searching for a medication that might decrease the damage from aortic regurgitation and thereby delay or eliminate the need for surgery. A recent randomized trial reports the first long-term positive results of such drug therapy.

New Role for Nifedipine

***Knowledge question:** What side effects might be caused by taking nifedipine?*

The drug used in this study was nifedipine—a medication that is used most commonly to treat high blood pressure and angina (the chest pain or discomfort that occurs when the heart muscle is not getting enough blood from the coronary arteries). Nifedipine (Procardia, Adalat) is a calcium-channel-blocking agent, which causes muscle cells to relax by blocking the movement of calcium across cell membranes. This medication is believed to help people with coronary artery disease, in part by dilating the coronary arteries and preventing spasm of these blood vessels. It also lowers blood pressure by dilating arteries in the rest of the body.

***Application question:** How does a vasodilator such as nifedipine delay the need for surgery?*

These vasodilator effects of nifedipine are believed to be the beneficial mechanism for patients with aortic regurgitation. The dilated arteries and the lowered blood pressure decrease the force that "pushes" blood back through the leaky aortic valve. Since less blood flows the wrong way, the strain on the left ventricle decreases.

***Analysis question:** How does nifedipine treat the symptoms of high blood pressure and angina?*

Two relatively short-term studies previously showed that nifedipine and another vasodilator, hydralazine, might have a beneficial effect on the heart's function, but whether these drugs could actually prevent the need for surgery remained uncertain. Therefore, a team of researchers from Padua, Italy, designed a long-term study to test this idea (New England Journal of Medicine, 494, pp. 689–694).

Before Symptoms Begin

All 143 people who were enrolled in this study had severe aortic regurgitation, which was documented by echocardiography, an examination that uses sound waves to produce a video of the beating heart (see *Harvard Heart Letter*). None of the patients started with symptoms or evidence of damage to the left ventricle. About half were assigned to receive daily digoxin (0.25 mg) to increase the strength of the heart's contractions; the rest took nifedipine (20 mg) twice a day.

Over the next six years, the patients who received nifedipine were about half as likely to need an aortic-valve replacement as those who took digoxin. During the first two years, there were no valve replacements in the nifedipine group versus about 10% of those who took digoxin. At the end of six years, 34% of the patients who took digoxin had undergone valve replacement compared with only 15% of those assigned to nifedipine. The decision to perform surgery was made according to specific criteria, so it is unlikely that knowledge of which drug the patient was taking influenced the rate of valve replacements.

Nifedipine's benefits were not without a price. At least one new mild symptom was reported during the first three months by 42% of the patients who took nifedipine versus 12% of those who used digoxin. The most common side effects were a sensation of a rapid heartbeat and headache among those who used nifedipine, and fatigue among those who used digoxin. At six years of follow-up, some side effects were still reported by 5% of those who used nifedipine, but no patient in this study discontinued medication because of complications.

Synthesis question: *How does the use of a drug such as nifedipine contribute to the treatment of cardiac patients?*

Encouraging Data

This encouraging study suggests that the course of aortic regurgitation can be altered and that nifedipine can delay the need for surgery if given early enough in the course of this disease. Whether other vasodilators can reduce the need for surgery is unknown; in theory, other drugs could be as effective, but none have been studied as comprehensively as nifedipine.

Evaluation question: *In what ways does research into the use of vasodilators appear to be promising?*

Vasodilator therapy is not a replacement for surgery. If medical therapy with a vasodilator is unsuccessful, patients and their physicians should not continue to rely on that treatment. If the left ventricle is substantially dilated or damaged, patients should have surgery before the problem becomes so severe that even replacing the valve cannot restore normal function. Nevertheless, this study represents very positive news to many of those with aortic regurgitation. People who have this condition should consult with their physician to determine whether the findings from this investigation are relevant to them.

A Drug Treatment for Aortic Regurgitation

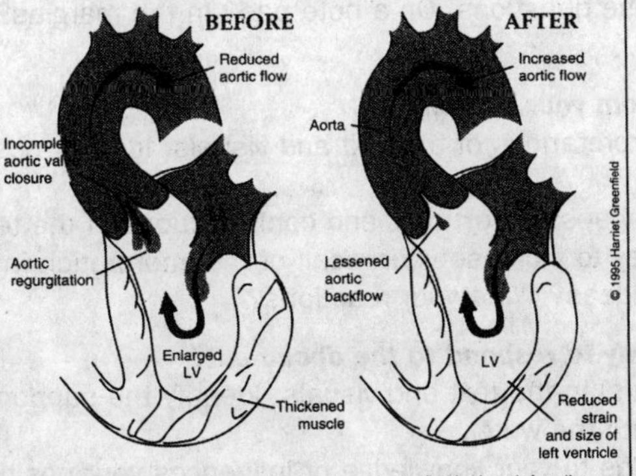

In aortic regurgitation, the leaking aortic valve allows blood to flow backwards from the aorta into the left ventricle. Nifedipine is believed to help patients with this condition by dilating blood vessels, encouraging the flow away from the heart, and decreasing the amount of backward flow. (LA = left atrium; LV = left ventricle)

FIGURE 3.10 **Practical Approaches for Reading Complex Technical Documents**

Before Reading

What pre-reading strategies are helpful?

- Skim the title, abstract, headings, opening and concluding paragraphs of major sections and visuals as well as their titles and captions,
- Mentally review what you already know about the subject. Identify what's likely to be difficult about the text and visuals. Complexity? Familiarity? Time constraints? Decide how you will manage these difficulties.
- Note and check meanings of unfamiliar terms or visual displays that catch your eye.
- Check the works cited or bibliography of the document to review the sources the writer used.
- Decide what's potentially relevant about the document.

What's your purpose(s) for reading a particular document?

- Determine your purpose for reading a particular document. *Reading to assess* (to decide whether to read thoroughly)? *Reading to learn* (to acquire background information)? *Reading to learn to do* (to understand a process you're supervising)? *Reading to do* (to complete a task or to make a decision)?

What's likely to be difficult about a particular document?

- Anticipate possible problems. Unfamiliar genre? New topic? Limited time to read? Difficult concepts? No supporting examples? Unfamiliar types of visuals? Complex visuals? Limited or inadequate visuals? Poor document design?

During Reading

How will you reduce (or prevent) distractions or interruptions during your reading?

- Given the difficulty and importance of the document, estimate the amount of time you'll need, and set other work aside during that time.
- Work in an isolated area, wear headphones, or post a DO NOT DISTURB sign.

How will you annotate your reading?

- Determine the approach you'll use for annotating important information: Take marginal notes? Highlight important phrases? Use self-stick notes? Make an outline? Create diagrams or charts?

How will you ask and record your questions about the reading?

- Determine the kinds of questions you should ask about the text and visuals: knowledge, comprehension, application, analysis, synthesis, and/or evaluation questions.
- Decide how you'll record these questions. On a note pad? In the margins? In a computer file?

After Reading

How will you make meaning from your reading?

- Determine the possible interpretations of the text and visuals. Identify possible alternative interpretations.
- Identify apparent omissions, gaps, distortions, and contradictions in the text and visuals.
- Decide the most effective way to increase your recall of the information in the text and the visuals. Summarize the key ideas? Write your reactions?

What is the most productive way to respond to the document?

- Identify the writer's key point(s) in the text and visuals. Identify the support for these points. Decide whether you agree with the writer.
- Consider how information adds to your knowledge or influences your position about the topic.

- Figure 3.12 presents the introductory paragraphs that embed the questions and comments made by Susan, who has a degree in journalism. Susan read the article to learn more about the interaction that takes place in smart rooms for a feature article she was writing for a local newspaper.

Can identical paragraphs mean different things to different readers? The questions posed by Clay and Susan show that from the very beginning they had different reactions. While their general purpose was the same (to learn), their specific purposes were quite different. Clay was interested in the technical interface and Susan in the human interaction and application. The meaning of a document is shaped by the reading process and interpretation brought to the document by the readers. As Figures 3.11 and 3.12 show, the opening paragraphs of this *Scientific American* article sometimes provoked similar comments and questions from Clay and Susan. At other times, though, their interpretations were startlingly different. The following list highlights some of their similarities and differences:

- Both remark that the term "smart room" sounds familiar. Both make connections to their prior knowledge, Clay mentioning a journal he reads and Susan drawing on her prior knowledge.
- Both are curious about who wrote the article. Susan immediately searches through the article until she finds the author's bio at the end. The information in this bio shapes Susan's reading, since she wonders whether the listed sponsors might influence the nature of the article.
- Clay and Susan both start eagerly, but they read the article in different sequences. Clay starts at the beginning and reads straight through the first three paragraphs, referring to photographs as he needs them. Susan reads the title, teaser, and author's name; then she searches for biographical information. Before moving back to the beginning of the article, she reads one of the article's sidebars, looks at a couple of the color photos in the article, and reads their captions.
- Clay and Susan both draw frequently on their prior knowledge, which shapes their reading. But their prior knowledge is remarkably different. Clay talks about UNIX-based systems, Silicon Graphic terminals, and limitations of VR goggles. Susan talks about the value of imperative mood, balanced examples, and personal anecdotes as well as ways to make information relevant to general readers.
- Clay and Susan form different views of the author. When Clay reads about software developed by the author and another programmer, he talks about the author's credibility going up: "This isn't a journalist trying to interpret an expert's words. . . ." Susan talks about the author's credibility having "taken a large dive" when she anticipates that he may be promoting his own work.

FIGURE 3.11 **Computer Scientist "Interrogating" a Text (Reader Comments in Blue)**

SMART ROOMS
Smart rooms. I heard about these in a *Communications of the ACM* a few years ago. The picture looks interesting. [Clay reads the caption.] **Okay, it's a giant screen and the user appears on it, sort of like a shadow projected on the wall, only more colorful. It's not 3D. How is it better?**

[article's teaser] In creating computer systems that can identify people and interpret their actions, researchers have come one step closer to building helpful home and work environments.
Not sure if I buy this. What do they mean by "interpret actions"? Physical actions, maybe — that's what the picture looks like. It reminds me of the haunted house ride in Disneyland; there's one point at which you pass a mirror and see ghosts sitting beside you in the reflection. You turn around and they're not there. Same with this screen.

by Alex P. Pentland
Who is this guy? Guess I'll find out.

Imagine a house that always knows where your kids are and tells you if they are getting into trouble. **Doesn't look like it'll be purely you facing the screen, then. I wonder how they're managing that? Cameras? How are they rendering the people they monitor — C++ objects? Shades of Big Brother here.** Or an office that sees when you are having an important meeting and shields you from interruptions. **Artificial intelligence — this isn't strictly graphical interface.** Or a car that senses when you are tired and warns you to pull over. **How?** Scientists have long tried to design computer systems that could accomplish such feats. **Examples? What research was this built from?** Despite their efforts, modern machines are still no match for babysitters or secretaries. But they could be.

The problem, in my opinion, is that our current computers are both deaf and blind; they experience the world only by way of a keyboard and a mouse. **And that's the way some of us like them.** Even multimedia machines, those that handle audiovisual signals as well as text, simply transport strings of data. **So this probably won't be referring to a UNIX-based system, since UNIX relies on data strings. Probably an object-oriented operating system. I see that the diagram has what looks like a Macintosh in it. Is this technology Mac-based? No, the next page shows someone rendering his face on a Silicon Graphics terminal, thank God.** [Clay skims the article looking for a mention of hardware or software.] **Here's a piece of software called Pfinder — apparently the writer and another programmer developed it. Well, the writer's credibility just went up: this isn't a journalist trying to interpret an expert's words, but someone who knows what he's talking about! But he doesn't want to tell us what OS he's using. Perhaps Pfinder IS the OS.**

They do not understand the meanings behind the characters, sounds, and pictures they convey. I believe computers must be able to see and hear what we do before they can prove truly helpful. **So is he talking about artificial intelligence? The experts say that true AI is a long ways away. Or is he speaking metaphorically?** What's more, they must be able to recognize who we are and, as much as another person or even a dog would, make sense of what we are thinking. **Yep, that's AI all right, or an impoverished imitation of it.**

To that end, my group at the Media Laboratory at the Massachusetts Institute of Technology has recently developed a family of computer systems for recognizing faces, expressions, and gestures. **That might be interesting. But maybe irritating. I mean, voice-activated technology at present involves having the user train herself to speak the way the computer wants him to — voice-pilots tend to sound pretty stilted when talking to the computer. Are we going to have to exaggerate our expressions to operate the software now? I don't like the idea of taking mime lessons just to get to my files. And different cultures use different expressions to express their emotions; would we have to have a library of expressions for each culture?** The technology has enabled us to build environments that behave somewhat like the house, office, and car described above. These areas, which we call smart rooms, are furnished with cameras and microphones that relay their recordings to a nearby network of computers. **Sounds expensive. High-end users, office security, etc. Could lessen need for security guards. Military installations? Corporate headquarters?** The computers assess what people in the smart room are saying and doing. Thanks to this connection, visitors can use their actions, voices, and expressions — instead of keyboards, sensors, or goggles — to control computer programs, browse multimedia information, or venture into realms of virtual reality. . . . **Arrgh. VR. Well, I have heard that VR goggles are too limiting for real work and collaboration — where was that, *Wired*? Makes sense. Maybe this would be useful, but I'd like to see more examples. This sounds too specialized and too expensive for the sort of tasks desktop users would perform — writing code, word processing, etc.**

FIGURE 3.12 Journalist "Interrogating" a Text (Reader Comments in Blue)

SMART ROOMS

OK, this is a term I have heard before, maybe in relation to missiles and other military applications. Hmmm. Wonder what smart rooms are like. Is this a virtual reality thing? I bet the subheads will help clarify.

[article's teaser] In creating computer systems that can identify people and interpret their actions, researchers have come one step closer to building helpful home and work environments.
Oh, my. This sounds incredible. So, how will the writer "sell" this to readers? Assume that they are sympathetic, excited about this technology? Approach the subject with soft sell? Do these work environments and home environments interact? Are they separate smart rooms?

by Alex P. Pentland
Who wrote this article? [Susan searches through the article to find a bio of the author.] **It's not at the bottom of the first page, which would have been more convenient; instead, it's at the end of the article next to the references. Geez. He has a Ph.D. from MIT — so, he's a technical person who writes rather than a reporter who's covering a technology beat. Awards, awards, awards. Honors, honors, honors. Oh, and he's a researcher on smart rooms. The sponsors of his research are listed; I'll be reading the article with an eye toward whether he mentions these sponsors explicitly. If so, I have to wonder about the piece.**

[Susan doesn't immediately go back to the beginning of the article. Instead, she looks at the PERSON FINDER sidebar and glances from it to the four-color photo to its right.]
So, now I know how this person finder application works. Why would I want to track this? A general reader of a feature article would be asking for this kind of answer, too.

[Susan's attention is attracted to the SURPRISED caption.] **The information is intriguing, but why? This looks a lot like the artists' renditions of suspects in crimes. Sort of the computerized drawings (a la Unabomber!) but these images are a comparison of "smart-room users" and the visual images of animated models. And, again, who are these smart room users?**

Imagine a house that always knows where your kids are and tells you if they are getting into trouble. **All right! The connection to the general reader of my feature! It's imperative mood. That's good. Those blasted question leads are deadly.** Or an office that sees when you are having an important meeting and shields you from interruptions. Or a car that senses when you are tired and warns you to pull over. **The three examples — that nice, odd number — offering general readers different, but recognizable examples.** Scientists have long tried to design computer systems that could accomplish such feats. **"Feats" makes me think that this technology is a good thing.** Despite their efforts, modern machines are still no match for babysitters or secretaries. **Pentland is reaching for the connection with the general reader with "babysitters and secretaries."** But they could be.

The problem, in my opinion, is that our current computers are both deaf and blind; they experience the world only by way of a keyboard and a mouse. **This is the same sentiment of the guy who wrote *Being Digital* — that computers are great, but they can be so much greater. So much more interactive.** Even multimedia machines, those that handle audiovisual signals as well as text, **Good. I needed a simple definition of what "multimedia machines" are.** simply transport strings of data. They do not understand the meanings behind the characters, sounds, and pictures they convey. I believe computers must be able to see and hear what we do before they can prove truly helpful. **Here's the opinion, an odd addition for the reporter to put himself into the story — even for a magazine. I guess I would have expected a first-person approach to be made explicitly from the start. Beginning with a personal anecdote.** What is more, they must be able to recognize who we are and, as much as another person or even a dog would, make sense of what we are thinking. **But why?**

To that end, my group at the Media Laboratory at the Massachusetts Institute of Technology **Uh, huh, here it comes. The ad for this guy's own work. His credibility has just taken a large dive.** has recently developed a family of computer systems for recognizing faces, expressions, and gestures. The technology has enabled us to build environments that behave somewhat like the house, office, and car described above. These areas, which we call smart rooms, **At last, a definition of smart room. I wonder if this wouldn't have been more effectively introduced earlier. I wonder if other readers remember the smart bomb rhetoric from the Gulf War and might have more easily connected with that. Probably endangers the negative rather than the positive for this guy's research.** are furnished with cameras and microphones that relay their recordings to a nearby network of computers. **Nearby, where?** The computers assess what people in the smart room are saying and doing. Thanks to this connection, visitors can use their actions, voices and expressions — instead of keyboards, sensors or goggles — to control computer programs, browse multimedia information or venture into realms of virtual reality. **The why? is missing . . . or at least not made explicit and real and desirable for general readers. Why do we want smart rooms?**

Explain why it's inaccurate to say that if a document is written clearly enough, each reader will gain the same meaning from it.

Regardless of the differences in the details of their reading, Clay and Susan both interrogate the article at about the same level of detail and for about the same amount of time, inserting occasional wry comments and regularly reminding themselves about their own purpose for reading. They both read critically; the meaning they create is shaped by their prior knowledge and their use of various reading strategies.

Individual and Collaborative Assignments

个人作业和小组作业

1. **Identify the purpose, methodology, result(s), and conclusion.** The abstract that follows is from the Web site of the journal *Medicine and Science in Sports and Exercise.* The headings have been removed from the abstract. Read the abstract and identify the purpose, methods, results, and conclusion. After you have identified them, check the Web site at **http://www.ms-se.com/** to see if your categories agree with the published version.[15]

   Abstract. Previous studies have found conflicting relationships between type of playing surface and injury in American football but have not taken into account possible variations in the surface conditions of outdoor stadiums due to changing weather. A total of 5910 National Football League team games between 1989 and 1998 inclusive were studied to determine associations between knee and ankle sprains, playing surface, and the weather conditions on the day of the game. There was reduced risk of significant ankle sprains (at least 7-d time loss) for games in natural grass stadiums compared with domes (indoor stadiums using AstroTurf) (RR 0.69, 95% CI 0.58–0.83). There was also reduced risk of significant knee sprains on grass compared with domes (RR 0.77, 95% CI 0.66–0.91), although most of this reduction was related to cold and wet weather on grass (RR 0.66, 95% CI 0.47–0.93 compared with hot and dry weather on grass). In open (outdoor) AstroTurf stadiums, cold weather was associated with a lower risk of significant ankle sprains (RR 0.68, 95% CI 0.51–0.91), significant knee sprains (RR 0.60, 95% CI 0.47–0.77) and ACL injuries (RR 0.50, 95% CI 0.31–0.81) compared with hot weather in the same stadiums. Weather did not have any significant effects on the injury risk in domes. The ACL incidence rate was lower during the later (cooler) months of the season in open stadiums (both AstroTurf and natural grass) but not in domes. Cold weather is associated with lower knee and ankle injury risk in outdoor stadiums (both natural grass and AstroTurf), probably because of reduced shoe-surface traction.

2. **Identify the purpose, methodology, result(s), and conclusion.** The example that follows is an abstract from the journal *Science.* Carefully read the abstract and identify the purpose, methodology, result(s), and conclusion.

Pollution Monitoring of Puget Sound with Honey Bees[16]

Abstract. To show that honey bees are effective biological monitors of environmental contaminants over large geographic areas, beekeepers of Puget Sound, Washington, collected pollen and bees for chemical analysis. From these data, kriging maps of arsenic, cadmium, and fluoride were generated. Results, based on actual concentrations of contaminants in bee tissues, show that the greatest concentrations of contaminants occur close to Commencement Bay and that honey bees are effective as large-scale monitors.

3. **Identify the main points.** The following abstract is from an internal technical report, *Correcting the Field Failure of the XC-2000.*[17] Read it carefully and then answer the following questions:
   - What is the main issue or problem?
   - Who and what are involved in the issue or problem?
   - What is the approach to the solution to the problem?
   - How will the approach be addressed or the solution be implemented?

Abstract. The XC-2000 display has a serious problem — a 20% field failure rate since July — that has resulted in a shipping delay. The failure is caused when the display's 4305 driver components short internally, producing smoke that concerned customers.

Failure evaluations of both the 4305 driver and the 4503 receiver have been conducted by Design Component Engineering. The evaluations included pin-to-pin electrical testing, external and internal visual inspection, and failure-mode duplication testing in and out of the application. The cause of failure is a 10,000-volt transient on the 12-volt supply (pin 8) of the 4305, and a similar transient on the input (pin 5) of the 4503 receiver.

Investigation confirms that the damage occurs in transit, between final system test and delivery to the customer site. Because of the difficulty encountered in locating the exact cause of the transient damage, efforts have been channeled toward protecting the parts rather than removing the cause.

XC-2000 display driver/receiver boards were tested with several bypass protection techniques. The most effective and economical protection is the placement of two 1N7211 zener diodes across selected pins on the J1 and J4 connectors. The 300 reworked units have been shipped through normal methods and have arrived in working order at the customer sites. Therefore, a corrective action has been identified and should be used on all future production of the XC-2000.

4. **Determine kinds of reading.** Read the following brief scenarios and determine the primary kind(s) of reading each workplace professional is doing: reading to assess, reading to learn, reading to learn to do, or reading to do.
   - Engineer reading a company newsletter to learn about what other research projects in the division have been funded

- Agronomy technician reading product label and instruction sheet to select proportions for mixing an herbicide to apply on an experimental plot
- Division manager reading a report about market trends in order to propose a new product line
- Chemical technician reading a product abstract to see if the report will be useful for herself and the rest of her research group to read
- Engineer reading an operator's manual to learn to calibrate a piece of equipment
- Mechanical engineer reading product descriptions to decide which spectrometer to order for the lab
- Hospital dietician reading product labels to see if any of the goods in the supply room meet the restricted needs of a new patient
- Office supervisor reading an operator's manual about ways to change the toner cartridge in the photocopying machine
- Lab technician reading an article from published conference proceedings to learn general background information about a process that a competing firm is using
- Equipment supervisor reading product safety sheets to learn to do the most appropriate first-aid treatment in the case of an emergency
- Maintenance team leader reading the online manual that identifies step-by-step troubleshooting procedures in order to repair a piece of equipment
- Microbiologist skimming specifications sheets to decide which air filtration systems to consider closely for a new clean room

5. **Compare differences in reading purposes.** (a) Work with a small group to obtain additional interrogations of the following excerpt — three paragraphs exactly as they appeared in the *Scientific American* article (or use another text of similar interest and length). Locate two people who would be interested in reading the document but have different purposes for reading it and who would bring different backgrounds to their reading. Ask the two to read and interrogate the text.

   You can access an online version of these paragraphs by going to **www.english.wadsworth.com/burnett6e** for a link to this excerpt. If you can, give the participants the online version, so they can write their comments directly into the online text, as Clay and Susan did. If they are reading a paper version, they can record their comments on a tape recorder or jot them in the margins. (b) With your group, compare the differences and speculate about the possible reasons for the differences. (c) Write a memo to the class in which you report what your group identifies as the key similarities and differences between the two readers' interpretations.

Rhetorical Elements Characterizing Technical Communication[18]

Smart Rooms

In creating computer systems that can identify people and interpret their actions, researchers have come one step closer to building helpful home and work environments.

by Alex P. Pentland

Imagine a house that always knows where your kids are and tells you if they are getting into trouble. Or an office that sees when you are having an important meeting and shields you from interruptions. Or a car that senses when you are tired and warns you to pull over. Scientists have long tried to design computer systems that could accomplish such feats. Despite their efforts, modern machines are still no match for babysitters or secretaries. But they could be.

The problem, in my opinion, is that our current computers are both deaf and blind; they experience the world only by way of a keyboard and a mouse. Even multimedia machines, those that handle audiovisual signals as well as text, simply transport strings of data. They do not understand the meanings behind the characters, sounds, and pictures they convey. I believe computers must be able to see and hear what we do before they can prove truly helpful. What is more, they must be able to recognize who we are and, as much as another person or even a dog would, make sense of what we are thinking.

To that end, my group at the Media Laboratory at the Massachusetts Institute of Technology has recently developed a family of computer systems for recognizing faces, expressions, and gestures. The technology has enabled us to build environments that behave somewhat like the house, office, and car described above. These areas, which we call smart rooms, are furnished with cameras and microphones that relay their recordings to a nearby network of computers. The computers assess what people in the smart room are saying and doing. Thanks to this connection, visitors can use their actions, voices and expressions instead of keyboards, sensors, or goggles to control computer programs, browse multimedia information or venture into realms of virtual reality. . . .

6. **Interrogate a document.** Use the World Wide Web to locate a document that addresses some controversial aspect of a subject in your professional discipline. As Dave Clark did with the online document in Figure 3.8, interrogate the document:
   - Identify the tacit assumptions on which you believe the document is based — what's presumed but not articulated?

- Extend the ideas to pose reasonable but unstated implications — what's implied but not articulated?
- Speculate on the impact of the implication — what's possible but not articulated?

Chapter 3 Endnotes

1 Some of the discussion in this section is based on types of reading identified in two articles that have become standards: Diehl, W., & Mikulecky, L. (1988). Making written information fit workers purposes. *IEEE Transactions on Professional Communication, 24,* 5–9; and Redish, J. C. (1988). Reading to learn to do. *The Technical Writing Teacher, 15*(3), 223–233.

2 Retrieved September 12, 2003, from www.extension.iastate.edu/foodsafety/rad/radura.html

3 The discussion related to Figure 3.3 is based on a synthesis of information from several sources.

- Dole, J. A., Duffy, G. G., Roehler, L. R., & Pearson, P. D. (1991). Moving from the old to the new: Research on reading comprehension instruction. *Review of Educational Research, 61*(2) 239–264.
- Duin, A. H. (1988). How people read: Implications for writers. *The Technical Writing Teacher, 15*(3), 185–193.
- Flower, L. (1990). Negotiating academic discourse. In Flower, L., Stein, V., Ackerman, J., Kantz, M. J., McCormick, K., & Peck, W. C. *Reading to write: Exploring a cognitive and social process* (pp. 221–252). New York: Oxford University Press.
- King, K. (n.d.). *Reading strategies.* Retrieved September 12, 2003, from http://www.isu.edu/~kingkath/readstrt.html
- Knuth, R. A., & Jones, B. F. (1991). *What does research say about reading?* Retrieved September 12, 2003, from http://www.ncrel.org/sdrs/areas/stw_esys/str_read.htm
- Mulcahy, P. (1988). Writing reader-based instructions: Strategies to build coherence. *The Technical Writing Teacher, 15*(3), 234–243.
- Slater, W. H. (1988). Current theory and research on what constitutes readable expository text. *The Technical Writing Teacher, 15*(3), 195–206.

4 *Journal of the American Medical Association (JAMA).* (1991). Structuring abstracts to make them more informative. *JAMA, 266,* 116–117.

5 Retrieved September 13, 2003, from http://www.foodprotection.org/

6 Sakchai, H., Suphachai, N., Riemann, H., & Cliver, D.O. (2001). Reduction of Escherichia coli O157:H7 and Salmonella Typhimurium in artificially contaminated alfalfa seeds and mung beans by fumigation with ammonia. *Journal of Food Protection, 64*(11), 1817–1819. Abstract retrieved, September 13, 2003, from Food Science & Technology Abstracts.

7 *NASA Tech Briefs,* Vol. 24, No. 3, March 2004.

8 Burnett, C. D. (1993). *How to grow shiitake mushrooms outdoors on natural logs.* (Marquette, MI: Big Creek Farm. Reprinted with permission.

9 This abstract is an amalgam of four slightly different versions of the published abstracts for this article. One is available on the Web site of Dr. Linnyer Beatrys Ruiz; retrieved September 13, 2003, from http://www.dcc.ufmg.br/~linnyer/linnyer.html; the second is on the IEEE Web site at http://www.comsoc.org/ci1/Public/2003/feb/current.html; the third is with the PDF version of the article; the fourth is available online through the Iowa State University Park's Library, connected to IEEE Xplore.

10 Bloom, B. S. (Ed.). (1956). *Taxonomy of educational objectives.* New York: David McKay.

11 Adaptation from Nelson, T. H. (1993) *The Xanadu Ideal.* Retrieved September 13, 2003, from http://xanadu.com.au/general/ideal.html. Originally retrieved June 1996, from http://www.xanadu.com/au/xanadu/idea.html/

12 Katz, S. (1992). "The Ethic of Expediency: Classical Rhetoric, Technology, and the Holocaust." *College English, 43,* 255–275.

13 © 1996 Scientific American, Inc. All rights reserved. Reprinted with permission.

14 Slowing the course of aortic regulation. (1995). *Harvard Health Letter,* (February), 3–4. Illustration © 1995 Harriet Greenfield.

15 Orchard, J. W., & Powell, J. W. (2003). Risk of knee and ankle sprains under various weather conditions in American football. *Medicine & Science in Sports & Exercise, 35*(7), 1118–1123. Retrieved September 27, 2003, from http://www.ms-se.com/

16 Bromenshenk, J. J., et al. (1985). Pollution monitoring of Puget Sound with honey bees. *Science 227* (February 8), 632–634. Copyright 1985 by AAS. Reprinted with permission.

17 Megnin, C. (n.d.). *Correcting the field failure of the XC-2000.* (Technical and Scientific Writing 42.225) University of Lowell. Reprinted with permission.

18 © 1996 Scientific American, Inc. All rights reserved. Reprinted with permission.

CHAPTER 4

Addressing Audiences
满足交流对象需求

任何一个话题都有可能成为技术文件或口头汇报的话题，但是如何呈现这些话题要依据不同的读者（客户）做调整。本章介绍了如何确定交流对象（如专家、非专业人士、技术人员、机器操作人员、学生、多面手或孩子）以及分析交流对象的特点（如工作环境、动机、教育背景、职业经历、阅读水平和工作职责）。然后，本章用实例说明如何根据交流对象的特点如专业知识水平和工作职责对交流内容的重点进行调整。

Objectives and Outcomes 学习目标

This chapter will help you accomplish these outcomes:

- Understand that professionals who plan, prepare, and present technical documents, presentations, and visuals usually have two broad purposes: to convey verifiable information and to persuade the audience to attend to this information
- Identify initial, primary, secondary, and external audiences, and determine whether these audiences are experts, professional nonexperts, technicians, equipment operators, students, generalists, or children
- Collect and analyze information about your audiences — the context in which they work, their attitudes and motivations, education, professional experiences, reading level, and organizational role
- Adjust material for different audiences in two broad ways: (1) address audiences with different levels of expertise by adjusting the complexity of the material; (2) address audiences with different organizational roles by shifting the focus of the discussion and the choice of details, including an acknowledgement of audiences' ethical stance or point of view

Nearly anything can be the subject of a technical document, oral presentation, or visual, but the treatment of that subject changes for different audiences. For example, the same polymer resin used to make baby bottles is also used for media storage disks. Many audiences could be interested in the same subject but with different purposes: Parents and pediatricians might want to know about polymer safety; media librarians and managers might focus on material stability; chemists might be interested in ways to modify material composition; production supervisors might want to know how to best extrude the resin.

The way you define and visualize your audiences influences your choices as you prepare documents, oral presentations, and visuals. This chapter discusses the importance of identifying your purpose, categorizing types of audiences, and analyzing factors that influence them.

Identifying Purposes
确定目的

Professionals who prepare technical documents, presentations, and visuals usually have two broad purposes: to concisely and accurately convey verifiable information and to persuade audiences to attend to this information. Figure 4.1 shows questions you need to ask yourself about your audiences during planning.

- *Do you think technical documents convey neutral or value-free information?*
- *In what ways are technical documents persuasive? How could you convince a colleague who thinks that technical documents are only to convey information that they also have a persuasive function?*

FIGURE 4.1 **Questions Stimulated by Purpose**

Purpose	Questions
To convey information	■ What information do I want my audience to learn? Why do I want them to learn this information? ■ What decisions does the audience need to make? What information does the audience need in order to make a decision? ■ What background information do I need to provide? What questions do I want to answer?
To argue/To persuade	■ What ideas or actions of the audience do I want to influence? ■ What information and approaches will persuade the audience? ■ What constraints will affect the persuasiveness of my argument? ■ What objections might the audience have? What logical argument would enable me to overcome those objections?

People may have both primary and secondary purposes for reading. As you read in Chapter 3, typical reasons include reading *to assess, to learn, to learn to do,* or *to do.* For example, a primary task might be to *do:* to make a decision that approves or rejects a proposal. A secondary task might be to *learn:* to gather information about important areas for future research and/or implementation.

Identifying Audiences
确定交流对象

Before you analyze an audience, you must identify it. For example, every technical document has an *intended audience,* a specific individual (Elizabeth Jones, research and development [R&D] director) or a category of users (owners of Dell computers), with identifiable needs. Audiences of technical documents often want information about specific rather than general issues.

Complicating matters, the same information is often read by a number of different audiences in several different ways. For example, a proposal for new product development could be read by people on various levels in several areas in a company — finance, marketing, engineering, manufacturing. As a result, you often are expected to create material that simultaneously meets the needs of several

These workplace professionals are all reading information about the same new product, but the situations are different and the form in which the information is accessed is different.

categories of audiences. You can accomplish this most easily by directing different audiences to particular sections of a proposal. For example, managers or executives would usually be most interested in the executive summary and the major recommendations, whereas engineers would usually be most interested in the application of these recommendations.

Audience roles can be separated into four general categories based on factors such as people's position in the organization, their connection to the particular issues, and their part in decision making. The same individual may be a primary audience in one situation and a secondary audience in another situation.

> *What might be the ramifications of misjudging who is the primary audience of a document?*

- The *initial audience* is usually the person to whom you submit a document, though not necessarily the ultimate decision maker. This initial audience directs your document to the appropriate primary audience.
- The *primary audience* is the person for whom your document is actually intended, the one who will actually use the information, the decision maker.
- *Secondary audiences* receive and read your document; they have an interest because they are affected by the information or by decisions based on it.
- Many documents also have *external audiences* who are outside the immediate organization but are affected by the information or by decisions based on it.

For example, a general contractor could be the initial audience of a request for quotation (RFQ) on wiring a condominium's new community center. The primary audience could be the electrical contractor. The secondary audiences might include the condominium's board of directors. An external reader might be a local building inspector.

Audiences also are distinguished by their level of expertise and form a continuum of knowledge about the subject, from those with expertise and interest to those with little knowledge and some interest. Audiences typically fit on more than one place on a continuum, especially if they have multiple interests and responsibilities.

> *Which audience(s) do you think you will address most frequently in your professional work?*

This continuum of audiences is not absolute; an individual reader often fits into more than one category. For example, a polymer engineer who is comfortable reading reports about composite materials may be a general reader or a professional nonexpert when reading about plant pathology, traffic patterns, or kidney failure. Similarly, a medical technician who is comfortable reading biopsy reports may be a general or a professional nonexpert when reading about astronomy, learning disabilities, or woodworking. A company vice president is an expert in business matters but may be a student reader in an aviation class and a general reader regarding agronomy or microwaves. Figure 4.2 identifies the level of familiarity these audiences typically have with various kinds of subject matter, the kinds of expectations they often hold, and the education many of them have. Such generalizations, of course, don't fit the profile of every reader, but may help you make preliminary decisions about ways to approach a particular audience.

> *What are specific examples of technical documents that target children as audiences?*

FIGURE 4.2 **Audience Familiarity with Subject, Expectations, and Education**

Readers	Familiarity with Subject	Expectations	Prior Knowledge
Experts	Most know theories, practical applications, jargon, and technical information in their own field	Most want an explicit purpose; prefer direct explanations; use information to assess, learn, learn to do, and do	Usually have undergraduate or graduate degrees or equivalent experience in specialized fields
	For example, engineers, ecologists, and economists typically read a wide range of print and electronic material pertaining to their field, from practical applications (specifications) to theoretical concepts (professional journals).		
Professional nonexperts	Most know general concepts of the field in which they're working	Most prefer definitions and explanations of concepts and procedures; prefer information for decision making	Usually have undergraduate or graduate degrees or equivalent experience, often in areas peripheral to those for which they are responsible
	For example, a department manager in a computer firm may have a degree in business but little specialized knowledge of computers. A manager of an engineering department may have earned an engineering degree twenty years ago or have a degree in industrial management, not engineering.		
Technicians	Most know the specialized area in which they're working; may have theoretical understanding	Most prefer straightforward definitions and explanations; prefer information that focuses on learning to do and doing	Usually have a degree from a two-year or four-year college or on-the-job training
	For example, chemical technicians helping R & D engineers develop applications for carbon fibers are able to contribute to the project because of their theoretical background in polymer chemistry.		
Equipment operators	Most know tasks they're assigned to do; may improve performance if they understand the way their job relates to broader processes	Most prefer explanations that let them focus on *doing*	Usually have on-the-job training (often oral rather than written) instead of formal education related to the job
	For example, machine operators do a better job if they know how their work is impacted by and impacts larger processes. Most equipment operators have no theoretical knowledge of the field.		
Students	Often know generalizations in a field; typically need technical details as well as implications for broader processes	Most prefer information that helps them assess, learn, learn to do, and do; interested in theory as well as practice	May have specialized training from summer or part-time jobs, internships, or co-op programs
	For example, students are interested in learning disciplinary knowledge and forming opinions in order to become professionals in a specialized field.		
Generalists	Often know generalizations in a field; want information that explains the how and why	Most prefer information that helps them assess, learn, learn to do, and do; varied interests	May be highly educated but not in what they're doing; may have specialized knowledge
	For example, general readers want to read about science and technology, but their interests usually have little or nothing to do with their job.		
Children	Often want information that explains how and why things happen; often have limited concepts and vocabulary	Most prefer information that helps them to learn, learn to do, and do; widely varied interests	Usually have completed some school; may have specialized knowledge from hobbies and activities
	For example, many children read science books, have their own subscriptions to children's science magazines, and regularly surf Web sites. They also read the technical documents that come with their DVD player and video games.		

WEBLINK

Identifying, analyzing, and adapting to your audiences is a major concern in government projects and presentations. Go to **www.english.wadsworth.com/burnett6e** for links to sites that include specific discussions about audience as part of preparing major projects and presentations. Access these links and examine the ways that audience is discussed. You might be surprised at the detailed attention that is given to audience.

CLICK ON WEBLINK

CLICK on Chapter 4/audience government

Analyzing Audiences

分析交流对象

Once you have identified the purposes for a document, oral presentation, or visual and the general category of the audience(s) (expert, technician, and so on), you need to learn more about the target audience(s). Several strategies exist for analyzing audiences. While no approach is foolproof, one of the most frequently used involves considering these characteristics as you plan to meet audiences' needs and expectations:

- Context in which a document is interpreted and used
- Purpose and motivation of the audiences
- Prior knowledge of the audiences, including education and professional experiences
- Reading level of the audiences
- Organizational role of the audiences

One of the most effective ways to assess your intended audiences is to talk with them and the people who work with them. Imagine that you are responsible for writing the user's manual and online help for a new computer system. Whether the manual and online help are usable for the intended audience is critical. So you need to find out about the actual users — what they're likely to have trouble with, what they'll probably find helpful, what they're likely to know and not know. To gain a sense of what should and shouldn't be included, you could talk with people in these areas:

- *Design and development* to learn what features the system will have and what kind of technical background a user would need
- *Marketing* to learn how the target market has been characterized

- *Sales* to learn how customers have reacted to similar manuals and online help systems
- *Customer service* to find out what causes the most difficulties for users of similar products

Even more useful would be talking with representative users — the actual people who will use the computer system and the manual and online help you plan to write. You can interview them about their needs, their expectations, and the problems they've had with other systems and documentation. You also should arrange for some users to test the manual at various stages during its drafting.

To help you collect information about the users of a document you're preparing, refer to the questions on the audience analysis worksheet in Figure 4.3. This worksheet will help you focus your audience analysis by answering specific questions. You will initially find it helpful to complete the entire worksheet. The more frequently you use it, however, the more familiar you will become with the questions. Eventually, you will automatically ask yourself the questions whenever you plan a document, oral presentation, or visual.

To use an electronic version of the Audience Analysis Worksheet, go to **www.english.wadsworth.com/burnett6e**.
CLICK ON WEBLINK
CLICK on Chapter 4/audience analysis

WEBLINK

Context 环境

An often ignored but vital consideration for technical communicators is the physical and political context and the general working conditions in which audiences will interpret and use documents, oral presentations, and visuals. Regardless of a person's cognitive ability or knowledge of the subject, accessing difficult material — that is, seeing or hearing it — may be nearly impossible if the physical context is distracting or noisy. In preparing a technical document, a writer might adjust elements such as paragraph division, headings, page design, type and size of illustrations, and binding to make it more accessible. For example, a repair manual used by technicians while they are troubleshooting manufacturing equipment needs a sturdy cover, pages that lie flat, a detailed and usable table of contents and index, and headings and visuals that can be scanned easily. Similarly, a technical report read by a busy executive needs an abstract, clear headings, an initial statement of conclusions and recommendations, and brief explanations and justifications.

Just as the physical context is important, so, too, is the political context. For example, the attitude people within an organization have toward particular documents affects how these documents are read. Is a new employee told, "The manager's

FIGURE 4.3 **Audience Analysis Worksheet**

Context: Where will the audiences access and use the material? What distractions will they face in the physical and political context? What are the audiences' working conditions (e.g., access to e-mail, available time)? ______

______

______

Audience: Who are the intended audiences? What are their purposes? Do you need to consider differences among the initial, primary, secondary, and external audiences? ______

______

______

Purposes, attitudes and motivations: What are the attitudes of the audiences? What factors might contribute to their resistance or receptivity? How might these factors influence the way they read a document, listen to an oral presentation, or view a visual? How can you decrease resistance and increase receptivity? ______

______

______

Prior knowledge: What level (high school, 2- or 4-year college, graduate school) and kind (theoretical or practical focus) of education do you anticipate that the audiences have? How does this affect your plans for the document, oral presentation, or visual? ______

______

______

How much on-the-job experience do the audiences have? How does this affect your plans? ______

______

______

Reading level: What is your best estimate about the level of material the audiences can handle without difficulty? How can you make the document more accessible to audiences? How have you used visuals and document design to aid reading? ______

______

______

Organizational role: What are the audiences' positions in the organization? What professional experiences and organizational roles do the audiences have? Job title? Areas of responsibility? Years of experience? Familiarity with the subject? How do these factors affect what they need to read? What constraints are at work? ______

______

______

memos are a waste of time; don't even bother reading them" or told, in contrast, "The manager's memos are important; make sure to keep them for reference"?

The general working conditions of an organization, including how information is presented to audiences, affect not only the way the documents and presentations are interpreted but whether they're attended to at all. For example, if important memos are simply posted on hallway or lunchroom bulletin boards, many audiences will skip them, thinking the memos are unimportant. If important internal documents are sent as attachments to e-mail, but some employees cannot access attachments, those readers may presume that they are unimportant, that the attachments are unimportant, or both. In these cases, audiences are making assumptions about information based on how it is disseminated, not on the content.

Another aspect of working conditions is the available time the audience has to read or listen to the material. Because time is valuable, documents, oral presentations, and visuals should be designed so that audiences can understand and use the information as quickly and easily as possible. Technical communicators use organizational or graphic devices that ease the audiences' task. The following strategies are particularly helpful:

- Initial abstracts or summaries
- Headings and subheadings
- Use of descending order so that the most important information comes first
- Definition of terms, if necessary
- Transitions that show how sections of the document relate to each other
- Visuals that make information easily accessible
- Page layout that is not crowded or cluttered

Purpose and Motivation 目的与动机

Analyzing an audience's purpose and motivation is relatively easy if you know the intended audience. Professional responsibilities can dictate a need to access and use particular information. For example, a computer technician might need to read an operations manual, whereas a manager might need to read theory about design or system architecture. A patient might need the instructions and side effects printed on a medication's package insert but probably would not care much about the chemical elements used to synthesize the medication, which might be of great interest to a pharmacist.

Knowing an audience's purpose and motivation helps you adjust the organization of information so that you increase audience receptivity and decrease resistance.

- *Receptive audiences:* You can present recommendations initially and then support them in subsequent sections.
- *Resistant audiences:* You can present the problem, discuss the alternatives, and then lead to the most appropriate and feasible solution, hoping audiences are persuaded by your interpretation.

Explain whether you think professional colleagues might ignore verifiable information in a report because they didn't agree with the overall position of the writer.

As the Baby Blues cartoon[1] shows, assessing and adjusting to your audience may make all the difference in whether the audience is receptive or resistant.

Receptivity is influenced by an individual's motivation, but motivation is an abstract quality that's difficult to quantify. So, how do you assess receptivity and motivation? Imagine an actual member of your intended audience. How will this person feel about the document — pleased, neutral, negative? How much does the person need the information? For example, a repair technician may be highly motivated in referring to the repair manual when equipment breaks down but may be unmotivated to check repair procedures if there's no problem. A manager may feel neutral about the proposal he has to read and completely unmotivated to begin reading it.

Prior Knowledge 背景知识

If you can estimate audiences' prior knowledge, you will be able to determine the appropriate vocabulary and content. Both education and workplace experience influence prior knowledge.

The level, type, and duration of a person's education strongly influence prior knowledge, affecting a person's comprehension of concepts and their application.

- *Vocational-technical training* focuses on providing a practical or applied knowledge.
- *Professional or academic training* focuses on providing a theoretical understanding as well as a practical experience.

People's education directly affects the kinds of documents they use. For example, a physician or nurse practitioner might consult the *Physician's Desk Reference* to review the side effects of a new medication. A patient would read the much less technical package insert accompanying the medication. A child might just see the Mr. Yuk poison symbol on the bottle and know enough to leave it alone.

"Mr. Yuk," developed in 1971 in Pittsburgh, has had a successful history of warning children to stay away from hazardous substances such as medication and household chemicals. However, occasional studies over a 20-year period suggest that Mr. Yuk is so familiar that children are sometimes attracted to rather than warned away from containers with a Mr. Yuk warning sticker. You can begin learning more about the this issue by going to **www.english.wadsworth.com/burnett6e**.

CLICK ON WEBLINK

CLICK on Chapter 4/Mr. Yuk

WWW

WEBLINK

People's organizational and disciplinary experience influences their reactions to a document. For example, experienced professionals are more likely than entry-level employees to be aware of corporate policies, politics, and personalities that may influence a document's recommendations. An equally important part of professional experience involves people's expertise in the subject. This includes the audiences' level of responsibility, years of professional experience, and familiarity with the field.

Although estimating audiences' prior knowledge is difficult, you can generalize about the amount of prior knowledge a person needs to hold a job; then you can make a reasonable guess about the kind of information that a person in such a position would need and respond to — appropriate vocabulary, technical complexity, and format.

Why is equating people's ability or intelligence with their amount of formal education a risky thing to do?

Reading Level 阅读水平

Reading level refers to the degree of difficulty of material that audiences are able to comprehend. Writing for an audience's level is important; if audiences cannot understand and act on the written information, it is useless. Technical accuracy, completeness, and logical organization are all irrelevant if the intended audience cannot comprehend the material.

Knowing an audience's reading ability helps you adjust content and approach. Writers should not automatically assume, however, that the smarter the audiences, the more difficult the material should be. A very intelligent person may not have a high reading level; another person may be able to read complex material in one specialized area but not in another. Someone capable of reading nearly any material might be constrained by lack of time or interest and thus prefer short, easy-to-read information. Your writing should be as easy as possible to read without oversimplifying or distorting the content.

Readability Formulas Your computer's word-processing program very likely comes with a function that supposedly calculates the readability of any text you write. The problem is that readability calculations simply use one of several formulas to determine a ratio between word length and sentence length. Despite its name, no readability formula tells you how easy or difficult a text is for audiences.

Readability formulas operate on the premise that shorter words and sentences are always easier to read. This is simply not so. The three-syllable word *elephant* is easier for virtually everyone to understand than the three-letter word *erg*. Such an oversimplified view of reading ignores many factors, including the complexity of the concepts; inaccuracies or biases in the presentation; the nature, development, and support of the argument; the use of visuals; as well as the document's overall design.

Using the Flesch-Kincaid formula to calculate readability for the paragraphs in this section of the text determines this section is appropriate for grade 11.9. However, with only a few changes to the text, the formulas can be manipulated to show a higher or lower level of difficulty. For example, making the text into many more short, simple sentences reduces the grade level. And other changes (such as making the entire section one long, dense, undifferentiated paragraph) result in no change at all to the readability results. Trusting readability formulas to assess the appropriateness of your documents for audiences is risky, at best.

If readability formulas don't really measure how easy or difficult a text is to read, why are they so widely used?

Although word and sentence length certainly do influence the accessibility of information and ideas in a document, readability formulas do not take into account many of the factors that affect reading. Figure 4.4 identifies some factors simply not considered by readability formulas that affect the ease or difficulty of a text. Of course, all the factors in Figure 4.4 have to be considered comparatively and in context. For example, for a food scientist, understanding how beans grow is probably as easy as understanding why beans cause flatulence; to a botany student, understanding how beans grow is probably much easier; and to a first-grade student, both topics are probably beyond reach.

Figure 4.4 provides questions that offer an alternative way to help you create documents, oral presentations, and visuals that are accessible, comprehensible, and usable. (See Figure 1.2 in Chapter 1 to review these critical concepts.)

Despite the value of understanding the factors in Figure 4.4, by themselves they do not make a text easy or difficult to read. In fact, how easy a document is to read depends largely on the interaction between the reader and the document, on the meaning that the reader creates during reading. As a writer, you can try to make a document accurate, accessible, appropriate, and appealing, but the ultimate readability test is what the reader gets out of the document. (Usability testing, discussed in Chapter 9, is a common method for making a document more accessible, comprehensible, and usable.)

FIGURE 4.4 Factors That Affect the Ease or Difficulty of a Text

Factor	Questions about Ease or Difficulty of Text	✓ Yes
Content	■ Is the content concrete?	❑
	■ Are abstractions supported with explanations and/or examples?	❑
	■ Do audiences have the necessary prior knowledge to understand the content?	❑
Context	■ Does the document, oral presentation, or visual sufficiently acknowledge and explain the context?	❑
	■ Is the type of document, oral presentation, or visual familiar to the audiences?	❑
Purpose	■ Is the purpose clearly stated?	❑
	■ Are audiences likely to agree with the stated purpose?	❑
Audience	■ Is the document, oral presentation, or visual adapted to the audience's level of understanding, needs and expectations, and organizational role?	❑
Organization	■ Is the content logically organized? Are audiences given cues about the organization?	❑
	■ Is the information coherent (for example, by using topic sentences and transitions)?	❑
	■ Is the argument clearly presented and well supported?	❑
Visuals	■ Is the verbal and visual information appropriately integrated?	❑
	■ Are the kinds of visuals appropriate and appealing?	❑
	■ Does the document, oral presentation, or visual conform to conventions?	❑
Design	■ Is information appropriately chunked and labeled? Is the hierarchy clear?	❑
	■ Are the choices for font, type style, type size, white space, and line length appropriate for the type of document, oral presentation, or visual as well as the audiences?	❑
	■ Is the overall design accessible and appealing?	❑
Usability	■ Is the information usable for the intended context, purpose, and audience?	❑
Language conventions	■ Does the document, oral presentation, or visual conform to conventions of language, both in grammar and mechanics?	❑

WEBLINK

The use of readability formulas has been highly controversial for at least three decades. For "everything you ever wanted to know about readability tests but were afraid to ask," go to **www.english.wadsworth.com/burnett6e** for links that provide more information about this issue.

CLICK ON WEBLINK

CLICK on Chapter 4/readability

Limited Literacy When people talk about "limited literacy," they can mean two different things: (1) people who are skillful readers in some circumstances (for example, reading engineering reports) but not necessarily skillful in other circumstances (for example, reading legal briefs); or (2) people who don't get much information from any written documents. This section discusses this second kind of limited literacy.

Workers with limited literary may see documents as difficult, intimidating, confusing, or even incomprehensible; thus, they may ignore the documents entirely. These workers can often read single words and short phrases, but they have great difficulty reading sentences, paragraphs, and entire documents. They also may not understand document conventions, which may result in literacy problems such as these:

- Not knowing how to use a table of contents or an index
- Not using headings to preview upcoming text
- Not treating boxed, shaded, boldfaced, or italicized text as more important than plain text
- Skipping parts of the text they don't understand
- Misreading parts of the text but believing they do understand it
- Expecting that all relevant information will be in the visuals

The problem of limited literacy is widespread in the workplace. The National Adult Literacy Survey reports the results of interviews with more than 26,000 randomly selected adults in the United States. Between 47 and 51 percent of the adult population (the equivalent of 90 to 94 million adults) could not complete very simple literacy tasks. These simple tasks included locating a single piece of information in a short article, entering a signature on a form, and locating information about eligibility for employee benefits in a table.

Surprisingly, the majority of people who performed at this level described themselves as being able to read and write English "well" or "very well," so their limited skills may "allow them to meet some or most of their personal and occupational literacy needs." In the same National Adult Literacy Survey, only 18 to

21 percent of the adult population (the equivalent of 34 to 40 million adults) performed at the highest literacy levels. More complex literacy tasks included interpreting information from an article, identifying patterns from information in a table, and summarizing information in a table.[2]

A more concrete example, reported by the Canadian Association of Speech-Language Pathologists and Audiologists, reinforces the seriousness of limited literacy. Specifically, adults with limited literacy skills often cannot read the labels and instructions on both prescription and over-the-counter medication; as a result, they sometimes take medication incorrectly. They also have difficulty following prescribed treatment plans from their physicians, such as complying with directions for treating diabetes or following preventative care, self-care, and follow-up care after an illness or injury. They also have difficulty understanding appointment slips, informed consent forms, discharge information and oral instructions.[3]

What compensatory skills might a person develop in order to make up for limited literacy skills?

As a person responsible for creating technical documents, you need to be especially careful if your audience has limited literacy skills. If time and budget allow, consider alternative forms of presentation such as one-on-one conferences, face-to-face small group meetings, training programs, videocassettes, videodisks, or multimedia computer programs.

If these options are out of the question, create documents that are largely visual. However, keep in mind that sequence of information on a page and ways of interpreting color are not universal; U.S. conventions are not worldwide conventions. Consider that moving through a document from left to right and from top to bottom is only a convention for reading in certain languages, including English. If a person doesn't read, this left-to-right, top-to-bottom movement may not be a familiar convention.

In many cases, design elements such as color and icons can help signal critical information. For example, arrows in addition to numbers may be useful for signaling sequence. Similarly, high risks can be signaled in words such as *Caution* or *Danger,* with yellow (caution) or red (danger) to reinforce the words. Color use should comply with standards advised by the American National Standards Institute (ANSI). (For more information on using color, refer to Chapter 12, Using Visual Forms.)

WWW

WEBLINK

You may need to prepare information for limited literacy audiences. If you want to know more about how to effectively address such audiences, go to **www.english.wadsworth.com/burnett6e** for links to sites that provide helpful suggestions and identify resources.

CLICK ON WEBLINK

CLICK on Chapter 4/limited literacy

Organizational Role 机构管理机制

Organizations are generally categorized as hierarchical or nonhierarchical. In practice, most organizations incorporate both hierarchical and nonhierarchical characteristics.

> *Explain where you would prefer to work — a hierarchical organization or a nonhierarchical organization. Why?*

- *A hierarchical organization* has bosses at the top, managers in the middle, and workers at the bottom. Hierarchical organizations generally assume that people work best when directed.
- *A nonhierarchical organization* has everyone contributing equally to the productivity of the organization. Nonhierarchical organizations regard people as most productive when they participate in decision making.

A hierarchical organization can be analyzed by examining where a person fits into the organizational structure of the company — who reports to whom, who is a decision maker, who holds ultimate responsibility for a process or a project. Curiously, e-mail is flattening hierarchies in some organizations because all employees are easily accessible simply by sending an e-mail message. But the ease of sending such a message doesn't mean it's necessarily appropriate. An assessment of hierarchy in an organization requires sensitivity to and awareness of any subtle differences between the formal structure and the actual working structure. For example, you cannot automatically assume that the most senior person in an organization is the most influential decision maker. A general manager or a CEO might collect all the relevant information and make decisions herself, or she might make decisions based largely on the recommendations of middle-level managers.

So far, the discussion has focused on internal audiences, those within the writer's organization. Frequently, however, audiences are external, belonging to another organization. Such audiences might be customers or a funding agency. They would not know many of the things that are apparent to internal audiences, so the writer needs to provide more background information than may be customary for an internal reader. This background might include elements such as definitions, a brief history, and the relation of the subject to the overall operation.

The tone used for external audiences is often more formal than the tone used for internal audiences. However, *formal* does not mean pompous; rather, the document just does not include casual language common in internal memos. For example, an internal memo might say, "I'll get back to you by Monday about the revised schedule," whereas a document for an external reader would be more likely to say, "I will send you information about the revised schedule by Monday, October 22" or "Information about the revised schedule will reach you by Monday, October 22."

Adjusting to Audiences
根据交流对象调整交流内容与形式

After you have identified and analyzed your audiences, you can prepare documents or oral presentations that respond to their need for information as well as to factors such as context, level of expertise, organizational roles, and prior knowledge. This section focuses on adjusting content complexity for different audiences in three broad ways:

- Address audiences with *different levels of expertise* by adjusting the complexity of the material.
- Address audiences with *different organizational roles* by shifting the focus of the discussion and the choice of details.
- Address audiences by designing Web sites that enable audiences to *construct unique sequences of information* to meet their own needs and interests.

Differences in Expertise 专业知识差异

Audiences vary in their level of technical knowledge. When you adjust material for audiences with various levels of technical competence, you need to change the complexity of the concepts, language, details, and examples. The following examples in Figures 4.5A, B, and C show how workplace professionals can adapt information to meet the needs of different audiences. The director of medical technology for an urban hospital produced three paragraphs about coagulation, each intended for a different audience.[4]

FIGURE 4.5A **Paragraph for High School Students**

What is coagulation? If a blood vessel ruptures, the blood thickens and forms a gel called a clot, which slows the flow of blood from the wound. This process is called *coagulation,* a mechanism to prevent blood loss when a blood vessel is ruptured. This process is initiated both by the damaged blood vessel tissue and by substances released from the damaged tissue. The substances activate proteins in the blood called *procoagulants.* The activated procoagulants act as enzymes in a series of chemical reactions that culminate in the conversion of a molecule of fibrinogen to a smaller molecule, fibrin. The fibrin molecules link together into strands. These strands form a tight mesh that is known as a *fibrin clot.*

COMPREHENSIBILITY
- *presumes a minimal level of prior knowledge about coagulation*
- *minimizes technical vocabulary*
- *defines new terms*
- *reviews common knowledge before presenting causal relationship*

USABILITY
- *signals key point with run-in heading*
- *italicizes new terms*

FIGURE 4.5B Paragraph for Medical Technology Majors in College

The Process of Coagulation. A major function of the hemostatic mechanism of the cardiovascular system is the coagulation of blood. Coagulation plays a vital role in preventing blood loss in episodes of vessel injury, allowing the body to maintain blood volume and retain blood products. The process of coagulation is achieved through the chain of chemical reactions of procoagulants (a group of plasma proteins) and tissue cell constituents. The procoagulants circulate through the bloodstream as inert enzymes, activated by damaged tissue, phospholipid from cell membranes, and calcium ions. After a series of enzymatic reactions, the procoagulants cleave a protein peptide from fibrinogen, a glycoprotein, to form a fibrin monomer. The fibrin monomers polymerize into strands that form an insoluble mesh known as a fibrin clot.

COMPREHENSIBILITY

- *presumes a modest level of prior knowledge about coagulation*
- *introduces and defines new technical vocabulary*
- *offers an explicit causal explanation of the process*

USABILITY

- *signals key point with run-in heading*

FIGURE 4.5C Paragraph for Professional Medical Technologists in a Hospital Review Course

Pathways in coagulation. Three pathways are involved in the coagulation of the hemostatic mechanism: intrinsic, extrinsic, and common pathways. Each pathway consists of a cascade of proteolytic enzyme reactions in which procoagulants, a series of inert circulating proteolytic enzymes called coagulation factors, activate one another. The *intrinsic pathway* is activated by the presence of damaged endothelium tissue and a high molecular weight activator, kallikren. The *extrinsic pathway* is activated by tissue factor, a phospholipid of endothelium, and calcium ions. The *common pathway* is activated by the resultant coagulation factors of the intrinsic and extrinsic pathways. The result of the common pathway is the conversion of fibrinogen to fibrin monomers, which polymerize into strands. The strands mesh through covalent bonding to form an insoluble fibrin clot.

COMPREHENSIBILITY

- *presumes a high level of prior knowledge about coagulation*
- *uses technical vocabulary consistently*
- *uses a parts/whole approach (types of pathways)*
- *provides a causal explanation of each type of pathway*

USABILITY

- *signals key point with run-in heading*
- *uses a topic sentence to state the main point*
- *italicizes key terms*

The first paragraph (Figure 4.5A) is for high school biology students learning new concepts. These students need to learn the vocabulary as well as the process of coagulation. The writer uses the run-in heading to pose a question to focus the students' attention and let them know what to anticipate. The writer then reviews common knowledge about clots before presenting and defining new terms. He organizes details using a familiar cause-and-effect organization.

The second paragraph (Figure 4.5B) is for college students majoring in a four-year medical technology degree program. These students can handle technical vocabulary and already understand the basic causal relationships. What they need to learn, though, are concepts that explain coagulation. The writer signals this focus with the run-in heading. The paragraph itself explains the process of coagulation, which includes introducing and defining new terms (such as procoagulants and fibrinogen) and providing specific details (for instance, procoagulants are activated by damaged tissue, phospholipids, and calcium ions).

The third paragraph (Figure 4.5C) is for professional medical technologists who are enrolled in a review course given in their hospital. These medical professionals understand the basic process of coagulation, but they need a review. After using a run-in heading to signal the topic, the writer uses a topic sentence to preview the content and the organization of the paragraph (intrinsic, extrinsic, and common pathways). Italicizing each main term provides a typographic cue that helps audiences keep track of where they are in relation to the whole.

Differences in Roles and Stances 交流对象职位差异

You should maintain a similar level of complexity for audiences with parallel roles in an organization — for example, people who are all managers but in different areas such as manufacturing, marketing, research and development, or quality control. One way to adjust to such audiences is emphasizing aspects of the subject that are relevant to their organization role. A second way is acknowledging their particular point of view.

The three brief e-mail messages in Figures 4.6A, B, and C, all written by the vice president of plant operations, are about the same subject: the purchase of a mill that is intended to increase product uniformity, reduce waste, and increase product availability. Each e-mail message is directed to a separate manager, each of whom has specialized interests and responsibilities. All three have approximately the same level of complexity, yet the focus shifts in each one to emphasize the content that is relevant to each reader's area of workplace responsibility.

In the first e-mail (Figure 4.6A) the writer addresses the production supervisor of the mill department. Because the recipient is interested primarily in production, the writer identifies a critical problem that will be eliminated with the new machine and identifies a series of benefits, including product uniformity and a reduction in rejections and downtime, that should increase productivity.

FIGURE 4.6A **E-mail from the VP of Plant Operations to the Production Supervisor**

To	Peter Smith, Prod. Supervisor, Mill Dept.
From	Thomas White, VP Plant Operations
Date	8 September 200-
Subject	Expected increase in product availability

The recently purchased mill is scheduled to be on line by October 15. This machine will solve the problems of the thermal stabilization times you have been plagued with, while increasing product uniformity. When the department has less product rejection and machine downtime, I look forward to seeing increased rates per shift. You will be notified of the new rate production schedule on October 15.

The writer focuses on the reader's interest — product availability. This topic is signaled in the subject line of the e-mail and is the primary topic of the paragraph.

The e-mail provides a critical date and identifies anticipated production benefits.

FIGURE 4.6B **Memo from the VP of Plant Operations to the Controller**

To	Elizabeth Daley, Controller
From	Thomas White, VP Plant Operations
Date	8 September 200-
Subject	New Wolverine Cereal Flaking Mill

The addition of the new mill to our production line is an effective solution to the production waste problems we have been experiencing. With the minimal waste expected combined with the machine's operating efficiency, the payback period should be within the next fiscal year. Preliminary information indicates that purchasing the mill has been a smart investment.

In writing to the controller, the writer focuses on financial matters.

Because the controller does not regularly work with production line equipment, she needs to be reminded (tactfully, in the subject line) about the specific machine.

The e-mail identifies ways the mill will save money and reviews the length of the payback period.

FIGURE 4.6C **Memo from the VP of Plant Operations to the Director of Marketing and Sales**

To	David Parker, Director of Mkting & Sales
From	Thomas White, VP Plant Operations
Date	8 September 200-
Subject	Expected increase in product availability

Due to the addition of capital equipment in the production department, product availability will increase by approximately 50%.

A short-term plan in marketing strategy should be initiated to increase sales and expand to new territories. Product stockpiling begins October 15.

The writer wants the director of marketing and sales to concentrate on a marketing plan.

Mentioning the increase in availability and the product stockpiling should reinforce the need for new territories.

What are the advantages and disadvantages of a writer preparing separate e-mail messages (or other correspondence such as memos) for audiences who need similar information?

The second e-mail (Figure 4.6B) is written to the controller, the person responsible for the company's financial operations. A controller is primarily concerned about money matters, so she would be interested in cost savings that come about because of waste reduction and increased equipment efficiency. The controller would also be interested in the payback period. The difficulty of the content, sentences, and vocabulary in this e-mail is much the same as that in Figure 4.6A.

In the third e-mail, to the director of marketing and sales (Figure 4.6C), the writer concentrates on product availability — amount, date, implications. The e-mail includes no mention of production details or costs, which are only peripherally relevant to this audience. The emphasis is on the need to develop a new short-term marketing plan.

Should you write three separate e-mail messages? Yes, if you have the time and believe that the special attention will increase reader comprehension and support. However, you may not have the time to write separate e-mail messages, and sometimes political realities dictate that all audiences receive an identical e-mail. In these circumstances, you need to write one e-mail for multiple audiences who differ in their interests, familiarity with the project, and levels of expertise. To make this one as effective as possible, consider these suggestions:

- *Identify and write for the primary audiences:* Organize the information for the people who need the information for activities or decision making, putting first what is most important to them. In Figures 4.6A, B, and C, all three recipients have the vested interest of a primary audience in the purchase of the mill. But their interests are different — manufacturing operations, finance, and marketing.

- *Identify and consider the secondary audiences:* Include information of interest to secondary audiences based on its value to the primary audiences and the influence these secondary audiences have on the primary audiences. In Figures 4.6A, B, and C, possible secondary audiences might include line supervisors, accountants, and sales reps. Their opinions about the new mill might well affect the perceptions of their managers.
- *Use design elements to make information accessible in both paper and electronic messages:* Use headings, typographic elements (such as boldface and italic), and typographic devices (such as bullets and boxes) to signal important topics.

> *Explain which is easier for you to do — write for audiences with different levels of expertise or for audiences with different organizational roles.*

So far, you've read about adjusting communication to meet needs established largely by audiences' organizational roles and responsibilities. Sometimes, however, concentrating solely on the verifiable information relevant to particular roles is not sufficient. For example, communication that ignores audiences' stance — their points of view, attitudes, values, and beliefs — is likely to be ineffective. In fact, audiences may dismiss documents and presentations that ignore affective concerns, feeling that such documents or presentations simply do not adequately consider them or the situation, despite being filled with verifiable information. The sidebar below addresses this important issue.

ETHICS 职业道德规范知识吧 **SIDEBAR**

"Their approaches are culturally insensitive": Ethics and Public Policies "他们的方式没有考虑文化因素"：职业规范与公共政策

Effective technical documents typically present clear, precise, verifiable information. Focusing on such details reflects the belief that the more audiences know, the better decisions they will make. However, technical professionals who rely too much on precise information sometimes ignore other, equally important aspects of a document. Focusing on precision can sometimes lead a writer to provide too much information or to present information in confusing or unfamiliar terms. Often, the result is a document that contains all the relevant information but does not sufficiently consider the ethics of the context, content, or purpose as it affects the audience.

Researchers Patricia Hynds and Wanda Martin, reviewing the public outcry over a city water project, outline how an unethical approach can derail a much-needed project.[5] Hynds and Martin describe a debate that arose when the City of Albuquerque, New Mexico, began the process of drilling a well in one of the city's suburbs, the South Valley. Albuquerque relies heavily on wells to provide water for its communities; city planners assumed that South Valley's residents would readily recognize the value of the new well. When South Valley residents voiced concerns about the effects of drilling the new well, Albuquerque's mayor asked the public works department to meet with South Valley residents to work out a new location, although resident approval for a new well's location was not legally necessary. Three community meetings later, communication between the city and residents had degenerated, and lawsuits were filed. The well has yet to be drilled.

How can you determine when your audience has concerns beyond the technical data?

Why did such a necessary project reach this impasse? Hynds and Martin believe the problem occurred because the city's representatives failed to adequately recognize the cultural and social viewpoints of the residents. The residents voiced concerns about the negative impact of the well; they did not want their small community to become too industrial or overcrowded with new construction. The city's representatives, however, viewed these concerns as simply a lack of understanding by the residents. In each meeting, the city's representatives continually emphasized the technical aspects of the well to support their position: they believed "that when the technical facts are clearly communicated, all reasonable hearers will arrive at similar conclusions." The residents, however, felt the technical explanations were patronizing and did not feel that their concerns were respected. For the residents, the issue was about more than facts; it was about respecting the traditions and heritage of the area. Eventually, the animosity the residents felt towards the city reached a point where the residents boycotted the last meeting and filed lawsuits to stop the drilling.

Hynds and Martin believe that despite the city's good intentions, the city planners failed to treat the audience ethically. Instead of talking to the residents about their concerns, they continually tried to make the residents see the situation from the city's point of view. They relied too much on precise facts and too little on the concerns of their audience. The unfortunate result was a breakdown in communication. If the city planners had used an ethical approach to communication, they would have considered more than their verifiable information about water needs and well locations.

How would you convince the city planners that listening to their audience matters? What would you do if your audience rejected carefully presented and verifiable information in favor of emotional and unverifiable opinions?

Individual and Collaborative Assignments

个人作业和小组作业

1. **Determine the audiences.** Read the following sets of sentences intended for different audiences. Determine the audience for each sentence and then answer the following questions:
   - How has the writer adjusted for the different audiences? Which set is adjusted for differences in audience expertise? Which set is adjusted for differences in organizational role?

- What information did the writer need to make these adjustments?
- Why are the changes necessary if the statements in each set convey essentially the same information?

Set 1 The sun damages many human-made materials.

The sun causes degeneration and weakening of many synthetic fibers.

Ultraviolet radiation causes polymer degeneration by attacking links in the polymer chain and reducing the molecular weight of the material.

Set 2 The shipment was delayed because of manufacturing equipment malfunction and misjudgment about the resulting delays.

Because your shipment has again been unavoidably delayed, we will credit your rental fee for fourteen days — the anticipated length of this second delay.

Occasional brief delays in shipping have a minimal impact on attaining projected third-quarter goals.

2. Determine the audiences. Visit the following Web sites and ask yourself these questions:

- Who are the various audiences for the Web site?
- How have the writer and designer adjusted for the different audiences? How have the writer and designer acknowledged and responded to the needs and interests of specific segments of the audience, such as people of color and international audiences?
- What information did the writer and designer need to make these adjustments?

www.discovery.com	www.science.doe.gov/bes/NNI.htm
www.ibm.com	www.sch-plough.com
www.dairynetwork.com	www.campbellsoup.com
www.ecotourism.org/	www.nsf.com
www.wipo.org/	www.aciic.org.au/
www.futureharvest.org/	www.scientact.gr/

3. For each of these three paragraphs about neonatal herpes (a venereal disease that is transmittable to newborns), identify a likely intended audience and explain your choice by using specific textual examples as support.

(a) Neonatal herpes simplex virus infections can result in serious morbidity and mortality. Many of the infections result from asymptomatic cervical shedding of virus after a primary episode of genital HSV in the third trimester. Antibodies to HSV-2 have been detected in approximately

20 percent of pregnant women, but only 5 percent report a history of symptomatic infection. All primary episodes of HSV and secondary episodes near term or at the time of delivery should be treated with antiviral therapy. If active HSV infection is present at the time of delivery, cesarean section should be performed. Symptomatic and asymptomatic primary genital HSV infections are associated with preterm labor and low-birth-weight infants. The diagnosis of neonatal HSV can be difficult, but it should be suspected in any newborn with irritability, lethargy, fever or poor feeding at one week of age. Diagnosis is made by culturing the blood, cerebrospinal fluid, urine and fluid from eyes, nose and mucous membranes. All newborns suspected to have or who are diagnosed with HSV infection should be treated with parenteral acyclovir.[6]

(b) About 25 percent of adults in the United States are infected with genital herpes. The virus is not curable. Babies born to mothers who have an active genital herpes infection at or near the time of delivery can become infected. This can be serious and sometimes fatal for newborns. If you have had genital herpes and are considering pregnancy or are pregnant, be sure to tell your doctor. He or she may give you antiviral medicines so you will be less likely to have an outbreak of herpes at or near the time you have your baby. If you do have an outbreak of genital herpes at the time of delivery, your doctor will want to deliver your baby by cesarean section so your baby will be less likely to get herpes infection.[7]

(c) Genital herpes is the most common cause of genital ulceration in developed countries, yet four in five people with HSV-2 go undiagnosed, either because they are truly asymptomatic or because they present with atypical symptoms which go undiagnosed.[8] It is now believed that what were previously regarded as atypical manifestations are, in fact, common presentations. Now it is becoming more important to support a clinical diagnosis of genital herpes with a diagnostic test.[9]

4. **Rewrite a paragraph.** Read the following paragraph and rewrite it to lower the difficulty.

A new concept that greatly improves the economics of outdoor storage of grain and other free-flowing bulk materials includes a self-erecting cover and new methods of aeration. The cover is laced together from triangular sections of vinyl-coated nylon fabric and raised to the top of a central filling tower before the filling operation is begun. During filling, it is lifted and spread by the growing grain pile and provides a form-fitting cover that completely encases the pile during all stages of fill. This form-fitting cover is highly resistant to lifting effects of high winds and protects the pile against rainfall. This protection allows the filling operation to be continued during the heaviest downpours. It also completely contains dust particles that would otherwise be carried into the atmosphere to settle on the surrounding countryside. When full, the covering, tightly fitted to the finished pile, is held in place without need of the usual tires or cable tie-downs and provides long-term protection against crusting and other surface spoilage effects caused by the weather. This protection is obtained at a very low cost, as the cost of the cover can be completely paid off by the spoilage eliminated by a single year of the cover's use.

5. Analyze audiences for different paragraphs.

(a) Read and analyze the audiences and some of the related factors for the following two paragraphs about the same subject — why stars twinkle.

Paragraph A. The stars twinkle because the earth's air scatters the light that comes from them. So during windy weather, stars appear to twinkle more than when the weather is calm. Also, stars near the horizon twinkle more than stars higher in the sky because the light has a thicker layer of air to go through. Observed from the moon, stars do not appear to twinkle at all because the moon does not have any air. Planets do not appear to twinkle as much as most stars because planets usually appear much brighter than most stars, making it harder for their light to be scattered.

Paragraph B. Stars twinkle because of atmospheric diffraction, the scattering of light caused by the earth's atmosphere. Stars appear to twinkle much more when the atmosphere is extremely turbulent, as it is just before a weather front passes through. Stars near the horizon appear to twinkle much more than those near the zenith because light has to pass through a thicker layer of atmosphere and has more of a chance to be diffracted. The moon's lack of an atmosphere causes a very small amount of diffraction. The light from planets is not diffracted as much as that from stars because planetary disks subtend a much larger area than do stellar disks (40 arc seconds as compared to 0.001 arc second). This larger area causes the light to be more intense and results in less diffraction.

(b) Complete a matrix based on your analysis of the paragraphs. Describe, explain, and illustrate each factor.

WEBLINK

Go to **www.english.wadsworth.com/burnett6e** for an electronic version of the matrix that follows.

CLICK ON WEBLINK

CLICK on Chapter 4/matrix

	Paragraph A	*Paragraph B*
Audience		
Context		
Content		
Purpose		
Vocabulary		

6. Contrast articles written for different audiences.

(a) Select an article from *Science Digest, Science News,* the *New York Times* science section (published on Tuesdays), or a local newspaper's science section, and then locate the original article from which it was abridged or on which it was based. Identify and comment on the changes.

(b) Create a table to present your analysis — one column to identify the features you examined and the other two columns (one for each publication) to present examples of the differences. Provide complete citation information for each article.

(c) Find a Web site that deals with the same information. Identify and comment on differences in the presentation of the information on the Web site. Revise your table (additional column and rows) to present the information from your Web site analysis.

7. Write memos for two audiences.

(a) Read the following two memos written by a production supervisor about the purchase of hand cutters for assembly workers on a production line. Note the places that make each memo appropriate for the intended audience.

- The first memo is to an engineer in manufacturing whose projects are affected by the quality of the work the assembly workers do. He wasn't involved in the testing, so he needs a summary of test information. He is particularly interested in the function and capability of the cutters.

- The second memo is to a finance representative. Her primary concern is cost — initially, total expenditure, then cost comparison. Least important to her is the reason for the choice.

(b) After reading the two memos, write two additional memos about the same subject. Direct one of the memos to the assembly workers themselves. Direct the other memo to the manager of the manufacturing division, who is the immediate supervisor of the production supervisor who is writing the memos.

(c) In a small group, choose people to role-play the responses of the recipients to the memos. Discuss your decisions as a group.

Memo from Production Supervisor to Engineer in Manufacturing Engineering

Memo

Marlborough Science, Inc.

October 11, 200 —

To Charles Faria
PCB Manufacturing Engineering

From Marty Holmann *mh*

Subject EREM Hand Cutters

From September 23, 200-, to October 10, 200-, the SPS assembly personnel evaluated three styles of EREM ergonomic hand cutters. The assemblers preferred cutter style 711E-BH to cutter styles 511E-BH or 512E-BH.

Nine line assemblers as well as six post solder operators had the opportunity to use the three styles of cutters. They all agreed that the 711E-BH cutter was the most comfortable, durable, and versatile. The padded handles and quick-action internal spring reduce the fatigue factor experienced by the assemblers with their current cutters. The cutters were used to cut leads varying from 0.019 inch to 0.050 inch and showed little sign of wear, even after being used to cut soldered leads.

In summary, the assemblers strongly preferred the EREM hand cutters to the Lindstrom or Utica cutters. They are still willing to evaluate any new cutters that you may consider equivalent or applicable to their needs.

Memo from Production Supervisor to Finance Department Representative

Memo

Marlborough Science, Inc.

October 11, 200 —

To Diane Martin
Finance Representative
From Marty Holmann *mh*
Subject EREM Hand Cutters

PCB Manufacturing Engineering and PCB Management are requesting approval from the Finance Department to purchase 400 EREM hand cutters for the assembly-line workers for a one-time total purchase price of $9,200.

From September 23, 200-, to October 10, 200-, three styles of EREM hand cutters were evaluated by the assembly-line workers and the manufacturing engineer of the department. The three styles are similar in size and shape and contrast only in material and price.

Style #	Unit Price	Discount Price (over 100)
711E-BH	**$30.00**	**$23.00**
511E-BH	$31.00	$25.00
512E-BH	$32.00	$25.00

The assemblers on the line preferred cutter style 711E-BH for its comfort, versatility, and durability. They also found that the cutter reduced their operator fatigue, which is a factor in our processes.

8. **Write for three audiences.** Write three separate paragraphs about the same subject for three different audiences.

Example: If you are writing about treating runners' knee injuries, you could write for any of these audiences. Each reader would be interested in some aspect of treating knee injuries, but the focus, as well as the amount and kind of detail, would differ.

EMT (emergency medical technician)
coach
athlete
athletic trainer
sports physician
physical therapist
therapy equipment manufacturer
running shoe designer

Be sure to make appropriate adjustments in content focus and complexity, clarity, diction, sentence structure, and organization. Label each paragraph to indicate the intended audience. Consider one of the following suggested topics, or select your own:

architecture for Web site
artificial insemination
cable TV operation
capability of computer software
conformation of show animal
construction of road bed
development of photographic film
effects of aerobic exercise
effects of cigarette smoking
fetal alcohol syndrome
gene splicing
hybrid seed development
laser optics
manufacture of plastic film
new treatment for cavities
operation of microwave oven
propagation of house plants
safety standards in paint shop
setting a fractured bone
shifting sand barriers
treatment for hangovers
weather tracking

Chapter 4 Endnotes

1 © 1996, reprinted with special permission King Feature Syndicate.

2 Kirsch, I. S., Jungeblut, A., Jenkins, L., & Kolstad A. (1993). *Adult literacy in America, Educational Testing Services and the National Center for Educational Statistics.* Washington, DC: Government Printing Office.

3 Myers, C. (n.d.). *Fact Sheets: Literacy, ESL, and Health Care.* Retrieved September 28, 2003, from http://www.caslpa.ca/english/resources/literacy.asp

4 Used with permission of James R. Carey, Lowell General, Lowell, Massachusetts.

5 Hynds, P., & Martin, W. (1995). Atrisco Well #5: A case study of failure in professional communication, *IEEE Transactions on Professional Communication,* 38.3, 139–145.

6 Rudnick, C. M., & Hoekzema, G. S. (2002). Neonatal herpes simplex virus infections. *American Family Physician, 65*(6), 1138.

7 American Academy of Family Physicians. (April 2003). *Herpes During Pregnancy: What You Should Know.* Family Doctor.org. Retrieved January 14, 2004, from http://www.familydoctor.org/x2425.xml

8 Herpes Web. (n.d.). *Issues in Genital Herpes.* Retrieved July 16, 2003, from http://www.herpesweb.net/profess/issues/issue.htm

9 Corey, L. (1994). The current trend in genital herpes: progress in prevention. *Sexually Transmitted Diseases, 21*(2 Suppl), S38-S44.

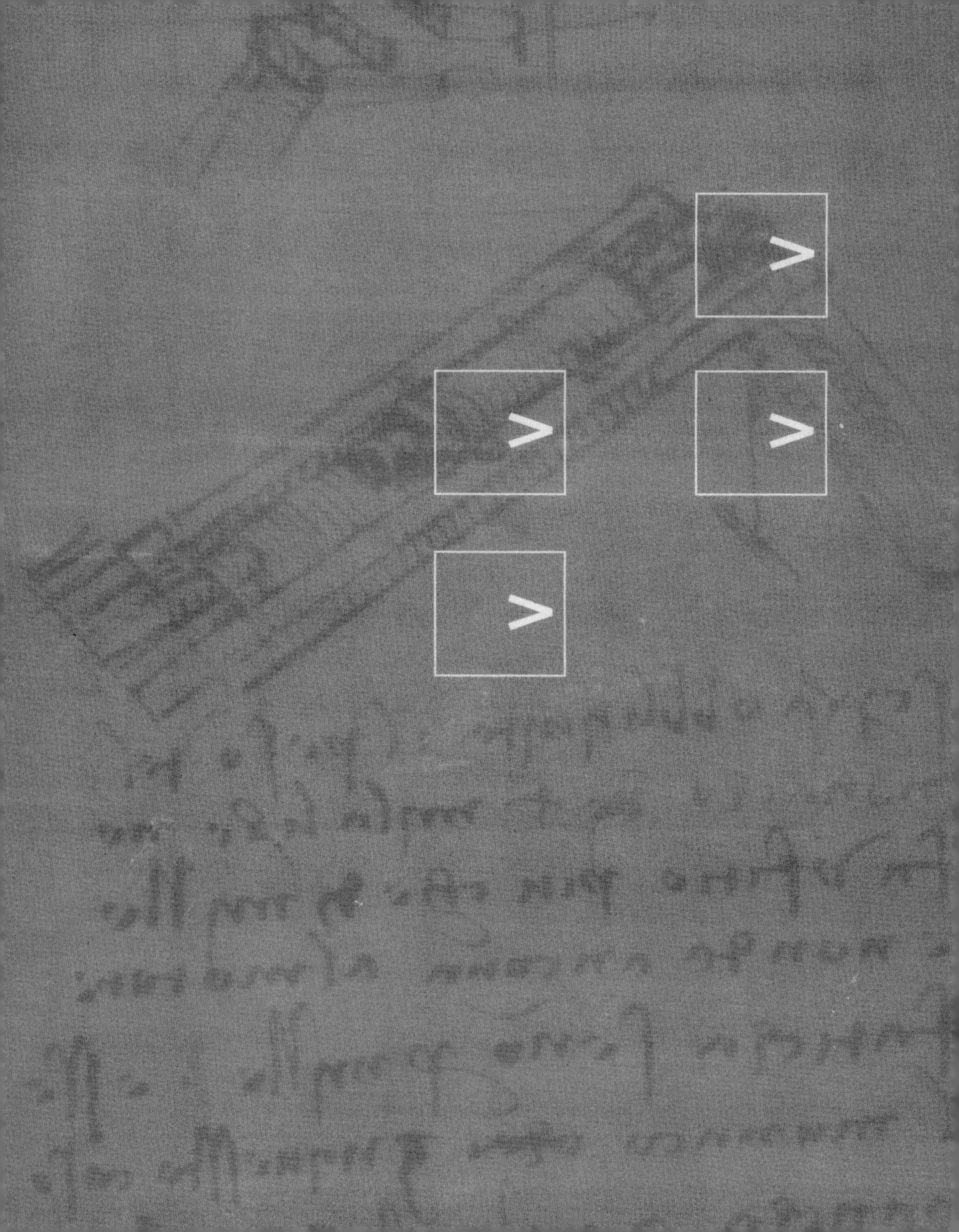

CHAPTER 5

Collaborating in the Workplace 职场中的合作

本章首先指出在职场中的大多数写作任务都需要与同事合作完成。然后介绍了参与合作的多种形式，如合著、咨询同事或协调项目等。同时介绍了如何成为好的合作者以及化解冲突。

Objectives and Outcomes 学习目标

This chapter will help you accomplish these outcomes:

- Understand that much of the writing you will do in the workplace will involve collaboration
- Recognize situations that make collaboration appropriate — subject, process, product, and benefits — as well as situations that cause problems
- Develop skills to participate in different types of collaboration: coauthoring, consulting with colleagues, and contributing to team projects
- Develop behaviors typical of skillful, engaged, and cooperative collaborators: listen, ask questions, share, use technology effectively, and reflect
- Discourage *affective* (interpersonal) conflicts; negotiate potential *procedural* conflicts; and encourage *substantive* conflicts. Recognize that conflicts are sometimes the result of differences in cultural attitudes, beliefs, and practices

"I look for a team player. . . . I want someone who understands that people are human and doesn't pick at the behavior of others until it becomes disruptive. I want someone who is not afraid to throw a bad idea out, in the hopes that it may spark a good idea." So says Sharon Burton-Hardin, the Chief Operations Officer at Anthrobytes Consulting in Riverside, California, and President of the Inland Empire chapter of the Society for Technical Communication (www.iestc.org). Burton-Hardin posted her comment on TECHWR-L, an electronic mailing list for professional technical communicators. "Too many times all the employees are doing what they want, regardless of what they have been told the joint effort is. Bickering, deception, destruction."[1] Her opinions give some indication of things that can go wrong with collaboration: disruption, bickering, deception, destruction. And she hints at another problem — the reluctance to be wrong.

Because 75 to 85 percent of the writing you will do in the workplace may involve collaborating with another person, knowing how to be effective is critical. What do you need to know to be an effective collaborator? What pitfalls do you need to be aware of in collaboration? In what ways can collaboration be more productive or effective than writing individually? This chapter helps you answer these questions. You'll learn about the reasons professionals give for collaboration, various types of collaboration, techniques for effective collaboration, and ways to deal with conflicts and resolve problems in collaboration.

Collaborative relationships generally have some common elements: two or more people cooperatively completing some agreed-on task and a specific goal or product to be accomplished over time. Physical proximity is not a necessity; in fact, computer-mediated communication makes long-distance collaboration commonplace.

While collaboration can take place with as few as two people, some collaborative efforts involve teams or networks with dozens or even hundreds of people. One profession that has large teams is high-energy physics (also known as elementary particle physics). Sometimes the teams are so large that the articles appear under the names of institutions rather than the individual authors. One big international high-energy physics collaborative, called H1, is conducting an experiment at HERA, a German national laboratory in Hamburg. The H1 collaborative has built and operates the H1 detector for collecting data with colliding positron-proton beams.

WWW

WEBLINK

Large-scale collaborations are often international. Go to **www.english.wadsworth.com/burnett6e** for links to a series of sites that describe large-scale collaborative efforts.

CLICK ON WEBLINK

CLICK on Chapter 5/teams and networks

DESY Hamburg

The people in front of the H1 detector are more than half of the members of the international H1 collaborative. This collaborative is comprised of about 400 people from 12 countries and about 40 institutes. Complex projects in particle physics require international teams to design, construct, and operate the detectors. The research focus of the H1 collaborative is "to measure the structure of the proton, to study the fundamental interactions between particles," and to "search . . . beyond . . . elementary particles."[2]

Reasons to Collaborate . . . or Not
合作与不合作的原因

Regardless of the number of people involved, professionals can enter collaborative relationships by individual choice, by circumstance, and even by management directive. Your reasons will generally fall into one or more of these four categories:

- Subject of the project
- Process used in the project
- Product that collaborators create
- Benefits of collaboration

Collaboration is widespread in the workplace. Go to **www.english.wadsworth.com/burnett6e** for links to several workplace publications tht provide additional reasons for collaboration.
CLICK ON WEBLINK
CLICK on Chapter 5/reasons to collaborate

WEBLINK

Despite all the reasons to collaborate, sometimes collaboration is inappropriate, inconvenient, or unsuccessful. After you review the reasons for collaboration, you'll have a chance to see some of the problems.

Subject 课题内容

The *subject* of some projects makes collaboration essential. Some tasks require expertise from more than one person. For example, a research project to help paraplegics walk might require professionals with backgrounds in biomedical engineering, electronics, neurophysiology, and physical therapy. An article resulting from such a collaboration could include input from all the individuals involved; thus, each could be acknowledged as a coauthor. Examining articles in professional journals for various branches of science shows that many are coauthored. Traditionally, collaboration in technical disciplines has been determined by calculating the percentage of published articles that are co-authored; for example, as long as 30 years ago, 83 percent of the journal articles in chemistry were co-authored.[3] More recently, however, collaborative has become so widespread that the National Science Board now determines collaboration by calculating the percentage of published articles that reflect cross-institutional authorship. Between 1981 and 1985, 35 percent of the published articles in science and technology worldwide reflected cross-institutional authorship; between 1991 and 1995, that increased to 47 percent.[4]

What subjects in your profession are well suited to collaboration?

More similar to what you'll probably do is an example from Kaufer Computing, Inc. The general manager heads a team that is preparing a proposal to install a new computer-aided design/computer-aided manufacturing (CAD/CAM) system in a lab for a local technical college. His team includes professionals with experience in drafting and design, education, electronics, computer systems and software, and, of course, technical communication — expertise unlikely to be found in a single individual. When you're working on a project that requires experience and expertise beyond your own, you should feel comfortable in forming or being a member of a team that works collaboratively to reach a common goal.

Process 过 程

Collaboration sometimes enriches the *process* of preparing a document in ways that are impossible for an individual working alone to experience. One major advantage of collaboration is considering a variety of alternative viewpoints. Imagine that an industrial engineer is exploring ways to improve the production capability for Northern Pacific Cabinet Company, Inc., an original equipment manufacturer (OEM) that provides handcrafted wood cabinets for high-quality electronic entertainment systems. The engineer realizes that this investigation will be much more productive if it involves materials buyers, cabinetmakers, schedulers, and shippers, all of whom can offer unique perspectives about ways to increase production.

Another way that collaboration can help you prepare documents is by providing feedback that is seldom available if you're working independently. Collaborators often reflect about the content and product as well as about the process. For example, the industrial engineer for Northern Pacific Cabinet Company not only will receive a variety of alternatives for improving production but also will receive feedback about all the proposed suggestions, her own as well as everyone else's. This type of feedback will enrich any work you do by providing you with reactions that you're not likely to think of alone. Your collaborators' ideas and reactions usually stimulate your own ideas and reactions, which not only makes the process more enjoyable but also improves the document.

How do you react when a collaborator poses an alternative that counters what you've already suggested?

Some companies build their reputations on specialized collaborative teams. For example, Omnica Product Development in Irvine, California, is a small company (25 employees) that promotes its industrial design team and its mechanical engineering team as the anchors of its design and engineering group. Their industrial design team creates concepts and designs, including photo-realistic renderings and working prototypes. Their mechanical engineering team makes sure that the most innovative designs can actually be manufactured.[5]

Omnica Corporation — Irvine, CA

Omnica's industrial design team says, "Much of the value of a product may come from the ability of the user to easily understand it."

Product 产 品

Sometimes the type of *product* signals the need for collaboration, simply because some products, such as Web sites, newsletters, user manuals, and proposals, are usually better if they're created collaboratively. Imagine that your task is creating a Web site for families of people with cystic fibrosis. The Web site might be more valuable and appealing if it contains topics written by a variety of health care professionals, by patients and their relatives, and by medical researchers. Written by you alone, this Web site is not likely to have the range of perspectives necessary to sustain the interest of such a variety of readers. Figure 5.1 presents an excerpt from a cystic fibrosis Web site published in English and Spanish by the Methodist Health Care System in Houston.

FIGURE 5.1 **Methodist Health Care System Cystic Fibrosis Web Site in English and Spanish**[6]

Accessibility

- *Since approximately one-third of the metro Houston area is Hispanic,[7] publishing the newsletter in both Spanish and English increases the number of readers.*
- *Media options for video, slides, and a model are clearly marked on the English-language site.*

Comprehensibility

- *Basic information is presented up front: definition, demographics, genetic explanations.*
- *Related information is logically chunked.*

Usability

- *The links are visible for the search engine, patient registration, scheduling, and appointments as well as a range of related services and basic medical background (anatomy, respiratory distress), equipment, and conditions.*

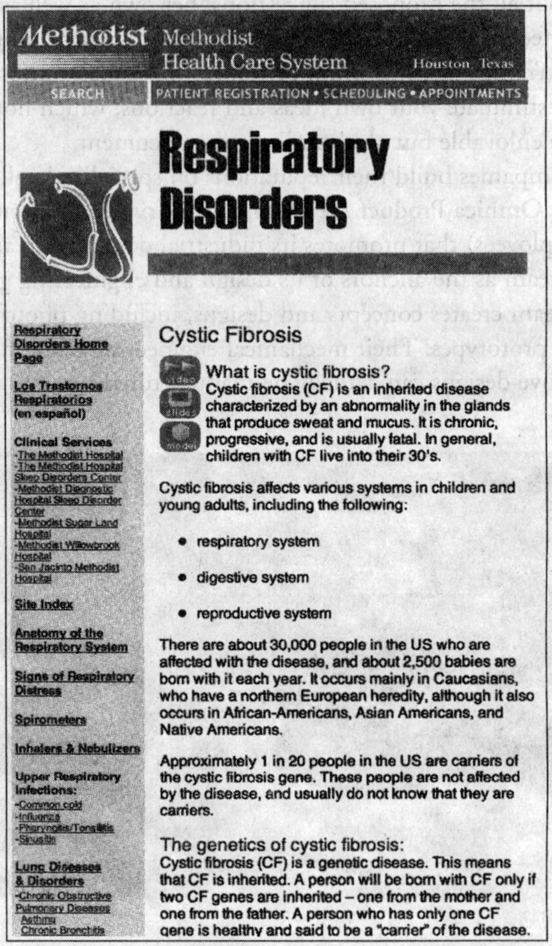

WWW

WEBLINK

The Methodist Health Care System Cystic Fibrosis Web site provides options for video, slides, and a model. To view these, go to **www.english.wadsworth.com/burnett6e** for links to the Web site in English and Spanish.

CLICK ON WEBLINK

CLICK on Chapter 5/CF

Typically, long documents such as user manuals or major proposals demand a collaborative effort because of the complexity of their content. For example, Ecological Recycling Associates wants to submit a proposal to the town of Sheffield for dealing with recyclable trash. One of the company's environmental engineers is responsi-

FIGURE 5.1 **Methodist Health Care System Cystic Fibrosis Web Site in English and Spanish[6] (continued)**

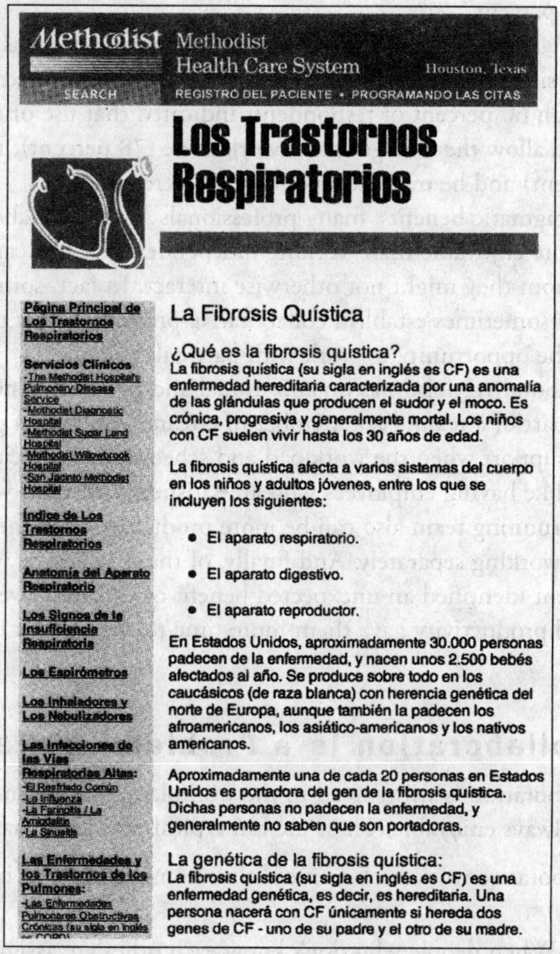
Methodist
Methodist Health Care System Houston, Texas
SEARCH
REGISTRO DEL PACIENTE • PROGRAMANDO LAS CITAS

Los Trastornos Respiratorios

Página Principal de Los Trastornos Respiratorios

Servicios Clínicos
-The Methodist Hospital's Pulmonary Disease Service
-Methodist Diagnostic Hospital
-Methodist Sugar Land Hospital
-Methodist Willowbrook Hospital
-San Jacinto Methodist Hospital

Índice de Los Trastornos Respiratorios

Anatomía del Aparato Respiratorio

Los Signos de la Insuficiencia Respiratoria

Los Espirómetros

Los Inhaladores y Los Nebulizadores

Las Infecciones de las Vías Respiratorias Altas:
-El Resfriado Común
-La Influenza
-La Faringitis / La Amigdalitis
-La Sinusitis

Las Enfermedades y los Trastornos de los Pulmones:
-Las Enfermedades Pulmonares Obstructivas Crónicas (su sigla en inglés es COPD)

La Fibrosis Quística

¿Qué es la fibrosis quística?
La fibrosis quística (su sigla en inglés es CF) es una enfermedad hereditaria caracterizada por una anomalía de las glándulas que producen el sudor y el moco. Es crónica, progresiva y generalmente mortal. Los niños con CF suelen vivir hasta los 30 años de edad.

La fibrosis quística afecta a varios sistemas del cuerpo en los niños y adultos jóvenes, entre los que se incluyen los siguientes:

- El aparato respiratorio.
- El aparato digestivo.
- El aparato reproductor.

En Estados Unidos, aproximadamente 30.000 personas padecen de la enfermedad, y nacen unos 2.500 bebés afectados al año. Se produce sobre todo en los caucásicos (de raza blanca) con herencia genética del norte de Europa, aunque también la padecen los afroamericanos, los asiático-americanos y los nativos americanos.

Aproximadamente una de cada 20 personas en Estados Unidos es portadora del gen de la fibrosis quística. Dichas personas no padecen la enfermedad, y generalmente no saben que son portadoras.

La genética de la fibrosis quística:
La fibrosis quística (su sigla en inglés es CF) es una enfermedad genética, es decir, es hereditaria. Una persona nacerá con CF únicamente si hereda dos genes de CF - uno de su padre y el otro de su madre.

ble for coordinating a five-member team to prepare the proposal. The team meets to plan the proposal, but various sections of the proposal are prepared individually by different members of the team. The comprehensive nature of the proposal and the amount of technical detail require expertise impossible to be found in one person, especially given the deadlines for submission. Having a project coordinator contributes to the collaborative proposal's consistency in style, tone, and format.

When you're working on a team in which each person is responsible for a separate section, how could you ensure overall consistency in style, tone, and format?

Benefits 利益

Many professionals advocate collaboration because of the *benefits,* both workplace and personal. Since the terrorist attacks of September 11, 2001, many workplace professionals are interested in alternatives to travel, including collaborative technologies. According to responses from approximately 700 business travelers to a poll conducted by Wainhouse Research, Web conferencing has increased 61.5 percent, video conferencing has increased 24.5 percent, and voice conferencing has increased 11.7 percent.[8]

While the initial increase in use of collaborative technologies was due to a concern for safety, since then workplace professionals have discovered additional benefits. "More than 60 percent of respondents indicated that use of conferencing technologies would allow them to get more work done (78 percent), make faster decisions (66 percent) and be more competitive (64 percent)."[9]

Beyond the pragmatic benefits, many professionals say the collaborative process is often more enjoyable than working independently. They can work with colleagues with whom they might not otherwise interact. In fact, some professionals admit that they sometimes establish collaborative projects, rather than individual ones, just for the opportunity to work with particular people.

How can you increase the interpersonal benefits of belonging to a team?

Working collaboratively also has organizational and personal benefits. Many people like being part of a team. As a member of a team, you have a group identity that provides support when the workload and schedule are especially difficult. While companies like having employees who are satisfied with their work environment, a smoothly running team also can be more productive than the same number of individuals working separately. And finally, of those polled by Wainhouse Research, 72 percent identified an unexpected benefit of collaborative technologies: The increased productivity gave them more time to spend with family and friends.

Reasons Collaboration is a Problem 合作产生问题的原因

Even though collaboration is widespread in the workplace, it is not necessarily easy, and it's not always enjoyable. These are ten typical problems that can occur:

- ***Time.*** Collaborative work is often more time consuming than individual work.
- ***Discomfort.*** When people who don't know each other are assigned to the same team, interaction may initially be awkward and frustrating.
- ***Control.*** Managers may be unwilling to let your team make its own decisions.
- ***Credit.*** Some individuals are unwilling to share credit, whether in the form of coauthorship, patents, royalties, or public acclaim (though they may be willing to let others take the blame).
- ***Conflict.*** Unproductive conflict can become overwhelming. Productive conflict may not be recognized and may be mistaken for unproductive conflict. (See "Negotiating Conflicts," beginning on page 164.)
- ***Criticism.*** Some people do not gracefully accept criticism or modification of their ideas.

- ***Ethics.*** You may observe attitudes, behaviors, or decisions of other team members that you believe are unethical.
- ***Style.*** People may have very different ways of approaching tasks and problems, so they may seem abrasive, unfocused, uncooperative, unavailable, shy, directive, or critical.
- ***Responsibility.*** If individuals are accustomed to being in charge, they may find working on a team to be uncomfortable because it requires sharing power and responsibility.
- ***Technology.*** The organization may not have the technology necessary to carry out efficient collaboration.

What can you do if faced with each of these problems? Can you pose at least two ways of dealing with each problem?

Despite these problems, collaboration has so many benefits that it's likely to play a large part in your professional life. Since you can anticipate that these problems will occur in some of your collaborations, you need to figure out ways to prevent or counter problems so that your collaborative efforts are not derailed or undermined.

Types of Collaboration
合作的种类

Collaboration in the workplace often takes many different forms. As long as the collaborators agree on their interpersonal roles and their tasks, numerous collaborative relationships are possible. For example, collaborators might work together during only one phase of a project, such as the planning stage, but then one person might draft and revise the entire document or oral presentation. Or, after the initial collaborative planning, each person might complete a different portion of a major document or presentation. Another example occurs when collaborators work together on only one portion of a project. An engineer might collaborate with a colleague in finance when preparing the budget section for a proposal and with another colleague in quality control when preparing the testing and evaluation section of the same proposal. Regardless of the nature of the collaboration, when collaborators assume unequal responsibility for different aspects of a project, they should expect to receive unequal recognition and compensation.

What typoo of collaboration are you likely to do as an entry-level professional? As a more senior professional?

One useful way to examine collaboration is to analyze the role of the individ ual in relation to the other collaborators. For example, consider the work of Paula Thompson, a manager at Dover Systems, a company that designs hardware and software for commercial architects and contractors. Three of Paula's current projects involve different types of collaboration: coauthoring, consulting with colleagues, and contributing to team projects.

Coauthoring 合 著

To many people, collaboration means that the contributions of the collaborators are equivalent and the exchange of information is reciprocal. In a coequal collaboration, each collaborator contributes ideas but is willing to abandon or modify them. Coequal collaborators both analyze the strengths and weaknesses of their own ideas and also evaluate the ideas of the other collaborator(s). Any arguments that arise are explored in light of mutually agreed-on purposes, tasks, and products. Because each collaborator assumes responsibility for creating and criticizing, the team is able to build new ideas by taking the best from each collaborator. Each collaborator takes equal responsibility and receives equal credit as coauthor.

One project Paula Thompson is responsible for involves working with a colleague, Chris McCaffrey, to prepare an article for publication in the company's technical report series. As coauthors, Paula and Chris share responsibilities for planning, drafting, and revising their technical report.

Paula and Chris have agreed to an initial meeting to discuss content, purpose, audience, organization, and evidence, as well as to plan their schedule. They agree to rough out ideas separately and then meet again. Although they each take responsibility for writing separate sections of the report, they read each other's drafts and make suggestions that influence the other's work. Because they both write on a networked computer system, they can share their drafts and exchange e-mail about them. Even though Paula and Chris communicate regularly by e-mail, they also have face-to-face meetings to resolve problems. Once the draft of their coauthored report is completed, they establish another series of collaborative relationships as the document moves through the review and editing cycles.

Consulting with Colleagues 咨询同事

Another of Paula's projects is preparing a packet of information sheets for a new product line. Paula initially creates thumbnail sketches for information sheets that should accomplish these five goals: draw attention to a new product or product line that solves a problem, unify the product conceptually with the design of the information sheet, create a sense of corporate competence, arouse customers' interest enough for them to seek additional information, and summarize the marketable features of the product.

Paula also knows that information sheets should not become merely a list of technical features, so she works with colleagues in a number of departments to complete her project:

- Engineering — to get accurate product specifications
- Marketing — to get information about the target market
- Graphic design — to work with the artist to design the information sheets and pocket folder they'll go in
- Communication — to work with the editor assigned to the project
- Publication — to get corporate publishing specifications and printing costs
- Quality control — to arrange for technical review and user testing

Although Paula is responsible for the development of the information sheet packet, she consults with a variety of colleagues who have expertise that she needs.

This type of collaboration — consulting with colleagues — is common and expected. You should willingly seek information from colleagues and be prepared to reciprocate when they need information from you. Naturally, Paula lets her colleagues (and their managers) know how helpful they have been.

Contributing to Team Projects 为团队项目献计献策

A third project Paula is responsible for is coordinating the efforts of a team of hardware engineers, software designers, systems analysts, information designers, and budget planners. She must organize their individual efforts into a proposal for a state-of-the-art laboratory. The team has had numerous planning meetings, but each person is responsible for an individual section of the document. Part of Paula's job is to facilitate the planning meetings and to coordinate the separate sections that people have prepared into a coherent, cohesive, persuasive proposal.

However, even on a team, collaboration does not necessarily mean coequal contributions. When one person assumes a greater responsibility, that person might initially identify the purpose of the collaboration, define the task, and perhaps even specify the product. Individual contributions do not have to be equivalent. However, if the collaboration is to be successful, all the individuals involved need to have some say in what responsibilities each person should assume and suggest the collaborative approach that should be used.

Being a Good Collaborator
成为一个好的合作者

Allan Ackerson, lead technical writer working for the Colorado Springs division of Logicon Applied Technology, Inc., commented on the TECHWR-L electronic mailing list that collaborators — especially if they're team leaders — should follow three guidelines:

1. Treat people like you'd like to be treated.
2. Identify strengths and weaknesses of team members and use them accordingly.
3. Insist on excellence.[10]

Ackerson's advice is valuable because it is a reminder that being an effective collaborator and team leader requires common sense and courtesy. Following Ackerson's advice is a good start. Whether you are preparing a document as a coauthor, as a consultant with colleagues, or as a member of a project team, you can do several things that will help you be more effective:

- Self-assess
- Be engaged and cooperative
- Listen
- Conform to conversation conventions
- Ask questions
- Share
- Use technology effectively
- Reflect

Self-Assess 自我评估

Before you consider the self-assessment in Figure 5.2, identify your strengths and weaknesses as a collaborator. What areas would you like to improve?

Being a productive collaborator means, in part, having a clear sense of what you bring to any project. Specifically, you need to consider your work style in general, collaborative style, sense of responsibility to projects, personality and prejudices, availability, skills, commitment, and expectations. A good place to begin is with the questions in Figure 5.2, which give you an opportunity to assess your own attitudes and behaviors that will influence your collaborative interaction.

WEBLINK

For an electronic version of Figure 5.2, go to **www.english.wadsworth.com/burnett6e** for a link to the questions.
CLICK ON WEBLINK
CLICK on Chapter 5/self-assessment

WEBLINK

Deciding what to tell your collaborators about yourself is sometimes difficult. The International Personality Item Pool (IPIP) is a questionnaire (50-item version or 100-item version) that makes no pretense of being scientific; it doesn't have norms or validity. However, if each member of your team completes the questionnaire, the responses will enable you to learn something about each other. Go to **www.english.wadsworth.com/burnett6e** for a link to the IPIP site.
CLICK ON WEBLINK
CLICK on Chapter 5/discussion inventory

After you have answered the questions in Figure 5.2 (on page 156–157), you can decide whether your attitudes and behaviors will probably have a positive or negative effect on your own collaboration, the collaboration of others on your team, and on the completion of the task itself. At that point, you and your collaborators might choose to discuss some or all of each other's self-assessments together.

Be Engaged and Cooperative 工作投入及善于合作

Several things increase the likelihood that your collaborations can be enjoyable and productive. You can begin by coming to the collaborative session with an open mind. Leave at the door any prejudices or negative preconceptions about the people you're working with or the project you're working on. Be receptive to the likelihood that the collaboration will improve whatever ideas you already have. Once you have an open mind and a receptive attitude, you will find the following general guidelines useful:

- Always *come prepared* for any collaborative meeting, which means gathering necessary information and having something to contribute to the collaboration.

- Be able to *articulate the purpose* of your collaborative work. What's the goal? What's the task? Do others on the team have similar ideas? What's the process you'll use to complete the project? How can you get all the collaborators in your group to represent or interpret the goals, task, and process in the same way?
- *Be articulate* in expressing your views. Don't assume body language or silence will sufficiently (or accurately) convey your views.
- *Be cooperative* and *supportive* rather than competitive and antagonistic.
- Be direct in stating your own opinions, but *don't trample* on the ideas of other collaborators.

Listen 倾 听

You can learn a great deal if you are an *active listener* instead of a passive listener. An active listener is engaged — attentive, involved, interested. Being an active listener means paying attention to what your collaborators say, and what they don't say. Be aware, too, of their manner of speaking. Tone of voice, pacing, and inflection all can reflect attitudes about the content. Sometimes knowing those attitudes is as important as knowing the content. (Refer to Chapter 2 for a discussion of cultural differences in listening behaviors.)

Being involved and interested while listening to your collaborators means asking questions when you're confused and periodically summarizing what you hear the speakers saying. Getting immediate clarification lessens the chance that you'll misinterpret what you hear. Paraphrasing what speakers say is a good way to verify that your understanding matches their intent.

Active listeners often have a number of ways to respond to and encourage ongoing conversation. Try some of the beginnings listed on page 158,[11] followed by the open-ended questions suggested in Figure 5.3 on page 160.

Despite background distractions, an active listener pays close attention, periodically reflects back what is being said, and follows up with open-ended questions.

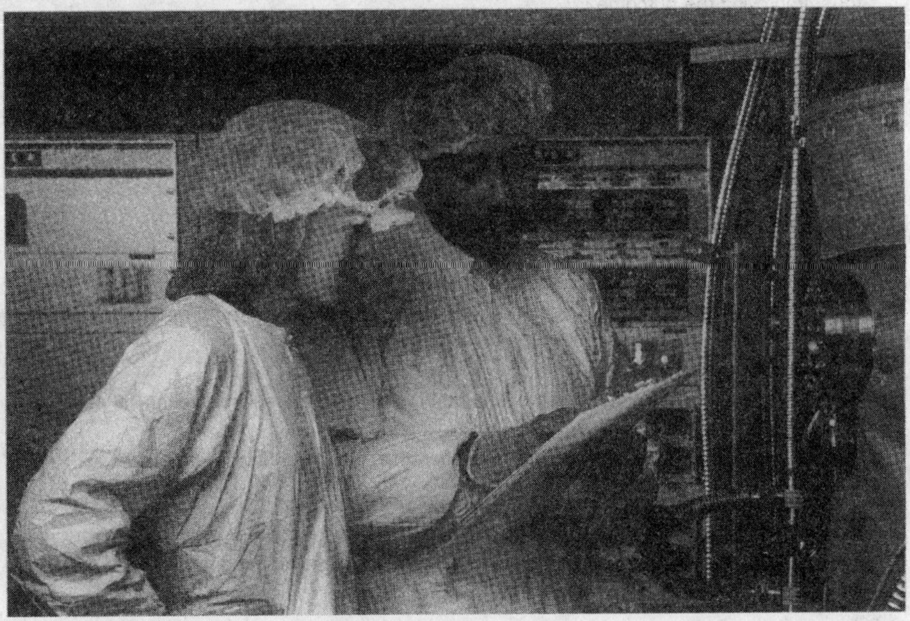

Lou Jones/Index Stock Imagery

FIGURE 5.2 **Questions for Self-Assessment about Collaboration**

Critical Factors	Self-assessment	Importance/Impact on Self, Team, Task?	Maintain or Change?
Your work style/work space: ■ How much do you procrastinate when starting or completing tasks? ■ What physical or psychological conditions do you have that could affect the work? ***Additional questions*** ■ Do you complete one task at a time (single focus) or work on several at once (multitask)? ■ When during the work process do you carefully check your work? ■ Do you work quickly? Slowly? ■ Are you fully engaged in tasks or do you lose concentration? ■ How do you prefer your workspace (sound, heat, light, interruptions)?			
Your collaborative style: How well do you listen and share? ■ How important is sharing the workload? How much do you expect collaborators to share the workload? How much of the workload will you share? ■ How do you prefer that collaborators inform you when you're not fairly sharing the workload? ■ How do you seek team input/agreement about team processes and procedures? ***Additional questions*** ■ How often do you challenge others' ideas for the purpose of considering alternatives and, thus, improving the outcome? ■ How do you prefer to resolve unproductive conflicts? ■ Do you prefer to share leadership or have a leader? How much do you like to be in charge? ■ What are your preferred strategies for communicating with team members? How often do you communicate about your progress? ■ How do you deal with team members who don't pull their own weight or assume their fair share of responsibilities?			
Your project responsibilities: How much of the work do you plan to do? ■ How active are you in establishing criteria to determine project quality? ■ What kind of project planning to you prefer to do? ■ What kind of written or oral feedback do you provide to others on the team? What kind do you expect them to provide you? ***Additional questions*** ■ How do you deal with team members who don't have the professional/technical skills to do their part of the project? ■ How do you deal with people who are uncooperative, belligerent, or unengaged?			
Your interpersonal/affective nature: How well do you get along? ■ What biases or prejudices of yours might influence team function or productivity (your reactions to race, gender, nationality, ethnicity, age, dialect, physical condition, sexual orientation, political preference, religion, etc.)?			

- How do you respond to criticism of your work?
- How do you respond to arguments or disagreements among team members?

Additional questions

- How important is having a friendly relationship with team members to your performance/productivity?
- How shy or outgoing are you? How likely are you to engage others in conversation? How reticent or voluble are you in conversation?
- How abrupt or welcoming are you when people contact you?
- How important is humor to you?

Your sense of time/availability: How much time will you put into the project?

- When are you available to work with the team?
- How much time each day/week are you planning to devote to this project?
- How easy are you to contact? How often do you check and respond to your voice mail? E-mail?

Additional questions

- What is your most productive time of day (or night) to work?
- Do you like to work for long or short periods? Do you take frequent breaks?
- What personal commitments might interrupt your work? Which cannot be changed?
- What do you think makes the most productive use of face-to-face meeting time?

Your skills or knowledge: What skills will you contribute to the team?

- Leadership skills?
- Project management skills?
- Problem-solving skills?
- Specialized technical knowledge?
- Writing and editing skills?
- Computer skills? Software? Hardware?
- Networking (people) knowledge?
- Knowledge of the organization(s)?
- Graphic design and document design skills?
- Translation skills?
- Usability testing skills?

Your commitment/expectations: How committed are you to the project?

- How important is doing excellent work? Is this a "done is good" project? How important is public acknowledgment of the project?
- How important is the implied or articulated commitment that comes with being on this team?
- How do you deal with free riders (team members who are lazy, careless, irresponsible, unproductive, or nonparticipating)?

Additional questions

- How willing are you to do the work of team members who don't do their work or don't do it well?
- What do you expect of other team members? How do you articulate these expectations?
- How will you find out what others expect of you?

- It sounds like you're saying . . .
- It seems that . . .
- I wonder if . . .
- Am I right that your main argument is . . . ?
- Am I right in thinking that your main points are . . . ?
- Tell me if I'm understanding that . . .
- I have the impression that . . .
- Am I right to think that . . . ?
- Do I understand that . . . ?
- You seem to be saying that . . .
- It seems to me that . . .
- Can you tell me if what's most important here is that . . . ?

An additional benefit is that if you listen actively to your collaborators, they're more likely to listen to you. As a result, you'll all have a better understanding of one another's views, and the project will have an increased chance of being successful.

Conform to Conversation Conventions 遵守对话规范

Collaboration requires conversation, either face-to-face or at a distance. Certainly having something to say matters, but, beyond that, following a few conventions makes face-to-face, telephone, and electronic conversations move more smoothly and productively.

All conversations

- Select an appropriate location with minimal background distractions.
- Look, sound, and act interested.
- State your points clearly.
- Provide explanations and examples as needed.
- Share the turn taking.
- Respond to the other person's ideas.

Face-to-face conversations

- Make direct eye contact (be aware of gaze, part of a person's cultural comfort zone).
- Respect personal space (be aware of proxemics, a person's spatial comfort zone).

Telephone conversations

- Don't eat, drink, or chew gum while you're on the phone.
- Don't put people on hold for more than a few seconds.

Electronic conversations (See Chapter 13 for netiquette about e-mail.)

- Keep in mind that all electronic messages can be forwarded, printed, or permanently stored by any recipient, so be sensible — even cautious — about what you send electronically.

- Copy only enough of the message you're responding to in order to provide a context or a reminder; do not copy the entire message unless you need a legal record.

What are your best habits — and your worst — in each kind of conversation?

Ask Questions 问问题

To be an effective collaborator, you need to ask questions to get the information you need. These questions can be powerful tools for helping you to assess what you already know and what you need to know to prepare an effective document. Two guidelines are particularly useful:

- Ask open-ended questions that require comments or discussions rather than questions that ask for *yes* or *no* responses.
- Ask questions that focus attention on a range of rhetorical elements important to the project: content, context, purpose, key points, audience, conventions of organization and support, and conventions of document design.

When you have primary responsibility for preparing a document, you can get a great deal of help from a supporter who asks you questions such as those in Figure 5.3. A good supporter encourages you to extend your ideas, questions you about points that seem inconsistent or contradictory, and offers suggestions about ways to improve the document. Of course, you can work with a supporter at any stage in planning, drafting, and revising a document. This kind of collaboration can help you focus your ideas, consider alternatives that may not have occurred to you if working alone, and give you feedback for improving the document. You can also reciprocate by acting as a supporter for colleagues.

The questions in Figure 5.3 are designed to help collaborators, whether they are acting as supporters for another writer, working as coauthors, or participating as members of a team. Although these questions are listed in separate categories, many concerns are relevant to more than one area. For example, the following question integrates several concerns: "How will the *organization* and *design* convey our *purpose* to the *audience*?" Periodically, you may want to consolidate two or more concerns into one question.

Share 分 享

Not only do you need to get information from your colleagues by listening and asking questions, but you also must be willing to provide them with detailed and accurate information. Unless prior agreements among all parties restrict sharing information (usually for proprietary reasons), you should make every effort to keep your collaborators informed about the work you're doing. You should also provide feedback to your collaborators about their work. This exchange of information should be done regularly.

The most effective way to ensure that information is exchanged regularly is to establish a schedule and a method when the project begins. For example, you can

FIGURE 5.3 **Questions to Help Collaborators Deal with Rhetorical Elements**[12]

Rhetorical Elements	Questions
Content	■ What critical information needs to be in this document or oral presentation? ■ What additional information might you/we include? ■ Have you considered including ________? ■ What content can be omitted?
Context	■ What is the context or situation in which this document or oral presentation will be used? ■ How will the situation be changed as a result of this document or oral presentation? ■ What aspects of the context or situation will influence the interpretation of the document or oral presentation?
Purpose and key point(s)	■ What do you see as your/our main purpose? ■ What main point(s) do you/we want to make? ■ How will the audience react to the purpose and points? ■ I see a conflict between ________ and ________. How can you/we resolve it?
Audience	■ Who is your/our intended audience? ■ What does the audience expect to learn? ■ How do you think the audience will react to ________? ■ What problems, conflicts, inconsistencies, or gaps might the audience see?
Organization and support	■ How can you/we organize the content to achieve the purpose? ■ What evidence can you/we use to support the purpose and appeal to the audience? ■ What examples (anecdotal, statistical, visual) should you/we use? ■ How are you/we going to connect ________ and ________?
Document design elements	■ How can design features be used to convey the main point(s)? ■ What design features will the audience expect? What will the audience respond to? ■ How can verbal and visual information be balanced? ■ How can the design be used to reflect the organization of the content?

What questions would you like to add to Figure 5.3? Why are these useful questions to add?

all agree to provide weekly update memos. Or you can provide read-only privileges for selected electronic files. Or you can have weekly meetings to discuss the status of the project. Or you can circulate updated drafts of the document, either on paper or electronically. The method is not nearly as important as the fact that regular communication occurs among collaborators.

How widespread are global teams? Here are just two examples. Intel helps top Malaysian engineers launch their own businesses and then contracts with these new companies to work alongside Intel's U.S. employees. Some Hewlett-Packard software teams rarely have face-to-face meetings because the engineers are from places as far apart as Colorado, Australia, Germany, India and Japan.[13]

Use Technology Effectively 有效运用技术

Most teams, especially global teams, depend on technology, specifically on groupware. This increased use of groupware draws attention to two important issues: awareness of collaborators and privacy. While these issues are important in any collaboration, they have the potential to be especially problematic in collaborative interactions that involve many people working asynchronously over long distances.

WEBLINK

Technologies that enable collaboration have moved from the experimental laboratories to test sites to large-scale implementation and integration in worldwide business and industry. Go to **www.english.wadsworth.com/burnett6e** for a link to a site that gives you access to a series of white papers about collaboration and technology from industry research groups and leading-edge companies. These papers are definitely about application and practice.

CLICK ON WEBLINK

CLICK on Chapter 5/white papers

Groupware *Groupware,* software designed to facilitate group interaction, usually changes the way collaborators plan, share documents, give and receive feedback, and make decisions. It enables the formation of groups for special projects. Two important factors characterize groupware:

1. *Time:* Are you and your collaborators working together at the same time (synchronous) or at different times (asynchronous)?
2. *Location:* Are you and your collaborators working in the same place (colocated; face-to-face) or in different places (noncolocated; distance)?

Whether you need synchronous or asynchronous communication, whether you and your collaborators are in the same room or separated by thousands of miles, groupware can bring together multiple perspectives and expertise. Figure 5.4 categorizes types of groupware that aid collaboration and teamwork.

Groupware designed for team interaction generally provides tools for a variety of complex activities: managing the information the team collects; managing factors that affect interaction, such as the context, agenda, and workspace; deciding access to information (who, when, and where); enabling team mobility so

FIGURE 5.4 **Common Types of Groupware**[14]

TIME

LOCATION: *Colocated interaction (same location)*; *Distance interaction (different locations)*

Synchronous interaction (same time)

- **Presentation support systems** aid speakers in formal or informal presentations with computer slides, often accompanied by audio and animation.
- **Decision support systems** (DSS) facilitate colocated and distance group decision making by helping collaborators with brainstorming, critiquing, weighing probabilities and alternatives, and voting. DSS may facilitate meetings by encouraging equal participation through anonymity or enforcing turn taking.
- **Shared whiteboards** permit two or more people to view and draw on a shared drawing from different locations. Color-coded telepointers identify each person.
- **Video communications systems** allow two-way or multiway calling with live video. Video is advantageous when visual information is being discussed.
- **Chat systems** permit multiple people in real time to write messages in a shared space. Many chat rooms control access or permit moderators for discussions. Issues in real-time groupware include anonymity, following the stream of conversation, scalability with number of users, and abusive users.

Asynchronous interaction (different time)

- **Shared computers** with word processing software enable collaborators to track changes and annotate each other's work.
- **E-mail** can send and forward messages to individuals or groups; filter, sort, and file messages; and attach files to messages.
- **Newsgroups and electronic mailing lists,** which deliver information to groups, are similar; however, newsgroups only show waiting messages when requested, while mailing lists automatically deliver messages as they're sent.
- **Hypertext** links related documents. Any authors can create links to new sites. Tools allow identifying visitors to a site and tracking the number of visitors on a site.
- **Group calendars** let people coordinate their schedules for projects, meetings, equipment and facilities use, out-of-town conferences and trips, and so on.
- **Workflow systems** help documents move through organizations electronically by a relatively fixed process. For example, employees can submit an expense report by routing it to a manager who electronically approves it for payment. The report is simultaneously debited from the group's account and then forwarded to the accounting department for payment.

- **Collaborative writing systems** provide both synchronous and asynchronous support. Collaborators can use various tools to plan and coordinate as well as link separately authored documents, track changes by various collaborators, and annotate their work in progress. Synchronous support usually provides an additional communication channel to the authors as they work, such as videophones or chat. Asynchronous support usually uses shared computers (see above).

members aren't restricted to a particular location; and encouraging team innovation and invention. Groupware also structures interactions, so aggressive people are less likely to dominate conversations.

Awareness Responding to what's happening is easier when team members are working face to face than when the team is separated by physical distance and by technology. Figure 5.5 describes a scenario in which two members of a team are using a shared, scrollable whiteboard. Sometimes awareness can be improved

FIGURE 5.5 **Increasing Awareness by Increasing Information[15]**

A *shared whiteboard* system allows two people to work on the same image at the same time. The changes that one person makes are copied to the other person's computer so that both people's workspaces contain the same object. If both people are able to scroll up, down, and across, . . . each person . . . [might have] a different view of the object . . . [with] only a small degree of overlap between the two views [as shown below]. In this situation, one could hardly say that either person is truly aware of the other's activity.

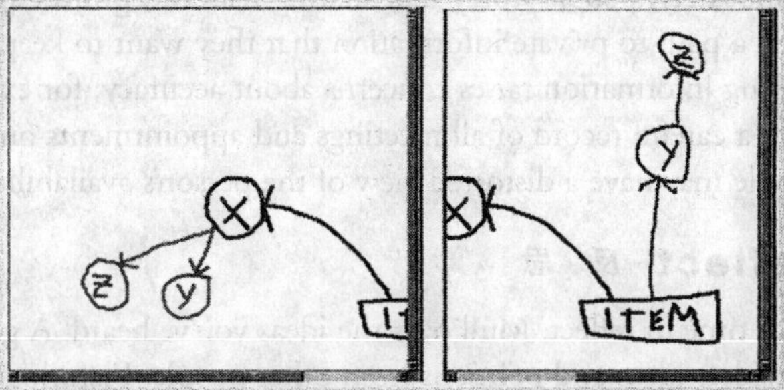

A's view B's view

In such a case, even the smallest piece of additional information regarding the other person's actions would constitute an improvement in the collaboration between the two. [The figure below] illustrates how a mutual understanding of the overall context can be facilitated if each . . . is aware of the other's activities, and can adjust his or her own activities accordingly.

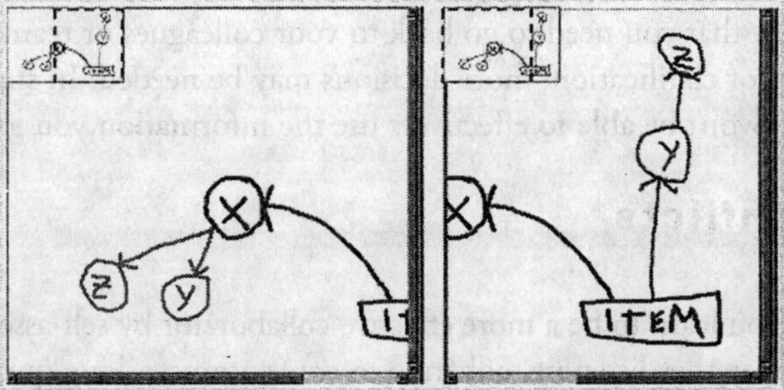

A's view B's view

when the collaborators simply pay more attention to the context, asking about things that would be understood in a face-to-face meeting.

Team awareness includes being tuned in to what's happening in the interaction, in the workspace, and with the information.[16] The team members, both individually and collectively, should consider responses to the questions in Figure 5.6. These questions are representative rather than comprehensive, so you might be able to add others to the list. Why so many questions? Worldwide practice indicates that *distributed teams* — that is, teams distributed across time and space — have many problems that don't affect face-to-face teams to the same extent. One way to reduce the problems is for team members to be aware of potential problems. A second way is for team members to develop strategies for either preventing those problems or managing them if they do occur.

What objections regarding privacy and accuracy might a person have about using a department-wide electronic calendar that helps schedule meetings, reserve rooms and equipment, manage projects, and coordinate activities among people?

Privacy Despite the convenience of groupware, users worry about privacy. Why? Security, control, safety, and accuracy. Electronically sharing information raises concerns about security: proprietary information needs to stay secure. Sharing information also raises concerns about control — that is, who has access to information and who decides what and how much to share. Sharing information raises concerns about safety; people worry that sharing relevant, project-specific information may open a path to private information that they want to keep private. And, finally, sharing information raises concerns about accuracy; for example, if a person doesn't keep a careful record of all meetings and appointments on a department calendar, people may have a distorted view of the person's availability.[17]

Reflect 反 思

Take time to reflect. Mull over the ideas you've heard. A good collaborator carefully considers ideas and opinions from other people. Planning a specific time for reflection is difficult when time is scarce — when deadlines slip, when your day is filled with back-to-back responsibilities, when you barely have time to eat lunch — but it is nonetheless an important part of the collaborative process. You need to sift through the information you've collected and assess its value, decide what information to use and what to discard, and pinpoint areas of confusion that should be clarified and areas of disagreement that should be resolved. Your reflection may also show that you need to go back to your colleagues or team for additional information or clarification; more decisions may be needed. In short, without reflection, you won't be able to effectively use the information you gain through collaboration.

Negotiating Conflicts
化解冲突

As you learn to be a more effective collaborator by self-assessing, being engaged and cooperative, listening, adhering to conventions, asking questions, sharing, using technology effectively, and reflecting, you'll also need to manage problems and negotiate the various kinds of conflicts — affective, procedural, and substantive — that arise.

FIGURE 5.6 **Team Awareness**

Areas for Team Awareness	Topics to Consider
Interaction	▪ **Who** — Who's involved on the team? Who's coordinating and facilitating team interaction? ▪ **What** — What might cause distortion or distraction in the interaction? ▪ **When** — When do people interact? How are differences in time zones and work schedules managed? How often do people interact? ▪ **Where** — Where is the interaction occurring? In virtual spaces? ▪ **Why** — Why might conflicts occur? How will conflicts be resolved? ▪ **How** — What will be the nature of the team interaction? How is the project history maintained so that team members can review who has done (or is doing) what? How are various versions of work being tracked or labeled? How will team members be able to see each other's planning sketches? Drafts?
Workspace	▪ **Who** — Who's in the workspace? Who's doing what? What's the order of authorship? ▪ **What** — What goals have been agreed on? What activities are necessary to achieve the goals? What activities are going on? ▪ **When** — When is the beginning and end of the project? What's the timeline? When are the various milestones? When does synchronous communication occur? How long is acceptable between asynchronous responses? ▪ **Where** — Where are team members located? How does the location affect participation and performance? ▪ **Why** — Why is each team member involved? What's the motivation? Purpose? Expectation? ▪ **How** — How will the team produce the deliverables?
Information	▪ **Who** — Who on the team already knows relevant information? ▪ **What** — What information is being gathered? By whom? What has been done so far? What does the entire picture look like (rather than a small segment)? ▪ **When** — When are the interim and final deadlines? When is the product and document testing? ▪ **Where** — Where are the most useful, reliable sources of information? What are people looking at? Using? Working with? ▪ **Why** — Why is the process being used to categorize, archive, disseminate the information the most appropriate? ▪ **How** — How is information being interpreted? How will the information be transformed into the deliverables?

WWW

WEBLINK

Is too big a deal made about workplace conflict? Go to **www.english.wadsworth.com/burnett6e** for a link to an article that summarizes more than ten years of workplace surveys and incidents about workplace conflict.

CLICK ON WEBLINK

CLICK on Chapter 5/conflict

Affective Conflicts 情感冲突

Affect involves your attitudes and biases, your personality and values. These factors shape your interpersonal communication and influence the way you approach collaboration. With effective interpersonal communication, your collaborations are more likely to be successful.

Interpersonal relationships are as important to collaboration as the task itself. A project is more likely to succeed if you respect your collaborators and get along with them, if you're comfortable working with them and feel free to share ideas and voice concerns. You and your collaborators need to trust one another; you can help build and maintain this trust by frequent contact and sharing of information.

Affective conflict, defined simply as interpersonal disagreement, can seriously impede any collaborative interaction, perhaps even signaling the end of the collaborative relationship. Simply put, it's unproductive. Affective conflicts might arise because of strongly held values and beliefs about religion, politics, business ethics, or gender, racial, or ethnic prejudices. For example, a collaborator who says, "I'll never work with a ____" (fill in the blank with some personal bias) has let affective conflict interfere with a working relationship.

Affective conflict may also occur in unexpected ways. For example, if your team is using a lot of technology to communicate and to complete your work, you may find that people have habits or behaviors that cause affective conflict, such as downloading software or music illegally, accessing porn sites, sending inappropriate jokes, or engaging in sexual harassment.[18]

One way you can avoid affective conflict is to first acknowledge your biases and prejudices and then make a special effort to not be negatively influenced by them during your collaboration. Think about the reasons that particular people or behaviors annoy or distress you and decide whether the reasons are relevant in a particular collaborative interaction. Sometimes people don't know their attitudes or behavior is causing a problem; in such situations, talking to your colleague privately may help. But sometimes it doesn't. And sometimes the problem is yours, not the other person's. In either case, you have a choice: Change your attitude or figure out professionally acceptable work-arounds so that prejudices don't derail the project.

Another way you can avoid affective conflict is by paying attention to differences and changes in footing during collaboration. *Footing* is a term used by cultural anthropologists to describe the underlying assumptions people make about a particular situation; those assumptions govern the way people act. Of course, your assumptions change as you learn new information about the people you're working with — their knowledge, their attitudes, their behavior — and the task you're working on. Even though you have established a relationship with your collaborators, you should recognize that changes are inevitable. In fact, as you react to new information and recognize subtle shifts in footing, your views about your collaborators and the task will gradually change. Being aware of this evolution will make it easier to handle.

What affective problems have you had when collaborating? What might you have done to decrease or eliminate those problems?

WWW

WEBLINK

For a quick read about ways to influence uncooperative people, go to **www.english.wadsworth.com/burnett6e** for a link to a short article with practical suggestions.

CLICK ON WEBLINK

CLICK on Chapter 5/conflict management

Procedural Conflicts 过程冲突

For a collaborative group to function smoothly, you and your collaborators need to discuss how the group sessions will run — that is, the procedures that will govern the group's operation. Many experienced collaborators find it efficient and productive to begin their work together by explicitly discussing and agreeing on several critical factors that affect procedures:

1. ***Meeting details***
   - Settle details of meetings: time, place, duration.
   - Agree on what preparation should be done for meetings.
   - Discuss the collaborative approach the group will use.
2. ***Team roles and responsibilities***
   - Identify the responsibilities each individual will assume.
   - Determine how to monitor the group's progress.
   - Decide on order of authorship based on some mutually acceptable criteria.
3. ***Productive management of conflict***
   - Agree on ways to minimize affective and procedural conflict.
   - Agree on ways to encourage substantive conflict.
   - Decide how to negotiate among alternatives and resolve disagreements.

Deciding such concerns up front can reduce your chances of having a group derailed by procedural conflict, which is usually unproductive. Open discussions about procedures can strengthen the group cohesiveness, both the feeling of group identity and the group's commitment to the task.

Anticipating procedural conflict can be critical to a group's success. Don't wait until your third 4:30 meeting to discover that one member always has to leave early because of family responsibilities or a second job. Don't wait until people are shouting at each other to agree that the team should withhold criticism until all the options have been presented. Don't wait until someone fails to meet a deadline to discover that he or she doesn't have the time or skills to do that part of the project effectively. Don't wait until the first progress report is due to discover that no one is keeping track of what's already completed, what is being done, and what needs to be done. Sometimes just asking questions about procedural concerns makes people aware of potential problems that can be easily managed by some preliminary discussions and agreements.

A group of workplace professionals in a course to study collaboration compiled a list of surefire ways to sabotage any collaborative effort. If you want to ensure failure, follow the suggestions in Figure 5.7.

FIGURE 5.7 **Ways to Sabotage Excellence in Collaboration**[19]

What would you add to this list of ways to sabotage collaboration?

Miss meetings.

Show up late.

Don't bother to talk about what the group goal is.

Don't ever allow discussion of anything not on the agenda.

Don't establish an agenda.

Ignore established agendas and procedures.

Disagree with everything just because you don't want to be there.

Agree with everything just because you don't want to be there.

Keep quiet, even when you have another idea.

Hoard your information.

Give up on your idea without even explaining it.

Make yourself responsible for everything.

Don't take responsibility for anything.

Plan to get everything done in one big work session.

Expect that many hands make quick work.

Keep meetings going for more than two hours.

Compete for individual recognition.

Elevate personal success above group success.

Don't bother to keep track of what is discussed.

Don't establish ways of communicating outside of scheduled meetings.

Rely solely on guesses to make decisions.

Don't establish any way to assess individual progress.

Attempt to include everything anyone ever said.

Expect the worst from your group members.

Don't let the group get to know you.

Strive for quick consensus on every issue.

Believe that everything runs smoothly in good collaboration.

Never laugh.

Other procedural concerns have to do with the costs and materials of a project — procedures regarding the allocation of resources. Because collaborative projects often take a long time to complete, they can be expensive. And because the projects are often complex, they require purchase of or access to a variety of equipment, tools, supplies, and services, which also can be costly. A limited budget can affect the nature of a collaborative project, restricting employee time and access to necessary resources. However, realistic long-range planning often allows an organization to budget for collaborative projects.

The extraordinary problems created by inattention to or short circuiting of procedural concerns are discussed in the ethics sidebar below. Initial discussions rather than assumptions about who would receive credit for important work would have reduced the chances that people would have been passed over. And as the situation discussed in the sidebar illustrates, procedural conflicts quite predictably spilled over into affective conflicts as well.

ETHICS 职业道德规范知识吧 SIDEBAR

"They were there to grasp all the credit for themselves": Ethics and the Culture of Credit

"他们来这儿索取功劳"：职业道德与文化

Picture the story of Susan Berget. Berget was a postdoctoral student researching human genes in a lab at the Massachusetts Institute of Technology (MIT). Berget's research revealed a puzzling connection between different strands of human chromosomes. Berget, working with Phillip Sharp, who headed the lab, later uncovered the concept of gene splicing, which was a major development in the field of molecular biology. The concept was so important that the 1993 Nobel Prize for medicine was awarded to its discovers: Phillip Sharp of MIT and Richard Roberts of New York's Cold Spring Harbor Laboratory (CSHL), a lab that had discovered gene splicing at about the same time. Notably missing from the list of prize winners was Susan Berget's name. Berget says that she and Sharp have settled their differences about the lack of acknowledgment for her role in the discovery, but "she acknowledges that the distribution of credit was not a perfectly smooth process."[20]

Reporters Jon Cohen and Gary Taubles investigated gene splice research and found that Berget was not the only researcher left out. As results from separate steps in the research were publicly released, contributions from many researchers went unacknowledged. John Hassell, a member of the CSHL group, believes that "[n]inety percent of the people at Cold Spring Harbor didn't get the credit they deserved." Cohen and Taubles attribute the winnowing of contributors to the "drive for individual credit — stoked by prize committees and the media." Focusing on individual credit "overshadows the collaborative nature of the scientific process, distorting the record and leaving researchers feeling bruised."[21]

How would you prevent the need for individual recognition from damaging a collaborative project?

How can technical professionals avoid these conflicts in giving credit? Researchers Mark Haskins, Jeanne Liedtka, and John Rosenblum believe a possible solution is to develop an ethic of collaboration that is based on relationships, not tasks. They identify four important elements in a collaboration that focuses on relationships:

- a caring attitude about the well-being of colleagues and about the work
- a recognition of the importance of the work for themselves and others
- a personal passion for the work
- a creative energy that fuels risk and innovation[22]

Focusing on relationships, Haskins and his colleagues believe, induces an ethic of collaboration that helps members see the advantages of group accomplishments over individual credit. If an ethic of collaboration had existed in Susan Berget's case, all the different researchers who played a role in the discovery would have been acknowledged for their role in the group's achievements.

Do you approach teamwork with an ethic of collaboration? Would you be willing to forgo individual credit for the sake of the group's success? Think of Susan Berget's story. How would you feel if your contributions to a project were not acknowledged?

Substantive Conflicts 实质性冲突

Substantive concerns deal with the substance of a document or presentation and include decisions about issues such as content, purpose, audience, conventions of organization and support, and conventions of design. Just as you may make preliminary agreements about procedural concerns, you should also adopt the practice of experienced collaborators who often address substantive concerns early in their discussions:

- Agree on the purpose of the collaboration.
- Agree on project objectives and outcomes.

Collaborators who do not agree about these substantive concerns run the risk of producing unfocused, poorly designed documents that don't respond to the needs or interests of any particular audience. Making decisions about these concerns doesn't lock you in; it gives you a direction. Replanning is always possible. You always have the flexibility to change any of your initial decisions, realizing that each one influences the others. For example, changing the purpose influences the organization and design of a document. Changing the design can change its impact on the audience.

Collaborators need to reach consensus, but not too quickly. One effective and productive way of deferring consensus is to engage purposely in substantive conflict. Unlike affective conflict (which deals with interpersonal tensions) or procedural conflict (which deals with disagreements about things such as meeting times), substantive conflict focuses on the issues and ideas of your collaborative work. Substantive conflict, which is usually productive, includes two specific types of interaction:

- ***Voicing explicit disagreements:*** For example, when one collaborator suggests, "Let's do Z," the other collaborator might respond, "No," or "I disagree," or "I think that's wrong."
- ***Considering alternatives:*** For example, when one collaborator suggests, "Let's do X," the other collaborator might respond, "Yes, X is a possibility, but let's consider Y as another way to solve the problem."

Deferring consensus can give you more time to identify and consider opposing points, more time to generate and critically examine issues and ideas. Resolution of substantive conflict can lead to increased commitment to your team effort and to a potentially better product. Because engaging in substantive conflict should be cooperative rather than competitive (after all, you're all going after the same goal: high-quality decisions and high-quality products), the resolution can be described as win-win. Here are some suggestions for engaging in substantive conflict during a cooperative collaborative session:

1. ***Ask provocative questions.***
   - Ask questions that focus on potential problems between various elements: "How can we use the design to help show our purpose?" "How can we explain these examples so the readers will be able to understand them?"
   - Ask your collaborators for elaborations, clarifications, and explanations of statements, and be prepared to offer clarifications and explanations of your own statements.
   - Ask for reasons to support arguments and work on developing and supporting well-formed arguments of your own.
2. ***Take a productive and critical perspective.***
   - Try never to settle on one solution or decision without first having considered a couple of alternatives.
   - Assume the role of devil's advocate.
   - When you disagree with something, say so; support your disagreement with a reason and, if possible, an alternative that will work.
   - If other collaborators don't generate substantive conflict by raising alternatives and voicing disagreements about your ideas, bring up alternatives and possible objections yourself.
3. ***Separate ideas and personality.***
   - Don't mistake an objection to your ideas as an attack on your character, personality, or intellect.

Substantive conflict should be viewed as a way to strengthen a project rather than weaken it. Such conflict enables collaborators to rethink their own positions, delineate the perimeters of their views, and make decisions about key issues. Collaborators who establish interpersonal relationships know that disagreements aren't personal attacks; instead, they're ways of reexamining issues critical to the project. Of course, as the Dilbert cartoon[23] shows, successful collaboration depends on an ability to think and communicate clearly.

Explain whether you believe the attitudes and behaviors in the Dilbert cartoon accurately reflect the workplace.

Successful collaboration depends on an ability to think and communicate clearly, but it also depends on all the participants being willing to interact and being receptive to the ideas they hear — even when they don't necessarily agree. Summarily dismissing collaborators when they disagree is not productive.

Where can agreement begin? Collaborators should agree about their project's goals, the conceptual core that reflects their ideas and ideals. Collaborators should be able to define their concepts and explain why they're important. Some documents are confusing because they seem to present inconsistent, sometimes even conflicting, views.

During planning, collaborators need to explore the concepts from a variety of angles: accuracy, logic, underlying theory, related issues, and implicit values. If the ideas aren't clear to the collaborators, they certainly won't be clear to the readers. Such investigating helps collaborators examine alternative views, bolster arguments against attack, refine explanations, delete weak positions, and clarify vague or misleading statements. Considering these alternatives makes the eventual agreement much stronger.

The International Online Training Program on Intractable Conflict offers very useful information about conflict management and constructive confrontation. For a link, go to **www.english.wadsworth.com/burnett6e**. Once you've read how to use the site and taken the quick tour, you'll probably find the problem-solving and self-study section the most useful place to start.

CLICK ON WEBLINK

CLICK on Chapter 5/constructive confrontation

WWW WEBLINK

Cultural Differences and Expectations 文化差异与期望

When a conflict arises, you need to ask yourself not only if it is affective, procedural, or substantive but also if it is generated by cultural differences. Drawing on what you learned about national and organizational cultures in Chapter 2, you can see that certain conflicts might occur during collaboration because attitudes and behaviors are unfamiliar.

Collaboration is a complex process of decision making and compromise that is influenced by cultural beliefs and practices. You can't assume that people from different cultural groups, backgrounds, or geographic regions will react the same way. Although all individuals have unique attitudes and behaviors that influence their collaborative style, within cultural groups you can often find common patterns of behavior.

Collaborators may inadvertently misjudge their colleagues' behaviors, not realizing that these behaviors are perfectly normal in another culture. For example, a colleague may agree with the clearly conflicting positions of two collaborators to avoid rejecting the ideas of either one. This behavior, regarded by some as indecisive or even wimpy, may simply be a reflection of the person's cultural practice of not insulting another by publicly rejecting his or her ideas.

In some cultures colleagues seldom directly express objections to problematic plans that are on the table for discussion. This reluctance to voice explicit disagreements may stem from a cultural practice that avoids criticizing others (which could embarrass them) and perceives disagreements as criticism or from a cultural perspective that values group harmony above potential benefits that substantive conflict might generate.[24] All sorts of behaviors — a reluctance to engage in substantive conflict, a hesitancy to spell out the procedural expectations, or an unwillingness to volunteer — may be the result of cultural practices different from yours.

You can help guard against inadvertent cultural bias by encouraging people you work with to exchange information about their collaborative patterns and practices, both their individual preferences as well as their cultural behaviors.

When your group is establishing the procedures to follow, collaborators can ask each other questions in categories such as these:

1. ***Moving the collaboration forward***
   - Are you willing to suggest an idea or plan that differs from the one accepted by the majority of the group?
   - When you don't understand something, do you ask for explanations and clarifications?
2. ***Reacting to disagreement***
   - When you don't agree with something, are you willing to express objections? Criticisms? How do you express your disagreement?
   - How do you think disagreements should be resolved?
3. ***Reacting to personal comments***
   - How do you react to being put on the spot?
   - How do you respond to criticism?
   - How do you respond to praise?
4. ***Considering team roles***
   - Do you think the group should have a leader? What are the responsibilities of the leader?
   - What are the responsibilities of the other collaborators?

Talking about these aspects of individual behavior may help collaborators understand that people respond in different ways. Understanding and perhaps even anticipating behaviors different from your own will help you be a more responsive and effective collaborator.

WWW

WEBLINK

If you want to learn more about collaboration, go to **www.english.wadsworth.com/burnett6e** for a link to tc.eserver.org, a portal that lists more than 60 workplace publications about collaboration.

CLICK ON WEBLINK

CLICK on Chapter 5/tc.eserver.org

Individual and Collaborative Assignments

个人作业和小组作业

1. **Address a complex problem.** Before coming to class or meeting with your collaborator, carefully read the case situation for Sundance Systems, Inc., and the Sundance information sheet. Before you meet with your collabora-

tor, prepare notes about a way to approach the technical memo and the information sheet redesign.

(a) **Write a memo.** Work with a collaborator to prepare a technical memo in response to the Sundance Systems case situation. The memo needs to include an analysis of the problems and propose a plan to address them. Take into account the task, the content, and concerns such as purpose, audience, organization and support, document design, and consolidation of these concerns. As part of your planning, discuss your approach to the issues and your collaborator's approach before you both decide how to prepare the memo.

Case Situation: Sundance Systems, Inc.

Examine the accompanying information sheet. In response to mail-in and telephone inquiries from potential customers (small businesses and homeowners), Sundance Systems, Inc., has sent out approximately 5,500 information sheets during the past 12 months. During this same period, the company has sold and installed 470 systems, at costs ranging from $5,000 to $25,000.

Unfortunately, a recent survey of customers indicates that although 47 percent of customers who purchased a Sundance System said they had read the information sheet, only 17 percent of customers who read it said it positively influenced their decision. In contrast, 22 percent of those who read it said it was confusing, and the remaining 61 percent said it didn't affect them one way or the other.

The information sheet was prepared by Lou Battle, founder of the company, who is considered an industry leader. Lou likes the idea of responding to inquiries with factual information. The current information sheet has been used for the past two years. In last week's staff meeting, Lou mentioned that he's heard some people want to update it, but he thinks it's pretty good as it is — it's short and accurate.

You've just been hired as an information designer in Sundance Systems' expanding corporate communication group. This group has consolidated the management of all published company documents, documents that until recently were handled by individual departments as needed. You were the top choice of Judith Dupras, the company's general manager. Part of your job is to work with another information designer to decide what to do about the survey results. What's the problem? What should be done? Present your collaborative assessment. (*Note:* You can create appropriate information to complete the assessment as long as it doesn't conflict with the minimal information provided.)

(b) **Revise the information sheet.** Continue working with the same collaborator. Your task now is to revise the Sundance information sheet. Take into account the content as well as purpose, audience, organization and support, visuals, and document design. Discuss your and your collaborator's approach to the issues as you decide how to revise the information sheet. Create a completely revised document.

SUNDANCE INFORMATION SHEET

Although most active solar systems are fairly simple in design and operation, the air-cooled system is the simplest. Unlike a liquid system, an air system needs needs no considerations for freeze protection, expansion, air bleeding, or vacuum relief. Since air-cooled systems run at lower operating temperatures than liquid-cooled systems, heat loss throughout the system is kept at a minimum while efficiency is kept at a maximum. The simplicity of the air-cooled solar system, its high efficiency, and its low cost should convince you to install a SUNDANCE SYSTEM in your home or business.

The heart of the air-cooled system is the solar collectors. The SUNDANCE solar collectors collect and convert the solar energy into usefull heat energy. The SUNDANCE collector is basically an air-tight insulated box. The inside of this box contains a black aluminum absorber plate, and the box is covered with a special transparent cover that allows light to pass through, but doesn't allow heat to escape. Light from the sun enters the box through the transparent cover, strikes the black aluminum absorber plate, and is converted to heat. Cool air enters the bottom of the solar collector, passes over the absorber plate, and exits from the top of the collector as heated air. Typically, this cool air entering the SUNDANCE collector is about 60F, and the heated air leaving the collector is about 140F. This heated air is brought via the ductwork into the building for water or space heating.

The ductwork is used to convey the cool air from the building (the return line) to the SUNDANCE collectors, and the heated air from the SUNDANCE colectors (the supply line) to the building. Ductwork is also used to connect the individual SUNDANCE collectors together to form an array and to vent this array during a period of nonuse such as a vacation. It is imperative that the ductwork system be thoroughly sealed from leakage. Leakage adversely affects the efficiency of the SUNDANCE SYSTEM by drawing cold outside air into the return line or by leaking heated air from the supply line. All ductwork done by SUNDANCE SYSTEMS is heavily insulated to keep heat loss at a minimum. Dampers are used to direct air into the house for space heating in the winter or to divert this heated air through a special water heater for summer operation.

A one-third horsepower two-speed blower provides air movement through the SUNDANCE SYSTEM. The fast speed is more suitable for winter operation since the system maintains a maximum output temperature of about 140F at this speed. This 140F air is usefull for space heating since it is about 70F warmer than the air already in the house. The difference between the temperature of the air leaving the house and the temperature of the air returning to the house is called the temperature differential. During summer operation however the lower operation speed is used since a higher operating temperature is necessary. The lower operating speed provides a collector output temperature of about 180F. This higher operating temperature is necessary for heating water since as the water becomes increasingly hotter the temperature differential and therefor the efficiency of the system are decrease. Therefore the SUNDANCE SYSTEM has a two-speed blower to maximize output year-round.

The SUNDANCE water heater is a three-shell design. The stainless steel inner shell contains the pressurized water. The middle shell provides the space for the heated air to circulate around the inner water tank. The outer shell contains the fiberglass insullation that is wrapped around the middle shell. Heated air enters the top of the water heater and circulates around the inner water tank, giving up its heat to the tank. Cooler air leaves the bottom of the water heater and is returned to the SUNDANCE collectors for reheating and the cycle continues. The heated water from the SUNDANCE solar water tank is piped into the existing electric hot water heater. By providing preheated water to the electric water heater, the amount of time this water water would be required to run is substantially reduced. This arrangement results in a continuous flow of hot water and an uncomplicated system

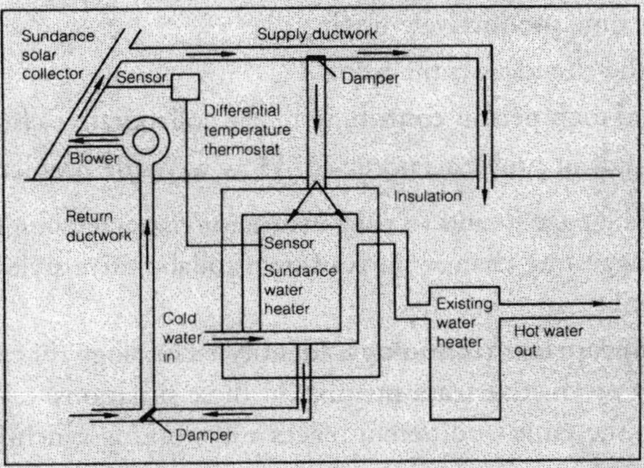

The differential temperature thermostat provides control over the entire SUNDANCE SYSTEM by controling the operation of the blower. In the winter operational mode, the unit turns the blower on when the collectors reach a preset temperature and off when they reach a preset minimum temperature. There is also a thermostat that will override the differential temperature thermostat and turn the system off if the building becomes too hot. In the summer mode, the operation of the temperature differential thermostat is a little more complex. The thermostat has two sensors connected to it. One from the SUNDANCE collector, and the other from the SUNDANCE hot water tank. The thermostat continuously monitors the temperatures at these two locations. The thermostat turns on the SUNDANCE SYSTEM when the temperature differential between the water tank and the collectors is greater than 40F, and off when the temperature differential is less than 20F. By maintaining a proper temperature difference between the collectors and the water tank and the collectors and the building, the SUNDANCE SYSTEM maintains maximum output and effeciency.

(c) **Write an analysis of the revised information sheet.** With your collaborator, prepare a memo to accompany the revised information sheet. This memo should identify the major changes you made and provide a rationale for them. Including "before" and "after" examples could illustrate your points. The memo should specifically address how the purpose, audience, organization and support, visuals, and document design affected your decisions.

2. **Evaluate your collaboration.** While conducting assignment #1, tape-record a planning session with your collaborator. After the assignment is completed, arrange a time when both you and your collaborator can listen to the tape together and then discuss the following questions. What interesting behaviors and patterns did you notice? Did anything surprise either of you when you listened to your collaboration? What does the tape reveal about the following issues:

   - Who was in charge? Was authority shared between the collaborators?
   - Was the time productively used?
   - Where did the ideas come from?
   - What did each person contribute to the collaborative effort?
   - What kinds of problems occurred? How were the problems resolved?

   Prepare a one-page memo to your instructor characterizing the the interaction and suggesting changes in your own collaborative style that you will work toward.

3. **Identify appropriate technology.** Identify technology that would enable you to be a productive team member in these situations: team members working in the same or different places and working synchronously or asynchronously.

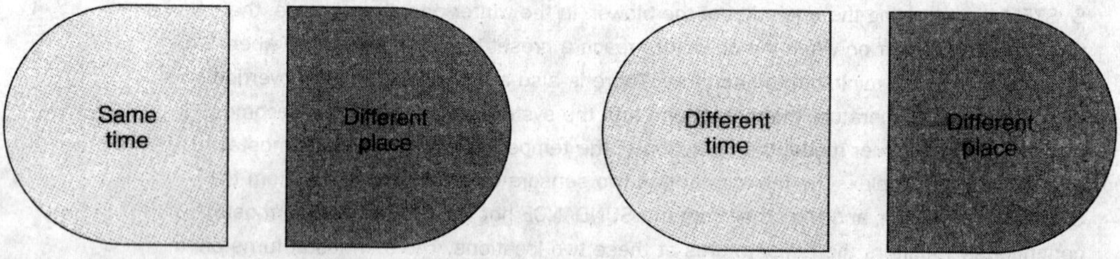

a. ______________________________

____

____

b. ______________________________

____

____

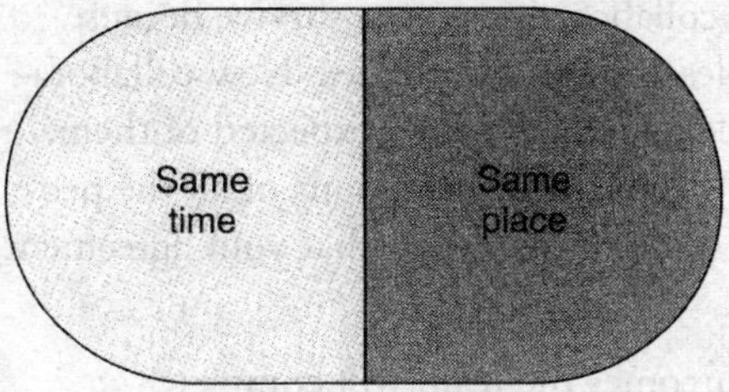

c. ______________________

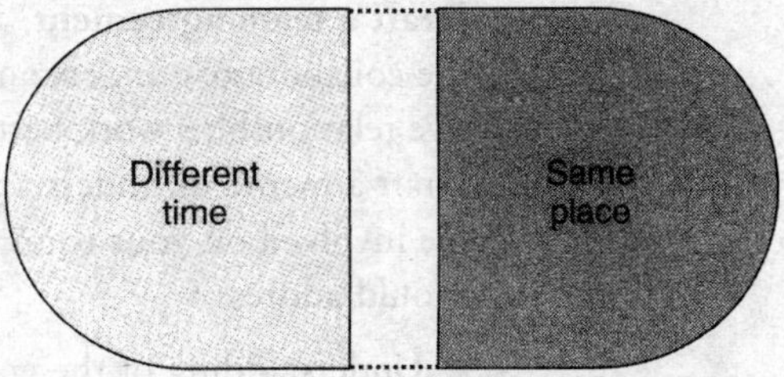

d. ______________________

To learn more about workspace awareness on teams, go to **www.english.wadsworth.com/burnett6e** for a link to an article that summarizes a number of issues about computer-supported cooperative work.

CLICK ON WEBLINK

CLICK on Chapter 5/team awareness

WEBLINK

4. Examine collaboration in your discipline.

(a) Survey a key professional journal in a specific discipline (your own field or another that interests you). Select three years — say, 1950, 1970, and 1990; 1960, 1980, and 2000; or 1983, 1993, 2003 — to determine changes in the percentage of coauthored articles. Present your findings in a table or a graph, and prepare a brief oral explanation of the results.

(b) Interview a professional in your discipline (or one that interests you) to learn about the kinds of collaboration in which you'll be expected to participate. Prepare a series of questions based on the information presented in this chapter. Ask for specific examples of collaboration. In a paper for your classmates, discuss the information you learn. Be prepared to give an oral summary of your findings.

5. Identify parallels in writing and design. The processes that Omnica's industrial design team (highlighted earlier in the chapter) follows in designing products[25] are similar to those that good communication teams follow when designing effective documents and presentations. Identify at least six ways in which product design and development teams are similar to document design and development teams in processes and outcomes. Prepare a list with examples to share during class discussion.

6. **Draft a team agreement.** Successful collaborations often survive because the collaborators understand their roles and responsibilities. New collaborative relationships work better when people know what's expected of them. Draft a memo of understanding that details the expectations of all the people involved on your team. Here are some of the things that your agreement should address:

   - Understanding of the goals and outcomes the team will complete
   - Tasks each person is responsible for completing
   - Dates drafts and completed work are due
   - Ways collaborators will communicate: phone, e-mail, face-to-face meetings
   - Frequency of collaborators' communication with each other
   - Process for resolving disagreements
   - Order of authorship
   - Process of peer review
   - Quality of work expected

7. **Evaluate computer software.** Establish criteria for the effectiveness of a software program that enables some form of collaboration. Then use your criteria to determine whether the software is effective. Based on your own testing and review, write a short review suitable for a trade publication.

8. **What kind of tools that can aid collaboration have you used?**

   - ☐ E-mail
   - ☐ Group e-list messaging
   - ☐ Whiteboard
   - ☐ Electronic calendars
   - ☐ Threaded discussions
   - ☐ Shared databases
   - ☐ Track Changes tool for response and editing
   - ☐ Document archive and management
   - ☐ Electronic meeting rooms
   - ☐ Web conferences
   - ☐ Video conferences
   - ☐ Project and task management
   - ☐ Real-time chats
   - ☐ Group-decision support
   - ☐ ____________
   - ☐ ____________

9. **Track your own collaborative behavior.** One way to learn more about your collaborative processes is to track yourself as you prepare a technical document or oral presentation. The tracking process has three basic steps.

   (a) Keep a log (in a notebook or online) in which you record every time you work on the document or oral presentation (even just thinking about it counts). Indicate whether you are working individually or collaboratively. Record the date and the time you start and stop. Describe what happens during the time — what gets accomplished, what goes wrong, what you expected to get done but didn't (and why), and so on. Focus particularly on the interaction. Record the facts, but also jot down your attitudes and feelings.

(b) Review and analyze the log, looking for interesting incidents and patterns of behavior that you believe characterize your collaboration.

(c) Use your analysis to describe the nature of your own collaborative behavior. Prepare a detailed memo that focuses on no more than four specific aspects of your own collaborative behavior — for example, the way you approach tasks, the way you handle disagreements, and the way you approach leadership. Include some discussion about the way the collaboration affected the document or oral presentation you prepared.

Chapter 5 Endnotes

1 Courtesy of Sharon Burton-Hardin.

2 H1. (n.d.). *The H1 Experiment at HERA.* Retrieved October 3, 2003, from http://www-h1.desy.de/

3 Meadows, A.J. (1974). Chapter 7: Scientific Collaboration and Status. *Communication in Science.* London: Butterworth. p. 197.

4 National Science Board. (1998). *Science and Engineering Indicators 1998.* Chapter 5: Academic Research and Development: Financial and Personnel Resources, Integration With Graduate Education, and Outputs. Retrieved January 14, 2004, from http://www.nsf.gov/sbe/srs/seind98/c5/c5s4.htm

5 Omnica Product Development. (n.d.). *Industrial design.* Retrieved October 4, 2003, from http://www.omnica.com/industrial_design.htm

6 Methodist Health Care System Cystic Fibrosis Web site in Spanish and English. Retrieved October 4, 2003, from http://www.methodisthealth.com/spanish/respiratory/cystic.htm and http://www.methodisthealth.com/pulmonary/cystic.htm

7 Klineberg, S. (2002, September). *The Houston area survey 1982–present: Demographic transformations.* Retrieved October 5, 2003, from http://cohesion.rice.edu/centersandinst/has/hasreport.cfm?doc_id=1238

8 Walker, B. *Is corporate America kicking the travel habit? Poll finds collaboration technologies taking hold as predicted.* Retrieved October 4, 2003, from http://www.phoneplusmag.com/articles/2b1collaborate2.html.

Wainhouse Research (2002, September 4). *Wainhouse survey of business travelers tracks use of collaborative technologues.* Retrieved October 4, 2003, from http://www.wainhouse.com/prtravhab0902.html

9 Walker, B. *Is corporate America kicking the travel habit? Poll finds collaboration technologies taking hold as predicted.* Retrieved October 4, 2003, from http://www.phoneplusmag.com/articles/2b1collaborate2.html.

Wainhouse Research (2002, September 4). *Wainhouse survey of business travelers tracks use of collaborative technologues.* Retrieved October 4, 2003, from http://www.wainhouse.com/prtravhab0902.html

10 Courtesy of Allan Ackerson.

11 Berdondini, L., & Fantacci, F. (n.d.). *Training on listening and peer support.* Retrieved October 5, 2003, from http://www.comune.torino.it/novasres/_private/ascolto.pdf

12 A version of these questions was originally developed as part of the author's work for the Making Thinking Visible Project for the Center for the Study of Writing, Berkeley and Carnegie Mellon, funded by the Heinz Endowment of the Pittsburgh Foundation.

13 © 1998 Massachusetts Institute of Technology Alumni Association.

14 Modified from information at usabilityfirst.com: (1) Brinck, T. (1998). *Groupware: Introduction.* Retrieved October 4, 2003, from http://www.usabilityfirst.com/groupware/intro.txl; (2) Brinck, T. (1998). *Groupware: Applications.* Retrieved October 4, 2003, from http://www.usabilityfirst.com/groupware/applications.txl.

15 This scenario is from Haeussler, A. (n.d.). *Supporting groupware with awareness.* Retrieved October 4, 2003, from http://www.sapdesignguild.org/editions/edition5/awareness.asp.

16 Team awareness is a widely considered computer-supported cooperative work (CSCW) topic. Information from these sources contributed to the discussion in this chapter: (1) Ferscha, A. (n.d.). *Workplace awareness in mobile virtual teams.* Retrieved October 4, 2003, from http://www.soft.uni-linz.ac.at/Research/Publications/_Documents/WETICE2000.pdf; (2) Jang, C. Y., Steinfield, C., & Pfaff B. (December 2, 2000). *Supporting awareness among virtual teams in a web-based collaborative system: The TeamSCOPE system.* Retrieved October 4, 2003, from http://216.239.37.104/search?q=cache:xajSfQOCiQsJ:cscw.msu.edu/reports/cscw2000.pdf+%22Supporting+awareness+among+virtual+teams+in+a+web-based+collaborative+system:+The+TeamSCOPE=system%22&hl=en&ie=UTF-8

17 Modified from information at (1) Brinck, T. (1998). *Groupware: Design issues.* Retrieved October 4, 2003, from http://www.usabilityfirst.com/groupware/design-issues.txl; (2) Haeussler, A. (n.d.). *Supporting groupware with awareness.* Retrieved October 4, 2003, from http://www.sapdesignguild.org/editions/edition5/awareness.asp

18 Ford, J. (2003, May). *Integrating the internet into conflict management systems.* Retrieved October 4, 2003, from http://www.mediate.com/articles/ford10.cfm

19 Adapted from Gillette, B., Johnson, R., Polashek, E., Thornburg, J., & White, C. *The art of working together: A guide to collaboration* (p. 5), Ames, IA: Iowa State University, Department of English.

20 Cohen, J., & Taubles, G. (1995). The culture of credit. *Science, 268*(5218), 1707.

21 Cohen, J., & Taubles, G. (1995). The culture of credit. *Science, 268*(5218), 1706.

22 Haskins, M., Liedtka, J., & Rosenblum, J. (1988). Beyond teams: Toward an ethic of collaboration. *Organizational Dynamics, 26*(4), 34–51.

23 Dilbert reprinted by permission of United Features Syndicate, Inc.

24 See Bosley, D. S. (1993). Whose culture is it anyway? *Technical Communication Quarterly,* (Winter), 186–200.

25 Omnica Product Development. (n.d.). *Ergonomics is more than a buzzword.* Retrieved October 4, 2003, from http://www.omnica.com/omniview_industrial_design2.htm

PART II

Managing Critical Processes

掌握信息筛选过程

CHAPTER 6

Locating and Using Information
搜集与使用信息

本章是关于知识管理的前期步骤，即为了帮助交流对象了解某一个主题而采取的发现、筛选、组织、综合及运用信息的体系。能否成为成功的交流者主要取决于对相关信息的掌握和使用以及把这些信息转化为自己的知识。本章首先介绍了通过一手和二手资料库找到与自己研究相关的信息。本章特别介绍了如何寻找并能运用与自己研究相关的电子资源库，如通过高级查询方法进行有针对性的电子文档搜索。另外，本章还阐释了通过内部档案记录、企业图书馆、个人观察、访谈、信件咨询及问卷调查等方法搜集相关研究信息。最后，本章强调在把研究结果写成文字的过程中要按照职业规范引用数据，避免抄袭。

Objectives and Outcomes 学习目标

This chapter will help you accomplish these outcomes:

- Identify and use electronic database resources relevant to your research
- Execute a specific, targeted electronic search using advanced search techniques
- Gather research data using several nonelectronic techniques
- Integrate research successfully into your text
- Avoid plagiarism

This chapter is about the beginning steps of *knowledge management*, which, broadly defined, is a system for finding, selecting, organizing, synthesizing, and using information in order to improve your audience's understanding of a particular topic.[1] Your success as a communicator depends in large part on your ability to master and use the information in this chapter, to turn it into knowledge for yourself. More specifically, the quality of your communication depends on your care and thoroughness in effectively using appropriate information. The credibility and completeness of this information affect the audience's acceptance of your points. The following diagram shows one way to think of the knowledge management process, which may be a new name for a process you already use.[2] Although this process is displayed as linear, it is in fact recursive, with the possibility of returning to any earlier step at anytime during the process.

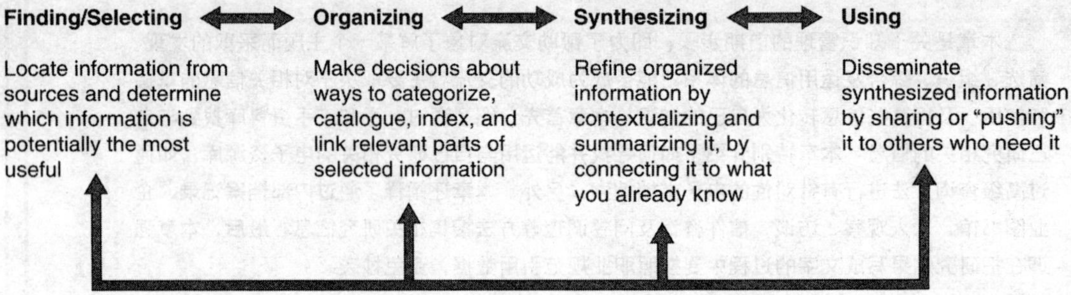

What's the difference between information and knowledge? The two terms are often used interchangeably, but many workplace professionals prefer not to use them as synonyms. *Information* is what we use as the building blocks for knowledge. We construct information from what we read, observe, hear, and experience in many other ways. *Knowledge* is what we *know.* It involves thinking about information, learning information, interacting with others as we shape and are shaped by information, and, probably most important, connecting information to other aspects of our prior knowledge. We construct both our tacit, unarticulated knowledge and our explicit, articulated knowledge. We express our knowledge in what we say, write, and design as well as in how we act — gestures, body language, and actions, including the attitudes we express and the processes we use.[3]

This chapter is about one of the first steps in knowledge management: finding and selecting information from a variety of sources. The following examples are typical of situations in which workplace professionals might collect information for technical documents, presentations, or visuals:

- A biomechanical engineer calculates the expected reduction in noise pollution in a call center office from using cubicles made primarily from recycled rubber and sends the results on to the marketing team.

- A polymer chemist spends several hours searching a computerized database to locate information for use in an internal proposal about new techniques to strengthen carbon fibers.
- An industrial engineer designs a survey for technicians as part of a study to assess the effectiveness of industrial degreasers, which will contribute to decisions about whether to change the current formula.
- A technical communicator has been corresponding with his senior application designer about changes made to the new version of their storage server management application, which he is documenting.
- A financial analyst examines online government documents to check details of recent changes in the tax code, which affects recommendations to the writers and graphic designers working on the organization's annual report.
- A hydrologist has spent 30 minutes reading abstracts in *Pollution Abstracts and Water Resources Abstracts,* an index that includes research on contamination of ground water, in order to decide what articles to read in their entirety.

How does each situation require knowledge management as it's defined on the preceding page?

What situations in your discipline require professionals to collect information?

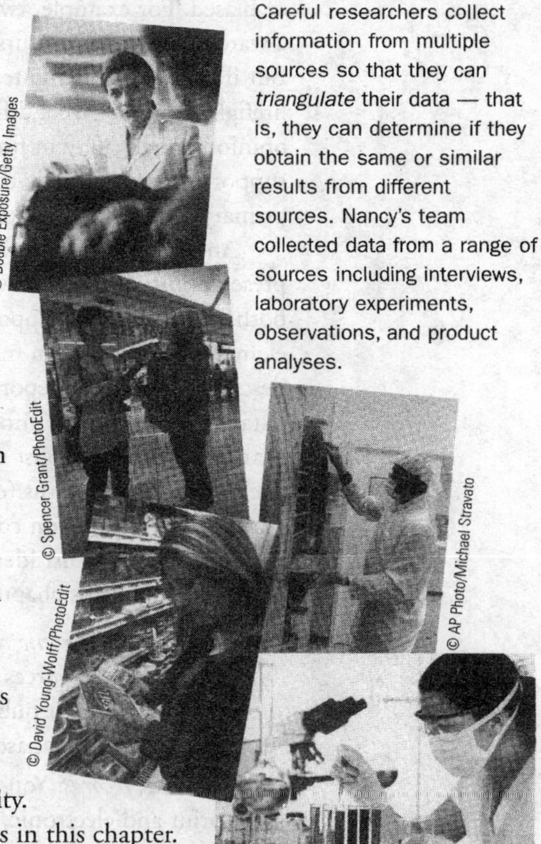

© Double Exposure/Getty Images
© Spencer Grant/PhotoEdit
© AP Photo/Michael Stravato
© David Young-Wolff/PhotoEdit
© Comstock Images/Alamy

Careful researchers collect information from multiple sources so that they can *triangulate* their data — that is, they can determine if they obtain the same or similar results from different sources. Nancy's team collected data from a range of sources including interviews, laboratory experiments, observations, and product analyses.

For major projects in your own discipline, you'll need to collect information in the workplace as well as in the library. For example, Nancy Irish, a nutritionist who has worked for government agencies as well as private groups, is investigating the ecological and nutritional benefits of soy protein and its potential for greater use in U.S. diets. Her preliminary work involves academic research, using library resources to review available literature about soy proteins and tofu. Then she conducts interviews and surveys to determine people's attitudes toward tofu and obtains tofu samples from local stores and food cooperatives to determine availability and quality. Some of her research techniques are included as examples in this chapter.

Locating Primary and Secondary Sources

找到第一手和第二手信息资源

Technical professionals can collect information and data from a variety of primary and secondary sources. Primary source information is first-hand information reported by people directly involved with an action or event, not interpreted by a second or third party. Secondary source information does not come directly from people involved in the action or event. Instead, the information is interpreted and reported by a second or third person. Most information has the potential to be both a primary and a secondary source. For example, if an engineer conducts an experiment and then reports her findings, her technical report is a primary source. However, if that same engineer is interviewed about her experiment by a technical writer who writes an article about the experiment, that article is a secondary source.

Whether you decide to use primary or secondary sources, check the credentials of the source, the sponsoring agency, and the date the information was obtained because both primary and secondary sources can potentially be slanted or biased. For example, two firefighters who worked to put out a chemical fire in a warehouse could give first-hand, primary reports about fighting chemical fires. But if one of the firefighters had been injured during the chemical fire, that firefighter might give a different account of the specific fire and have a different opinion about safety in firefighting. On the other hand, a local politician supported financially by the company where the fire occurred might try to use the primary sources to downplay the company's accountability for the fire.

Another important point to consider when planning a technical document, presentation, or visual is whether it calls for quantitative or qualitative data, or both, as evidence to support your positions. *Quantitative data* describe measurable elements (quantities) in mathematical or statistical terms. *Qualitative data* describe observed or reported information (qualities). However, after qualitative data are recorded, the information can sometimes be treated quantitatively. For example, a field biologist might record observations of a cane toad population over a period of months (qualitative data). The number of observations of a particular phenomenon could then be counted (quantitative data).

The following list identifies some of the ways of managing the information you collect that this chapter discusses:

- *Print and electronic resources.* You can search, read, and analyze information from print resources (college, corporate, and community library resources and government publications) and large digital databases (library and government databases, as well as Web sites).
- *Internal records.* You can analyze an organization's proprietary records, both print and electronic, in order to gather information about practices and activities.
- *Personal observations.* You record and analyze information that you see, smell, taste, or feel in order to document a process or experience first-hand.
- *Interviews and letters of inquiry.* You can use face-to-face meetings or correspondence with knowledgeable people to gather information not readily available.
- *Surveys and polls.* Using a list of targeted questions, you can gather information from a large representative sample of people.

- *Empirical research.* You can collect information by conducting empirical research, which is an observational study or an experiment to answer a question, address a problem, or test a hypothesis or observable pattern. During empirical research, you collect various kinds of data, including physical samples and specimens that you categorize and analyze in order to identify features, and use standard formulas to help analyze, interpret, and assess your data. You record and categorize information, analyze and interpret data in ways that make sense to others, and then develop various narratives to explain your interpretation.

Empirical and experimental are not synonyms: Empirical research is the superordinate category; experimental research is one of the subcategories. What is an example of a research project in your professional area that is empirical but not experimental? What is an example of a research project that is empirical and also experimental?

All of these common ways to collect information are not mutually exclusive. For example, you could conduct an empirical investigation that involves an analysis of an organization's internal records. During a face-to-face interview, you could make specific reference to that person's Web site and online publications. The primary value of this list is in providing you with a range of options for collecting technical information when you have a problem to solve. The next section of the chapter focuses on electronic resources.

Keeping a list of useful portals will make your work life much easier. Go to **www.english.wadsworth.com/burnett6e** for links to useful portals.
CLICK ON WEBLINK
CLICK on Chapter 6/portals

WWW
WEBLINK

ETHICS 职业道德规范知识吧 SIDEBAR

On-the-Job Pressures: Ethics and Technology in the Workplace 工作压力：职业道德与技术

Consider the following on-the-job actions:

- Sabotaging the systems or data of a current or former coworker or employer
- Accessing private computer files without permission
- Listening to a private cellular phone conversation
- Accessing pornographic Web sites using office equipment
- Using office equipment to search for another job
- Copying the company's software for home use
- Wrongly blaming an error on a technological glitch

Have you engaged in any of the unethical actions listed on the previous page?

Did you consider them unethical at the time?

What would be the most effective deterrent to keep you from engaging in them in the future?

- Making multiple copies of software for office use
- Using office equipment to shop on the Internet for personal needs

Which of these actions would you find unethical? All of them are unethical, according to the Ethics Officer Association (EOA), the professional association for managers of corporate ethics and compliance programs. In 1998, the EOA, along with the American Society of Chartered Life Underwriters and Chartered Financial Consultants, conducted a nationwide survey of American workers "to measure whether or not the presence of new technologies in the workplace increases the risk of unethical and illegal business practices."[4] Nearly half (45%) of the respondents to the survey indicated they had engaged in at least one unethical act.

The survey found that business and technical professionals feel pressured by new workplace technologies. The pressures caused by workplace technologies include increased productivity expectations; the continual need to change or update the technology; increased frustration with coworkers who are not up to date on the technology; less tolerance for errors; inadequate manuals and/or training; and the fear of losing data. Female respondents felt more pressure (70%) than male respondents (51%), largely due to a "lack of understanding terminology or lingo." "New technologies have changed the way we do our jobs and the way we work with one another," said EOA Executive Director Ed Petry when the survey results were announced. "We're expected to do more, to do it faster, and we're also working more independently."

What are some solutions to these ethical problems? Survey respondents offered several, including creating guidelines for the personal use of company technology resources, installing Internet-blocking software, and encouraging employees to police themselves. For technical professionals, perhaps the best individual advice is to be aware of how these actions can cause unnecessary workplace conflicts. Avoiding these conflicts will help make workplace technology more of an asset and less of a liability. (See discussion of unproductive conflicts in Chapter 5.)

Finding Information Using Electronic Resources

运用电子资源发现信息

Odds are that whenever you begin research for a new paper or project, you probably start on the World Wide Web or in your university's online catalog. But less than 15 years ago, electronic resources were available only for a fee and with the assistance of a specially trained librarian. Now, electronic resources are widely available — not only in public, college, and corporate library databases, but also through the Internet. Knowing where to look for information can be a daunting task in the face of the thousands of available research databases and millions of public Web sites. The following section describes several types of electronic databases and catalogs where you can begin your research; the section after that offers specific pointers to help you search these electronic resources effectively.

Scientific and technical databases are remarkably important when you're searching for information. Go to **www.english.wadsworth.com/burnett6e** for a link to a detailed discussion of databases.

CLICK ON WEBLINK

CLICK on Chapter 6/databases

WWW

WEBLINK

Finding Electronic Resources 发现电子资源

Your college, company, and community libraries, as well as your link to the Internet, give you access to a vast array of computerized databases and indices, which are searchable digital repositories of published material. Electronic databases have largely replaced print card catalogs and reference books in most well-funded libraries because they can be far more easily and cheaply updated on a regular basis. Because available information is increasing at a rate faster than anyone can manage to read it, professionals in most fields learn to use computerized databases that give them an overview of current information and research in their fields. Database searches can be helpful to you in several different ways:

- To prepare a literature review
- To stay abreast of current information and research
- To locate answers to specific questions
- To locate resources in the form of citations, abstracts, or full-text articles

When using electronic resources, you receive specific types of information for each returned "hit." You receive the name of the book or article, its author(s), and the date of publication. Other bibliographic information depends on the database. For example, library catalogs often include the publication's call number, ISBN or ISSN, and location in the library, as well as the category of a particular book. External databases generally do not provide call numbers but do identify where the article was originally published, so you can locate it in the library.

Most electronic databases return three types of hits to your topical search: citations, abstracts, and full-text articles. A *citation* provides only bibliographic information such as title, author(s), and journal or publisher; to use the article or book you must locate it in the original form. An *abstract* lists bibliographic information about the article and a short summary, either provided by the author(s) or written by a database indexer. Abstracts can be used to eliminate articles that are not related or are only tangentially related to your research, which can save a great deal of time when you are conducting a broad search. And finally, a *full-text article* is usually an HTML version of the entire article as it was published in the original setting, including the full bibliographic citation. Full-text articles are easy to print and use immediately but can pose problems when you attempt to appropriately cite page numbers from the article in your final document. Whether your search returns a citation, abstract, or full-text article depends on the database, the library holdings, and that company's agreement with the original source.

When researching a new topic, consider searching electronic sources in the following order:

- Library's online catalog
- Online reference materials
- General reference databases
- Discipline-specific databases
- Government databases
- The Internet and World Wide Web

What do you think is the rationale for this order of investigtion?

What specific electronic resources are available in your own college or university library?

Online Catalog. The online catalog in a specific library is a database that lists all of the library's holdings: books, bound periodicals (a year's issues of a particular journal bound into a single volume), audiovisual (AV) holdings (films, records, audio- and videotapes), and electronic resources (e-books, e-journals).

You can use the online catalog to determine if the library has books, bound periodicals, or AV materials relevant to your subject.

Each book or other item is assigned an individual number based on either the Dewey decimal system or the Library of Congress classification system. Public libraries generally use the Dewey decimal system, whereas college and university libraries use the Library of Congress system. The Dewey decimal system divides books into ten categories, each identified by a range of numbers. The Library of Congress system divides books into twenty categories, each identified by a letter followed by specific numbers. The broad letter categories represent major subject areas.

In both the Dewey decimal and the Library of Congress systems, the broad categories are further subdivided until each book has an individual number — the call number — that helps you locate specific volumes in library stacks. Being familiar with call numbers enables you to go into the stacks and browse though the books in your specific field of interest. Browsing does not constitute efficient use of time, but you often find volumes of interest that you might have ignored had you only read the online information about a book.

Nancy Irish began her search using the online catalog at Iowa State University in order to locate current resources about nutritional benefits of soy protein. Following the on-screen directions, she had several choices: She could search for information by author, title, subject, or keyword. The keyword option is the one Nancy decided to use. Figure 6.1 shows selected screens that appeared when Nancy was conducting her search.

© Frank Chmura/Index Stock Imagery

FIGURE 6.1 Online Catalog Screen[5]

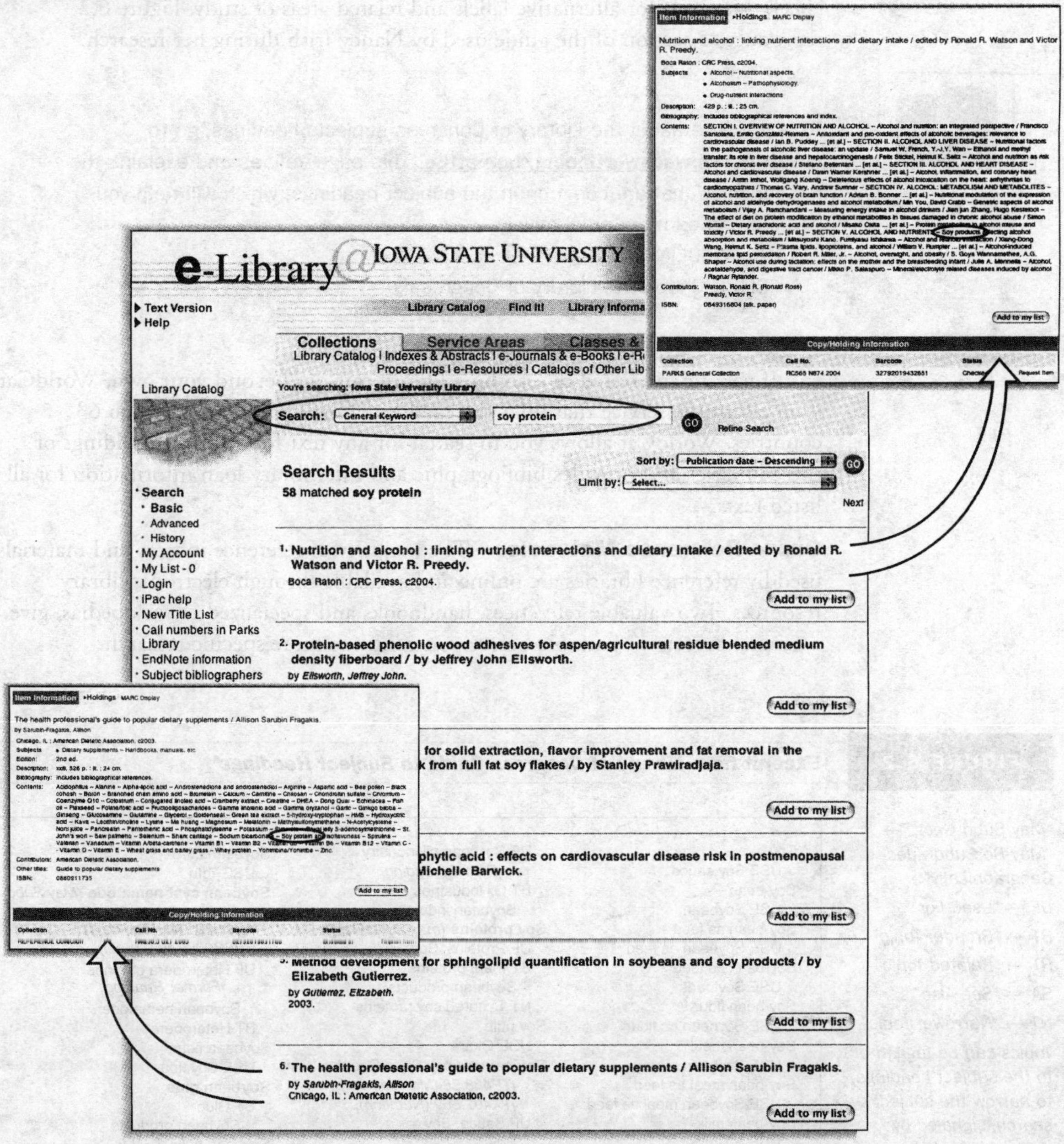

The *Library of Congress Guide to Subject Headings* is also valuable to use. After one or two attempts at identifying the topic(s) under which a subject is cataloged, check this guide for alternative labels and related areas of study. Figure 6.2 reproduces a section of the guide used by Nancy Irish during her research.

WEBLINK

To learn more about the Library of Congress subjects headings, go to **www.english.wadsworth.com/burnett6e.** This page defines and explains the relationships that are common in the subject headings, which will help you use the entries more productively.

CLICK WEBLINK

CLICK Chapter 6/Library of Congress

If you are interested in searching library catalogs beyond your own, WorldCat is an electronic service that links the catalogs of over 23,000 libraries in 63 countries. WorldCat allows you to search for any text found in the holdings of these libraries and provides bibliographic and interlibrary loan information for all listed texts.

Online Reference Materials. The majority of reference indices and materials used by reference libraries are online and available through electronic library resources. Two valuable references, handbooks and specialized encyclopedias, give a general overview of a topic before you continue more specific research.

FIGURE 6.2 **Excerpt from *Library of Congress Guide to Subject Headings*[6]**

"May Subd Geog" → "May Be Subdivided Geographically"
UF → "Used For"
BT → "Broader Topic"
RT → "Related Topic"
SA → "See Also"
NT → "Narrower Topic"
Topics can be tagged on to the subject headings to narrow the subject search, signaled by dashed lines (- -).

Soy
  USE Soy sauce
Soy-bean
  USE Soybean
Soy-bean as feed
  USE Soybean as feed
Soy-bean as food
  USE Soyfoods
Soy-bean flour
  USE Soybean as flour
Soy-bean meal
  USE Soybean meal
Soy-bean meal as feed
  USE Soybean meal as feed
Soy-bean milk
  USE Soymilk
Soy-bean mosaic virus
  USE Soybean mosaic virus
Soy-bean oil
  USE Soy oil
Soy... oil mills

  UF Soybean oil industry
    [Former heading]
  BT Oil industries
    Soybean industry
Soy proteins *(may Subd Geog)*
  UF Proteins, Soy
  BT Plant proteins
    Soybean products
  NT Textured soy proteins
Soy pulp
  USE Okara
Soy sauce *(may Subd Geog)*
  [TP438.56 (Manufacture)]
  [TX407.569 (Nutrition)]
  UF Sauce, Soy
    Soy
    Soya sauce
  BT Fermented soyfoods
  RT Cookery (Soy sauce)
Soy sauce industry *(may Subd Geog)*

Soybean curd
  USE Tofu
Soybean cyst nematode *(May Subd Geog)*
  [QL391.N4 (Zoology)]
  [SB9098.S68 (Pest)]
  UF Heterodera glycines
    [Former Heading]
    Soybean nematode
  BT Heterodera
Soybean flour
  USE Soy flour
Soybean glue
  BT Glue
    Soybean products
Soybean hulls
  USE Soy bran
Soybean industry *(May Subd Geog)*
  [HD9235.S6-HD9235.S62]
  BT Vegetable trade
  NT Soy oil industry

Handbooks usually present compact, carefully organized information in tables, charts, diagrams, graphs, and glossaries. Handbooks in both print and electronic format are available in astronomy, biological science, biomedical science, chemistry, computer science, engineering, environmental science, geoscience, mathematics, physics, and virtually every other major field of technical and scientific inquiry. Electronic handbooks include *CHEMNetBASE* for chemists and *ENGNetBASE* for engineers; however, using the print form may be easier since you can flip to the section very quickly.

Specialized encyclopedias and a variety of business and industry guides are invaluable for initial inquiries because the entries provide an overview, summarizing and discussing essential facts and theories about a subject. The entries also often present statistical data in various visual forms, provide historical background, and list bibliographic references. Encyclopedias for a wide range of technical topics are published in both print and electronic versions. For example, the *Encyclopedia of Life Science* and the *Encyclopedia of Virology* are available in both print and electronic forms.

General Reference Databases. Once you have completed a general topic search in the library catalog and reference books, you can do a topic search to look for published articles in one of the common general reference databases available at most college, corporate, and community libraries. Libraries usually pay a per-student fee to gain permission to link to the online database through their computers or Web site. These reference databases, specifically designed for undergraduate researchers, cull citations and articles from a variety of academic journals, periodicals, and newspapers. They can provide a good overview of a topic from popular academic journals and the popular press but generally do not index the more research-oriented technical publications and journals. Three common general reference databases found in libraries are *Expanded Academic ASAP, LexisNexis,* and *Web of Science.*

- *Expanded Academic ASAP* is a highly generalized database that indexes citations, abstracts, and full-text articles from journals, periodicals, and national newspapers in a wide variety of disciplines, including the humanities, social sciences, general sciences, and technology.
- *LexisNexis* is a general topical database that pulls articles, usually in full text, from global newspapers, business and news periodicals, and government publications. It is an excellent resource to investigate current topics or issues that are frequently in the news, such as cloning or global warming.
- *Web of Science* is a metaindex of over 8,500 journals that searches three smaller indexes: *Science Citation Index Expanded, Social Sciences Citation Index,* and *Arts & Humanities Citation Index.* It provides citations and abstracts, as well as the list of works cited for each article. This allows you to search for articles that cite a particular article. Accessing these databases can provide you with an overview of a topic so you can narrow and define your research as you work through a project.

Discipline-Specific Databases. Most academic disciplines have electronic databases that index research and publications in that discipline. Some are published by professional organizations in the field, others by for-profit companies. These databases allow you to search publications and reports specific to the field and often include publications that are not listed in more general databases. Depending on your library's funding, you may be able to find many of these resources in print, CD, and online format. These are only a few of the hundreds of discipline-specific indexes available:

- *AGRICOLA* (AGRI) is a database of the National Agricultural Library, indexing more than 3,300,000 citations in the agricultural literature since 1970.
- *Avery* is an index of architectural periodicals, covering architecture, interior design, and city planning since 1977.
- *Compendex* is a general database for engineering, known in its print version as the *Engineering Index.*
- *MEDLINE* is a general index of the National Library of Medicine, covering over 4000 international biomedical journals.
- *NTIS* (National Technical Information Service) is a database of unrestricted technical reports for U.S.- and non-U.S.–government-sponsored projects.
- *ScienceDirect* is a general, massive, electronic database covering all sciences and some social sciences.

In many cases, several abstracting indexes are available for a single discipline. Because these indexs may not draw from the same sources, you should check the publications to ensure that particular journals are covered. For example, biology abstracts and citations can be found in many indexes, including *Biological Abstracts, Biological Abstracts/RRM, Biological and Agricultural Index, Biology Digest,* and *BioOne.*

Government Documents and Offices. Another source for valuable information on a variety of topics is the U.S. government, which is required by law to publicly post many of its documents, research findings, and proceedings. Virtually all agencies of the U.S. government have public Web sites that are updated regularly, making their information easily and cheaply accessible. For example, the U.S. Census Bureau has the most recent census online (**http://www.census.gov**), the FBI posts its Most Wanted list (**http://www.fbi. gov/mostwant.html**), and the Federal Aviation Administration publishes many of its regulations (**http://www.faa.gov**). Several other government sites are interesting and useful:

- Federal Deposit Insurance Corporation (FDIC) — **http://www.fdic.gov**
- Fish and Wildlife Service — **http://www.fws.gov**
- Library of Congress — **http://www.loc.gov**
- Patent and Trademark Office — **http://www.uspto.gov**

- Securities and Exchange Commission (SEC) — **http://www.sec.gov**
- Smithsonian Institution — **http://www.si.edu**

An extremely useful resource for federally funded government research is supported by the Office of Scientific and Technical Information (**http://www.osti.gov**), which enables users to search across multiple collections of preprint, noncommercial, and peer-reviewed journal literature with a focus on physical sciences and technology. For example, the *EnergyFiles* collection (**http://www.osti.gov/EnergyFiles/**) provides information, tools, and technologies to facilitate the use of scientific resources in planning and conducting energy-related research from over 500 databases and Web sites.

While some government documents that may be of value to you may not be available electronically, many national repositories for government documents have electronically indexed their holdings. For example, Iowa State University (ISU) is one of many national repositories; its electronically indexed holdings are searchable through ISU's library catalog.

Which repository of government documents is closest to you?

Web Research. While the terms *Internet* and *World Wide Web* are often used synonymously, they actually refer to two different things. The Internet is the technical infrastructure over which content in the form of Web pages, chat relays, and newsgroups flows.[7] The Web enables anyone with access to a Web server (a computer that connects a group of users to one another and to the Web) to publish documents on it. Because of the Web, very little time is needed to make new information available around the world, with minimal printing or delivery costs.

Photographs from the Hubble telescope were made available by NASA on the Web minutes after they were taken. In contrast, most of a day is needed for photographs to be published in newspapers, months to be published in professional journals, and sometimes years to be published in scholarly books.

What are the trade-offs to online publication, which makes information available to users more quickly than traditional print media?

Search engines, both general and discipline-specific, are a good place to start doing Web research. Many engines are available online today, but some of the most reliable and well-respected include **www.google.com**, **www.yahoo.com**, **www.excite.com**, and **www.metacrawler.com**. Disciplines may also have their own free or subscription-based search engines on the Web, which can usually be located through a discipline's professional organizations. For example, SPIN Web (**http://ojps.aip.org/spinweb/**) is a subscription search engine for physics journals and research records, and EEVL (**www.eevl.ac.uk**) is a free search engine for engineering, mathematics, and computer science sites.

Newsgroups allow users to correspond by "posting" and "replying to" messages from other users on the Internet through a special newsreader interface. Lists (e.g., LISTSERV and Majordomo) are automatic mailing list servers that transmit e-mail only to individuals who have subscribed to the list. Newsgroups are separated into more than 25,000 different subjects. Their titles usually begin with a prefix followed by a period and then a suffix such as *alt, soc, comp, misc, rec,* or *sci.* Lists are often associated with professional organizations or particular professions. (See Chapter 13 for netiquette for newsgroups and lists.)

Searching Electronic Resources 搜索电子资源

The amount of information available in print and online is astounding — and growing exponentially every year. Researchers at Berkeley have estimated that between 1 and 2 exabytes (an exabyte = one billion gigabytes) of unique information is produced by the world every year, and printed documents of all kinds make up only 0.03% of the total.[8] Corporations, universities, research institutions, and even governments are moving more and more print information to online formats, which makes searching for information both easier and more complicated. With these vast electronic resources available, you must develop advanced electronic search techniques to effectively sort and select relevant information. This section explores techniques that can help you more effectively search, sort, and find information in electronic resources.

We often don't think about "the best way" to execute a search as being dependent on the particular preferences of a search engine, but understanding how to effectively word and punctuate a request can save you a great deal of time. Before you begin a search in a new database or electronic resource, take a minute to read the Help or About page that is usually located in the main navigation bar of the site. Nearly all respectable electronic resources have these pages, which are designed to give users suggestions about the best ways to complete effective and targeted searches. The Help page tells you which search strategies and punctuation are most effective in that resource and explain how to limit or broaden your searches using search menu options.

Once you are familiar with a particular electronic resource, you should also consider ways to approach your search. Developing a search strategy helps you focus your ideas so that you get information that is useful, but it also saves you time (and money). Consider the following critical questions:

- What are your key terms? What are synonyms for these terms? What alternative terms are used to refer to the topic?
- What indexing source does the database use?
- How do you want to combine the terms?

Many electronic resources allow to you search in a variety of ways, including by keyword, subject, author, or title. Author and title searches allow you to quickly find pieces by one author or a particular piece. But more often than not, you will not know a specific author or title; therefore, you will use a keyword or subject search. Though they may seem like synonymous terms, keyword and subject searches return very different results.

Before you read the next two subsections, consider why keyword and subject searches return different results.

Keyword Searches. *Keywords* are flexible search terms that can be words, parts of words, phrases, or some combination of these that relate to your topic. You can generate a list of possible keywords when you develop your topic search strategy; consider not only exact topic phrases but also synonyms or related words that might generate hits in the database. Use keyword searches at the beginning of your search when you are trying to get a feel for the type of information that is available about your topic. Because keyword searches search the database for particular words, not specific topics, they often return results that might not be directly related to your topic. At that point you can use the search limiters offered by the resource or add additional keywords to narrow the field.[9]

To complete a keyword search, choose "keyword" from the resource's search menu and type your keywords in the search field. Figure 6.3 illustrates some advanced and Boolean search techniques you can use to combine or eliminate keywords in your search, depending on the preferences of the database as noted on its Help page.

Subject Searches. Subjects are different from keywords because *subjects* are predetermined categories that you can search within the database. Figure 6.4 shows how subject and keyword searches produced different results for Nancy Irish. Many databases use the subject headings defined by the U.S. Library of Congress. These subject headings are listed in alphabetical order in the *Library of Congress Subject Headings (LCSH),* which is available in both print and online editions. The *LCSH* lists both the subject headings and other common phrasings with pointers to the appropriate subject heading. Some disciplines have their own published subject listing guides, so be sure to ask your reference librarian about these resources. To complete a subject search, browse through the *LCSH* or the subject guide provided by the electronic resource, choose Subject Search from the search menu, and type the exacting wording of the subject heading in the search field.[10]

While keyword, subject, author, and title are the most common criteria for general topic searching, many electronic resources offer several ways to further

FIGURE 6.3 **Advanced and Boolean Search Limiters[11]**

Be sure to read the Help or About page for each database to determine which advanced search techniques a particular search engine recognizes.

Search Goal	Strategy	Example	Variation
Search for exact keyword phrase	Group words by enclosing in quotation marks or linking words with underscores	"BT plant proteins"; BT_plant_proteins	
Search for multiple keywords in same document	Type all keywords without punctuation or group terms by Boolean AND	Soymilk Soyfoods Tofu; Soymilk AND Soyfoods AND Tofu	Some engines use + rather than AND
Exclude keywords from search	Use the Boolean AND NOT	Soyfoods AND NOT Tofu	Some engines use − rather than AND NOT
Include spelling or synonym variations	Use the Boolean OR and/or parentheses	Tofu AND (soybeans OR soy-beans)	The combination or elimination of OR or parenthesis depends on the search engine
Search for variation of word endings	Use * after the stem	Soy* will return all results including Soybean, Soymilk, Soyfood, etc.	

limit your hits. For example, many resources allow you to specify important parameters:

Which parameters are important for searches you might conduct?

- *Time frame.* Do you want information from the past ten years? Five years? Only the current year?
- *Types of materials.* Do you want only books? Articles? Articles in refereed publications? Audiovisual materials? Presentations?
- *Language(s).* Do you want materials only in English? Also in German? French? Russian? Spanish? Chinese?
- *Print format.* Do you want only the titles? The full citation? The complete record with the abstract if it's available? The full text?

Developing a search strategy and using these advanced search techniques will help you make effective use of your time.

FIGURE 6.4 Comparison of Search with Subject and Keyword[12]

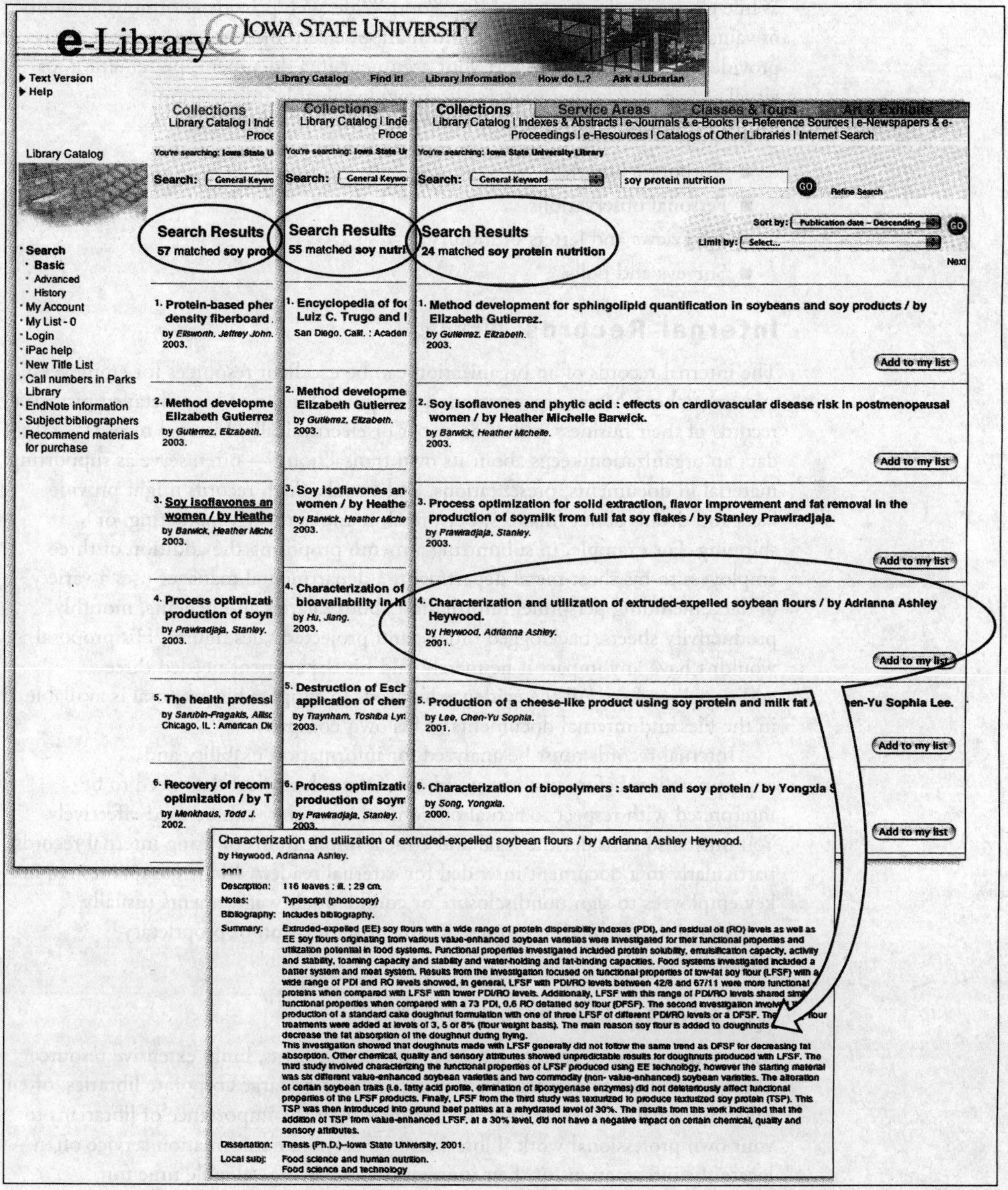

Finding Information Using Other Resources
运用其他资源发现信息

While electronic databases and the World Wide Web provide enormous amounts of valuable (and not so valuable) information, electronic resources cannot always provide specific data to support your argument in a document, presentation, or visual. A variety of other sources also provide valuable information:

- Internal records
- Corporate libraries
- Personal observations
- Interviews and letters of inquiry
- Surveys and polls

Internal Records 内部记录

The internal records of an organization can be excellent resources for employees and researchers. Many organizations are required by law to keep detailed historical records of their business, either on paper or electronically. Internal records — the data an organization keeps about its own transactions — often serve as supporting material in documents, presentations, and visuals. Such records might provide facts and details about finances, personnel, manufacturing, marketing, or shipping. For example, in submitting a memo proposing the addition of three employees to his sheet metal department, a departmental manager uses a variety of data, including personnel information about salaries and benefits, monthly productivity sheets, backlogged orders, and projected sales figures. His proposal wouldn't have any impact if he merely said his department needed three additional workers. All the evidence he needs to support his proposal is available in the files and internal documents of his own company.

Internal records must be analyzed for information usability and appropriateness before you can use them. Often, historical data need to be interpreted with respect to actual outcomes before they can be used effectively. You must also consider the legal and ethical implications of using internal records, particularly in a document intended for external readers. Many companies require key employees to sign nondisclosure or confidentiality agreements (usually considered legally binding) to restrict the dissemination of proprietary information.

Corporate Libraries 企业图书馆

Many organizations, such as law and engineering firms, build extensive resource libraries for their employees. The services offered by large corporate libraries, often called information services, give a clear picture of the importance of librarians to your own professional work. Librarians in a corporate information service often locate the information for their internal clients, saving valuable time for employees. The Information Services division of 3M Corporation, headquartered in St. Paul, Minnesota, estimates that, on average, it saves employees some 28 hours per project. Barbara Peterson, Director of Information Services for 3M, explained in an interview how the 75 professionals in Information Services help meet her division's four distinct responsibilities:[13]

1. Responding to three kinds of inquiries:
   - *What are current facts?* Information Services answers fact-based questions that range from locating potential consultants for a project to identifying regulatory requirements that may affect project development.
   - *What are relevant sources?* Information Services identifies publications related to a particular topic, from state-of-the-art sources to newspaper articles.
   - *What are recent developments?* Information Services monitors ongoing developments with selective dissemination of information so that searches can be tailored to an individual's information needs.
2. Providing 3M professionals with easy access to library materials, ranging from print journals to the Internet.
3. Organizing and maintaining systems that track two kinds of R&D information for 3M:
   - Internal research and development documents, such as research proposals, laboratory notebooks, research reports;
   - An online database of skills of 3M's scientists and engineers so that project teams have a good chance of locating a needed expert from among the company's 8,000 technical employees.
4. Providing ongoing education to help 3M employees use, manage, and share information effectively.

Although corporate libraries in other companies may provide a different range of services, you can depend on a good corporate library to be a tremendous help to you in identifying and collecting information useful for your projects.

Personal Observations 个人观察

Personal observations are legitimate primary sources if the observer is trained in the area of investigation. For example, botanists can identify a bog by observing and classifying the vegetation in a geographic area, and opticians can make remarkably accurate judgments about the flatness of a mirror surface by observing light refraction.

Personal observations of experts and experimenters were the basis for scientific and technical knowledge long before the days of sophisticated testing and measuring equipment. For instance, in 1628, William Harvey wrote *De Motu Cordis (On the Motion of the Heart),* part of which is quoted in Figure 6.5, based entirely on his personal observations. In fact, modern medicine still uses some of the same observational strategies that Harvey used almost 400 years ago. Notice how Harvey describes the motion of the heart using common but specific terms and draws specific conclusions based on specific examples.

FIGURE 6.5 **Translated Excerpt from Harvey's *De Motu Cordis*[14]**

In the motion, and interval in which this is accomplished, three principal circumstances are to be noted:

1. That the heart is erected, and rises upward to a point, so that at this time it strikes against the breast and the pulse is felt externally.
2. That it is everywhere contracted, but more especially toward the sides, so that it looks narrower, relatively longer, more drawn together. The heart of an eel taken out of the body of the animal and placed upon the table or the hand shows these particulars; but the same things are manifest in the hearts of small fishes and of those colder animals where the organ is more conical or elongated.
3. The heart, being grasped in the hand, is felt to become harder during its action. Now this hardness proceeds from tension, precisely as when the forearm is grasped, its tendons are perceived to become tense and resilient when the fingers are moved.
4. It may further be observed in fishes, and the colder-blooded animals, such as frogs, serpents, et cetera, that the heart when it moves becomes of a paler color; when quiescent, of a deeper blood-red color.

From these particulars it appeared evident to me that the motion of the heart consists in a certain universal tension – both contraction in the line of its fibers and constriction in every sense. It becomes erect, hard, and of diminished size during its action; the motion is plainly of the same nature as that of the muscles when they contract in the line of their sinews and fibers; for the muscles, when in action, acquire vigor and tenseness, and from soft become hard, prominent, and thickened: in the same manner the heart.

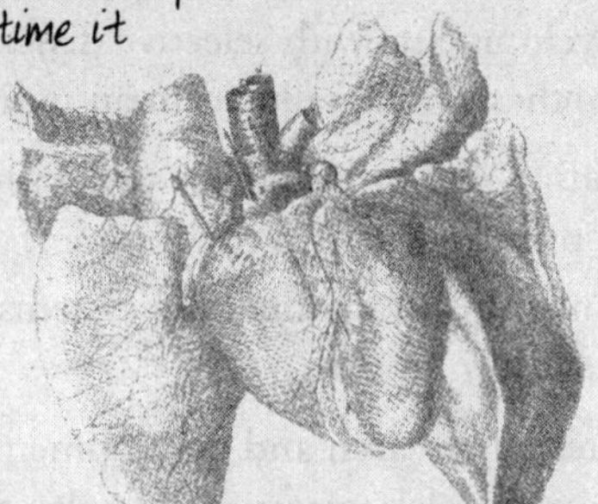

To learn more about William Harvey's treatise, *On the Motion of the Heart* go to **www.english.wadsworth.com/burnett6e** for a link to Harvey's treatise.
CLICK WEBLINK
CLICK Chapter 6/William Harvey

WWW
WEBLINK

Even if you are not a specialist, your own involvement and observations are important and valid sources of primary information. We make mental personal observations, usually subconsciously, all the time; for example, you might speak up without raising your hand in class once you've observed that the instructor prefers a conversational classroom or observe and model a mentor's behavior as you make a transition into a professional environment. Consciously observing relationships, cultural and social factors, behaviors, and repeated processes can provide a great deal of information in your research efforts.

Also, do not underestimate the value of your hands-on experience. For example, technical communicators who can use the computer software they are documenting are better equipped to explain how to accomplish tasks with the software than is a colleague who merely watched someone else use it. Similarly, if you are a supervisor who can actually run the equipment in a machine shop, you are better qualified to train new employees than is a colleague who knows the theory but not the actual operation. A nutritionist experienced in dietary analysis is better equipped to teach such analysis than is an inexperienced nutritionist.

When personal observations are appropriate, consider the following guidelines to increase the likelihood that data will be accepted as credible:

- Identify the situation, the context.
- Indicate the expertise and the disciplinary or social biases of the observer.
- Determine if you are an observer in a situation or if you are what ethnographers call a "participant-observer" — someone who is studying a culture or situation by interacting with it.
- Take extensive descriptive notes so you can identify trends or key points for analysis.
- Look for trends in the data rather than trying to make the data fit your assumptions.
- Select observations for a final report that are representative of the situation as a whole.
- Quantify observations whenever possible and use standard notation and terminology.
- Support generalizations you make based on your observations with specific details and examples from your notes.

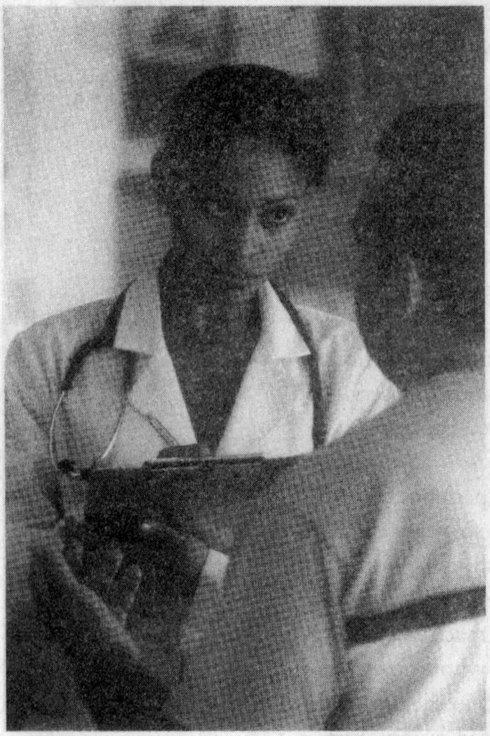
© Jose Luis Pelaez, Inc./CORBIS

Interviewing is one of the most important professional skills. Often the information you need is not written in any book or article but is in the mind or indecipherable notes of another person.

> *What are the advantages and disadvantages of submitting questions you'll ask in an interview in advance to the person you're interviewing?*

When you're conducting an information interview, you need to be prepared and persistent about asking the right questions in order to elicit the information you need. Preparing effective questions for an interview requires some homework. You need to prepare in three ways:

- Gather necessary information about the subject: What do you already know? What do you need to know? What do you expect this particular person to be able to tell you?
- Approach the person you want to interview: How should you contact the person? What's the best place for the interview? What's the most convenient time? Be aware when you select the site that time and place can affect the quality of the interview. How should you refer to the person?
- Identify the categories of questions you want to ask, and plan the specific topics that you want to explore. Listing topics rather than specific questions gives you more flexibility.

The answers to these questions provide a focus for the interview. An essential courtesy is learning to pronounce the name of the person you're interviewing. You should also be familiar with the terminology you'll use during the interview.

Questions can be divided into two broad categories: *convergent questions,* which have only one correct answer, and *divergent questions,* which are open-ended and therefore more useful in problem solving. The more prepared you are before you enter an interview, the more likely you are to conduct an effective, focused interview that will uncover the information you are looking for (if, that is, the person being interviewed can answer your questions). Several useful guidelines for asking effective interview questions are illustrated in Figure 6.6 by some of the questions that Nancy Irish revised for her interviews.

What you ask is important. How you ask it is also important. Figure 6.7 identifies actions and attitudes that will make your interviews more efficient and effective. Far more than the content of the questions is important: You also need to consider your behavior and body language, respect conventions of interviewing, and decide ways to manage mechanical considerations.

Interviews can be conducted in a number of ways depending on time and geography. Face-to-face interviews are usually the best because you can easily gauge reactions or clarify meaning. If time is limited or distance is a problem, telephone or e-mail interviews are alternatives. Telephone and e-mail interviews

FIGURE 6.6 Guidelines for Asking Effective Interview Questions

Guidelines	Negative and Positive Examples
Design questions whose answers require a definition or an explanation rather than a simple yes or no.	***Weak:*** Are people's diets improved by using soy protein? ***Effective:*** In what ways are people's diets improved by protein?
If you must ask a yes or no question to establish a position, follow it with a question requiring some explanation. Generally, you should know the answers to basic questions. Don't waste interview time asking questions when you already know the answers except when a confirmation attributed to the person would be useful. Instead, use the basic information you already know to develop more fruitful questions.	***Weak:*** Has there been an increase in the past five years in soy protein used in processed food for human consumption? ***Effective:*** Has there been an increase in the past five years in soy protein used in processed food for human consumption? What has contributed to this increase (or decrease)? ***Better:*** What has contributed to the increase (or decrease) in the past five years in soy protein used in processing food for human consumption?
Ask questions that require a focused response, not a broad, rambling discussion.	***Weak:*** What do you think of the public attitudes about soy use? ***Effective:*** What specific strategies work to persuade the public to incorporate soy into regular meals?
Ask a single question at a time, not combined (complex) questions that require multiple answers.	***Weak:*** Describe the progress that has been made in identifying those components responsible for undesirable flavors and colors and in developing processing technology to eliminate these from food products. ***Effective:*** Describe the progress in identifying components responsible for undesirable flavors and colors in soy products. ***Follow-up:*** What processing technology has been developed to eliminate these from food products?
Use terminology that narrows the area of response.	***Weak:*** In what ways have soybeans been improved? ***Effective:*** In what ways has the nutritive value of soybeans been improved, specifically the amino acid profile and the digestibility?
Prepare questions to tactfully redirect a respondent who has begun to ramble.	***Weak:*** Getting back to the subject, I'd like to ask you again to describe the ways in which soybeans have been improved. ***Effective:*** I'd be interested to hear more of the ways in which the nutritive value of soybeans has been improved.
Research other interviews in the field to avoid asking what have become cliché questions; instead, find a new angle so that the respondent will be interested in what you ask and will know you have done your homework.	***Weak:*** What are the ecological benefits of soy foods? ***Effective:*** How do you think the ecological benefits of soy foods could be used in marketing to increase the American public's interest in them?
Refer specifically to the respondent's published work.	***Weak:*** I liked your recent article on soybeans for human consumption. ***Effective:*** Your article in last month's *Soy Research Journal* effectively supports the importance of increasing human consumption of soybeans.
Prepare questions the respondent might perceive as hostile so that the respondent is not offended but, instead, answers.	***Weak:*** How can you carry out objective research on soy foods when your research is funded by the National Soy Growers of America? ***Effective:*** I understand that your research is funded by the National Soy Growers of America. Does that make it difficult for you to conduct your research objectively?

may allow the possibility of a series of shorter interviews rather than one long personal interview; this is sometimes valuable because it gives both the interviewer and interviewee time to research stronger questions and responses during the interim. These alternatives also present their own challenges, though, such as the lack of visual cues to determine comprehension and the less personal nature of these media.

When a person is simply not available in person or on the telephone, an e-mail request or a letter of inquiry is an appropriate vehicle for collecting information. In some situations, a person may even agree to record answers on an audiotape that you provide so that he or she is spared writing detailed responses or working within a short timeframe. Figure 6.8 displays a letter of inquiry that Nancy Irish wrote to Chris Morgan.

FIGURE 6.7 **Actions and Attitudes for Effective Interviewing**

Category	Actions and Attitudes
Interpersonal behavior	■ Be attentive and courteous. ■ Know how to pronounce the person's name. ■ Generally address the person formally ("Dr. Greenough" rather than "Pat") unless you know him or her personally.
Body language	■ Convey interest through your tone of voice, facial expressions, and body language. ■ Make direct eye contact with the person you're interviewing. ■ Note the person's body language as a signal to how well the interview is going.
Interviewing conventions	■ Confirm arrangements beforehand regarding the time, place, and duration of the interview. ■ Arrive or call on time, and do not exceed the agreed-on length. If you want to record the interview, ask for permission; it's usually granted. ■ Prepare questions in advance. You can modify or extend them if you need to, but don't go into the interview unprepared. ■ Give the person time to respond to your questions. ■ Don't interrupt unless the person strays off track or becomes too long-winded.
Mechanical considerations	■ Be prepared to take notes, paraphrasing the person's comments, in case there are mechanical problems with the recorder or the person prefers that you don't use it. ■ Consider asking the person to prepare responses to statistical questions prior to or after the interview itself.

FIGURE 6.8 **Letter of Inquiry**

Make sure to include your return address so the person can contact you.

112 North Riverside Drive
Ames, IA 50010-5971
October 30, 20—

Chris Morgan, Research Director
National Soybean Institute
731 Jefferson Street
Dubuque, IA 52086

If you don't know the gender of the person (because of a name such as Robin, Pat, or Chris), use the full name.

Dear Chris Morgan:

Identify your role and goal.

As part of my work designing educational programs for members of food co-ops, I am investigating the role of soybeans in an ecologically and nutritionally sound food system. I am particularly interested in the increased use of soybeans in the American diet.

State specifically what you want.

Could you please provide information on the following topics?

1. Percentage of annual U.S. soybean crop consumed by humans vs. livestock; domestic vs. foreign markets
2. Percentage of U.S. arable land (acreage) planted in soybeans
3. Nutrient composition of traditional Asian soy foods
4. Resource efficiency of soybean products vs. grain-fed livestock production
5. Current research to develop new soy products for human consumption

I appreciate your assistance. If you wish, I will be glad to send you a copy of my final report outlining program options.

Thank the person for assisting you.

Sincerely,

Nancy Irish

Nancy Irish
515-555-1234 (office)
515-555-6779 (fax)
nirish@iastate.edu (e-mail)

Provide a telephone number and, if available, a fax number and e-mail address to give the person alternative and perhaps more convenient ways of contacting you.

Should you agree to submit material written from the interview to the person you interviewed for clarification? For approval?

Whether you obtain your information through a personal interview, telephone interview, e-mail interview, written questionnaire with taped response, or written response to a letter of inquiry, take the time to write a thank-you letter, acknowledging your appreciation for the time and effort the person took to assist you. You can give the letter a personal tone by mentioning one or two things that were particularly helpful. If the person is someone you regularly see in your company, you can write an informal note or send an e-mail message; even a person you see every day appreciates a brief thank you. If the person is someone you do not see every day, make the thank you more formal.

Surveys and Polls 问卷调查

Surveys and polls are extremely useful tools for gathering information about opinions and preferences from large groups of people. They are usually based on a predetermined set of questions called a questionnaire, which can be administered on paper, through e-mail or the Internet, or in personal interviews. If you use a random sample of the target audience, you can make statistically acceptable generalizations about the entire population. If you are conducting your own survey, take care in constructing the questions, selecting the test group, and compiling the results in order to generate ethical and statistically significant results. If you are using data from surveys by others, investigate how carefully the surveys were constructed and conducted to ensure the reliability and validity of results.

Survey design is important. The questions should be both valid (the questions really ask what the survey takers intend to ask) and reliable (the questions are likely to be interpreted in a similar way by people completing the survey). Surveys can be designed using any of six different types of questions; each type has advantages and disadvantages you should consider when designing a questionnaire for a survey or poll:

- *Dual alternatives,* the simplest questions to tabulate, offer only two choices: yes/no, positive/negative, true/false, and so on. Such questions adequately address simple issues, but they often unrealistically limit the range of responses needed to portray complex situations. If you want to use this type of question, assure yourself that there really are only two possible answers so that the respondent does not feel as if the choices are inadequate.
- *Multiple choice questions* give respondents alternatives, sometimes limiting them to a single answer, at other times permitting them to check all applicable answers. Because the survey designer provides all the choices, multiple choice questions may not offer an answer with which respondents agree, thus distorting the results. A well-designed multiple choice question does not have two or three choices that are obviously wrong, nor does it have choices in which the distinctions are so slight that the respondent must guess the correct answer.

- *Rank ordering* provides respondents with a series of items and asks them to order the items according to preference, frequency of use, or some other criterion. Tabulating rank ordering is easy, but distortion may occur if the mean (arithmetic average) differs significantly from the mode (most frequently occurring number). If the items in a particular grouping are similar, respondents will have a difficult time ranking them and may assign an arbitrary value rather than an actual preference.
- *Likert scales* provide a method for respondents to express their opinion by rating items either numerically or verbally on a continuum. As with rank ordering, tabulation is easy but may give distorted results if the mean and mode are significantly different. Scales are most effective if they have an even number of choices (usually four or six). If a scale has a middle choice (as occurs when the scale has an odd number of choices), respondents will choose it a disproportionately large percentage of the time.
- *Completions* expect respondents to fill in information to complete an item. The answers are simple to tabulate if the responses are quantitative, such as age, frequency, or amount. But even short, open-ended opinion questions present problems in tabulation if respondents give a variety of answers; the evaluator must decide which terms respondents use are synonymous.
- *Essays or open-ended questions* give respondents the opportunity to fully express themselves, presenting both facts and opinions, but the responses are difficult to tabulate. Essays are much more effective if they ask respondents to focus on specifics rather than request general opinions or reactions.

How much difference do the types of questions really make? Imagine that Nancy Irish read a claim that 23 percent of people questioned agreed they would include tofu in their diets. The statistic doesn't mean much unless she knows the question. That same answer may be a response to several variations of the same question. Dual alternatives, for example, could elicit far more positive responses than completion questions. Figure 6.9 illustrates some of the possible questions that could have elicited such a response. In order to determine the validity and reliability of your questions, test them with a small representative sample. If changes are necessary, you can make them before officially administering the survey.

Designing an effective series of questions is only the first step in preparing a survey. After you have designed and tested your questions, you need to administer the survey to a representative random sample of the target population. Compiling and reporting the results should not be difficult if your questions have been carefully designed. Even when the questions are valid and reliable, the population sample random and representative, and the data compiled accurately, the results may be disappointing, particularly with mail-in surveys, which have a very low return rate.

FIGURE 6.9 **Variations of Questions That Could Produce the Same Response**

Dual Alternative

Would you include tofu in your meals if you knew good recipes?

❑ Yes (23 percent) ❑ No

Single Multiple Choice

Tofu is a traditional Asian soybean food high in protein and low in calories and fat. Considering the high nutrient value of tofu, check the one item you most agree with.

❑ Willing to try tofu if I had a good recipe (14 percent)
❑ Use tofu regularly (9 percent)
❑ Tried tofu and didn't like it
❑ Not interested in trying tofu
❑ Never heard of tofu

Rank Order

Rank order the following soy items in order of preference as additions to your current diet.

__ Soy sauce
__ Tofu (23 percent ranked tofu second)
__ Miso
__ Natto
__ Tempeh

Continuum (Likert)

Mark your preference for each food item on the scale.

Tofu: Would not ever use — Might consider — Would if knew how — Use now

(23 percent)

Completion

Which soy product are you most willing to include in your meal planning?

________ ("tofu"-23 percent)

Using Sources Ethically

使用资源应符合道德规范

As a writer and reader, you are responsible for assessing and using information ethically. The ease with which any person with a computer and server access can post information online means that readers must be much more careful when assessing the reliability and validity of electronic information. And the proliferation of electronic and Web resources has made plagiarizing information increasingly frequent. Ethically using information means understanding ways to assess information on the Web for credibility and understanding ways to incorporate information into your documents, presentations, and visuals without plagiarizing, which is the literary equivalent of stealing.

Assessing Credibility 评估可信度

Many readers assume that information published in professional journals or books is reliable and valid because the peer-review process authors must go through usually eliminates misinformation. Readers of online journals usually assume that these articles have been through similar peer review and editing. But not all online publications are peer reviewed or carefully edited. The Web makes possible the publication of documents with little or no editing or review; thus, you may have difficulty judging the credibility of online information.

The ease of posting information on the Web has changed how you need to approach online information. You need to consider possible biases and inaccuracies in information obtained from the Web and to think critically about a document's origin. For example, documents published by companies may be biased in favor of their own products; documents published by individuals may be partially or entirely based on unsubstantiated personal beliefs or opinions. While a particular bias may not be a sufficient cause to reject a source, you do need to recognize ways in which a bias can influence a source. Consider the following elements when assessing the credibility of Web documents:

1. ***Authorship***
   - Can you identify the author or webmaster on the site?
   - Is the author identified as a person, a corporation, a university?
   - What do you know about the credentials of the author or organization?
   - Does the site have a sponsor that might have a vested interest?
2. ***Timeliness***
   - When was the site originally posted?
   - When was the site last updated?
   - How regularly is the site updated?
   - Is the information current or outdated for your needs?
3. ***Purpose***
   - Can you determine from the design and content if the site is intended to inform, persuade, or sell?
   - Can you determine the intended audience?
   - Does the site have advertising banners? Do they affect the content?
4. ***Content***
   - How detailed and well-researched is the content?
   - Does the new information confirm or disconfirm your prior knowledge?
   - Does the author fully cite sources and link to respected sources to support assertions?
   - Can you verify the author's claims using other resources?
   - Does the content contain spelling and grammatical errors?
   - Can you identify a particular slant or bias to the information?

Avoiding Plagiarism 避免剽窃

Avoiding plagiarism is just as important in the workplace as it is in academia. Cutting and pasting information from an original source into a second document has become extremely easy to do with today's word processing programs. But the law in the United States is on the side of the original author. Stealing text from other sources — whether published or unpublished — is unethical and illegal.

WWW

WEBLINK

Go to **www.english.wadsworth.com/burnett6e** for a link to learn more about ways to avoid plagiarism.
CLICK ON WEBLINK
CLICK on Chapter 6/plagiarism

What is plagiarism? Using work that is not your own without attribution.

- Using exact quotations from documents, presentations, Web sites, or visual designs and images without attribution
- Using someone else's unique or distinctive ideas without attribution
- Using someone else's unique or distinctive processes without attribution
- Using words, images, or processes, that have only been changed slightly without attribution. What counts as an insufficient change? Changing verbs from past to present tense. Changing nouns from singular to plural. Reordering items. Omitting some information but keeping some of it as it was in the original.

Figure 6.10 provides practical guidelines for avoiding plagiarism. The guidelines can be summarized quite simply: Give credit for ideas, words, and visuals that are not your own, whether they are directly quoted or paraphrased.

Just as Web sites peddling academic term papers for sale are flourishing, so are sites used to combat plagiarism. You can type in a long phrase in the search engine **www.google.com**, and it will return any online document that uses that exact phrasing. Several universities are building searchable databases of student papers for faculty who suspect plagiarism. And many companies are designing software for faculty and research libraries that searches student papers against online materials. The Internet may have made plagiarism easier, but it has also made plagiarism easier to combat.

What's exempt from plagiarism? Using common knowledge, widely known historical facts, or company boilerplate (for company purposes) is usually not considered plagiarism, but a courtesy acknowledgment doesn't hurt. The best guideline you can use is, "When in doubt, include a complete citation."

WWW

WEBLINK

The notion of "common knowledge" often causes remarkable problems in deciding what to cite. Go to **www.english.wadsworth.com/burnett6e** for a link to learn more about what constitutes common knowledge.
CLICK ON WEBLINK
CLICK on Chapter 6/common knowledge

FIGURE 6.10 **Ways to Avoid Plagiarism**[15]

To take accurate, usable notes, clearly signal all quoted material with BIG quotation marks, a bold Q (for quotation), and the complete citation information.	. . . and then later	Proofread the final document with clearly marked notes at hand to make sure that all ideas, words, and visuals that are not your own, whether directly quoted or paraphrased, are clearly cited in in-text references, footnotes, or endnotes and the bibliography or works cited.
To avoid plagiarism when you're writing a summary, close the journal or book. When you've finished drafting the summary, check the original source for accuracy. Write the complete citation information next to the quotation in your notes.	. . . and then later	In the text of your document, give credit to the source. Use quotation marks for unique words or phrases. Use parenthetical citations (author, date, page) immediately after quoted and paraphrased information.
To accurately use a direct quotation, use the exact words and quotation marks.	. . . and then later	Refer directly to the person or source in introducing or commenting on the quotation. Check that the quotation marks are in the correct places.

When integrating information from another source into your document, you have several options, all of which require documentation. You can directly quote a phrase or sentence(s) from the source in quotation marks and support that quote with an introductory phrase such as "According to . . ." or "Jones says . . . ." If the information you want to quote is longer than a few sentences, paraphrase the information into one or two sentences that summarize the information without borrowing exact wording. Paraphrases do not require quotation marks but do require an introductory phrase to identify their source. Both quoting and paraphrasing require that you cite the source in a parenthetical citation at the end of the sentence and that you include a bibliographic reference to the original source at the end of the entire document. Documentation formats vary across disciplines but include MLA, APA, and Chicago style. *Avoiding Unintentional Plagiarism* on the next two pages shows examples of quoted, paraphrased, and plagiarized materials as well as proper documentation forms.

AVOIDING UNINTENTIONAL PLAGIARISM
避免无意剽窃

Part of your professional ethos comes from using information correctly and ethically, which means knowing how to avoid plagiarism by properly citing, attributing, paraphrasing, and integrating information from other sources. Plagiarism is not only an academic offense; it's a legal offense. Companies view plagiarism as unacceptable, unethical, and illegal. The following examples show both plagiarized and acceptable uses of information. The brochure was published by the United Soybean Board and reports a portion of an independent research firm's findings about consumer attitudes toward health and nutrition.

In each box, A–D, decide which example is plagiarized. Check your answers in the key on the next page.

CONSUMER PERCEPTIONS AND KNOWLEDGE OF ORGANIC FOODS[16]

Forty-four percent of consumers buy organic food products either frequently or sometimes, while 30 percent do so rarely and 25 percent never purchase organics. More consumers aged 35-54 (20 percent) frequently buy organic products than do consumers aged 18-34 (13 percent) or 55 and older (14 percent).

The majority of consumers concerned about biotechnology are not aware of the alternatives they already have. Only three percent of consumers know, without prompting, that organic foods can't contain genetically modified ingredients by law, compared to the much larger 41 percent who are aware that organics must be grown without pesticides or herbicides. Additionally, 33 percent cannot name any requirements for a food to be called "organic."

REQUIREMENTS FOR A FOOD TO BE CALLED "ORGANIC"

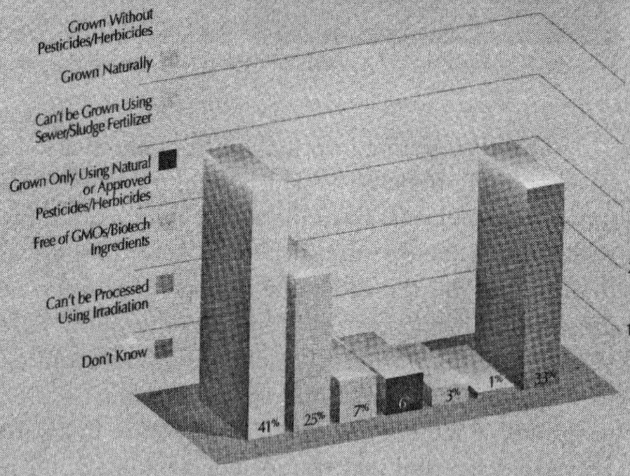

On an aided basis, 48 percent know that organic foods can't contain genetically modified ingredients and 64 percent know that organics must be grown without pesticides and herbicides.

A1 Organic foods are growing in popularity in the United States as 44% of consumers buy organic food products either frequently or sometimes. More consumers aged 35–54 (20%) frequently buy organic products than do consumers aged 18–34 (13 percent) or 55 and older (14 percent). This suggests that the food industry may not be doing enough to target and increase organic food awareness among younger people.

A2 According to a report sponsored by the United Soybean Board (USB) (2002), "44% of consumers buy organic food products either frequently or sometimes" (Organic Foods section, para 1). The report also notes that more middle-aged consumers regularly purchase organic food than younger and older consumers (Organic Foods section, para 1). This research suggests that the food industry may not be doing enough to target and increase organic food awareness among younger people.

CONSUMER ATTITUDES ABOUT FATS

Consumers continue to show confusion about the health profile of fats and oils. While 90 percent of consumers recognize that saturated fats are unhealthy, most remain uncertain about unsaturated fats with nearly half perceiving mono- and poly- unsaturated fats as unhealthy. Additionally, four in 10 consumers believe that *trans* fatty acids are healthier than saturated fats, while two in 10 believe that saturated fats are healthier and three in 10 do not know which is healthier. In contrast, consumers are much more sure about Omega-3 fatty acids, with 67 percent stating that they are healthy.

On an unaided basis, only three percent of consumers mentioned *trans* fats or hydrogenation as a health concern in relation to soy and fewer than one in 10 perceive any negative health effects of soy or soyfoods. However, when consumers were asked specifically to rate the healthiness of *trans* fats and hydrogenation, seventy-seven percent ranked *trans* fatty acids as very or somewhat unhealthy, compared to the 66 percent who rated hydrogenated vegetable oils as unhealthy. In contrast, 22 percent now feel that *trans* fats are very or somewhat healthy, while 34 percent believe that hydrogenated vegetable oils are healthy.

Sixty-two percent of consumers say they are somewhat or very unlikely to buy products labeled as containing *trans* fatty acids. While this percentage is higher than in 1999, it is significantly smaller than just last year. One-half of consumers (51 percent) feel they are unlikely to buy products featuring hydrogenated vegetable oils on the label.

C1 Even in a very health-conscious society, consumers are still confused about the health benefits and drawbacks of most fats. "While 90 percent of consumers recognize that saturated fats are unhealthy . . . four in ten consumers believe that trans fatty acids are healthier than saturated fats" (USB). This statement shows that consumers have difficulty defining the types of fats and determining which are healthy.

C2 A study sponsored by the United Soybean Board (2002) reported that 90 percent of consumers recognized that saturated fats were bad for their health but were torn about the health value of mono- and poly- unsaturated fats (Attitudes about Fats section, para 1). The study also stated that consumers are unsure of the health value of trans fatty acids but "are much more sure about Omega-3 fatty acids, with 67 percent stating they are healthy" (Attitudes about Fats section, para 1). Credit for the view about saturated and Omega-3 fats can be credited to the extensive coverage these fats have had in the popular media in the last 20 years.

D1 According to a USB report, consumers remain confused about the advantages of fats and oils in one's diet. When speaking about soy, a small number of consumers (3%) thought trans fats or hydrogenation was a health concern. Less than 1 in every 10 people thought soy or soyfoods had negative health effects.

D2 According to a USB-sponsored report (2002), fats and oils still confuse many consumers, most of whom are unsure which fats and oils are healthy for their diets. The report noted that a miniscule number of respondents thought trans fats were unhealthy and that less than 10 percent presumed soy and soyfoods would be harmful to their health (Attitudes about Fats section, para 2).

B1 Consumers cannot agree on the definition of organic, but the majority know it has something to do with how food is grown. Over 50% of consumers think "organic" has something to do with fertilizer, while many have no idea what makes food organic.

B2 According to the USB-sponsored study, 33 percent of consumers cannot define characteristics of organic food, while over 50 percent relate the term to the use of herbicides, pesticides, and unnatural fertilizers during growth (Organic Foods section, graphic). Only three percent were able to determine that organic foods must be free of genetically modified organisms, one of the key requirements for food to be termed organic (Organic Foods section, graphic).

Key

A1 **Plagiarism** — uses the original source without quotation marks, attribution, or citation

A2 **Acceptable** — uses quotation marks to signal directly quoted material and appropriately paraphrases other material; uses attributions and citation

B1 **Plagiarism** — distorts information in the figure and does not attribute or cite the source

B2 **Acceptable** — accurately interprets information in a way readers can understand, provides attribution, and cites the source

C1 **Plagiarism** — does not introduce or attribute the partial, and therefore potentially misleading, quotation even though an in-text citation is provided

C2 **Acceptable** — integrates direct quotation into the text and appropriately attributes and cites quoted and paraphrased information

D1 **Plagiarism** — uses the paraphrased statistics and conclusions from the original with attribution but without citation

D2 **Acceptable** — maintains the attribution but now cites the source

Individual and Collaborative Assignments

个人作业和小组作业

1. **Learn about your own academic library.** Some academic libraries have cooperative arrangements with local businesses so that the library facilities are available for practicing professionals. Work in small groups with others who share your academic major (or a closely related one).

   (a) Design questions for a librarian about services and resources available to local businesses and industries.

   (b) Select a representative to arrange and conduct an interview with a college librarian.

   (c) Design a hands-on library orientation for local business professionals to develop skills in using library references and resources. Go beyond the usual orientation by including information about the services of reference librarians, database searches, periodical and abstract indexes, technical reference materials, government documents, microfilm and microfiche files, and audiovisual materials. Present the information in a guidebook that also serves as a convenient reference for professionals after the orientation.

2. **Learn about a corporate library.** Learning about corporate library resources is important for technical professionals and for technical writers. Work in small groups with others who share your academic major (or a closely related one).

   (a) Design questions for a corporate librarian about the differences between a university and a corporate library, frequency of use, and the types of professionals who use them.

   (b) Select a representative to arrange and conduct an interview with corporate librarians at different local businesses and industries.

   (c) Design a hands-on library orientation to introduce new professional employees to the references and resources in a corporate library. Include information about services of professional librarians, available books and periodicals, loan privileges, database searches, periodical and abstract indexes, technical reference materials, government documents, microfilm and microfiche files, and audiovisual materials. Present the information in a guidebook that also serves as a convenient reference for employees.

3. **Recommend resources.** Corita Muir of GeoTech, Inc., is investigating the cost effectiveness of her company's instituting a longer lunch hour and flex-time. Its goal is to have a variety of company-sponsored fitness programs available to all employees from 6:00 to 8:00 a.m., 11:00 a.m. to 1:00 p.m., and 4:00 to 7:00 p.m. She plans to use the following resources to prepare her proposal:

   - Company records providing the number of sick days employees used in the past 24 months

- Recent articles in the local newspaper describing the benefits of regular exercise
- Articles in business or science journals about the benefits of company-sponsored exercise

What additional resources would you recommend?

4. **Identify keywords and subject headings.** You are trying to locate information about one of the following topics. Before looking in the Library of Congress Subject Headings (LCSH), brainstorm possible alternative keyword terms for the topic. Determine subject search headings as well.

   - Midwives
   - Medical applications of lasers
   - New coal-mining techniques
   - Proper use of farming equipment
   - Wellness programs

5. **Compare sources in your field.**

   (a) Do a search for information on a particular topic in your field using the library catalog, electronic databases, and the World Wide Web. Use both keyword and subject searches where applicable and compare the different results generated. Determine what you believe are advantages and disadvantages of each type of information source and each search strategy.

   (b) Compile and then annotate a list of reference books, electronic journals and databases, and Internet sources that are particularly helpful to a person in your career field.

6. **Compare Internet sources.** Visit the following Web site, http://www.nist.gov/weblinks.htm, and choose three different government Web sites to visit and analyze. Determine what you believe are the purposes, audience, and advantages or disadvantages of each. In a memo to the class, report your analysis.

7. **Interview a professional, part I.**

   (a) Arrange to interview a professional technical writer or a technical professional in your field who writes frequently. During the first part of the interview, inquire about the person's approach to locating information from a variety of sources. Ask some of the following questions and add additional questions relevant to the specific person and organization:

      - Where/how do you get the information you use?
      - Do you ever have problems getting the information? How do you handle these problems?

- How available and cooperative are your informants?
- What kind of bias tends to be part of the data you collect?
- What's your background? Technical communication? Science? Engineering?
- How does this background affect the way you locate and collect information?

(b) Organize the information you find as part I of a brief oral or written report intended for other members of the class. This report can be posted on the class Web site or made available in print form in a class notebook in the library.

8. **Identify and correct plagiarism.** Several original passages and the related paraphrased and/or quoted passages follow. Read each pair. Then decide how you can revise the paraphrased and/or quoted passages so that the quoted segments and citations are correct.

(a) ***Original passage***[17]

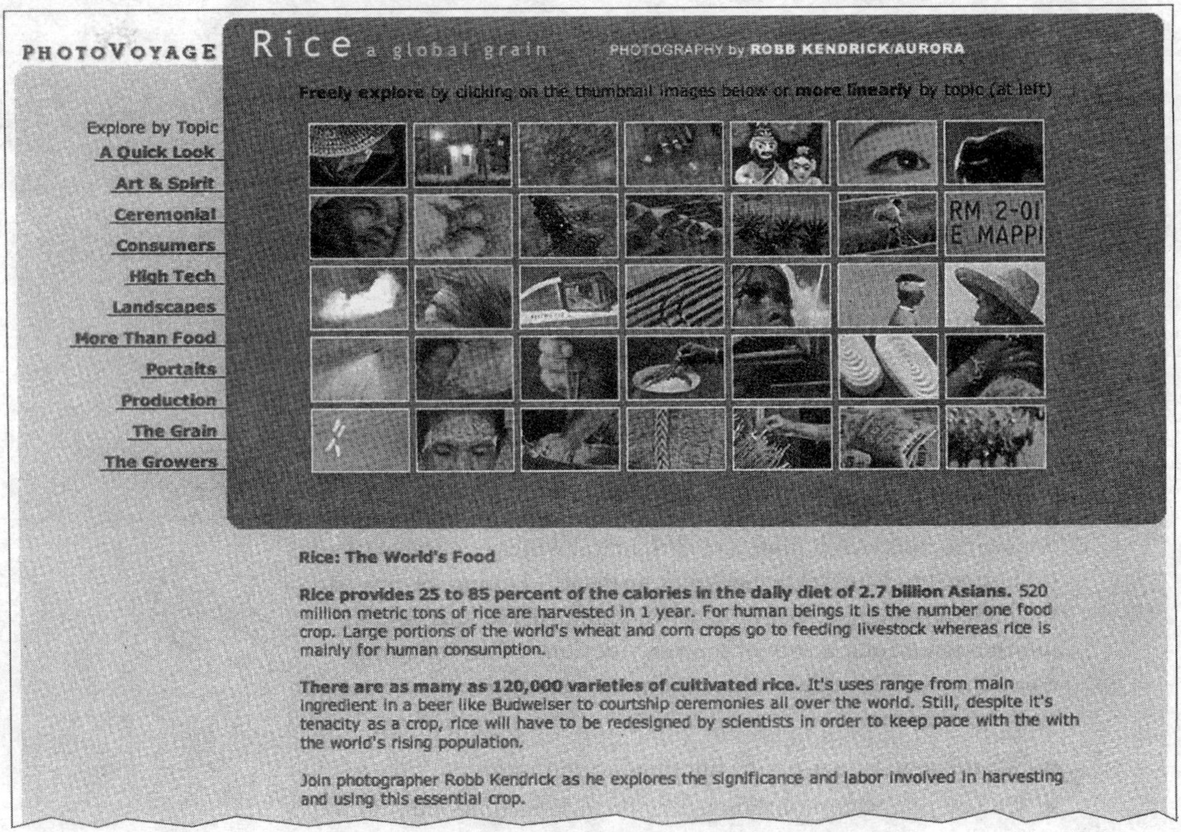

Quoted or paraphrased passage

During one year, approximately 520 million metric tons of rice are harvested, making it the number one food crop for people. The more than 120,000 varieties of rice currently being cultivated have many uses, including being the main ingredient in a beer. Food scientists are working to create new ways to use rice, which provides between 25 to 85 percent of the calories in the daily diet of 2.7 billion Asians.

(b) ***Original passage***[18]

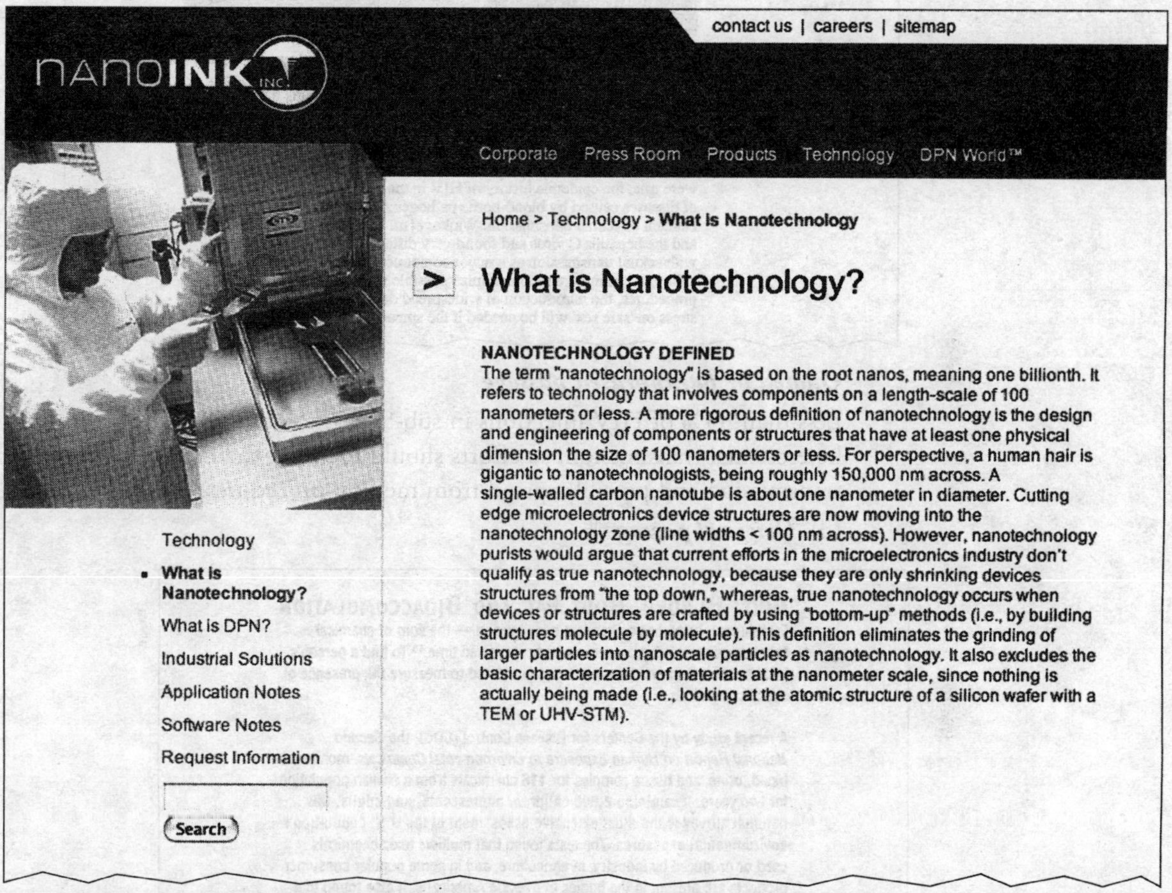

contact us | careers | sitemap

nanoINK INC.

Corporate Press Room Products Technology DPN World™

Home > Technology > **What is Nanotechnology**

> What is Nanotechnology?

NANOTECHNOLOGY DEFINED

The term "nanotechnology" is based on the root nanos, meaning one billionth. It refers to technology that involves components on a length-scale of 100 nanometers or less. A more rigorous definition of nanotechnology is the design and engineering of components or structures that have at least one physical dimension the size of 100 nanometers or less. For perspective, a human hair is gigantic to nanotechnologists, being roughly 150,000 nm across. A single-walled carbon nanotube is about one nanometer in diameter. Cutting edge microelectronics device structures are now moving into the nanotechnology zone (line widths < 100 nm across). However, nanotechnology purists would argue that current efforts in the microelectronics industry don't qualify as true nanotechnology, because they are only shrinking devices structures from "the top down," whereas, true nanotechnology occurs when devices or structures are crafted by using "bottom-up" methods (i.e., by building structures molecule by molecule). This definition eliminates the grinding of larger particles into nanoscale particles as nanotechnology. It also excludes the basic characterization of materials at the nanometer scale, since nothing is actually being made (i.e., looking at the atomic structure of a silicon wafer with a TEM or UHV-STM).

Technology
- **What is Nanotechnology?**

What is DPN?
Industrial Solutions
Application Notes
Software Notes
Request Information

Search

Quoted or paraphrased passage

The word "nanotechnology" comes from the root *nanos,* meaning one billionth, which involves components on a length-scale of 100 nanometers or less. Nanotechnology involves the design and engineering of components with at least one physical dimension of 100 nanometers or less. How small is this? A human hair, which is roughly 150,000 nm across, is gigantic to nanotechnologists. In comparison, a single-walled carbon nanotube has a diameter of about one nanometer. Innovative microelectronics devices are now moving into the nanotechnology zone; however, current efforts don't qualify as true nanotechnology. True nanotechnology occurs when devices are crafted molecule by molecule.

(c) ***Original passage***[19]

nature   **nature** 17 April 2003

highlights

home
search
? help

nature structural & molecular biology

this week's highlights

← item →

Epidemiology: Controlling AIDS in Africa

A recent suggestion that heterosexual transmission accounts for no more than 35% of HIV infections in sub-Saharan Africa proved controversial. Critics argued that the situation would be worsened by focusing on the risks of parenteral transmission (contaminated blood, unsterile medical equipment) and downplaying the 'safe sex' message. If the hypothesis were true, the epidemic history of HIV in the region should resemble that of diseases caused by blood-borne pathogens known to have only a small element of sexual transmission. Walker *et al.* compared the data for HIV and the hepatitis C virus and found very different histories, consistent with sexual transmission as a major component of HIV spread. So although it is important to minimize possible spread via medical procedures, the introduction of widespread drug treatment and continued stress on 'safe sex' will be needed if the spread of HIV is to be halted.

Quoted or paraphrased passage

Less than 35% of HIV infections in sub-Saharan Africa result from heterosexual transmission, so efforts should focus on the risks of parenteral transmission and possible spread from medical procedures.

(d) ***Original passage***[20]

BODY BURDEN, BODY FAT, AND BIOACCUMULATION

Each human being has a chemical body burden — the sum of chemical substances detected in a person's body at a given time.[46] To find a person's body burden, fluid and tissue samples are tested to measure the presence of specific chemicals.[47]

A recent study by the Centers for Disease Control (CDC), the *Second National Report on Human Exposure to Environmental Chemicals*, monitored blood, urine, and tissue samples for 116 chemicals from a civilian population for two years. Examining 2,500 children, adolescents, and adults, this national survey is the most extensive assessment of the U.S. population's environmental exposures. The tests found that multiple toxic chemicals used or produced by industry, in agriculture, and in some popular consumer products are present in the bodies of average Americans. It also found that children and minorities have more chemicals in their bodies than do other Americans. The chemicals found in the test group included ones that are no longer produced or used domestically, but which clearly remain in the environment and in human tissue.[48]

Body fat is considered an especially sensitive indicator of exposure to persistent environmental contaminants. A number of synthetic chemicals are soluble in fat and collect in tissues with high fat content — such as breasts, the liver, bone marrow, and the brain. Many fat-soluble synthetic chemicals are classified as probable or known carcinogens. Women, on average, have a two to 10 percent higher proportion of body fat.[49] Mothers pass their body burden to their unborn children in utero and to newborns through breast milk.

The writer using this report did not verify or read any of the sources cited in its endnotes, which included these in the passage below.

46 *Living Downstream*, 226.
47 Ibid.
48 Department of Health and Human Services, Centers for Disease Control and Prevention, "Second National Report on Human Exposure to Environmental Chemicals," (Washington, D.C.: CDC, 2003) [online]; available from: <http://www.cdc.gov/exposurereport/pdf/SecondNER.pdf>.
49 Margaret Reeves and Terra Murphy, Pesticide Action Network North America and Teresa Calvo Morales, Organización en California de Lídres Campesinas, *Farmworker Women & Pesticides in California's Central Valley* [online]; available from: <http://www.panna.org/resources/gpc/gpc_200304.13.1.08.dv.html>.

Quoted or paraphrased passage

According to a report published by the Centers for Disease Control and Prevention, the body fat of average Americans shows evidence of toxic agricultural and industrial chemicals, including ones that are no longer produced or used in the United States. This recent study examined 2,500 children, adolescents, and adults, monitoring blood, urine, and tissue samples. Many of the tissue samples contained carcinogens.

Chapter 6 Endnotes

1 *Knowledge management glossary.* (n.d.). Retrieved October 30, 2003, from http://www.mccombs.utexas.edu/kman/glossary.htm

2 *Knowledge management.* (n.d.). Retrieved October 30, 2003, from http://searchcrm.techtarget.com/sDefinition/0,,sid1 1_gci212449,00.html

3 Wilson, T. D. (2002). The nonsense of "knowledge management." *Information Research, 8*(1), Paper 144. Retrieved October 30, 2003, from http://informationr.net/ir/8-1/paper144.html

4 EOA national study finds nearly half of American workers engaged in unethical hi-tech behavior last year. (1998). *EOA News,* (Spring), 1, 4–5.

5 Office for Subject Cataloguing Policy, Collection Services. Library of Congress Subject Headings, 15th ed., vol 1 A-C. Washington, DC: Cataloguing Distribution Service. Library of Congress.

6 e-Library@Iowa State University. Collection Search Page. Retrieved on April 7, 2004, from www.lib.iastate.edu

7 Tech Web: The Business Technology Network. (n.d.). *Tech encyclopedia.* Retrieved July 6, 2003, from http://www.techweb.com/encyclopedia

8 Lyman, P., & Varian, H. R. (2000). *How much information?* Retrieved July 15, 2003, from http://www.sims.berkeley.edu/how-much-info

9 Adatped from ISU's *Instruction Commons Guide* by Vega Garcia, S. A. (2000, October). Searching by subject or by keyword. Retrieved July 15, 2003, from http://www.lib.iastate.edu/commons/resources/lcsh.index.html

10 Adapted from ISU's *Instruction Commons Guide* by Vega Garcia, S. A. (2000, October). Searching by subject or by keyword. Retrieved July 15, 2003, from http://www.lib.iastate.edu/commons/resources/lcsh.index.html

11 Adapted from UC Berkley-Teaching Library Internet Workshops. (n.d.). *Finding information on the internet: A tutorial.* Retrieved July 17, 2003, from http://www.lib/berkeley.edu/TeachingLib/Guides/Internet/Strategies.html

12 e-Library@Iowa State University. Collection Search Page. Retrieved on April 7, 2004, from www.lib.iastate.edu

13 Barbara Peterson, Director of 3M Innovation Services (personal communication, 1995, 2001).

14 Harvey, W. (1960). On the motion of the heart and circulation of the blood. In F. R. Moulton and J. J. Schifferes, (Eds.), *The autobiography of science* (2nd ed., pp. 106–107). Garden City, NY: Doubleday.

15 The suggestions include information from these sources:

- Purdue University Online Writing Lab. (n.d.). *Avoiding plagiarism.* Retrieved October 20, 2003, from http://owl.english.purdue.edu/handouts/research/4_plagiar.html
- Baylor College of Medicine. (n.d.). *Plagiary and the art of skillful citation: How to cite!* Retrieved October 20, 2003, from http://www.bcm.tmc.edu/immuno/citewell/artcite.html

- Reference and Instructional Services, Young Research Library, UCLA. (2002, October). *Preventing plagiarism: YRL seminar program.* Retrieved October 20, 2003, from http://www.library.ucla.edu/yrl/referenc/plagiarism.htm

16 *Consumer attitudes about nutrition: Insights into nutrition, health and soyfoods.* (n.d.). Retrieved July 21, 2003, from http://www.talksoy.com/pdfs/Consumer-Attitudes-2002.pdf

17 Robb Kendrick/Aurora. (n.d.). PhotoVoyage: Rice: A global grain. Washingtonpost.com. Retrieved October 30, 2003, from http://wpni01.auroraquanta.com/pv/rice

18 NanoInk, Inc. (n.d.). What is nanotechnology? Retrieved October 30, 2003, from http://www.nanoink.net/4100_whatis.html

19 Epidemiology: Controlling AIDS in Africa. (2003, April 17). *Nature.* Retrieved October 30, 2003, from http://www.nature.com/nature/links/030417/030417-3.html

20 Eshaghpour, T. (2003). *Confronting toxic contamination in our communities.* The Women's Foundation of California. Retrieved October 30, 2003, from www.womensfoundca.org/fullreport10_7.pdf

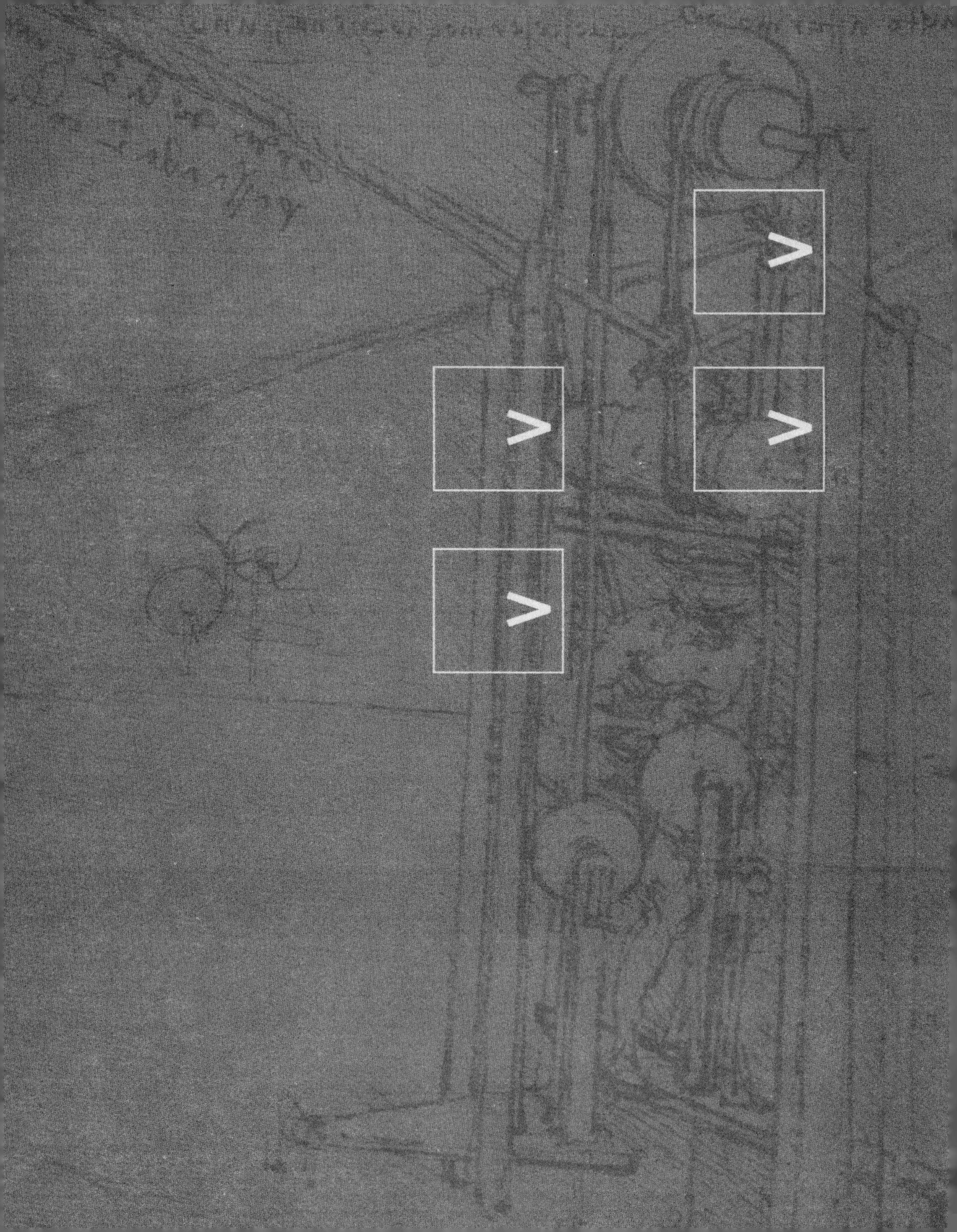

CHAPTER 7

Planning and Drafting
设计与起草

写作研究发现有经验的作者很注意花足够的时间调查研究主题、设计方法以及整理信息。他们非常重视信息的准确性以及能否引起交流对象的关注。本章注重介绍了有经验的职场人士在准备文本过程中采取的写作步骤。

Objectives and Outcomes 学习目标

This chapter will help you accomplish these outcomes:

- Learn the strategies used by experienced writers as they explore, plan, and draft documents, oral presentations, and visuals
- As part of *inventing and exploring,* use a problem-solving process with proven strategies: brainstorming, 5 *W*s plus *H,* cause-and-effect analysis, and synectics
- As part of *planning,* consider types of planning, use project-management tools, make decisions about rhetorical elements (content, purpose, task, audience, constraints, organization, and design), assess the logic
- As part of *drafting,* select the appropriate person and verb mood, use plain language, avoid density, and use given-new constructions

Research about writing shows that experienced writers recognize the importance of taking time to investigate their subject, plan their approach, and organize the draft of their information. They are concerned with accuracy as well as with the appropriateness and appeal of the information for the intended audience. They typically ask whether their documents, oral presentations, and visuals are accessible, comprehensible, and usable. In contrast, inexperienced writers tend to be concerned with whether they have enough content, minimize their planning, and not think much about the audience.

Let's look at the details of a process that you might use to create a document, oral presentation, or visual. Although the specific steps will change to suit your individual approach and the requirements of a particular project, experienced professionals typically move through these steps during their process:

- Inventing and exploring
- Planning and organizing
- Drafting and designing
- Revising
- Editing

This chapter focuses on what happens in inventing/exploring, planning/organizing, and drafting and suggests a number of strategies to help you become more expert-like in these parts of the process. Revising and editing are the focus of Chapter 8.

Differences Between Writing Processes
写作过程差异

What do skillful writers do when they write? The writing process used to be described as three linear stages: prewriting, drafting, and revising. However, as researchers have charted the actions and ideas of actual writers through the writing process, the notion that the process is linear has been dispelled. Writers say things like, "Lots of times while I'm in the middle of writing, I'll get a terrific idea — something I've never thought of before, something that's not part of my outline." Or, "I'll write one word and immediately know it's not quite right, so I'll scratch it out and write a new one." These people are saying that the steps in this creative process do not necessarily happen consecutively; rather, they are typically recursive — that is, steps happen more than once, and more than one step can happen at the same time.

Producing a technical document, oral presentation, or visual isn't a solitary process, either. You collaborate with other people for many different reasons (as you read in Chapter 5): to get the necessary information, to verify your approach, to confirm technical accuracy, and to check readers' reactions. Figure 7.1 identifies some of the major categories you need to consider and some of the questions you need to ask throughout every project. You can learn good questions to ask by starting with any category in Figure 7.1.

FIGURE 7.1 **Questions to Ask about Communication Relationships**

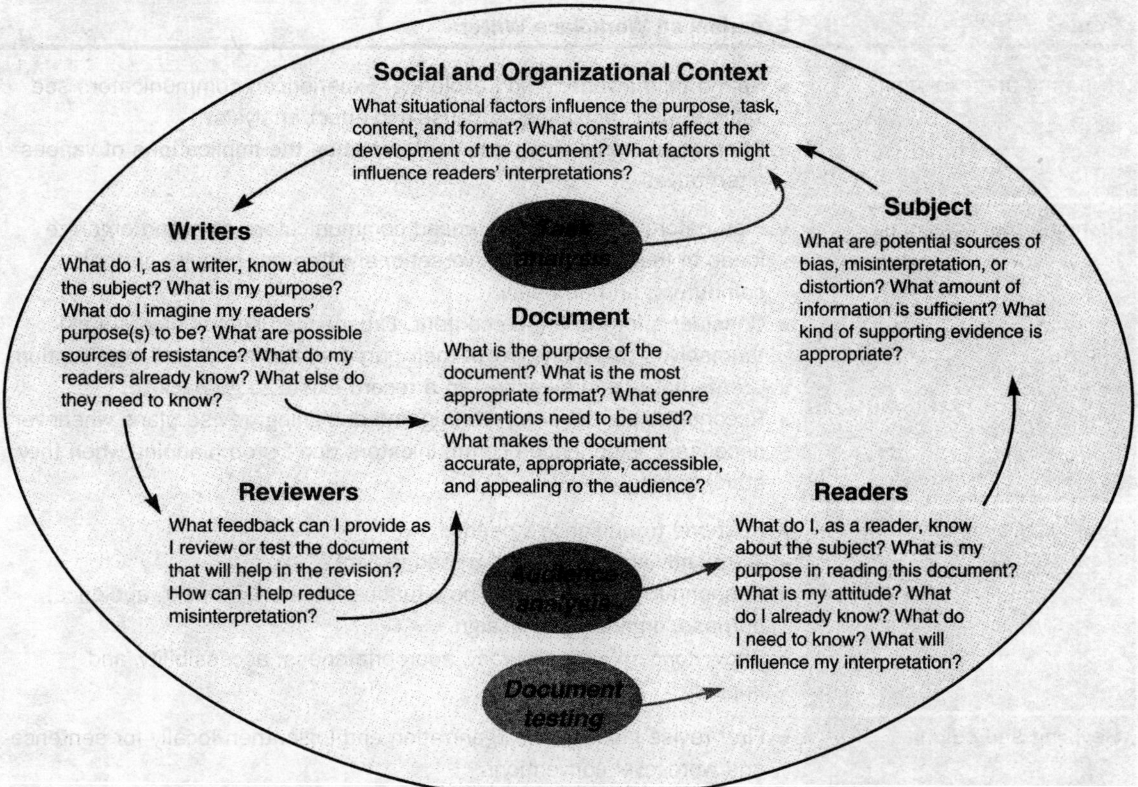

Many skillful communicators begin by asking about the context, the subject, and the document, oral presentation, or visual itself. But you can also start with yourself, depending on whether your role is as a writer (or speaker or designer), reader (or listener or viewer), or reviewer. Take time to carefully read the questions in Figure 7.1 and get accustomed to asking them every time you plan a document, presentation, or visual. When you're working for a specific organization, you'll add questions to those suggested here based on the people and politics of that organization.

When you find processes for inventing/exploring, planning, and drafting that work for you, examine them, use them, develop them. Once you're confident of an approach, branch out and try another one. If it works, integrate it with your writing practices. Figure 7.2 reviews some of the habits, concerns, and working procedures that are used by experienced workplace writers. You goal should be to develop these expert processes.

FIGURE 7.2 Composing Processes of Experienced Writers

Stage	Experienced Workplace Writers
Inventing and exploring	■ Spend time inventing and exploring. Experienced communicators see value in such activities as cause-and-effect analysis. ■ Spend time considering and contemplating the implications of various alternatives.
Planning and organizing	■ Plan before drafting. Experienced communicators plan and organize ideas in their heads, in conversations with other people, on their computers, and on paper. ■ Consider a lot more than content. Experienced communicators ask themselves questions about their purpose, audience, and organization. ■ Create notes and sketches so a record exists to go back to. ■ Reconsider plans during drafting and designing; revise plans whenever necessary. Experienced communicators don't stop planning when they start drafting.
Drafting/Designing	■ Respond to audience's needs. ■ Frequently stop to rescan, reread, reflect. ■ Respond to all aspects of the situation: content, context, audience, purpose, organization, design. ■ Show concern with accuracy, appropriateness, accessibility, and appeal.
Revising and editing	■ First revise globally for organization and logic, then locally for sentence- and word-level conventions. ■ See revising as ongoing throughout the process of preparing a document, oral presentation, or visual. ■ Proofread with care.

Inventing and Exploring
创作与探索

Communicators really do talk to themselves; they invent an idea and listen to how it sounds. During your inventing and exploring, you may assess your knowledge, read and review available background references, ask questions and discuss ideas, make observations, conduct experiments, and take notes. You may make tentative decisions about your task. Thinking about your options and your approach is part of this stage, one that you will return to many times while preparing a document, presentation, or visual.

Problem-Solving Processes 解决问题过程

Inventing and exploring offer an opportunity to investigate problems related to a particular document, oral presentation, or visual; as you consider possible solutions, effective problem solving can make your work easier. For example, you may have problems identifying good alternatives or determining the focus. One way you can be a more skillful problem solver is to go through a problem-solving process (which, like writing, is recursive, with overlapping stages).

Productive individuals and groups in the workplace consciously follow a problem-solving process. They initially (1) identify the context (politics, policies, parameters for solutions) and the problem (which may be defined differently by different people). Then they (2) gather and evaluate information in order to set priorities. Next they (3) typically formulate alternative possible solutions that may differ from conventional approaches, being careful to defer judgment about the preferred solution. Individuals (4) draw on their prior knowledge and experiences with similar problems in order to determine the preferred outcome and the criteria for success. Then they (5) assess the alternatives and select one plan of action. At that point, the group can (6) get started on the most appropriate, efficient solution, considering technical as well as organizational and interpersonal factors. As the solution is implemented, people need (7) to monitor individual and group performance against the outcome. Finally, they can (8) evaluate their performance to determine success of the problem-solving process and final product.

Which of these four problem-solving strategies have you used? How useful have they been? Which ones do you think you'll try in the future?

Problem-Solving Strategies 解决问题策略

This section of the chapter applies problem solving to four commonly used and successful strategies: brainstorming, 5 *Ws* + *H,* cause-and-effect analysis, and synectics.

To learn more about problem-solving strategies, ones that reinforce a constructive process as well as engage your creativity, go to **www.english.wadsworth.com/burnett6e** for useful links.

CLICK ON WEBLINK

CLICK on Chapter 7/problem-solving steps

WEBLINK

You're probably already familiar with the first problem-solving strategy, *brainstorming,* which encourages you to suggest as many ideas as possible about a given problem or situation without making any judgments until after a number of ideas have been suggested. Despite being remarkably simple, brainstorming is a problem-solving strategy that often works.

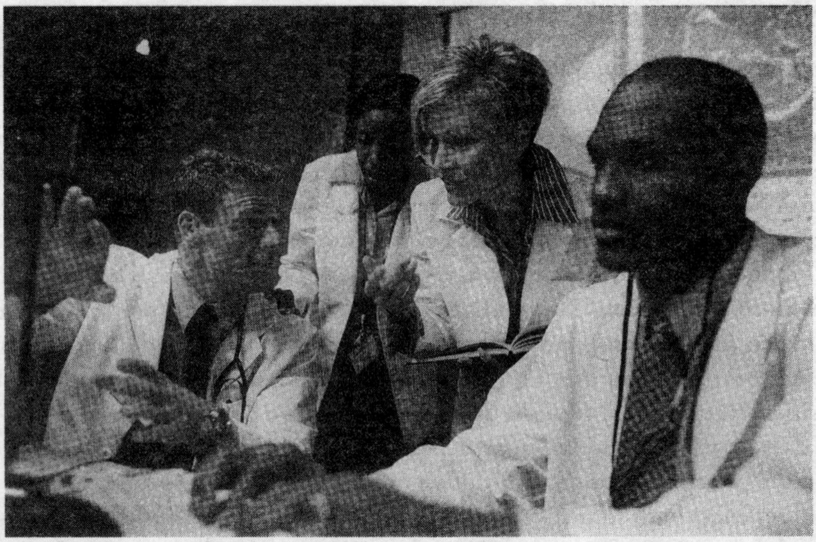

© Comstock Images/Getty Images

In a productive problem-solving situation, team members usually follow an established process, which means that along the way they consider lots of alternatives and engage in a considerable amount of substantive conflict (see Chapter 5). People working independently can also follow the same productive process, asking themselves tough questions.

Two other strategies are commonly used by quality control circles.* One of these strategies is also a formula frequently associated with journalism: *5 Ws plus* H. These questions are effective for approaching any problem you are examining:

- WHO — Who is involved? Who should be involved?
- WHAT — What is involved? What should be changed? What should remain the same?
- WHEN — When should it be done? When is the most appropriate or convenient time?
- WHERE — Where should it be done?
- WHY — Why should it be done?
- HOW — How should it be done?

Another strategy recommended by quality control circles is *cause-and-effect analysis,* which focuses on the causes of a particular problem. The initial causes are often separated into four categories: *machine, employee, material,* and *method.* Any of these possible causes can be expanded with additional headings. *Cause-and-effect charts* (also called *fishbone charts*) are a useful way to summarize causal relationships.

*A *quality control circle* is a group problem-solving process used in many companies. Small groups of people doing similar work go through a training period and then meet regularly to identify, analyze, and solve problems connected to the work they do. Many companies have established quality control circles, using research pioneered in Japan, to improve productivity as well as employee involvement.

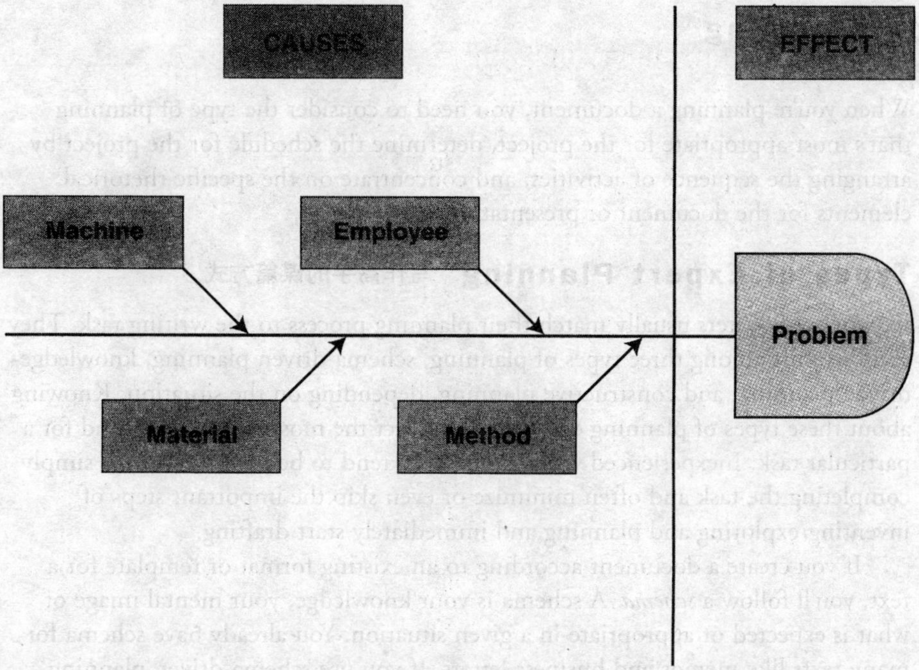

A final problem-solving strategy is *synectics,* often used collaboratively to stimulate creative thinking. *Synectics* is a coined word, from the Greek *syn* (meaning "to bring together") and *ectos* (for "diversity"), which, combined, suggest bringing together diverse people and ideas.[1] This "bringing together" encourages workplace professionals to, for example, combine two unrelated ideas as a means of analyzing a particular problem. The goal is to develop new perspectives and solutions. Using a variety of techniques, including metaphors, analogies, role-playing, and simulations, participants first define a particularly difficult problem. Then they put themselves *into* the problem by creating a metaphor or an analogy or by acting out a component of the problem. In synectics, participants are encouraged to engage in a variety of strategies: search for ideal solutions, imagine that they are the subject, compare the subject to something concrete, and compare the subject to something abstract. You can, of course, use similar problem-solving strategies at any time during the writing process.

To learn more about synectics, a widely used corporate problem-solving process (which developed from William Gordon's book, *Synectics,* published in the 1960s), go to **www.english.wadsworth.com/burnett6e** for useful links.
CLICK ON WEBLINK
CLICK on Chapter 7/synectics

WWW
WEBLINK

Planning and Organizing

谋篇与组织

When you're planning a document, you need to consider the type of planning that's most appropriate for the project, determine the schedule for the project by arranging the sequence of activities, and concentrate on the specific rhetorical elements for the document or presentation.

Types of Expert Planning 写作高手的谋篇方式

Experienced writers usually match their planning process to the writing task. They seem to shift among three types of planning, schema-driven planning, knowledge-driven planning, and constructive planning, depending on the situation. Knowing about these types of planning can help you select the most appropriate kind for a particular task. Inexperienced writers, however, tend to be concerned with simply completing the task and often minimize or even skip the important steps of inventing/exploring and planning and immediately start drafting.

If you create a document according to an existing format or template for a text, you'll follow a *schema.* A schema is your knowledge, your mental image of what is expected or appropriate in a given situation. You already have schema for many texts like memos and business letters. If you use schema-driven planning, you can often complete a document without much thought about format or the kind of information to include. For example, if you have a memo schema, you can quickly produce a memo announcing a meeting. If you have a business letter schema, you can quickly produce a letter requesting product specifications. Writers who use schema-driven planning can usually produce successful documents if their schema is appropriate for the situation.

In another situation, you might not have a schema, but you might have a great deal of knowledge about the subject. In this case, planning a document becomes a matter of your telling what you know about the subject. For *knowledge-driven planning* to work, your information must be well organized and appropriate for the task. For example, a chemist who has a great deal of experience with gas chromatography has the procedural knowledge to write instructions for technicians to operate the equipment fairly easily.

In contrast, if you have a difficult writing problem, you probably can't depend on existing schema or knowledge. Instead, you'll have to do *constructive planning,* which requires careful analysis of the purpose, audience, task, and a variety of constraints. Although constructive planning usually requires more time and effort than other kinds of planning, it helps you set goals and criteria as well as establish procedures for composing your document.

Often you may use a combination of schema-driven planning, knowledge-driven planning, and constructive planning. For example, writers preparing a proposal for municipal recycling of refuse need to be familiar with the format and language of proposals (their schema) and also need to have extensive knowledge about the subject. But the specific problem of preparing a proposal for recycling in a particular community requires constructive planning, so that the writers can solve the problems of the task and establish procedures for completing it.

Project Planning 项目设计

Inadequate project planning is one of the most common reasons that projects fail to produce excellent results. Early in the process of planning, workplace professionals often manage their time by sketching out what needs to be done and when it needs to be done. Your informal plan may be nothing more than a self-stick note stuck on a bulletin board or on the edge of your computer screen. Or you may prefer notes jotted on a calendar or electronic organizer. Maybe your style is to make a list of tasks that you paper clip to the front of a manila folder containing notes for the project. Whatever the form you choose, though, project planning serves an important time-management function by encouraging you to make a preliminary assessment of the tasks that need to be done, their order, and their deadlines.

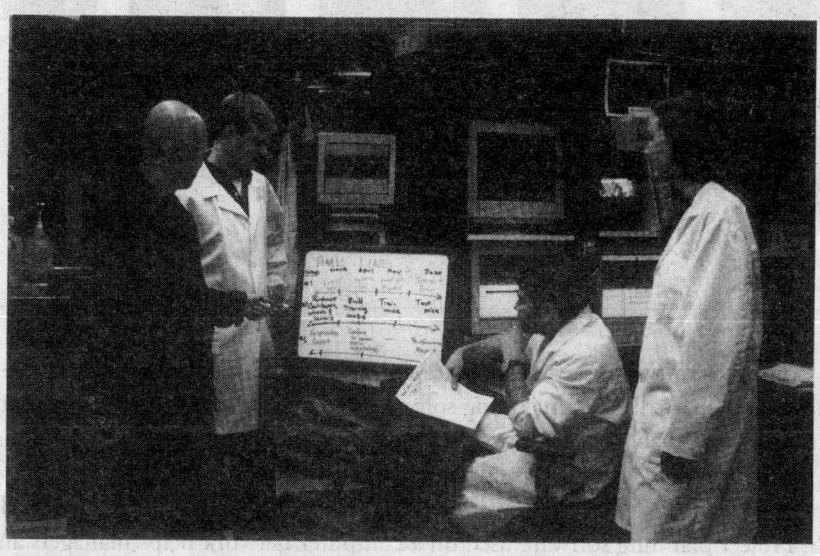

© Christina Micek Photography

Planning and updating the schedule for a complex project requires input from all the major players on a team. Checking the milestone dates on the schedule with the actual progress should be a regular weekly task.

For larger projects, professionals often turn to more formal time- and project-management tools. Two common tools are Program Evaluation Review Technique (PERT) charts and Gantt charts, both of which keep track of the various project tasks. PERT charts not only track project activities but also show how these activities depend on each other. Gantt charts track project activities on a timeline. Both of these project management tools enable you to plan projects and determine what should be accomplished at each stage. Figure 7.3 (PERT chart) and

Figure 7.4 (Gantt chart) illustrate the same project so that you can easily compare the two tools.

FIGURE 7.3 **PERT Chart Showing Steps in Revision of Mitsubishi TV Manual[2]**

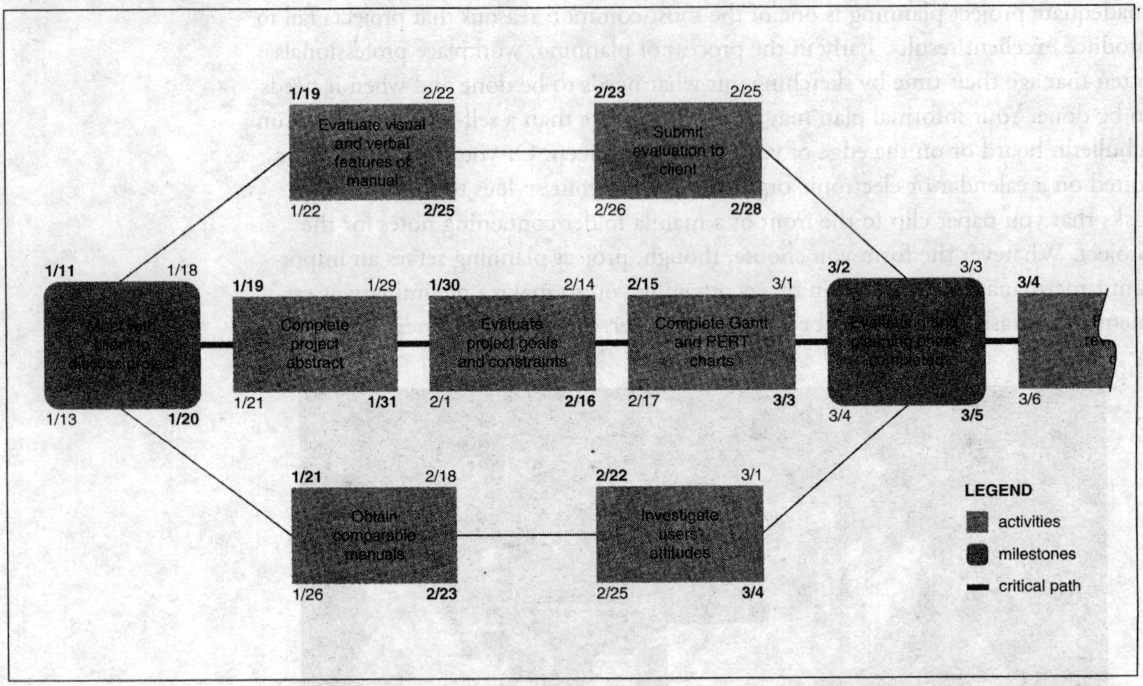

Computer software is available that helps you construct both kinds of time-management charts. Project planning software can make creating PERT and Gantt charts very easy; managers can print up-to-date charts, status reports, and graphs of the project's progress. More sophisticated packages allow users to link the charts for various projects so that managers can see conflicts in deadlines and balance work-loads. Project planning software used on a computer network helps managers automatically update the schedule and inform project members. For example, when a manager changes the project schedule, all project members are first notified and then receive e-mail reminding them of changes in upcoming deadlines.

WWW

WEBLINK

To see examples of project-planning charts as well as other useful visual displays, go to **www.english.wadsworth.com/burnett6e** for links to these project management tools.

CLICK ON WEBLINK

CLICK on Chapter 7/project management

FIGURE 7.4 Gantt Chart Showing Phases of Revision of Mitsubishi TV Manual[3]

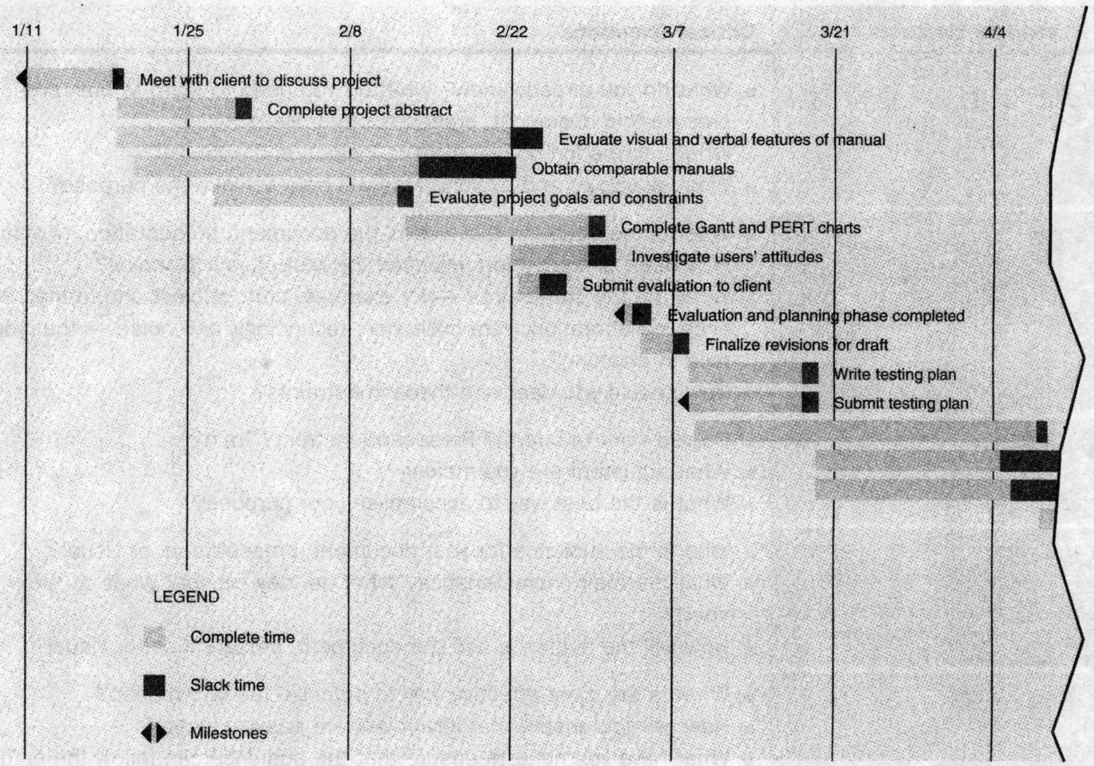

Considering Rhetorical Elements 考虑修辞方式

When you plan, you need to make decisions about a variety of rhetorical elements (which you have read about in Chapter 1). Figure 7.5 lists these rhetorical elements again, this time as areas that skillful communicators consider as they plan their documents, oral presentations, and visuals. The critical questions in Figure 7.5 provide suggestions you can use as you make decisions. As you use these questions, you should jot down additional ones that also help.

What planning questions do you believe will be useful for the kinds of communicating you expect to do in your career?

What you read at the beginning of this chapter about the overall process of writing being recursive also applies to the process of planning: Each element affects the others. The sequence in which you consider these elements has no best order. As your work on a document, presentation, or visual progresses, you can change your plans, but you need to begin with a sense of what you're doing and where you're going, in part because changes in one element influence the other elements. Although skillful communicators plan often and replan as their work progresses, careful planning can minimize the number of major changes that are

FIGURE 7.5 Critical Questions to Ask during Planning

Rhetorical Elements	Critical Questions
Content	■ What do you already know? What do you need to learn to plan and prepare this document, presentation, or visual? ■ What information do you want to include and exclude? ■ What examples and explanations will help achieve the purpose?
Context	■ What is the situation that needs the document, presentation, or visual? How does this situation influence the rest of your planning? ■ What are the constraints — for example, time, subject and format, audience, collaboration, data collection, technology, and noise — that you face in planning? ■ How should you deal with these constraints?
Purpose	■ Do you want to inform? Persuade? Instruct? Train? ■ What argument are you making? ■ What is the best way to accomplish your purpose?
Audience	■ Who is the audience for your document, presentation, or visual? ■ What are their characteristics? What do they expect? What do they need? ■ How will the audience use the document, presentation, or visual?
Organization	■ What is the most effective way to organize the information? ■ How will you ensure that key points are easy to locate? ■ What have you done to ensure that the audience can follow the argument? That the points are coherent?
Visuals	■ Which information should be presented verbally, and which should be presented visually? ■ What visual conventions need to be followed?
Document design	■ How can the design reinforce the purpose of the document, presentation, or visual? ■ What design features will appeal to the audience? ■ What design conventions need to be followed?
Usability	■ How will you determine that the information is accurate? ■ How will you determine that the information in the document, presentation, or visual is usable for all of the intended users?
Language conventions	■ What professional standards are you using? ■ What will the audience expect?

needed later. Simply put, you'll find changing a plan easier than changing a completed document, presentation, or visual.

Planning is often more productive if it is collaborative, even if you are going to draft independently. Working with someone else often generates ideas and approaches that you might not come up with when working alone. Unfortunately, you will almost always be under a deadline, so make time for planning, whether a few minutes alone as you develop ideas for a short letter, or two-minute oral update during a meeting, or a few weeks with others as you collaborate on a complex proposal or an important conference presentation. Despite temptations to jump right into the actual work, you should not skimp on exploring and planning.

One of the most important things you should pay attention to during planning is the ethics of the situation. The ethics sidebar below specifically addresses ethical questions you need to answer early in your planning. Having accurate content or an appealing design doesn't much matter if you're perceived as unethical. The sidebar focuses on achieving a balance between your personal (or private) positions and your public positions.

What issues in your discipline might cause inconsistencies between your private and public positions?

ETHICS 职业道德规范知识吧 SIDEBAR

"Is the communication honest?": Ethics and the Writing Process "交流是诚实的吗?"：职业道德与写作过程

Technical professionals face ethical decisions throughout the writing process. From initial brainstorming through the creation of the document, to post-production distribution, technical professionals must continually be aware of the ethical aspects of their communication. Researcher Brenda Sims provides a useful list of questions to ask yourself as you plan, draft, and revise documents and presentations:[4]

- Is the communication honest and truthful?
- Am I acting in the organization's best interest? In the public's? In my own?
- What if everybody acted or communicated in this way?
- Does the action or communication violate the rights of any of the people involved?
- Am I treating similar situations similarly?
- Am I willing to take responsibility for the action or communication publicly and privately?

Asking yourself these questions helps you look at your communication from personal and public perspectives. Ethical problems can occur when we don't look at how communication is perceived privately and publicly.

If you are willing to take responsibility for a communication privately but not publicly, then your behavior may be viewed as unethical by your colleagues or the general public. For example, if you send a private memo to a colleague objecting to company hiring practices but you are unwilling to voice the same concerns publicly, you may be perceived by some colleagues as acting unethically because you will not take a public position.

If, on the other hand, you take a public position but it conflicts with your private view, then your personal ethics may also be in question. For example, if you tell sales representatives that an owner's manual covers all possible problems that owners will encounter, but you neglect to mention that you personally believe that some explanations are very difficult to understand, some people may question your ethics.

How can you revise documents so that they are acceptable privately and publicly?

Ethical problems like these affect your professional standing and credibility. In most companies, organizations, and agencies, you will be held responsible for what you communicate. Using checklists like the one provided by Sims helps you avoid potential ethical problems that could negatively affect your writing and career.

Assessing the Logic 逻辑检测

One of the most difficult parts of planning is making sure your document, oral presentation, or visual is logical. You must first recognize potential problems in logic and then know how to correct them. Problems in logic generally fall into four categories:

- Using data from authorities
- Presenting facts without drawing inferences
- Drawing inferences
- Establishing causal relationships

Once you recognize these pitfalls, you are likely to judge your data more critically. The following discussion defines these four categories of logic problems, analyzes examples, and suggests possible ways to eliminate the problems before they find their way into a draft.

What problem(s) have you observed that involved using data from authorities?

Using Data from Authorities Your audience will often respond positively to data from a recognized authority in the field. However, the data lose their effectiveness if the expert's qualifications are suspect or if the expert has a vested interest in the subject. If people or organizations have a vested interest (that is, a proprietary concern in supporting a particular position), their views might be more self-serving than objective. For example, imagine that the New England Soy Dairy prints a flier that states, "People everywhere are excited about the prospect of adding tofu to their diets." The business of the New England Soy Dairy is to market soy products, so it is in their interest to promote positive attitudes about soy products. Before accepting their word about the widespread excitement regarding soy products, you should verify the information with less vested sources.

What problem(s) have you observed that involved at least one of the following kinds of presenting facts without drawing inferences?

Presenting Facts without Drawing Inferences You present verifiable information (what we usually call *facts*) in the form of statistics, quotations, or visuals intended to support points in a document or oral presentation. If the facts you present are incomplete, out of context, oversimplified, or distorted, the audience will be misled.

- ***Omitted or Incomplete Data.*** Omitted or incomplete data, whether deliberate or accidental, affect the accuracy and credibility of a document or oral presentation. Imagine a novice computer user trying to follow instructions that omit a critical piece of information, such as "Press Enter after completing each step" — information that is second nature to anyone who has some computer experience. Having omitted or incomplete data sometimes results from failure to check and recheck facts, but the problem also occurs when a writer hopes to influence the audience by omitting discrepant or conflicting data, as the following example shows:

Statement	Soy-based infant formula is generally the best food for infants with milk allergies.
Comment	The statement fails to mention that breast milk is the best food for infants and greatly reduces the likelihood that an infant will develop milk allergies.
Revision	When breast-feeding is impossible or is not the feeding method of choice, soy-based infant formula is generally the best alternative for infants with milk allergies.

- ***Out-of-Context Data.*** Out-of-context information may be accurate in itself, but if relevant background or related information is omitted, the audience will have a distorted view. Out of context, even indisputable information can be misleading, as seen in this example:

Statement	American farmers often prefer planting corn to soybeans.
Comment	Although the statement is true, taking it out of context ignores both the important reasons that influence farmers' decisions and the relationship between soybeans and other major crops.
Revision	Soybean crops compete with other major crops in the principal production areas, so the amount of land planted with soybeans depends on a complex interaction of factors that affect both soybeans and the competing crops. Most significant appears to be the price relationship between corn and soybeans in the major Midwest area, and between cotton and soybeans in the Mississippi Delta. This relationship, in turn, depends on world market factors, which most recently have tended to favor corn over soybeans and soybeans over cotton.[5]

- ***Oversimplified or Distorted Data.*** Oversimplification reduces a complex situation or concept to a few simple ideas, ignores relevant details, and gives the audience a distorted view, as the following example illustrates:

Statement	Adding soy protein to a person's diet improves the quality of the diet.
Comment	Many factors determine the quality of a diet; the interrelationships of all dietary components must be considered. Adding soy protein to some diets may result in an excess protein intake, limit the intake of other necessary nutrients, and so on.
Revision	The inclusion of soy protein in a person's diet may have economic, nutritional, and sensory benefits.

What problem(s) have you observed that involved at least one of the following kinds of drawing inferences?

Drawing Inferences During your planning of a document, oral presentation, or visual, you obtain data and then draw inferences based on that data. These inferences will be faulty if you make hasty generalizations, assume irrelevant functions, or fall prey to fallacies of composition and division. Data should represent the general condition or situation.

- ***Hasty Generalizations.*** A hasty generalization occurs when a particular case or situation is mistakenly assumed to be typical or representative of a group. This error usually takes place when you have not examined enough cases to warrant a generalization, as in the following example:

Statement	In a survey of members of food cooperatives, 90 percent stated they would like to increase the amount of soy in their diets. Therefore, Americans are willing to eat more soy foods.
Comment	Members of food cooperatives may not be representative of the greater population.
Revision	The willingness of co-op members surveyed to increase soy food intake suggests a potential for increased soy food consumption in at least some segments of the American population.

- ***Irrelevant Functions.*** When you criticize something for not having a characteristic it was never intended to have, you are guilty of assuming an irrelevant function:

Statement	Tofu and tempeh (a traditional Indonesian cultured soybean food) do not taste like meat.
Comment	Tofu and tempeh, traditional foods in several cultures, should be appreciated for their own characteristics. They are not intended to taste like meat.
Revision	Tofu and tempeh are alternative sources of protein for people who choose to eat less meat in their diet.

- ***Composition and Division.*** The fallacy of composition assumes that the characteristics of the individual components can be attributed to the whole. The reverse occurs in the fallacy of division, in which the characteristics of the whole are attributed to each of the individual components composing the whole. The following example illustrates the fallacy of division:

Statement	Peanut butter on wheat bread is a protein dish of high biological value (it is a "complete protein"); therefore, peanut butter alone or wheat bread alone has a high biological value (is a "complete protein").
Comment	In this example of the fallacy of division, the basic assumption is faulty. In fact, peanuts (peanut butter) and grain (bread) proteins complement each other to together provide protein of high biological value.
Revision	Peanut butter combined with wheat bread is a protein dish of high biological value.

What problem(s) have you observed that involved at least one of the following kinds of causal relationships?

Establishing Causal Relationships One of the most frequent relationships employed in technical documents, oral presentations, or visuals establishes causes and resulting effects. Your audience can be misled by several kinds of poorly drawn causal relationships, including a condition not being sufficient cause, variables not being correlated, and the fallacy of *post hoc, ergo propter hoc.*

- ***Condition Not a Sufficient Cause.*** An effect that results from multiple causes must have sufficient causes, and it may also have contributing causes. A *sufficient cause* is one that by itself can produce the effect. A *contributing cause* may help bring about the effect, but if all other causes are eliminated, any one contributing cause by itself cannot produce the effect. The following example demonstrates how poorly established cause–effect relationships can mislead an audience:

Statement	The patient's heart attack was caused because his diet contained too much cholesterol.
Comment	Heart disease is caused by a number of contributing factors, such as diet, obesity, smoking, heredity, hypertension, and amount of exercise. Evidence has not yet shown that cholesterol alone is a sufficient cause, but it is usually a contributing cause.
Revision	High cholesterol may have contributed to the patient's heart disease.

- ***Variables Not Correlated.*** Even though a number of factors frequently occur in sequence, a cause–effect relationship does not necessarily exist:

Statement	In the 1970s, the U.S. production of soybeans rose, and soon after, Americans began eating more soybeans.
Comment	The increase in soy production was primarily to help the balance of trade. Most of the soy was exported and used as animal feed. Americans' increase in soy consumption has resulted from a number of factors such as increased awareness, marketing, and availability.

Revision	In the 1970s, the U.S. production of soybeans rose to help the balance of trade. At the same time, Americans began eating more soybeans in response to a combination of factors, such as increased awareness, marketing, and availability.

- ***Fallacy of* Post Hoc, Ergo Propter Hoc.** This line of reasoning (usually simply called *post hoc*) claims that because one event follows another, the first event must cause the second. The Latin translates as "after this, therefore because of this." The following example demonstrates how such fallacious logic can undermine a document's credibility:

Statement	Japanese women eat a high proportion of soy protein in their diets. Japanese women also have a low incidence of breast cancer; therefore, eating soy lowers the likelihood of breast cancer.
Comment	Even though eating soy precedes the low incidence of breast cancer, the chronology does not necessarily indicate a causal relationship. Japanese women also have a high intake of fish. Does eating fish also lower the risk of breast cancer?
Revision	Japanese women eat a high proportion of soy protein in their diets. Japanese women also have a low incidence of breast cancer. Emphasizing low-fat foods in the diet (such as soy and some types of fish) may be a contributing factor in lowering the risk of breast cancer.

When you're finished revising a document or presentation, checking the statements in Figure 7.6 will help you evaluate whether the information will withstand scrutiny.

FIGURE 7.6 **Questions about the Logic of a Document to Ask Yourself During Revision**

If you answer "I agree" to each of these statements, you can be fairly sure the logic in your document, oral presentation, or visuals will withstand scrutiny.	***I agree***
All the evidence and data are accurate.	❑
No information has been deliberately or accidentally omitted, oversimplified, or distorted.	❑
No sources have special vested interests.	❑
Examples and cases are representative of the general condition(s) or situation(s).	❑
Data are presented with appropriate background information or discussion so that they are meaningful to readers.	❑
Sources have expertise in the area being discussed.	❑
Visuals are presented without distortion of any kind.	❑
Nothing is criticized for something that is not part of its nature or function.	❑
Causes and effects are clearly differentiated and not mistakenly assumed because of a sequence of events.	❑

Drafting involves writing the text and preparing the visuals. Writers, speakers, and designers have many different ways of approaching this stage of the process:

- You may create bits and pieces of a draft during the planning stage, recording key sentences or making preliminary sketches of things you don't want to forget. When your planning seems to be done, you take these ideas, develop them, and fill in the spaces.
- You may sit down to compose or design from beginning to end without interruption.
- You may prepare an outline and notes or a rough thumbnail sketch, then set them aside and start to write or draw, checking your planning materials only when you get stuck.
- You may generate an online outline or a sketch as the framework of your document or visual and then stick to this outline or sketch.
- You may work slowly, pondering and polishing every phrase and sentence or every line and figure as you go along.
- You may work rapidly, encouraging the ideas to flow quickly, tumbling onto each other.

One key to drafting is trying several approaches in order to find out which ways work best for you. A second key is seeing drafting as recursive, something you do throughout the process of preparing a document, oral presentation, or visual. You draft as you think of new ideas, as the nature of the project changes, as sections need to be elaborated, as new information become available. Drafting is seldom a "do it once" part of the process.

Selecting Person 人称选择

Choosing among first, second, or third person depends on the purpose and audience of the document, oral presentation, or visual. First person (*I, we*) is appropriate if, for example, you are narrating the events in a sequence in which you were involved. If your role in the action was significant, the use of first person emphasizes this. Second person (*you*) is usually reserved for instructions, since readers are being directed to complete a particular action. Third person (*he, she, one, it, they*) is most common, allowing you to emphasize the sequence of action rather than yourself or the readers.

While the guidelines above are appropriate for default decisions, you should follow the conventions of the organization or journal that is the primary audience for your document, oral presentation, or visual. For example, some organizations and journals require third person, while others accept and sometimes even expect first person.

WWW

WEBLINK

To read about ways to manage gender problems with pronouns, go to **www.english.wadsworth.com/burnett6e** for a link to a discussion about ways to avoid sexist language.
CLICK ON WEBLINK
CLICK on Chapter 7/sexist language

Verb Mood 动词语气

Mood refers to the characteristics of verbs that convey a speaker's or writer's attitude toward a statement. During drafting, you should select the verb mood that's appropriate for the situation.

- Indicative mood states facts or opinions or asks questions.

fact	Nurses *use* a rectal thermometer to take a baby's temperature.
opinion	Child-care providers *prefer* a thermometer strip rather than a rectal thermometer for taking a baby's temperature.
question	Why should child-care providers *use* a thermometer strip to take a baby's temperature?

- Imperative mood expresses commands or gives a direction.

command	(You) *Use* a rectal thermometer to take a baby's temperature.
direction	(You) *Get* a thermometer from the drawer labeled "Thermometers" in Utility Room II.

- Subjunctive mood expresses recommendations, wishes, conjectures, indirect requests, and statements of conditions contrary to fact.

recommendation	When children are hospitalized, we recommend that parents *be* with them. [not *are*]
wish	I wish the clinic *were* able to provide more well-baby classes. [not *was*]
conjecture	If the budget *were* not cut, we would have electronic thermometers. [not *was*]
indirect request	If the rectal thermometer *were* to break, a baby could be seriously injured. [not *was*]
condition contrary to fact	The parent asked if the examination *were* almost over. [not *was*]

Because process explanations deal with observable, verifiable information, they are written in indicative mood. But you also need to be able to recognize and use imperative mood (especially for directions) and subjunctive mood (useful in correspondence and reports).

Selecting Active or Passive Voice 主动或被动语态

Your selection of active or passive voice depends on the subject, the purpose and focus, and the audience. Active voice emphasizes the doer of the action (sometimes called the agent) and de-emphasizes the receiver, which is appropriate in most situations. Such emphasis is appropriate when readers are more interested in the doer or in the action itself than in the receiver or result of the action. Material presented in active voice is also more interesting to read, in part because the subject of the sentence is responsible for the action. Active voice is more direct; the audience does not have to work as hard to figure out who does what. Active voice is less wordy because the "to be" verb form necessary to create a passive construction is omitted. In general, you can use active voice unless you have a specific reason not to. You need to think about active and passive voice while you're drafting a document. The agent (the doer) in active voice does not always have to be a person, or even a living organism, as the following example illustrates:

> Solid-state computer scanners maintain a file of fingerprints. When a fingerprint is put into the file, the computer scanner identifies the characteristic "points" of a fingerprint (up to 150 points, though only 12 are needed for legal identification) and then converts them to a series of numbers that are stored on a computer disk file. When a fingerprint from a crime scene is digitized in a similar manner, the scanner attempts to match the "numbers." Each disk drive stores up to 90,000 fingerprint cards, each card with 10 prints. The computer can riffle through 1,200 such points every second. The computer can increase arrest rates based on fingerprints 10 to 15 percent above the current levels.[6]

In this example, the agent is the computer scanner, which can maintain a file, identify characteristic "points," convert them for storage, and, later, match the numbers.

Passive voice also has appropriate uses. When the receiver is more important than the agent, passive voice is usually correct. In this following example, the agent ("by Hollywood lore") is less important than the concept ("the fingerprint").

Passive voice	The fingerprint is overrated by Hollywood lore as a way to catch criminals.

Passive voice is also appropriate when the agent is unknown or insignificant.

Passive voice	Fingerprints are collected only between 25 and 30 percent of the time, even though they are usually the most prevalent form of physical evidence at the scene of a crime.

In this sentence the agent is not identified ("Fingerprints are collected [by unknown detectives]"), so passive voice is not only appropriate but necessary.

When you are deciding whether to use active or passive voice, consider your purpose and audience. If you want the focus to be on the receiver of the action rather than on the agent, then use passive voice. If, on the other hand, you want to emphasize the agent, use active voice. The following two examples illustrate the difference.

Passive voice masks or minimizes the agent of action and emphasizes the receiver of the action. Argon lasers and household "super glue" are now used by some dactylography experts to collect fingerprints. A small, highly concentrated, single-wavelength light beam is produced by the laser. Fluorescence is induced by the laser in such fingerprint chemicals as riboflavin. Prints — even old ones — can be lifted from paper, something that has been impervious to traditional dusting, by the laser. The benefits of super glue were discovered by accident. The fumes from the glue interact with the amino acids and outline the print. A fingerprint is raised and preserved by super glue on just about any surface. The glue is used on surfaces such as skin, plastic, coarse metal, and leather.	**Active voice** emphasizes the agent of action. Some dactylography experts now use argon lasers and household "super glue" to collect fingerprints. The laser produces a small, highly concentrated, single-wavelength light beam that can induce fluorescence in such fingerprint chemicals as riboflavin. The laser can lift prints — even old ones — from paper, something that has been impervious to traditional dusting. Experts discovered the benefits of super glue by accident. The fumes from the glue interact with the print in a way that raises and preserves it on just about any surface, including skin, plastic, coarse metal, and leather.

Using Plain Language 使用通俗语言

Plain language communicates information — even very complex information — so that it makes sense to most people. As you draft, you should make plain language a goal. Many experts in both law and technical communication agree that plain language has a number of characteristics:

- It eliminates unnecessary or inappropriate formalisms ("wherefore," "whereas"), archaic expressions ("herein," "thereof"), redundancies ("consent and agree," "each and every"), and Latin words.
- It uses strong verbs that eliminate nominalizations ("classify" rather than "classification").
- It is direct and eliminates wordiness.

Plain language is more than a good idea; it's a presidential order that has been in effect since 1998 for all U.S. federal documents (though most people acknowledge that getting all government documents in plain language is not an easy task):

> The Federal Government's writing must be in plain language. By using plain language, we send a clear message about what the Government is doing, what it requires, and what services it offers. Plain language saves the government and the private sector time, effort, and money. . . . Plain language documents have logical organization, easy-to-read design, [and these language features]:
>
> - common, everyday words, except for necessary technical terms
> - "you" and other pronouns
> - the active voice
> - short sentences[7]

To read the full text of the "Presidential Memorandum on Plain Language," go to **www.english.wadsworth.com/burnett6e** for a link to the original order.
CLICK ON WEBLINK
CLICK on Chapter 7/Presidential Memorandum

WEBLINK

The federal agency charged with helping departments and agencies use plain language, the Plain Language Action & Information Network, says that "[p]eople should be able to understand what we write the first time they read it, especially materials that tell people how to obtain benefits or comply with requirements."[8]

To learn more about ways to use plain language, go to **www.english.wadsworth.com/burnett6e** for a link to sites with guidelines and strategies to make technical documents, including legal documents, more usable.
CLICK ON WEBLINK
CLICK on Chapter 7/creating plain language

WEBLINK

Efforts in government, business, and industry to increase the use of plain language have been under way for nearly a decade. Does plain language really make a difference? One dramatic situation shows how complex technical language can affect people's lives. The U.S. Court of Appeals for the Ninth Circuit heard the case *Maria Walters and Others v. United States Immigration and Naturalization Service* (INS).

> In this case, the court found that certain government forms were so difficult to read that they violated due process requirements that people be given "notice"

of possible legal actions against them, and of the legal consequences of their own actions. In brief, the 9th Circuit Court of Appeals found that aliens subject to deportation based on INS charges that they committed document fraud did not get due process. The forms used by INS to tell the plaintiffs that they might be deported did not "simply and plainly communicate" legal consequences to the plaintiffs. The court ordered INS to redo the forms to communicate better. The court also ordered INS to refrain from deporting any alien whose case had been processed using the deficient forms.[9]

WWW

WEBLINK

To read more about the case *Maria Walters and Others v. United States Immigration and Naturalization Service*, go to **www.english.wadsworth.com/burnett6e** for a link to the complete text of the decision.

CLICK ON WEBLINK

CLICK on Chapter 7/Walters vs. Reno

How else can plain language make a difference? Which of these pairs of sentences would you prefer to read? Which would you prefer to write?

When the process of freeing a vehicle that has been stuck results in ruts or holes, the operator will fill the rut or hole created by such activity before removing the vehicle from the immediate area.	***or this . . .***	If you make a hole while freeing a stuck vehicle, you must fill the hole before you drive away.
The Secretary of the Interior may, in specific cases or in specific geographic areas, adopt or make applicable to off-reservation Indian lands all or any part of such laws, ordinances, codes, resolutions, rules or other regulations of the State and political sub-divisions in which the land is located as the Secretary shall determine to be in the best interest of the Indian owner or owners in achieving the highest and best use of such property.	***or this . . .***	We may apply state or local laws to off-reservation lands. We will do this only if it will help the Indian owners make the best use of their lands.[10]

Using plain language will increase the comprehensibility and usability of your documents, oral presentations, and visuals.

Is plain writing just "dumbing it down"? To learn more about whether using plain language in government, business, and industry really makes any difference, go to **www.english.wadsworth.com/burnett6e** for links to the results of a study that discusses the cost saving and microeconomic reform that can result from plain writing, as well as a straightforward discussion about the myths and benefits of plain writing.

CLICK ON WEBLINK

CLICK on Chapter 7/It's not "dumbing it down."

WWW

WEBLINK

Avoiding Density 避免晦涩

One of the ways to draft comprehensible, usable documents is to avoid dense text. For example, sometimes a paragraph you draft focuses on a single topic and has appropriate sentence structure, yet it is difficult to read because you have packed the ideas so tightly that the connections are obscured. As a result, the audience will have trouble following your reasoning. Several techniques can help you draft to reduce the density in your writing:

1. ***Suggestions about verbal elements***
   - Separate information into several sentences rather than a few very long sentences.
   - Develop important points in separate paragraphs.
   - Add examples and explanations to illustrate points.
   - Use direct diction.
   - Add transitions within paragraphs and between paragraphs and sections of a document.
2. ***Suggestions about visual elements***
   - Use headings and subheadings to identify key sections.
   - Illustrate objects and concepts to aid understanding.
   - Use selected visual devices to highlight key ideas: lists, bullets, tables, underlining, italics, boldface.

In Figure 7.7, the notes for the paragraph are so dense that readers have trouble absorbing the information. The sentences are long and wordy, with few transitions to establish relationships among the ideas; in some places, additional information is needed. Careful drafting of this paragraph in Figure 7.8 considers sentence length, separates information into several paragraphs, adds a clarifying figure, and includes transitions to signal relationships.

One of the interesting things about this example is that the comprehensibility has more to do with organization of information than with adherence to mechanical or grammatical conventions.

FIGURE 7.7 **Dense Notes**

Separate each chunk into sentences to give equal emphasis to each point.

Too much new information in each sentence.

A robot hand can perform rapid, small motions by human-like finger actions—independently of its manipulator arm, be attachable to many different manipulators without any modifications to the arms, and has the potential as a prosthesis for humans. The hand employs three opposed fingers, each one with three joints and a cushioned tip on the outer segment, controlled by four sheathed cables running to motors on the forearm. The motor drives on the forearm impose no loads on the hand actuators, and the drives are more easily accommodated on the forearm and have a much smaller effect on its response than they would if located on the hand. The robot-hand fingers can provide more than three contact areas since more than one segment per finger can contact an object; thus, the robot hand can move objects about, twist them, and otherwise manipulate them by finger motion alone.

Separate into paragraphs to reduce density.

Add a figure so readers can visualize the robot hand.

FIGURE 7.8 **Draft of a Paragraph That Avoids Density[11]**

Applying given-new principle places "hand" in the subject position.

A robot hand currently under development performs rapid, small motions by human-like finger actions—independently of its manipulator arm. Without modification, the robot hand attaches to many different arms. The hand even has the potential as a prosthesis for humans.

As shown in the figure, the hand employs three opposed fingers. Each has three joints and a cushioned tip on the outer segment. Each finger is controlled by four sheathed cables running to motors on the forearm.

The use of an analogy — comparing the robot hand to a human hand — helps readers understand key distinctions.

The topic of the paragraph (eliminating problems) is placed first.

The new hand eliminates some problems with previous designs. Its motor drives are on the forearm (rather than on the hand itself), where their weight and inertia impose no loads on the hand actuators. The drives are more easily accommodated on the forearm and have a much smaller effect on its response than they would if located on the hand.

Like the fingers on the human hand, the robot-hand fingers provide more than three contact areas since more than one segment per finger contacts an object. Thus, like the human hand, the robot hand moves and manipulates objects by finger motion alone.

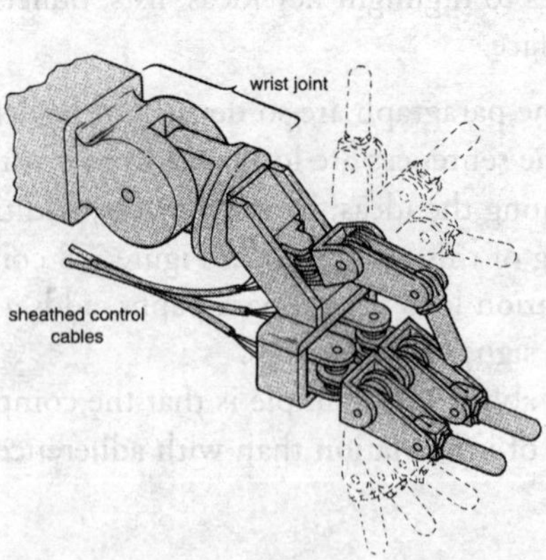

A figure helps readers visualize the robot hand.

Using Given-New Analysis 采用已有—新增信息构建写作模式

Another problem that occurs during drafting is working toward document coherence — that is, making sure that one idea logically or clearly relates to the following idea. Connections that aren't obvious to audience must be articulated. This problem often occurs when a writer presumes too much about the readers' prior knowledge. In these situations, a writer forgets (or neglects) to include background and connecting information that readers need.

One way to ensure that you provide the audience with the cues is to use *given-new constructions,* which strengthen the coherence of a document. In such constructions, new information is connected to what the audience already knows, either from background knowledge or from immediately preceding text. Given-new analysis aids drafting by providing a quick, effective way to spotlight the new information you have introduced. These are three of the many variations of given-new that are possible, with *A, B, C,* and so on representing pieces of information:

EXAMPLE 1[12]

sentence	**given-new**	
(1)	given A: new B	(1) The *ink* of a squid [A] is *brown or black viscous*
(2)	given A: new C	*fluid* [B], which is contained in a reservoir. (2) The
		ink [A] is *ejected through the siphon when a squid is*
(3)	given A: new D	*alarmed* [C]. (3) This *ink* [A] not only forms an *effective*
		screen behind which the animal can escape [D], but
	given A: new E	*it* [A] contains *alkaloids that paralyze the olfactory*
		senses of the enemy [E].

EXAMPLE 2

sentence	**given-new**	
(1)	given A: new B	(1) All *squids* [A] propel themselves by *taking in and*
		forcibly expelling water from the mantle cavity
(2)	given B: new C	through the siphon [B]. (2) The *force and direction of*
		the water expelled [B], plus the undulation of the fins
		and body, determine the *direction and rapid move-*
(3)	given C: new D	*ment* [C] of the animals. (3) The *rapid movement*
		[C] is always in the opposite direction of the *water*
(4)	given D: new E	*ejected from the siphon* [D]. (4) The *ejection of the*
		water [D] also *oxygenates the gills,* located in the
		mantle cavity [E].

EXAMPLE 3

sentence	**given-new**	
(1)	given A: new B	(1) The unusual *coloration* [A] of squid is caused by
		the presence of *integumental pigment cells* [B].
(2)	given B: new C	(2) These *cells, called chromatophores* [B], contain
(3)	given A: new D	red, blue, yellow, and black *pigment* [C]. (3) *Coloration*

(4)	given B: new E	[A] is *specific to each species* [D]. (4) The *chromatophores, color cells,* [B] are controlled by m expand or contract in relation to visual stimuli, thus *changing the color of the*
(5)	given B: new F	(5) The *pigment cells'* [B] release of color into th flesh of a dead animal indicates the *onset of spoilage* [F].

Information in drafts that follow given-new structures is typically easier to read and remember. In addition, given-new structures make the relationships between ideas clear to the audience.

Individual and Collaborative Assignments
个人作业和小组作业

1. **Track your writing process.** One way to learn about your writing process is to track your own process as you prepare a document. You will need to maintain careful records. Use one of the following methods.
   (a) Tape-record your planning or drafting. (Note: Trying to track the entire process of preparing the document takes too much time; pick just one part of the process.) Afterward, listen to the tape to identify interesting patterns you can note in your log.
   (b) As you were encouraged to do in Chapter 5, keep a log in which you record every time you work on the document. Record the date and time as well as what happens during the time. Try to be as accurate and complete as possible.

2. **Analyze your writing process.**
   (a) Use the data you have collected in Assignment 1 to write a one- to two-page discussion about one aspect of your writing process. Focus on some specific aspect — for example, the way you defined the task, the way you considered your audience, the way you organized or designed the document. Reread your log, looking for patterns in your oral interaction and your writing. Determine what problem-solving strategies you found useful in your writing. Use quotations from the tape or log to support your decision.
   (b) Write a memo to your instructor in which you describe the productive patterns that you hope to continue and the unproductive patterns that you hope to change. Then speculate about the relationship between your process and the quality of your writing.

(c) Assume the time from the beginning to the end of the writing project in Assignment 1 is 100 percent. Design a chart that will be part of the memo in which you show the typical proportion of time you spend on each stage of your writing process. Explain in which stage(s) you're most effective, in which you're the weakest, and what might you do to improve your process.

3. **Create a rubric.** The only way to make sure that your writing is effective is to analyze it (as in Assignment 2) to determine what areas you need to improve. Use the rubric from Chapter 1 to analyze a document that you created (modify it to fit your document) so that you can assess your own skills as a technical communicator. Each time you create a new document, use the rubric to establish where you have made improvements.

4. **Interview a professional, part II.**

(a) Arrange to interview a professional technical writer or a technical professional in your field who writes frequently. During the second part of the interview (Part I of the report is an assignment in Chapter 6), inquire about the person's approach to planning and drafting. Ask some of the following questions and add additional questions relevant to the specific person and organization:

- What kind of planning do you do? How much time does it take? How important is it? Could you reduce or omit planning of your documents with little negative effect?
- How important is project planning and project management in the successful completion of a project?
- What factors influence decisions about what content you include? How important are factors such as context, purpose, audience, organization of information, overall argument, design of the document?
- How important is the creation of a document or presentation that doesn't have errors in logic?
- How much does a draft change from the initial plan to the penultimate version?
- How does your background affect your planning and drafting?

(b) Organize the information you find as part II of a brief oral or written report intended for other members of the class. This report can be posted on the class Web site or made available in print form in a class notebook in the library.

5. **Look at the process of translation.** Because your audience is not always made up of native English speakers, you need to consider how to translate your documents into the language that your audience uses. Translation of technical documents is not as easy as it may sound. In order to test your translation, you should have a native speaker of that language read your original document and its translation to check for errors or miscommunications caused by direct translation. This is called back-translation. In this assignment, you will be asked to look at the process of translation and back-translation. Visit the following Web site: www.babelfish.altavista.com/.
   (a) Type in a short paragraph from a document that you have written in English.
   (b) Ask the "translator" to translate your paragraph to another language.
   (c) Find a native speaker of that language on your campus and ask her or him to read the translation and the English original.
   (d) Write a short memo to your classmates about the process of translation. Consider the effectiveness of the Web site translation program and the value of the native speaker.

6. **Determine the appropriate voice.** Work in a small group with your classmates to determine whether you would use active or passive voice for each situation and audience listed below.

   Example: A document about the grading of pearls could be written in active voice if the document is intended for trainees learning how to grade pearls, because the focus should be on what the person does. However, the document could be written in passive voice if it's for customers who are more interested in the pearls than in the grader.

   (a) blood donation, for a potential donor
   (b) purification of water from sewage treatment plant, for an ecologist
   (c) grading of diamonds for jewelry, for a consumer
   (d) professional dry cleaning of antique clothing, for a dry cleaner
   (e) an operation, for a child in hospital for surgery
   (f) filing a claim, for a new insurance adjuster
   (g) a change in manufacturing procedures, for a customer
   (h) formation of sebaceous cysts, for patient with cysts
   (i) operation of a heat exchanger, for a homeowner

7. **Explain active and passive voice.** Carefully read the following two paragraphs. Explain the context, purpose, and audience that makes active voice appropriate for one paragraph and passive voice appropriate for the other.

active voice The neonatal nurse can decrease the chances that a newborn will suffer from cold stress by following several standard procedures. The nurse should monitor the baby's temperature regularly and should not bathe the baby until the temperature is stabilized. A careful nurse coordinates all medical procedures that expose the baby to cool air and will be certain to remove all wet bedclothes and diapers that cool the skin by evaporation.

passive voice A newborn will not suffer from cold stress if the neonatal nurse follows several standard procedures. The baby's temperature should be monitored regularly. The baby should not be bathed until the temperature is stabilized. A baby should not be exposed to cool air while undergoing medical procedures and should not be left with wet bedclothes or diapers that cool the skin by evaporation.

8. Revise an explanation to eliminate density. Read the following dense paragraph and revise it to make it more coherent. You may separate the material into shorter paragraphs, use lists, and add or delete material. This information was part of a memo informing employees about changes in procedures dealing with scrapped parts.

Several steps must be taken to separate and stage inventory to be scrapped. The first step is to locate and stage all excess parts. The white tag on each part will identify the part as either EXCESS, GOOD or EXCESS, DAMAGED. Parts tagged EXCESS, GOOD should be staged in bin #020185. Parts tagged EXCESS, DAMAGED should be staged in bin #020186 for further sorting and staging by code. The code is etched into the frame of each part: 1A — defective consumable, 1B — unidentified damage, 1C — vendor return/unrepairable, 1D — identifiable damage. Parts labeled code 1A, defective consumable, are staged in bin #020188, to be automatically scrapped without further investigation. Parts labeled code 1C, vendor return/unrepairable, are staged in bin #020189; these parts can also be automatically scrapped. If a part is labeled code 1B, additional information is required. Code 1B parts should be visually examined for signs of damage such as broken chips or split jumper cables. Parts with observable damage should be placed on a skid in bin #020187. Parts with no observable damage should be hand carried to the Repair Center where each part will be tested to determine the extent of damage. Parts the Repair Center determines cannot be repaired are staged in bin #020187. Parts the Repair Center believes are repairable are placed in the Repair Stockroom and scheduled for repair. Parts labeled with code 1D are staged in bin #020190. When ten or more skids have accumulated, the manager should be notified to check the accumulated parts and fill out a justification form to scrap each part.

9. Revise using given-new structures. Read the paragraph below, following these steps:

(a) Analyze to identify the current given-new structure, which will help you see why the paragraph is not coherent.

(b) Revise the paragraph to more closely reflect given-new structures.

(c) Identify the given-new structure of your revised paragraphs.

(1) Hot Isostatic Processing makes metal more dense. (2) Dense metal is more durable. (3) Metal parts cannot be cast without unavoidable small cracks and air pockets. (4) Imperfections lead to wear and breakage. (5) These flaws can be eliminated with Hot Isostatic Processing. (6) The parts are heated in special units, then pressurized with gas to minimize flaws. (7) A controlled cooling process ensures that the parts retain their original shape. (8) Hot Isostatic Processing produces stronger parts, able to withstand greater pressures for a longer span of time.

Chapter 7 Endnotes

1 Synectics. (n.d.). http://www.synectics.com/chicago.html. Retrieved October 12, 2003.

2 Downes, N. (n.d.). Mitsubishi Project PERT Chart (Carnegie Mellon University).

3 Downes, N. (n.d.). Mitsubishi Project Gantt Chart (Carnegie Mellon University).

4 Sims, B. (1993). Linking ethics and language in the technical communication classroom. *Technical Communication Quarterly, 2*(3), 285–299.

5 Adapted from Johnson, V. A., et al. (1978). Grain crops. In M. Milner, N. S. Scrimshaw, & D. I. C. Wang (Eds.), *Protein resources and technology: Status and research needs* (p. 244). Westport, CT: AVI Publishing. Used with permission of AVI Publishing Company.

6 Examples modified from McMillan, G. (1984, January 30). Technology finger-printing moves into the computer age. *Boston Globe.*

7 Plain Language Action & Information Network. (n.d.). *Presidential memorandum on plain language.* Retrieved October 18, 2003, from http://www.plainlanguage.gov/

8 Plain Language Action & Information Network. (n.d.). Retrieved October 18, 2003, from http://www.plainlanguage.gov/

9 Plain Language Action & Information Network. (n.d.). *Maria Walters and others v. United States Immigration and Naturalization Service.* Retrieved October 18, 2003, from http://www.plainlanguage.gov/cites/ins.htm

10 Plain Language Action & Information Network. (n.d.). *How to comply with the president's memo on plain language.* Retrieved October 18, 2003, from http://www.plainlanguage.gov/cites/vpguid.htm

11 Three-fingered robot hand. (1983). *NASA Tech Briefs, 8*(Fall), 99.

12 Modified from Bardach, J. E., & Pariser, E. R. (1978). Aquatic proteins. In M. Milner, N. S. Scrimshaw, & D. I. C. Wang (Eds.), *Protein resources and technology: Status and research needs* (p. 461). Westport, CT: AVI Publishing.

CHAPTER 8

Revising and Editing
修改与编辑

修改与编辑是文件撰写成功的关键步骤。尽管不同的专家和公司对修改与编辑的定义可能不同，但是根本的目的是一致的，即增强文件的可访性、理解性及可用性。本章阐释了修改与编辑的内容、过程及注意事项。

Objectives and Outcomes 学习目标

This chapter will help you accomplish these outcomes:

- Differentiate various types of revising and editing and develop the skills required to complete these tasks
- Revise and edit to make documents, presentations, and visuals more accessible, comprehensible, and usable
- Understand that revising is a global function involving complex, interrelated strategies and decisions
- Identify and correct inconsistencies and errors in a draft
- Review a draft of a document that has been carefully edited and then analyze the resulting final version to study the impact of the changes

Revising and editing are critical to the success of your documents. Although these processes often overlap and definitions vary slightly from expert to expert and company to company, their fundamental purposes remain the same: to increase the accessibility, comprehensibility, and usability of documents, presentations, and visuals.

- *Revising* generally refers to the process of changing overall (or global) elements of documents.
- *Editing* generally refers to (1) changing specific (or local) elements of documents and (2) managing administrative details necessary for document publication.

Because of the complexity of editing tasks, a range of skills is necessary. As you can see in Figure 8.1 on the next page, all aspects of revising and editing require attention to detail and an eye for consistency, which can mean a number of things. For example, in revising and substantive editing, these skills can mean recognizing repetitious or discrepant content that may be dozens of pages apart. In proofreading, however, attention to detail and an eye for consistency can mean recognizing vertical alignment or knowing the difference between 0 (the numeral) and O (the letter), between 1 (the numeral) and l (the letter), and between a hyphen (-), an en dash (–), and an em dash (—). This range of tasks also requires remarkably different skills. For example, revising and substantive editing require subject matter expertise related to the topic of the document, oral presentation, or

© Christina Micek Photography

Not even the very best professionals know everything, so they use invaluable print resources such as these for checking facts and language conventions. They also have technical handbooks for the areas they work in, technical communication handbooks, dictionaries in English and other languages as well as references for checking general facts.

visual, which is not a necessity for proofreading or administrative editing. Administrative editing typically requires knowledge of drafting and arranging contracts with a range of vendors, including designers and printers, which is not usually necessary knowledge for copy editors.

FIGURE 8.1 Types of Revising and Editing

Types	Necessary Knowledge
Revising focuses on global aspects of the document such as content, organization, argument, and design. ***Substantive editing*** also focuses on global aspects of the document.	■ Subject matter expertise ■ Organization/logic of argument ■ Disciplinary/professional expectations and conventions ■ Ability to revise a document ■ Document design conventions ■ Attention to detail and an eye for consistency
Design review focuses on the overall design of the document. ***Copyediting*** focuses on global aspects such as logic and format and local aspects such as language conventions and consistency.	■ Organization/logic of argument ■ Document design conventions ■ Ability to craft sentences and paragraphs ■ "Macro" features of a document ■ Language conventions: grammar, punctuation, capitalization, spelling, symbols, numbers, usage, style ■ Attention to detail and an eye for consistency
Traditionally, proofreaders compare a manuscript of a document with the typeset version to identify typographical errors. In electronic publishing, ***proofreading*** usually involves eliminating typographical errors in the electronic version (and any paper version) without comparison to the original.	■ Language conventions: grammar, punctuation, capitalization, spelling, symbols, numbers, usage, style ■ Citation practices ■ Proofreading marks to save time and avoid ambiguity ■ Skill with technology ■ Attention to detail and an eye for consistency
Administrative editing focuses on the aspects of compliance with the organization's policies and management of a range of tasks related to electronic or print publication.	■ Organizational policies ■ Publication and printing processes ■ Prepress/publication technology and procedures ■ Intellectual property ■ Contracts with vendors ■ Attention to detail and an eye for consistency

WEBLINK

Skillful editors as well as technical professionals and managers who have to edit a great deal make their job easier and faster by having a list of readily available resources to answer questions. Go to **www.english.wadsworth.com/burnett6e** for a list of URLs to a variety of useful professional resources for revision and editing.

CLICK ON WEBLINK

CLICK on Chapter 8/editing resources

Revising

修 改

Important documents, such as instructions, politically sensitive memos and letters, major reports, and proposals need to be reviewed by experts who can assess factors such as accuracy, audience appropriateness, and design.

Important documents should be tested by actual users who can assess factors such as accessibility, comprehensibility and effectiveness.

This chapter focuses on two levels of revision — *global revision* (redesigning and reorganizing the overall document) and *local revision* (revising individual paragraphs and sentences). Both kinds of revision depend on chunks of text rather than on individual words and phrases. The information for making revisions can come from various kinds of document testing (see Chapter 9), reviewer feedback, and careful self-assessment.

During revision, you'll read and reread your draft critically to examine choices in content, structure, organization, coherence, logic, and design. You can add, delete, and rearrange material in order to produce a document that is more accurate and effective for the audience. You may be the kind of writer who begins revising almost as soon as you start planning, or you may defer most of your revising until you have drafted a substantial chunk of text.

Ideally, you'll have time to compose the draft and then set it aside for a while before thoroughly revising it. All documents are improved when you check them to verify the accuracy and logic of the content, note needed changes in the examples or organization, and keep an eye open for violations of mechanical and grammatical conventions. In other words, you need to maintain the minimum specifications for good writing identified in Chapter 1.

The Revision Process 修改过程

Revision is more difficult than most inexperienced writers realize. Part of the difficulty comes from not necessarily understanding what to revise and how to change an acceptable draft into an excellent one. A researcher who studies revision strategies, Barbara Sitko, developed a decision tree that identifies six steps you go through during revision. At each step in the process, you can decide to move to the next step — or bail out. Figure 8.2 shows the steps and provides a

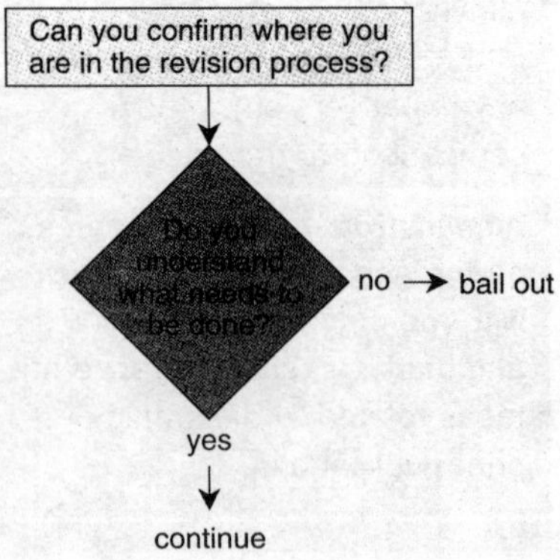

clear explanation of the options you have at each decision point.

Understanding these six steps gives you considerable flexibility in assessing your revision process. Once you realize the kind of knowledge you need in order to revise a document, you are more likely to actually complete the revision.

FIGURE 8.2 **Decision Points Leading to Revision**[1]

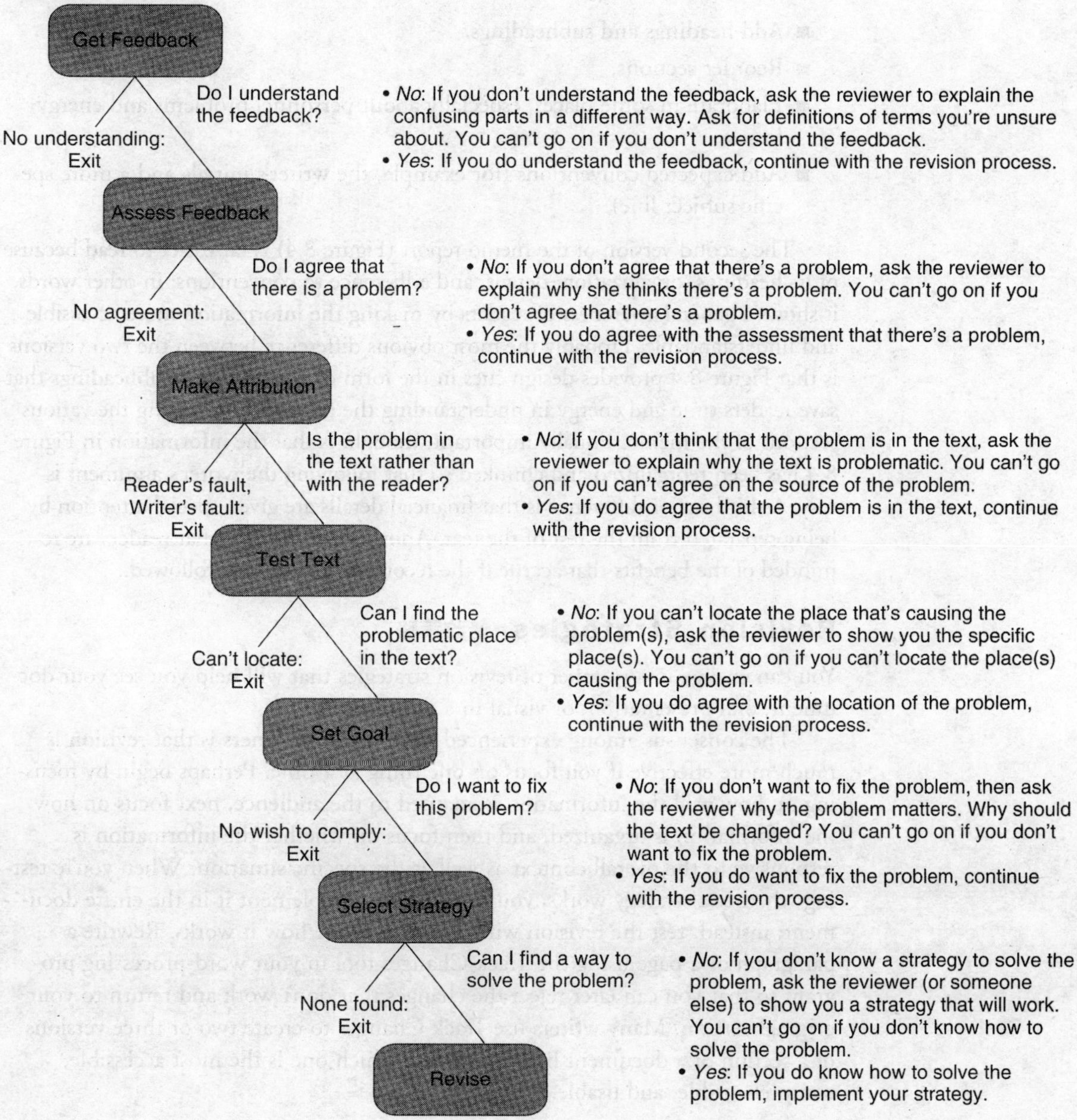

Redesigning Documents 重新设计文件

The organization and format of a report have a strong impact on readers' reactions. Figures 8.3 and 8.4 are different versions of the same memo report, which requested that automatic garage doors be installed in a shop area constantly exposed to harsh weather. Both reports were accompanied by several attachments that are not included here. In the first version of the report (Figure 8.3), readers have to work too hard to get the information they need. This version has been marked for the following revisions:

- Add headings and subheadings.
- Reorder sections.
- Elaborate in some places, especially about personnel problems and energy losses.
- Add expected conventions (for example, the writer's initials and a more specific subject line).

The second version of the memo report (Figure 8.4) is far easier to read because of its headings, organization, details, and adherence to conventions; in other words, it shows a general awareness of readers by making the information more accessible and understandable. Probably the most obvious difference between the two versions is that Figure 8.4 provides design cues in the form of headings and subheadings that save readers time and energy in understanding the relationships among the various sections of the memo. Equally important, though, is that the information in Figure 8.4 has been reorganized and chunked so that following the writer's argument is easy. A third major difference is that financial details are given special attention by being separated from the rest of the text. Another difference is that readers are reminded of the benefits that accrue if the recommendations are followed.

Revision Strategies 修改策略

You can engage in a number of revision strategies that will help you see your document, oral presentation, or visual in a new way.

The consensus among experienced writers and designers is that revision is much more effective if you focus on one thing at a time. Perhaps begin by focusing on how well the information is adapted to the audience, next focus on how the information is organized, and then focus on whether the information is responsive to the overall context as well as the specific situation. When you're testing whether a strategy works, you don't need to implement it in the entire document; instead, test the revision with a section to see how it works. Rewrite a paragraph or a page using the Track Changes tool in your word-processing program so that you can later reject the changes that don't work and return to your original version. Many writers use Track Changes to create two or three versions of a section of a document before deciding which one is the most accessible, comprehensible, and usable.

FIGURE 8.3 **Report without Carefully Designed Information**

*Add headlines and subheadings to help readers identify issues and recommendation.

MEMO

Add job titles

Make subject line more specific

To: Charles Malatesta
From: Tom Mansur
Subject: Purchase and installation of automatic roll-up doors
Date: September 27, 20—

*Reorder sections to create a stronger argument (see numbers)

Overview of unacceptable conditions

① The R&D Model Shop moved to its current location—next to the rear shipping and receiving dock of the Colebrook facility—15 months ago. Since then, we have been subjected to excessive heat in summer and extreme cold in winter. Most of the day the loading doors are open, and the heat or air conditioning is lost through the two connecting doorways. This is both expensive and a health risk.

⑤ Previous attempts to solve the problem.

Swinging Metal doors:

One attempt to control the temperature was swinging metal doors, which kept out the weather but were dangerously noisy. These doors banged loudly against the chain link fence outside. Machinists would jump at the sound, presenting the danger of severed fingers. Eventually these doors were knocked of their hinges, leaving us no protection from the outside elements.

Plastic Flap Doors:

We next installed clear plastic strip doors, which flap in the breeze and offer no protection from extreme temperatures. They also present a safety risk to fork truck drivers, in that the flexible strips swing down from the fork truck extensions and slap the drivers on the face and arms.

② Background on current problems

Personnel Concerns: (expand!)

Cost of Lost Energy:

The approximate cost of the lost heat and air conditioning is $5,970.00 per year. (See attached cost breakdown.) In human terms, in the summer when the air conditioners are on, we are sweating; in the winter when the heaters are blowing, we are shivering. These conditions are unacceptable.

Energy Loss: (add info)

Recommendation for Automatic Garage Doors

③ We, therefore, recommend the purchase and installation of two electric garage doors with both wall-mounted and pull-chain openers. These doors would be equipped with pneumatic safety stops at the bottom to prevent injury. In compliance with the fire safety egress requirements, we recommend the installation of two regular doors, with pneumatic closers, as common entry/exit ways. The total cost to purchase and install the equipment to correct the situation is $4,262.00. This would account for $1,708.00 in savings at the end of one year. Please refer to the attached estimates for prices of the garage doors and regular doors. Refer also to the attached building layout that identifes the recommended locations of the proposed doors.

④ Financial Evidence

Purchase and Installation Costs:

Potential Savings:

Discussion

⑥ We need these doors now, since winter is rapidly approaching. (Expand!)

TM/db
Attachments

FIGURE 8.4 **Revised Report**[2]

MEMO

To: Charles Malatesta
Plant/Facilities Administration
From: Tom Mansur *TM*
R&D Model Shop Group Leader
Subject: Justification for the purchase and installation of automatic roll-up doors for the R&D Model Shop
Date: September 27, 20—

A detailed subject line helps orient the reader to the purpose of the memo.

Overview of Unacceptable Conditions

The R&D Model Shop has been in the Colebrook facility, zone 5 (see Figures 1 and 2), for 15 months, adjacent to the shipping and receiving dock. The dock's loading doors are open approximately 8–10 hours a day, so the heat or air conditioning escapes from the R&D Model Shop through the two connecting doorways. The Model Shop machinists are exposed to excessive heat during the summer and extreme cold during the winter.

Establishing the problem—the seriousness and the background—helps the reader see the need for immediate action.

Background on Current Problems

This situation poses personnel concerns as well as energy losses, both of which are influential in analyzing and addressing the current problem.

Personnel Concerns: Machinists working in the R&D Model Shop are exposed to temperature extremes for up to 10 hours a day, causing discomfort and decreasing resistance to colds and flu. Employee satisfaction with the working conditions is low, influencing shop productivity. Additionally, use of sick days by R&D Model Shop employees has increased 7% since we moved to the Colebrook facility, costing the company money.

Energy Loss: Because the loading dock is open to the outside for up to 10 hours a day, the energy expended to heat or air condition the R&D Model Shop is wasted.

Reordering of sections clearly establishes and labels the problems before making a recommendation that addresses the identified problems.

Specific headings and subheadings ease reading.

Recommendation for Automatic Garage Doors

The purchase and installation of two electric garage doors with both wall-mounted and pull-chain openers would eliminate the problem with temperature extremes. These doors would be equipped with pneumatic safety stops at the bottom to prevent injury. In compliance with the fire safety egress requirements, two regular doors (with pneumatic closers) would be installed as common entry/exit ways.

Financial Evidence

This recommendation for automatic garage door openers takes three financial factors into consideration

Cost of Lost Energy: The cost of BTU loss in zone 5—based on heating and air conditioning expenses for the last fiscal year and cost formulas (see Figures 3, 4, and 5)—is approximately $5,970.00.

FIGURE 8.4 **Revised Report[2] (continued)**

Reviewing the previous attempts reminds the reader that the problem is long term and that various solutions have been tried.

Purchase and Installation Costs: The total cost to purchase and install the equipment to correct the situation is $4,262.00, based on quotations from Dempsey Door Company and Jackson Lumber Company. (See Figures 6 and 7.)

Potential Savings: The payback period would be less than one year.

Estimated annual cost of problem	$5,970.00
Estimated cost of solution	-4,262.00
Savings the first year	$1,708.00

All the financial information is chunked and labeled so that the implications are easy to see.

The recommended solution would account for more than $1,708.00 in savings at the end of one year. Please refer to the attached estimates for prices of the garage doors and regular doors. Refer also to the attached building layout that identifies the recommended locations of the proposed doors.

Previous Attempts to Solve the Problem

The two previous attempts to address the problem have not been successful.

Swinging Metal Doors: Swinging metal doors were in place for the frst six months that the R&D Model Shop was in the present location. They kept out the weather but were dangerously noisy. When fully loaded fork trucks passed through, these doors banged loudly against the chain link fence that surrounds the shop. Machinists in the area would jump at the sound, presenting the danger of severed fngers or worse, not to mention the rattled nerves. The constant traffic of fork trucks eventually knocked these doors off their hinges.

Plastic Flap Doors: The swinging metal doors were replaced with clear plastic strip doors. These doors flap in the breeze and actually provide no protection at all from extreme temperatures. They also present a safety risk to fork truck drivers. As the fork trucks move through the doorway, the flexible strips swing down from the fork truck extensions and slap the drivers on the face and arms.

Figures, which provide supplementary information, are attached if the reader needs to check any details.

The figures that accompanied the original report are not included here.

Discussion

Implementing the recommendation in this report will benefit both the R&D Model Shop employees as well as the Colebrook operation in general. The comfort of the work environment and job satisfaction will increase for employees in the R&D Model Shop. Sick time should decrease. The impact on the heating and air conditioning expenses should be felt almost immediately.

This report has been approved by Raphael Calvo, Manager of the R&D Model Shop, and Max Freeport, Director of Colebrook Operations.

So that work can begin immediately, a working print (Figure 8) and the completed work request form (Figure 9) are attached.

The brief discussion acts as a conclusion that reminds the reader about benefits that are gained if the recommendations are followed.

Another good way to begin the revision process is to get feedback from the intended audience — an actual or simulated one. For example, you can get feedback from an actual reader, invite feedback from a peer reviewer, or even role-play the intended audience. Various people will have a perspective different from yours, which may give you some insight about what works and what needs to be changed. Writing audience-based prose is difficult if you never check audience reactions.

Sometimes you know something isn't quite right with a document, oral presentation, or visual, but you can't put your finger on the problem. You know it's not the basic grammar, mechanics, or sentence structure that's wrong, but something simply isn't working. If the piece is particularly important, taking extra time to investigate whether some other approach will work is worthwhile. Reading the document aloud is one excellent way to hear problems that you can miss if you're reading silently.

Another way to start the revision process is to play with the draft in unexpected ways. Seeing the information presented in another way gives you opportunities to move forward in a potentially productive manner. Try any combination of these outside-the-box approaches to re-visioning text and design to help you think of your work in new ways:

1. ***Text changes to encourage re-vision:***
   - Put the end section at the beginning . . . and start to revise from that point.
   - Keep the same major argument but make it half the length.
   - Select different supporting evidence — different quotations, different statistics.
   - Change the intended audience (which necessarily changes things such as the emphasis and the kind of details).
   - Change the genre. Try it as a newsletter article, journal article, lab report, letter to a former colleague, after-dinner speech.

2. ***Design changes to encourage re-vision:***
   - Change points in a paragraph into a bulleted list.
   - Change a dramatic example into a sidebar.
   - Change the headings from descriptive labels to questions.
   - Convert critical information in paragraphs to visual displays: charts, diagrams, tables, maps, graphs.
   - Add captions to the visuals (and delete information from the text).
   - Redesign the document. Try it as a two-column piece with callouts, as a Web page with hyperlinks, as a script for a National Public Radio feature report.

A skillful editor pays as much attention to the design of a document, PowerPoint presentation, or visual as to the words. For some very useful guidelines about visual proofreading, go to **www.english.wadsworth.com/burnett6e**.

CLICK ON WEBLINK

CLICK on Chapter 8/visual proofreading

WWW WEBLINK

Editing 编辑

Most people think of editing as having to do with correctness — avoiding errors in mechanics and grammar. You might find a more useful approach is to think of editing as adhering to conventions and assuring consistency. *Conventions* are what a particular group of people agrees is acceptable, expected usage. *Consistency* involves ensuring that a document conforms to those agreed-on conventions. Conventions differ from country to country and from company to company. Skillful editors seldom make absolute decisions; instead, they make situated, contextualized decisions. So, for example, in the United States, *color* is conventional; in the United Kingdom and much of the rest of the English-speaking world outside the United States, *colour* is conventional. Similarly, U.S. currency uses commas ($1,000 = one thousand U.S. dollars) in places where UK currency uses periods (£1.000 = one thousand British pounds).

Excel lets you change the Windows Regional Settings in order to apply foreign currency formats with the appropriate monetary symbols and use of commas and decimals for various national denominations.[3]

Levels of Edit 编辑层次

Effective editing improves a document's technical or textual accuracy as well as its appropriateness and appeal to the audience. The term *editing* as it is used in this text refers to four functions that describe the nine levels of edit identified in Figure 8.5. These functions, which typically take place in the final stages of preparing a document, help writers adhere to conventions and ensure consistency.

If the information in a document is accurate and complete, why does a writer need to revise the document so that it's accessible and adapted to the audience?

In some organizations *content accuracy* is the responsibility of the writer, in others it is the responsibility of an editor, and in still others writers and editors act as safety checks for each other. In situations in which the editor does make changes in content, final approval for the changes usually remains with the writer (unless the changes involve institutional policies and practices more familiar to the editor). Regardless of who controls content, little point exists in completing any other level of edit until the content accuracy is established by a subject-matter expert.

Design review typically includes assuring the consistency of all elements of design, from "macro" elements, such as assuring the same font type, style, size,

READABILITY FORMULAS DON'T DO WHAT THEIR NAME CLAIMS

可读性方程

Readability formulas reputedly assess a text's level of difficulty: How easy the text is to comprehend. Readability formulas are used in government, industry, and education. The question is whether they do what they claim.

How Readability Formulas Work

Readability formulas are based on the relationships between average word length (number of syllables per word) and average sentence length (number of words per sentence). The principle presumes that both the higher the average number of syllables per word and the greater the average number of words per sentence, the more difficult the document is to read. The formulas yield a ratio between word length and sentence length that estimates a document's readability by level of difficulty or grade level.

Problems with Readability Formulas

Because readability formulas are based on a ratio, they do not adequately address several rhetorical elements of writing.

Content complexity plays a critical role in audience comprehension. But readability formulas do not consider difficulty of content. A paragraph may be labeled "seventh-grade readability" because of relatively short words and sentences; but the ideas may be extremely difficult to comprehend. For example, this sentence has only 15 words: "Boards with tight lines and spaces required reworking due to shorts caused by solder bridging." According to some reading scales, the sentence falls between fairly easy and standard because most of the words are short and the sentence has a total of only 21 syllables. However, the terminology is unfamiliar to general readers, and the sentence is not easy to understand — despite formulas that indicate otherwise. Or consider what grade level you would assign for "I think; therefore, I am."

Sentence length can affect material's comprehensibility. Generally, shorter sentences are easier to read than longer ones. Some reading experts assign levels of difficulty to sentence length, as the following examples show. However, the content in these sentences does not vary much in difficulty since all of the sentences are from the same article in *Aviation Week and Space Technology*,[4] a magazine for professionals and experts in aerospace-related industries. The practical difference in difficulty between the sentences is small, a factor ignored by readability formulas.

> The cockpit instrumentation is well designed. (6 words) *very easy, 8 words or less*
>
> This aircraft is equipped with combined dual navigation and communication systems. (11 words) *easy, 11 words*
>
> All controls are within easy reach of the pilot and have readily discernible functions. (14 words) *fairly easy, 14 words*
>
> The DO 228 has easy access to cockpit seats by an optional door located on either side of the cockpit. (19 words) *standard, 17 words*
>
> The aircraft's fuel, electrical, deicing and starting systems controls are color coded and shown in clearly styled flow diagrams on the overhead panel. (23 words) *fairly difficult, 21 words*
>
> The front instrument panel is not cluttered, partly due to the large center console located between the pilots that contains most of the avionics controls. (25 words) *difficult, 25 words*
>
> Dornier's DO 228–200 commuter and utility twin turboprop offers operators a versatile-mission aircraft with short-field performance combined with excellent flight performance characteristics and easily maintained aircraft systems. (28 words) *very difficult, 29+ words*

Variety of sentence length affects comprehensibility. A document with sentences all of the same length quickly becomes repetitious and boring. Variation maintains readers' interest and potentially increases comprehension. Although a single document might not have the tremendous variety shown in the previous examples, effective technical communicators try to vary sentence length, but readability formulas do not account for this.

Subordination of ideas can increase comprehension. Short, separate sentences that treat all ideas equally may be more difficult to comprehend than sentences that have subordinate and main ideas clearly established. Two versions of the same information illustrate this point.

> **Original.** A decayed woven linen robe was found in 1981. The robe dated from c. 1000 B.C.E. It is the oldest known piece of cloth found in Greece. The robe was found by a Greek-British excavation team. The team was digging on the island of Euboeoa. Euboeoa is about 40 miles from Athens.
>
> **Revision.** A decayed woven linen robe from c. 1000 B.C.E., the oldest known piece of cloth found in Greece, was unearthed in 1981 during a Greek-British excavation on the island of Euboeoa, 40 miles from Athens.[5]

Although readability formulas indicate that the original version is easier to read, most adults prefer the revision because relationships are established clearly and repetition is eliminated.

Word length is a central factor in readability formulas, which equate short words with simplicity, without regard to word meaning or audience knowledge. However, shortness is not always a measure of reading ease, for short words do not necessarily have simple meanings. For example, *quark* and *erg*, although short, are more difficult words than *satellite* or *occupation*. And some very long (and sometimes technical) words have a high recognition factor. For example, some multisyllable medical and chemical terms are easily and immediately recognized by all professionals in their respective fields. Likewise, a fourth-grader recognizes the words *Mississippi* or *Massachusetts*.

© Roger Ressmeyer/CORBIS

Editing is done by professional editors as well as by peers who are often willing to provide feedback on drafts. The more specific you are in telling these peer reviewers what needs attention, the more help they're likely to be. Should they look at organization? At adaptation to the audience? At the evidence you use? At the tables and figures?

Such multisyllable, high-recognition words can give a false high grade-level equivalency compared with the difficulty of the content when evaluating readability for adult professionals.

Word length is less important in comprehension if the words are familiar to the audience. Some technical words are long and appear complex to the general reader, but they are easily understood by experts. In many cases a technical term is exactly the correct word; an explanation comprised of shorter, more recognizable terms would be less precise. The following sentence probably won't make sense to general readers, but to plastics engineers it is both accurate and easy to understand.

> Polysulfones comprise a class of engineering thermoplastics with high thermal, oxidative, and hydrolytic stability, and good resistance to aqueous mineral acids, alkali, salt solutions, oils and grease.[6]

Document design is not part of readability formulas. Closely spaced, small printing with little visual relief is more difficult and takes longer to read and comprehend — regardless of the content — than carefully designed, visually pleasing pages.

FIGURE 8.5 **Functions of Editing and Levels of Edit**[7]

Functions of Editing	Levels of Edit
Substantive editing and revising	■ ***Substantive edit*** — reviews the document globally for accuracy, logic, completeness, coherence, consistency, organization, and tone.
Design review and copyediting *Proofreading*	■ ***Format edit*** — establishes consistency in "macro" physical elements such as headings, fonts, page design, use of visuals. ■ ***Integrity edit*** — matches text references to corresponding figures, tables, references, footnotes, and appendixes.
Administrative editing	■ ***Mechanical style*** — edit establishes consistency in "micro" physical elements ■ ***Screening edit*** — corrects language and numerical errors. ■ ***Language edit*** — changes grammar, punctuation, usage, and sentence structure to meet conventions, such as symbols, citations, and numerical copy.
	■ ***Policy edit*** — ensures that institutional policies are enforced. ■ ***Clarification edit*** — provides clear instructions to the compositor and graphic artist. ■ ***Coordination edit*** — deals with the administrative aspects in publishing technical documents.

Which of the nine levels of edit are you skillful at? Which of these levels of edits would help you be successful in your career?

and placement of headings, to details, such as assuring that numbers of figures and their textual references match. Individuals who assume this responsibility need to understand the general principles of document design as well as have a keen eye for inconsistencies in mechanical details.

If "correctness" is often a matter of conforming to conventions, why do people make such a big deal about not following these conventions?

Proofreading encompasses a broad range of responsibilities, including those most typically considered editing. All of the problems and errors in numeracy and language use fall into this category. Individuals who proofread documents need to have a thorough command of language appropriateness as well as the skill and sensitivity to create reader-based documents.

Some writers try to decrease their editing/proofreading burden by using software tools to flag potential problems in style, mechanics, and usage. Most word-processing software comes with built-in spelling and grammar checkers that catch glaring problems. However, such tools cannot guarantee that a document will be error-free or that it will communicate effectively with its audience. Writers should never depend on software tools to identify all the errors in a document, but should consider the following benefits and limitations of software tools for editing:[8]

Benefits	***Limitations***
Software can identify	Software cannot identify
■ misspelled words	■ correctly spelled words used incorrectly
■ passive voice	■ inconsistent writing styles
■ complex sentences	■ confusing sentence structures
■ wrong part of speech	■ what the audience needs to know
■ redundancy	■ every grammar/mechanical problem
■ potentially difficult wording (based on word and sentence lengths only)	■ poorly organized documents
■ slang/colloquialisms	■ missing or faulty information
■ potentially sexist language	■ potentially offensive ideas
■ negative wording	■ how a document will be used

When preparing a document that will be read online, most professional editors recommend that you print everything for final editing and proofreading. Why is this a good practice to follow?

Finally, a number of *administrative responsibilities* are often considered editorial tasks. An individual who assumes these responsibilities needs to be familiar with corporate policies, understand the production and publication processes, and be a skillful manager of people and tasks.

These nine levels of edit are functions that in a small organization may be performed by a single individual. In very large organizations, several people may be responsible for these editing functions. However, whether one person or several are responsible, the functions are completed in several passes through a document. No editor tries to look for everything at the same time. So, for example, an editor who is doing a substantive edit for content accuracy typically ignores the other areas. Similarly, an editor who is checking for consistency in headings or documentation tends to set other problems aside temporarily.

People who work on a networked computer system often use the network's capabilities to help with *document cycling,* the part of the process that takes a document through several rounds of reviewing, revising, and editing. They can electronically send their document to several reviewers simultaneously and receive the reviewers' comments the same way. Using the network can potentially speed document cycling, which in many organizations is a required part of preparing important documents, especially ones for external readers.

Your responsibilities as an editor are not always clear-cut. Although you often have rules and guidelines to follow (e.g., Does the document have problems in

© Helen King/CORBIS

Editing is done by professional editors and peers. The more specific you are in telling peer reviewers what areas of your draft need attention, the more help they're likely to be. Should they look particularly at organization? At adaptation to the audience? At the kind of supporting evidence you use? At your discussion of the tables and figures?

punctuation? Is all the documentation correct?), an even bigger part of your editorial role requires judgment. You may make recommendations to a writer based on the response you imagine readers will have. Rather than having a rule to enforce, you'll ask, "Is the design accessible?" "Is the document easy to read?" "Is the document easy to understand?"

Common Copyediting Problems 常见编辑问题

The discussion in the remainder of the chapter identifies four common copyediting problems for writers. They are areas that need a final check before a document is complete: concrete details, directness, positive phrasing, and the elimination of several kinds of wordiness.

Use Concrete Details Concrete words that refer to tangible objects are usually easier for your readers to understand than abstract words. Thus, you can generally make your writing more precise if you use specific details and examples. An effective technique for reducing abstract writing is to insert specific details in place of vague or general statements. The list in Figure 8.6 identifies some of the questions you can ask yourself as you edit a document to make abstract statements precise and concrete, to make your statements quantifiable and verifiable.

Use Direct Language Indirect language often results from inappropriate attempts to be formal or to use inflated or abstract language. In general, direct language is better. Direct language is typically plain and simple. However, no word is inherently right or wrong until you take the context, audience, and purpose into account. For example, the word *feel* would be appropriate in a pamphlet for women on breast self-examination that stated, "If you feel your breast tissue and detect a lump, contact your doctor." However, in a document for medical personnel, the more technical *palpate* would be a better choice than *feel.*

One way to be direct is to use straightforward terms. The revision of the following sentence substitutes simple language for needlessly ornate language.

Why might a writer purposely obscure meaning in writing?

Inflated Language	Revised: Direct Language
Your conceptualization of our aggregate capability may enhance our marketing position.	Your ideas about our capability may improve our marketing.

FIGURE 8.6 **Selecting Concrete Details**

Abstract Information		Concrete Details
important client	Who?	Jean Thompson, PPI president
a new development	What?	developed a blight-resistant chestnut
schedule early	When?	schedule before 9 a.m.
ideal location	Where?	Southfield, MA
a substantial profit	How much?	a 37 percent profit
a broken part	Which one?	a broken camshaft
limited leg mobility	What percentage?	lift his leg 40 percent of normal extension
high-temperature environment	What degree?	up to 2,000°F
a small wingspan	What size?	a 7.0-mm wingspan
few changes in the procedure	How many?	three changes in the procedure
corrosion-resistant metal	What kind?	stainless steel

Another guaranteed shortcut to improved writing involves changing abstract nouns into verbs. One example is listed below, but many others appear in technical documents. If you change abstract nouns back to verbs and delete words that add little to the meaning, you'll greatly improve your writing. (Refer to the Usage Handbook on the Companion Web Site for additional examples.)

Abstract Language	Revised: Direct Language
The judge provided the required authorization for the search.	The judge authorized the search. (*Authorize* identifies the action.)

Use Positive Phrasing Effective writers often employ positive phrasing for several reasons. Psychologists and linguists know that readers and listeners understand positively phrased sentences more quickly and accurately than negatively phrased sentences, which the human brain takes slightly longer to process. Also, positive phrasing generally is more direct and appealing because eliminating negatives also eliminates words.

The most obvious negative words, which include *no, not, none, never,* and *nothing,* are added to a positive sentence to negate the idea. When you edit, consider replacing a negative word with a less overtly negative term, often an antonym for the word in the "not" phrase:

not many	few
do not accept	reject
do not succeed	fail

Other negative words are created by adding a common negative prefix to a word. The words with the prefixes are more indirect; they're less overtly negative. However, when you want to emphasize a negative point, use *not:*

inefficient	not efficient
impossible	not possible
unreliable	not reliable

In what situations might you choose to word directions positively? Negatively?

While one negative word or phrase only slightly delays a reader, multiple negatives significantly decrease reading speed and inhibit comprehension. Also, possible confusion results from multiple negatives. The following sentences illustrate how replacing negative wording with positive wording lessens the chances of confusion arising from multiple negatives.

Negative Phrasing	More Positive Phrasing
The production line changeover will not be ready on time.	The production line changeover will be delayed.
The manager could not approve the decentralization of the tool crib because there would be no inventory control or centralized maintenance checks.	The manager denied decentralization of the tool crib because it provides a regular inventory control and maintenance check.

In some situations, however, you'll find that positive phrasing is inappropriate because it is not emphatic enough. The following set of directions presumes that many users will do the wrong thing unless specific *do nots* are presented, as the following example illustrates.

Failure to follow standard procedures in using a disk will have detrimental results. Follow these guidelines:

- Do not turn drive on or off with disk in the drive.
- Do not bend disk.
- Do not touch disk surfaces with fingers or objects.
- Do not store disk out of protective envelope.
- Do not expose disk to heat, magnets, or photoelectric beams.

Such phrasing cautions computer operators to treat disks carefully. Although the wording is negative, experience has led manual writers to realize that some readers ignore cautions that use positive wording.

Eliminate Wordiness Wordiness can make your writing difficult to understand because readers are forced to plow through unnecessary text to read essential information. Your readers may lose patience. The most effective way to reduce wordiness is to avoid redundancy — the unnecessary repetition of concepts, words, or phrases. Sometimes readers cannot discern the point because it is hidden underneath layers of language. At other times redundancy is so annoying or time consuming that readers give up without completing a document.

The memo in Figure 8.7 has numerous instances of redundancy. Section manager Carl Saunders typed the memo directly into his word processor and read a copy after it was printed. When he proofread his draft, he was appalled by its redundancy, which he eliminated by crossing out unnecessary terms and making minor changes in wording. Figure 8.7 shows the editing he did on his memo. Producing a new copy constituted very little work on his word processor; within a few minutes, he printed the revision (Figure 8.8). You may encounter several redundant elements that you can edit out of the final drafts of technical documents — modifiers similar to those in Mr. Saunders's initial memo.

FIGURE 8.7 **Redundant Language in Memo**

MEMO

August 3, 20—

To	Production Supervisors
From	Carl Saunders CS
Section	Manager
Subject	Staff Meeting

~~The~~ staff meeting ~~will start at~~ 10 a.m. Tuesday ~~morning~~, August 6, in Conference Room 317 ~~on the third foor.~~

~~First and foremost,~~ our ~~primary~~ goal ~~of the meeting will be~~ is to reach a consensus ~~of opinion~~ about the best way to use ~~utilize the high degree of expertise of~~ the consultant's advice ~~we brought in. The consultant advised us about future plans for implementing new state-of-the-art developments in~~ about production techniques.

At this ~~point in~~ time, we must determine the priorities for changes to ~~prioritize in order of importance those basic and fundamental changes we believe are most important to modify in~~ our production system.

- ***Redundant Pairs.*** Some common terms contain two words, both of which mean the same thing. Some writers use such redundant pairs to give their writing what they think is an air of elegance. Because both terms mean the same thing, only one is necessary. You could appropriately write *first* or *foremost,* but using both terms is repetitive. Sometimes, as in Mr. Saunders's memo, neither term is necessary because there is only one stated goal. Some other common redundant pairs include *null and void* and *final and conclusive.*

WEBLINK

For additional examples of redundant pairs, go to **www.english.wadsworth.com/burnett6e**.
CLICK ON WEBLINK
CLICK on Chapter 8/redundant pairs

FIGURE 8.8 **Revised Memo**

MEMO

August 3, 20—

To Production Supervisors
From Carl Saunders *CS*
Section Manager
Subject Staff Meeting
10 a.m., Tuesday, August 6
Conference Room 317

Our goal is to reach a consensus about the best way to use the consultant's advice about production techniques.

At this time, we must determine the priorities for changes to our production system.

- ***Redundant Modifiers.*** Phrases in which one term implies the other are known as redundant modifiers. For example, *collaborate* implies "together," so *collaborate together* is redundant. Some other common redundant modifiers include *initial preparation* and *most unique.*

Mr. Saunders's memo contains the phrase "high degree of expertise of the consultant brought in," which has three redundant features. A consultant is assumed to have expertise and is also brought in from outside the company; saying a consultant has expertise and is brought in is doubly redundant. Also, expertise assumes a high degree of competence; repeating "high degree" is unnecessary.

For additional examples of redundant modifiers, go to **www.english.wadsworth.com/burnett6e**.
CLICK ON WEBLINK
CLICK on Chapter 8/redundant modifiers

WEBLINK

- ***Redundant Categories.*** When one term in a phrase is in the general category to which the other term belongs, it's known as a redundant category. For example, the expression *bitter taste* is redundant because bitter is one of four tastes; the word *bitter* is sufficient. In Mr. Saunders's memo, the initial "a.m." implies the category stated in the second term, so "morning" is unnecessary. You could appropriately write "at 10 a.m. Tuesday" or "at 10:00 Tuesday morning." Some other common redundant categories include *reliability factor* and *red in color.* The following examples show how eliminating redundant categories makes sentences less wordy.

Redundant	Improved
The reliability factor of the equipment was guaranteed.	The equipment's reliability was guaranteed.

For additional examples of redundant categories, go to **www.english.wadsworth.com/burnett6e**.
CLICK ON WEBLINK
CLICK on Chapter 8/redundant categories

WEBLINK

Revise Noun Strings Your writing can be improved by eliminating noun strings, which are a series of two or more nouns in which the first nouns modify the later ones. For example, in the string "circulation pump filter," both *circulation* and *pump* modify *filter.* Noun strings are distinguished by the absence of both apostrophes and connecting words that show relationships (such as *of, for, in*).

You'll run into problems if you use noun strings, particularly when the reader is unable to determine exactly how the nouns relate to each other. Strings that are only two words long seldom present difficulties. For example, *data analysis* is easily understood; saying "the analysis of data" is unnecessary. When the strings are three words long, the reader can usually figure out what is meant, but reading may be slowed slightly. When the strings reach four words, extra time is required to figure out the relationship among words. Although your reader probably will accurately interpret the string, this takes unnecessary time and effort, which may distract and annoy the reader. Strings that are five or more words long are open to multiple interpretations and can be indecipherable. The reader may never guess exactly what you intended.

Noun Strings	Revision
standardization blending	controller that standardizes blending
test module specification review	the specifications review for the test module
scanner head motion control	control of the scanner head's motion

Revisions of noun strings usually require additional words to clarify the relationships; however, these extra words eliminate ambiguity.

The issues of conventions and correctness addressed in this chapter are often more difficult to apply in workplace situations, which are nearly always complicated by politics and personalities. The ethics sidebar below addresses some of these complications, which often force writers and editors to make difficult decisions. The sidebar suggests that identifying the values that are in conflict will aid decision making.

ETHICS 职业道德规范知识吧 SIDEBAR

Author, Audience, and Company: Ethics and Technical Editing

作者，读者和公司：职业规范与技术编辑

Imagine a technical editor in the following scenario:

> Sam is a technical editor, working for a software development company. As she edits the draft of a manual for the company's newest product, she realizes that large sections are very technical, making them unclear and difficult to understand. When Sam talks to the writer, a programmer, she finds him very reluctant

to revise the manual; he argues that the technical information, as it is written, is necessary. The deadline for the manual is looming; Sam has little time to revise the manual without the writer's help.

What are the technical editor's responsibilities in this situation? As this scenario indicates, technical editors, because of their unique position in the document production process, must balance obligations to several different groups. First, they have an obligation to the audience to ensure that documents are clear and accurate. Second, they are expected to safeguard the employer's reputation and protect the company from legal liabilities. Finally, they have to respect the author's intellectual independence, especially if the editor is not an expert in the subject. In most situations, each of these different obligations works toward a collective goal of clear, accurate, professional documents.

When these obligations do conflict, however, the editor is faced with an ethical dilemma. To which group does he or she have the greater responsibility: author, audience, or employer? For example, in the situation above, the editor faces several different ethical obligations:

- *To the audience* — they expect the manual to be clear and readable but also expect it to be technically accurate
- *To the author* — the author is an expert on the product but may not appreciate the audience's lack of technical expertise
- *To the employers* — they could lose money if the product is delayed but could also suffer if the documentation is inaccurate or misleading

This situation does not have one simple solution. Researchers Lori Allen and Dan Voss, however, provide a process that allows editors to at least clearly identify the values that are in conflict.[9] The outline of their process includes parenthetical notes about ways in which each step fits the scenario in this sidebar.

- Define what is at issue (producing a clear text) and the groups involved (audience, author, and employer)
- Determine the different groups' interests (clarity, experience, profit)
- Identify the relevant values (usability, integrity, capitalism)
- Determine the values that conflict (usability vs. integrity, capitalism vs. usability)
- Determine which value has greater importance (usability)
- Resolve the conflict for that value (require the writer to revise the document)

Requiring the writer to revise the document is one possible resolution for this dilemma. If the greater value is capitalism, then the ethical decision may be to improve as much of the quality of the manual as time allows. No matter which they choose, editors should heed Allen and Voss's final point: Editors carry a greater ethical responsibility because they are experts with language. Editors have the advantage of looking at a situation from different perspectives, but that advantage comes with weighty ethical responsibilities.

Reread the scenario at the beginning of this sidebar. Using Allen and Voss's six-step process, how would you resolve this conflict? What value(s) would you emphasize?

How would you edit a poorly written technical document that the author does not want altered?

Proofreading 校 对

Before any document, accompaniments for an oral presentation, or visuals get approved for final distribution, display, or publication, you need to do careful proofreading — a final check. This isn't a time to add new information or to do rewriting. It's a straightforward check for accuracy and consistency in five broad areas:

- mechanical conventions (e.g., , punctuation, capitalization, spelling)
- grammatical conventions (e.g., grammar, usage)
- design conventions (e.g., typography, visual displays, headings)
- disciplinary conventions, (e.g., abbreviations, citations)
- typographical conventions (e.g., symbols, numbers)

Reading aloud helps catch problems — omissions, awkward phrasings, grammatical errors — that you might miss when proofreading silently, especially proofreading on-screen.

The proofreading marks in Figure 8.9 are widely used by editors as a common system for identifying specific things to change in a document. Learning and regularly using these symbols will enable you to understand editorial marks on documents returned to you as well as to similarly mark documents you are asked to proofread.

Examining Revision and Editing Decisions
检查修改和编辑内容

Figure 8.10 shows the first few pages of a draft of a feasibility report (pages 288–292). This particular report evaluates two anchor bolts and recommends one for the company. Suggestions for revision and copyediting are marked on this draft. Marginal annotations comment on some of the other problems with the draft. Figure 8.11 shows the final revised and edited version of the same report (pages 293–302).

To assess the effectiveness of this document, you need to know about the purpose of feasibility reports, which is to advocate the best solution to a problem, and their structure. The introduction of the report usually gives an overview of the feasibility study (the work that results in the report) by briefly stating the purpose of the study, describing the problem being investigated, and presenting the scope of the report. An optional background section, which is included when the audience is not likely to be familiar with the situation that necessitated the feasibility study, can contain information such as the history of the problem, the possible long-range impact of not correcting the problem, and relevant work that has already been done in the field.

The criteria and solutions sections are the most important. The criteria allow readers to evaluate the various solutions fairly, so their selection is important. Some of the following criteria are often used:

- cost of purchase, installation, and maintenance
- ease and frequency of servicing
- ease of operation

FIGURE 8.9 **Proofreading Marks**[10]

Symbol	Meaning	Example	Symbol	Meaning	Example
(delete marks)	delete	take it out	lc	set in lowercase	set South as south
⁀	close up	print as o ne word	ital	set in *italic*	set oeuver as *oeuver*
	delete and close up	closse up	rom	set in roman	set *mensch* as mensch
^ or > or ⋏	caret	insert here (something)			
#	insert a space	put onehere	bf	set in **boldface**	set important as **important**
eq#	space evenly	space evenly where indicated	= or -/ or	hyphen	multi-colored
stet	let stand	let marked text stand as set	1/N or en or /N/	en dash	1965–72
			1/M or em or /M/	em (or long) dash	Now—at last!—we know.
tr	transpose	change order the			
/	used to separate two or more marks and often as a concluding stroke at the end of an insertion		∨	superscript or superior	as in πr^2
			∧	subscript or inferior	as in H_2O
			or	centered	for a centered dot in $p \cdot q$
[	set farther to the left	too far to the right		comma	
]	set farther to the right	too far to the left		apostrophe	
			⊙	period	
⌢	set as ligature (such as æ)	encyclopaedia	; or ;/	semicolon	
=	align horizontally	alignment	: or	colon	
‖	align vertically	align with surrounding text	or	quotation marks	
			(/)	parentheses	
X	broken character	imperfect	[/]	brackets	
□	indent or insert em quad space		OK/?	query to author: has this been set as intended?	
¶	begin a new paragraph				
sp	spell out	set 5 lbs as five pounds	or	push down a work-up	an unintended mark
cap	set in CAPITALS	set nato as NATO	9	turn over an inverted letter	inveṛted
smcap or s.c.	set in SMALL CAPITALS	set signal as SIGNAL	wf	wrong font	wrong siZe or style

- kind and duration of operator training
- performance specifications
- dimensions
- compatibility with existing systems
- flexibility for expansion
- environmental impact

Writers should select only criteria that identify significant differences in the solutions, and the solutions offered should be feasible. Including impractical or weak solutions as a way to make a preferred solution look better borders on the unethical and can destroy the credibility of the entire document.

The final section of a feasibility report incorporates the conclusions and recommendations. These sections may be presented separately or together; in either case, the points are often bulleted or enumerated. Sometimes the conclusions in a feasibility report present both advantages and disadvantages of each solution, synthesizing rather than just summarizing the information. The recommendations identify the best solution based on the criteria used in the feasibility study. The recommendations should be clear, precise, unambiguous, and logical.

As you read the draft in Figure 8.10 and the final report in Figure 8.11, consider both global revisions (redesigning and reorganizing the report) and local revisions (revising paragraphs and sentences). Then consider the editing decisions that focus on word- and phrase-level usage that affect the report's accuracy as well as its appropriateness and appeal.

FIGURE 8.10 **Draft of Feasibility Report Marked for Revision and Editing**

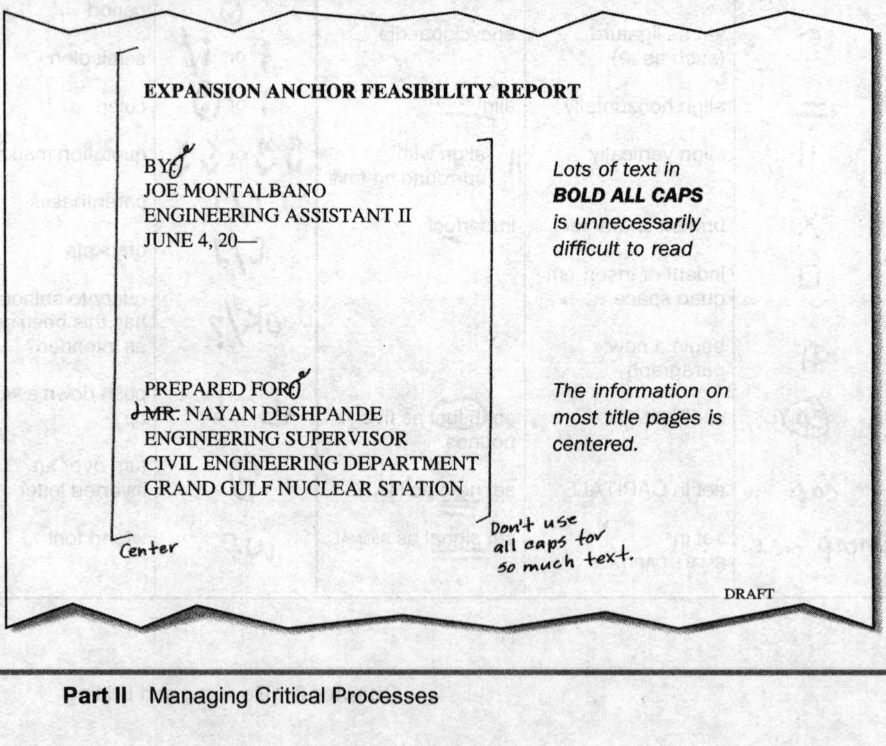

FIGURE 8.10 **Draft of Feasibility Report Marked for Revision and Editing (continued)**

TABLE OF CONTENTS

DRAFT

Make "Criteria" and "Methodology" into level-1 heads and reverse their order.

Headings (which are also sections in the table of contents) should present content, not just section labels.

Use only the first page number of a section in the table of contents.

Inconsistencies and problems in the organization of a document often show up in the sequence of sections in the table of contents.

Provide names of the appendixes.

The changes in the table of contents should be reflected in the reorganization of the text and the retitling of the sections.

FIGURE 8.10 Draft of Feasibility Report Marked for Revision and Editing (continued)

Add an abstract

INTRODUCTION : Nonductile Expansion Anchors at GGNS

By convention, the first page of the main body usually doesn't have the page number on it.

~~Background~~

The nonductile expansion anchor has a long history of use at Grand Gulf Nuclear Station (GGNS). The nonductile expansion anchor~~, which has been~~ used almost exclusively~~, is~~ has been the Hilti Kwik Bolt anchor bolt. This wedge-type anchor is essential for installation of a wide vriety variety of components including conduit supports, pipe supports, instrument supports, and ventilating and air conditioning supports.

~~However,~~ replacement of the Hilti Kwik Bolt is required because the manufacturer recently discontinued production ~~of it~~. ~~Therefore,~~ As a result, I conducted a search for a replacement ~~anchor bolt. This search consisted of~~ by evaluating ~~several types of~~ two anchor bolts: ~~they are~~ the Hilti Kwik Bolt II anchor bolt* and the Drillco Maxi-Bolt anchor bolt.*

Double spacing takes up an unnecessary amount of space. Space-and-a-half will maintain the ease of reading but save room as well.

Criteria for Selecting Anchor Bolts

I established three criteria that ~~best~~ describe the desired characteristics of the new anchor bolt. ~~These criteria are listed~~ in order of importance:

- Favorable design characteristics
- Ease of installation
- Lowest cost

Readers may more easily follow the logic of the report if the general approach (the methodology) is presented before the specifics (the criteria for evaluation).

What additional problems have you identified in this report?

Methodology for Evaluating Anchor Bolts

In evaluating the Hilti Kwik Bolt II anchor bolt and the Drillco Maxi-Bolt anchor

*~~See Glossary for definitions of terms.~~ All terms marked with an asterisk are defined in the Glossary in Appendix A on page 11.

DRAFT

bolt, I used several methods of gathering information. The main method I used was reading vendor brochures, technical guides, and a technical standard. This provided a substantial amount of information about the two bolt types. Also I gathered information by distributing an expansion anchor preference questionnaire and by interviewing an engineer familiar with the two bolt types.

CONCLUSIONS

The evaluation of the Hilti Kwik Bolt II and the Drillco Maxi-Bolt produced the following results.

Generally single space the items in a list and double space between these items.

- In terms of design characteristics, the Hilti Kwik Bolt II has four of the most important characteristics. The Drillco Maxi-Bolt has only one and it is the least important characteristic.
- In terms of ease of installation, the Hilti Kwik Bolt II satisfied both installation requirements. The Drillco Maxi-Bolt satisfied neither of them.
- In terms of lowest cost, the Hilti Kwik Bolt II satisfied this criterion because it was at least 20% cheaper in cost than the Drillco Maxi-Bolt.

RECOMMENDATION

I recommend that the Civil Engineering Department approve the Hilti Kwik Bolt II for future use at GGNC. This bolt is suitable for use at GGNS because it adheres to all the established criteria, with the exception of load capacity. Although this bolt type does not have the highest load capacity, it is acceptable. The load capacity is very similar to that

The word- and sentence-level editing makes the report easier to read.

FIGURE 8.10 **Draft of Feasibility Report Marked for Revision and Editing (continued)**

Repaginate to eliminate orphan.

of the Hilti Kwik Bolt which was used at GGNS for a long time.

Make sure that the visual cues allow readers to easily and quickly distinguish between levels of headings.

DISCUSSION

Description of Bolts

The Hilti Kwik Bolt II and the Drillco Maxi-Bolt represent two different anchor designs with each having an ultimate tensile stress of 125,000 psi. The primary difference between the two bolts is the anchoring mechanism. The Hilti Kwik Bolt II has a wedge anchoring mechanism and is classified as a wedge anchor.* (See Figure 1.) Also it is a nonductile expansion anchor because of its nonductile failure characteristics. The Drillco Maxi-Bolt has a sleeve anchoring mechanism and is classified as a sleeve anchor.* (See Figure 2.) This anchor has ductile failure characteristics and is also called a ductile expansion anchor. ← Insert Figures 1, 2 here

Incorporate critical figures and tables as close to the text reference as possible after the end of the paragraph.

Criterion 1:
Favorable Design Characteristics) close up spacing

The new anchor bolt must have five characteristics. ~~They are~~ listed here, in order of importance:

- Largest assortment of bolt diameters and bolt lengths
- Minimum bolt embedment
- Minimum bolt spacing*
- Minimum free edge distance*
- Highest load capacity

Eliminate unnecessary repetition by changing the first mention of the glossary to include references to all succeeding asterisks.

(ital)
Hilti Kwik Bolt II. The bolt diameters for this bolt type range in sizes from $^1/_4$" to 1" in $^1/_8$" increments excluding $^7/_8$". Also each bolt diameter is available in ~~a~~ at least two lengths. For example, the $^1/_2$" diameter bolt is available in $2^3/_4$", $3^3/_4$", $4^1/_2$", and $5^1/_2$" lengths. The large variety of sizes for this bolt type broadens the number of its applicable uses.

~~*See Glossary for definitions of terms~~

FIGURE 8.11 **Final Version of a Revised and Edited Feasibility Report**[11]

*The choice to use **BOLD ALL CAPS** draws attention to the title. The brevity of the title makes **BOLD ALL CAPS** acceptable in this situation.*

The title clearly informs readers about the topic (expansion anchors) and the approach (feasibility).

EXPANSION ANCHOR FEASIBILITY REPORT

Joe Montalbano

Engineering Assistant II

June 4, 20—

Prepared for

Nayan Deshpande

Engineering Supervisor

Civil Engineering Department

Grand Gulf Nuclear Station

FIGURE 8.11 **Final Version of a Revised and Edited Feasibility Report[11] (continued)**

The headings identify the content of each section rather than simply specify the section of the report—that is, Methodology for Evaluating Anchor Bolts rather than just Methodology.

Page numbers are right justified.

Dot leaders help readers visually track from the topic to the page number.

The organization and typography of the table of contents match what appears in the report itself.

Only the first page number of a section is listed in the table of contents.

TABLE OF CONTENTS

FIGURE 8.11 **Final Version of a Revised and Edited Feasibility Report[11] (continued)**

The abstract should preview both the content and the organizational structure of the feasibility study.

The specific headings help readers anticipate the content to be discussed in each section.

ABSTRACT

This report presents the result of a feasibility study of two anchor bolts—the Hilti Kwik Bolt II and the Drillco Maxi-Bolt—and recommends the Hilti Kwik Bolt II for use at Grand Gulf Nuclear Station. The study evaluated both bolt types in terms of three criteria: design characteristics, ease of installation, and low cost.

INTRODUCTION: NONDUCTILE EXPANSION ANCHORS AT GGNS

The nonductile expansion anchor has a long history of use at Grand Gulf Nuclear Station (GGNS). The nonductile expansion anchor used almost exclusively has been the Hilti Kwik Bolt anchor bolt. This wedge-type anchor is essential for installation of a wide variety of components including conduit supports, pipe supports, instrument supports, and ventilating and air conditioning supports.

Replacement of the Hilti Kwik Bolt is required because the manufacturer recently discontinued its production. As a result, I conducted a search for a replacement by evaluating two types of anchor bolts: the Hilti Kwik Bolt II anchor bolt* and the Drillco Maxi-Bolt anchor bolt.*

The report uses first person ("I") because the individual engineer is making a recommendation. By using first person, he accepts responsibility for his recommendation.

Placing the Methodology before the Criteria helps readers understand the overall approach before they learn about the specifics.

METHODOLOGY FOR EVALUATING ANCHOR BOLTS

In evaluating the Hilti Kwik Bolt II anchor bolt and the Drillco Maxi-Bolt anchor bolt, I used several methods of gathering information. The main method was reading vendor brochures, technical guides, and a technical standard. This information provided a substantial amount of background about the two bolt types. I also gathered information by distributing an expansion anchor preference questionnaire to engineers and by interviewing an engineer familiar with the two bolt types.

Glossary terms are easy to identify because they're marked with an asterisk and clearly defined.

What additional strengths have you identified in this report?

*All terms with an asterisk are defined in the Glossary in Appendix A on page 9.

CRITERIA FOR SELECTING ANCHOR BOLTS

I established three criteria, in order of importance, that describe the desired characteristics of the new anchor bolt:

Bulleting the criteria helps readers see their importance.

- Favorable design characteristics
- Ease of installation
- Low cost

CONCLUSIONS

The conclusions and recommendation are put up front so that readers know the critical information first. The supporting discussion follows for readers who want more information or who want to understand the rationale for the decision.

My evaluation of the Hilti Kwik Bolt II and the Drillco Maxi-Bolt led me to the following conclusions.

- In terms of design characteristics, the Hilti Kwik Bolt II has four of the most important. The Drillco Maxi-Bolt has only one, and it is the least important.
- In terms of ease of installation, the Hilti Kwik Bolt II satisfies both installation requirements. The Drillco Maxi-Bolt satisfies neither of them.
- In terms of lower cost, the Hilti Kwik Bolt II satisfies this criterion because it is at least 20 percent lower in cost than the Drillco Maxi-Bolt.

RECOMMENDATION

I recommend that the Civil Engineering Department approve the Hilti Kwik Bolt II for future use at GGNS. This bolt meets all the established criteria, with the exception of load capacity. Although this bolt type does not have the highest load capacity, it is acceptable. The load capacity is very similar to the Hilti Kwik Bolt, which was used at GGNS for a long time.

DISCUSSION

In this section, I provide an overall description of the two different bolts and then discuss the three criteria that influenced my recommendation.

Description of Bolts

The Hilti Kwik Bolt II and the Drillco Maxi-Bolt represent two different anchor designs, each having an ultimate tensile stress* of 125,000 psi. The primary difference between the two bolts is the anchoring mechanism. The Hilti Kwik Bolt II has a wedge anchoring mechanism and is classifiedas a wedge anchor.* (See Figure 1.) Also it is a nonductile expansion anchor because of its nonductile failure characteristics. The Drillco Maxi-Bolt has a sleeve anchoring mechanism and is classified as a sleeve anchor.* (See Figure 2.) This anchor has ductile failure characteristics and is also called a ductile expansion anchor.

Figures 1 and 2 are proportional in size and placed side by side for fair and easy comparison. Note that both are referred to in the text.

FIGURE 1:
Hilti Kwik Bolt II
Source: *Hilti Technical Guide*

FIGURE 2:
Drillco Maxi-Bolt
Source: *Drillco Maxi-Bolt Brochure*

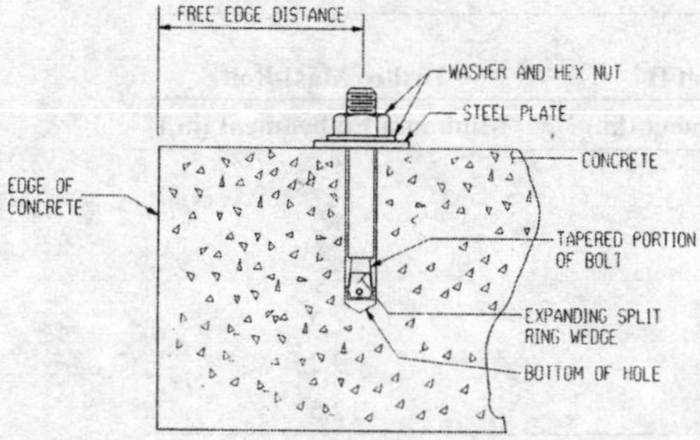

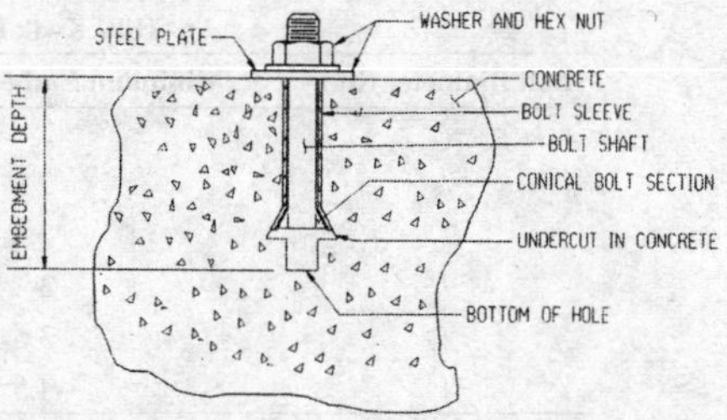

Criterion 1: Favorable Design Characteristics

The new anchor bolt must have five characteristics, listed here in order of importance:

Using a bulleted list to specify the favorable design characteristics helps readers know what to look for in the assessment of each bolt.

- Largest assortment of bolt diameters and bolt lengths
- Minimum bolt embedment
- Minimum bolt spacing*
- Minimum free edge distance*
- Highest load capacity*

Differentiating heading levels — on this page a level-3 heading — helps readers understand the hierarchical relationships in your discussion.

Hilti Kwik Bolt II. The bolt diameters for this bolt type range in size from $^1/_4$" to 1" in $^1/_8$" increments excluding $^7/_8$". Also each bolt diameter is available in at least two lengths. For example, the $^1/_2$" diameter bolt is available in $2^3/_4$", $3^3/_4$", $4^1/_2$", and $5^1/_2$" lengths. The large variety of sizes for this bolt type broadens the number of its applicable uses.

The bolt embedment is the portion of the bolt's overall length that is embedded in concrete (Standard 6). Each bolt diameter has a minimum embedment as indicated in Table 1. In comparing the embedment values given in Table 1, you will notice that the Hilti Kwik Bolt II has at least 33 percent shallower embedment than the Drillco Maxi-Bolt. Shallower embedments allow faster bolt installation.

Table 1 provides readers with an easy-to-read comparison that summarizes information. Note that the table is referred to in the text.

TABLE 1:

A Comparison of Embedments

	Hilti Kwik Bolt II	Drillco Maxi-Bolt
Bolt Diameter (in.)	**Minimum Embedment (in.)**	**Minimum Embedment (in.)**
$^1/_4$	2	3
$^3/_8$	2	4.5
$^1/_2$	2.5	6
$^5/_8$	3	7.5
$^3/_4$	3.5	9.25
1	4.5	12.5

Source: Standard No. SERI-CS-03, "Standard for Design of Concrete Expansion Anchors"

Providing the citation for the information in Table 1 helps readers assess its credibility.

The bolt spacing and free edge distance represent minimum spacing requirements. These design characteristics are smaller for the Hilti Kwik Bolt II than the Drillco Maxi-Bolt. The smaller bolt spacing means the bolts can be installed close to each other. The small free edge distance means that the bolt can be located closer to the edge of a concrete structure. Instances where these design characteristics can be advantageous are on concrete walls or floors of the plant where there is limited room for additional items.

Readers are referred to the attached appendixes, which increases the likelihood that they'll check that information.

The load capacity of the Hilti Kwik Bolt II is measured in terms of pullout force* and shear force.* For each bolt diameter, Appendix B shows the maximum pullout forces produced at the maximum embedment. Appendix C shows the maximum shear force for each bolt diameter. These two appendixes indicate that pullout forces and shear forces for the Hilti Kwik Bolt II are consistently lower than the yield forces and shear forces for the Drillco Maxi-Bolt. (The pullout forces and shear forces are also lower than for the original Hilti Kwik Bolt.) The lower forces mean that the Hilti Kwik Bolt II is not as strong as the other two bolts.

Drillco Maxi-Bolt. This bolt is available in the same bolt diameters as the Hilti Kwik Bolt II. But for each bolt diameter there are fewer alternate bolt lengths. The lengths of the bolts range from $4^1/_2$" for $^1/_4$" bolts to $16^1/_2$" for 1" bolts.

The embedments for the Drillco Maxi-Bolt are shown in Table 1 on page 4. The embedment for each diameter Drillco Maxi-Bolt is consistently larger than for the Hilti Kwik Bolt II. These deeper embedments are unfavorable because when bolts are installed in reinforced concrete, there is an increased probability of damaging or severing the reinforcing steel.

Like many paragraphs in this report, this paragraph uses given-new principles to provide coherence for readers.

The bolt spacing and the free-edge distance for this particular bolt type are dependent on bolt embedment. Because the embedment of the Drillco Maxi-Bolt is deeper than the Hilti Kwik Bolt II, it follows that the bolt spacing and free edge distance are larger. These larger spacing characteristics are a disadvantage because a larger area is required to produce the rated load capacity of the bolts.

Like many paragraphs in this report, this paragraph uses a clear topic sentence to help readers anticipate what is coming in the next few sentences.

The load capacity of the Drillco Maxi-Bolt is measured in terms of yield force* and maximum shear force. For each bolt diameter, Appendix B shows the yield force corresponding to the maximum embedment. Appendix C shows the maximum shear force for each bolt diameter. Both appendixes indicate that the yield forces and the shear forces of the Drillco Maxi-Bolt are consistently higher than the forces shown for the other two bolt types. The higher forces mean that this bolt type is stronger.

The conclusions are clearly labeled and formatted in a bulleted list so they are easy to distinguish from the rest of the text.

Conclusions about Design Characteristics. Based on the information provided for each design characteristic, I have made the following conclusions:

- The Hilti Kwik Bolt II has the largest assortment of bolt diameters and bolt lengths because it provides more alternate bolt lengths for each bolt diameter.
- The Hilti Kwik Bolt II has the desired minimum embedment characteristic because it requires a shallower embedment than the Drillco Maxi-Bolt.
- The Hilti Kwik Bolt II has the desired minimum bolt spacing and minimum free edge distance characteristic because this bolt type provides the smallest distance dimension.
- The Drillco Maxi-Bolt has a higher load capacity than the Hilti Kwik Bolt II.

The Hilti Kwik Bolt II is preferred in terms of design characteristics over the Drillco Maxi-Bolt because it satisfies four of the most important design characteristics. Its load capacity is only slightly lower than the Hilti Kwik Bolt.

A summary conclusion for criterion 1 removes any ambiguity that might have remained if the writer had simply presented the bulleted list of conclusions.

The same structure used to organize the information for criterion 1 is used here to organize the information for criterion 2: required features, compliance of Kwik Bolt II, compliance of Drillco Maxi-Bolt, and conclusion.

Criterion 2: Ease of Installation

Because of the anticipated high frequency of use of the new anchor bolt, it must meet the following installation requirements:

- Easy installation process
- Average installation time of less than 2 hours

Hilti Kwik Bolt II. The process of installing the Hilti Kwik Bolt II consists of three easy steps:

1. Drill a hole in hardened concrete.
2. Insert the bolt in the hole to the desired embedment.
3. Set the anchor by torquing the nut down.

The installation process is so simple that it takes an average of only $1^1/_4$ hours with a few standard tools.

Drillco Maxi-Bolt. The installation of the Drillco Maxi-Bolt is a more involved, four-step process:

1. Drill a hole in hardened concrete.
2. Cut the undercut shape at the appropriate location in the hole.
3. Insert the bolt in the hole to the desired embedment.
4. Set the anchor by torquing the nut down.

This more involved process takes $2^1/_2$ hours and requires special tools such as the Maxi-Bolt undercutting tool and the Maxi-Bolt setting tool.

Conclusion about Installation. The Hilti Kwik Bolt II satisfes both ease of installation requirements, while the Drillco Maxi-Bolt does not satisfy either of them.

Criterion 3: Low Cost

The new anchor bolt must be the less expensive of the two bolt types being evaluated. Since the different bolt sizes are packaged in various quantities, I needed to determine a per unit cost for the Hilti Kwik Bolt II and the Drillco Maxi-Bolt. Table 2, which shows the per unit cost, indicates that for each bolt diameter the cost for the Hilti Kwik Bolt II is a minimum of 20 percent less than the Drillco Maxi-Bolt.

Table 2, referred to in the text, summarizes the critical information about cost, in a display that is far more efficient and effective than using sentences. Whereas Table 1 came from a single source about industry standards, this table has been constructed by the author from two different sources, both of which are noted.

TABLE 2:
Cost Comparison

	Hilti Kwik Bolt II	Drillco Maxi-Bolt
Bolt Diameter (in.)	**Cost[1]**	**Cost[1]**
1/4	$2.20	$2.65
3/8	3.05	4.00
1/2	4.30	5.55
5/8	5.10	6.35
3/4	6.15	7.40
1	7.50	9.45

[1]cost per bolt

Source: *Hilti Technical Guide* and *Drillco Maxi-Bolt Brochure*

Conclusion about Cost. Based on the available cost information presented in Table 2, I recommend the Hilti Kwik Bolt II.

Because the overall conclusions were presented near the beginning of the report, when the discussion of the criteria is completed, the report simply stops (with appendixes added).

The appendixes that accompanied the actual feasibility report are not included here.

1. **Edit sentences for wordiness.** Work in a small group with a few classmates. For each of the following sentences, prepare a less wordy revision. Explain to your classmates why you think your revision is an improvement given the context, audience, and purpose that you envision.

   - It has come to my attention that the lights in my office have not been working.
   - Subsequent modifications will be disseminated to all users.
   - The deterioration of her condition led to the determination that surgery was necessary.
   - When the inspector did not accept this data, claiming it was unreliable, we were not so inefficient as to reject suggestions for alternative testing methods.
   - A 35mm SLR (single lens reflex) camera is a camera (a light-tight box that uses a physical means of reproducing an image and a chemical means of preserving it) that uses film of 35mm width and allows the photographer to see the image to be photographed through a single lens, the one used to expose the film, rather than through a second one used only for viewing the image.
   - A single-lens method of viewing the image to be photographed is preferable to the viewfinder or rangefinder method, in which the user "finds the view" through a separate lens because it eliminates the problem of parallax error, or not seeing precisely what will be photographed.

2. **Revise law to make more comprehensible.** Read the following state law explaining fishing regulations and then revise to clarify, while maintaining necessary information.[12]

   Lake or Pond Partly in Another State. If, in the case of a lake or pond situated partly in this state and partly in another state, the laws of such other state permit fishing in that part thereof lying within such other state by persons licensed or otherwise entitled under the laws of this state to fish in that part of such lake or pond lying within this state, persons licensed or otherwise entitled under the laws of such other state to fish in the part of such lake or pond lying within such other state shall be permitted to fish in that part thereof lying within this state, and, as to such lake or pond, the operation of the laws of this state relative to open and closed seasons, limits of catch, minimum sizes of fish caught and methods of fishing shall be suspended upon the adoption and during the continuance in force of rules and regulations relative to those subjects and affecting that part of such lake or pond lying within this state, which rules and regulations the director is hereby authorized to make, and from time to time add to, alter and repeal.

3. **Use a software editing program.** Select a document that you have written that still needs careful editing — that is, you still need to clean up stylistic problems as well as eliminate errors in mechanics and usage. Then go to your school (or company) computer lab and select one of the software packages that does this kind of editing. Run the software program to identify problems in style, mechanics, and usage. Make the corrections that you believe will improve your document.

4. **Evaluate a software editing program.** Write a review of the software you used in Assignment 3 and evaluate the effectiveness of the software. Prepare this review for publication in a local Society for Technical Communication newsletter so that other technical communicators and professionals who might use this software may have access to it.

5. **Interview a professional, part III.**

   (a) Arrange to interview a professional technical writer or a technical professional in your field who revises and edits frequently. During the third part of the interview (Part I of the report is an assignment in Chapter 6, and Part II is an assignment in Chapter 7), inquire about the person's approach to revising and editing. Ask some of the following questions and add additional questions relevant to the specific person and organization:

   - What kind of revising and editing do you do? How much time does it take? How important is it? Could you reduce or omit revising and editing of your documents with little negative effect?
   - What factors influence what you decide to revise?
   - How do you use revision and editing to create more accessible, comprehensible, and usable documents, presentations, and visuals?
   - How much does a draft change from the initial plan to the penultimate version?
   - What technology/software do you use for revising and editing?
   - How does your background affect your revising and editing?

   (b) Organize the information you find as part III of a brief oral or written report intended for other members of the class. This report can be posted on the class Web site or made available in print form in a class notebook in the library.

Chapter 8 Endnotes

1 Sitko, B. (1992). Exploring feedback: Writers meet readers. In A. M. Penrose & B. M. Sitko (Eds.), *Hearing ourselves think: Cognitive research in the college writing classroom* (pp. 170–187). New York: Oxford University Press.

2 Mansur, T. (n.d.). Justification for the purchase and installation of automatic roll-up doors for the R&D model shop. *Technical Writing, 42,* 225.

3 Microsoft Press. (n.d.). *Troubleshooting Excel® spreadsheets.* Downloaded October 21, 2003, from http://www.microsoft.com/mspress/books/sampchap/4757b.asp

4 Klass, P. J. (1982, January 11). Software augments manual readability. *Aviation Week & Space Technology, 116,* 106.

5 Adapted from Robe from 1000 BC found on Greek Island. (1983, July 5). *The Boston Globe.*

6 Fried, J. R. (1983). Polymer technology — part 7: Engineering thermoplastics and specialty plastics. *Plastics Engineering, 39*(May), 39.

7 Modified from the work originally done by Buehler, M. F. (1981). Defining terms in technical editing: The levels of edit as a model. *Technical Communication, 28*(4), 13–15. Based on a system developed and used at the Jet Propulsion Laboratory, Pasadena, CA.

8 Modified from a study conducted by Kohut, G. F., & Gorman, K. J. (1995). The effectiveness of leading grammar/style software packages in analyzing business students' writing. *Journal of Business and Technical Communication, 9*(July), 341–361.

9 Allen, L., & Voss, D. (1998). Ethics for editors: An analytical decision-making process. *IEEE Transactions on Professional Communication, 41*(1), 58–65.

10 *Proofreaders' marks.* (n.d.). Downloaded October 20, 2003, from http://www.m-w.com/mw/table/proofrea.htm

11 Montalbano, J. (n.d.). *Expansion anchor feasibility report.* Grand Gulf Nuclear Station, Port Gibson, MS. Used with permission.

12 New Hampshire State Fishing Laws, 1983, 6.

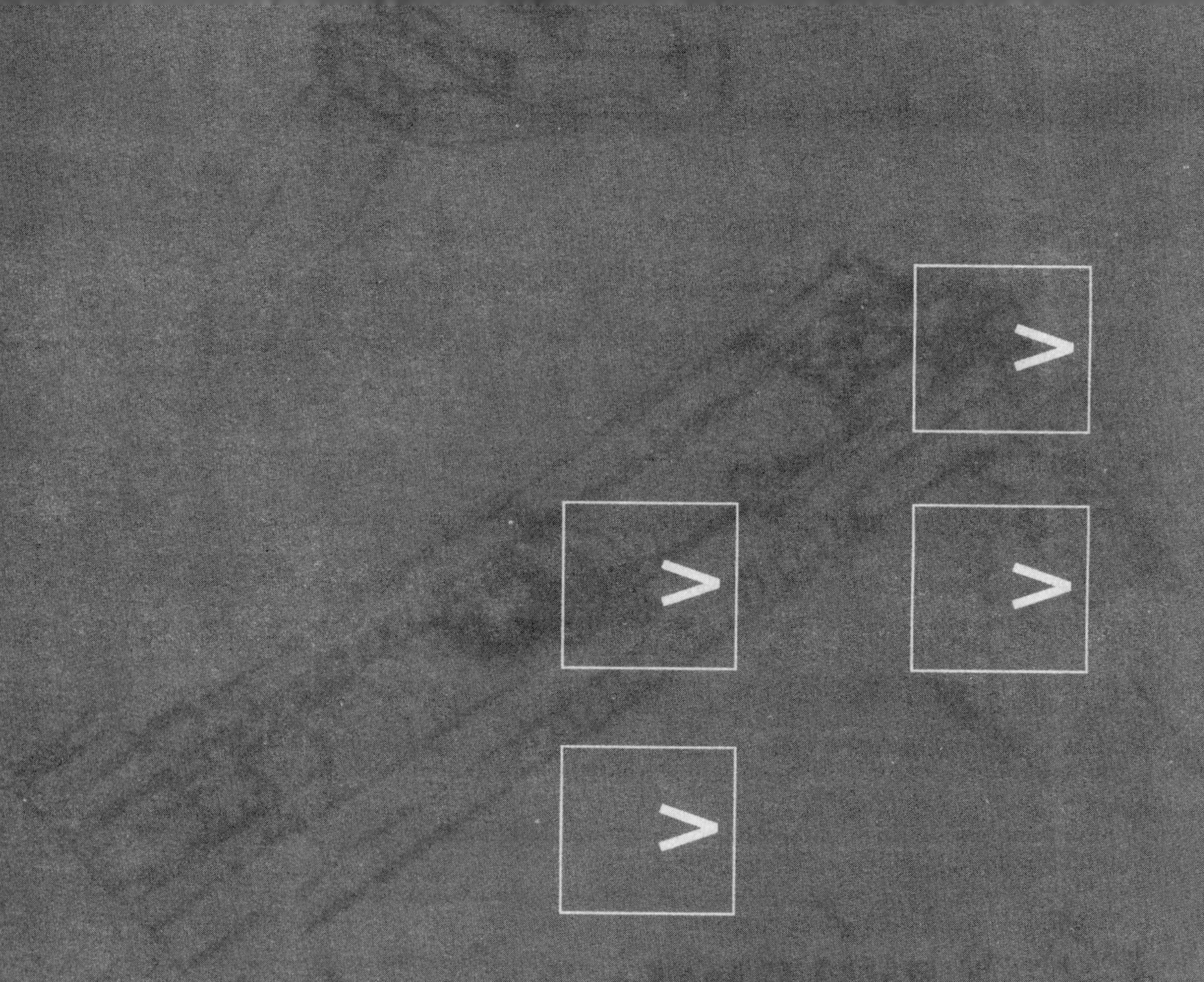

CHAPTER 9

Ensuring Usability
确保可用性

确保可用性是文件撰写、网站设计及软件程序开发的一个重要环节。但是，在产品开发的过程中，时间限制、预算紧张或缺乏确保可用性方面的技能会经常导致各种文本的可用性测试，导致产品使用过程中的修复费用。可用性的确保可以减少对客户服务的开销及增加客户满意度。本章首先讨论了确保可用性的指导原则，然后对可用性测试的概念进行了界定，并阐释了几种可用性测试的方法。本章重点介绍了如何进行可用性测试和报告结果。本章最后讨论了确保可用性的一个重要环节——确保可访性，即如何保证客户能够找到相关信息和服务。

Objectives and Outcomes 学习目标

This chapter will help you accomplish these outcomes:

- Characterize usability and understand the crucial role that its principles play in allowing people to accomplish tasks
- Understand factors that characterize usability and usability testing
- Differentiate and use text-based testing, expert-based testing, and user-based testing
- Identify, plan, and conduct various types of usability tests based on user and task analyses
- Define accessibility and understand the relationship between accessibility and usability

Think about the last time you used directions to assemble or use a piece of equipment. Were the directions clear, well organized, and helpful? Now consider the last time you encountered new computer software or used a Web site to accomplish a task. Did the design of the software or Web site help or hinder your ability to complete your task? Documents and interfaces that are difficult to understand or use or that make your experience unpleasant indicate poor usability. To be *usable,* communication — including documents, software interfaces, Web sites, and other media — must successfully meet the needs of the people using them in complex situations.

Although ensuring usability is an important step in creating documents, designing Web sites, and developing software interfaces, it too often receives inadequate attention or may even be overlooked during product development. Time constraints, tight budgets, and lack of expertise in usability often limit usability testing of print and online texts. In the long run, however, attending to usability throughout the design and development processes saves time and money. Good usability reduces costs incurred through fixing problems later, reduces the need for user support, and increases customer satisfaction. Within a company, high usability also reduces costs by increasing employee productivity.

WEBLINK

Usability is a complex and critical topic in technical communication. For a link to many valuable, even essential, usability sites, go to **www.english.wadsworth.com/burnett6e**.

CLICK ON WEBLINK

CLICK on Chapter 9/usability sites

This chapter begins with a discussion of principles that guide usability and then defines usability testing, identifies various types of usability testing, and considers their importance. The majority of the chapter focuses on conducting usability tests and reporting the results. The final section discusses accessibility, which is an important corollary of usability.

Characterizing Usability
可用性特点

The goal of usability is to place user concerns, rather than text features, at the center of the design and development processes. Usability responds to the needs, goals, skills, and contexts of people who are completing a process or using a product.

This chapter focuses on the way that texts interact with users to affect usability. Texts affecting usability may be displayed in various *materialities* and, thus, necessarily expand the meaning of the term "text." For example, the texts can be printed (usually on paper or plastic) in a manual, on a product package insert, on the packaging itself, on a tag wired to the product, or on a small label glued to a product. Or the texts can be printed or embossed on the products themselves, from face protectors for welders to hypodermic needles. Or the texts can be displayed on an LCD screen on devices ranging from laptop computers to SIDs monitors.

Equally important, texts affecting usability appear in various modes. They may be written, visual, graphic, oral, signed (as in American Sign Language), or a combination, further expanding the meaning of the term "text." For example, texts may be entirely in written language, which is typical of many technical reports and proposals. Texts may be a combination of written language and visual displays, typical in specification sheets. Texts may be largely visual and graphic, such as many Web sites. Texts may be entirely graphic, such as airline evacuation instructions for international audiences. Texts may be entirely oral, which is typical of a considerable amount of workplace training. Texts may be oral and signed, such as a presentation to an audience that includes hearing and deaf people. Texts affecting usability may take any or all of these forms, regardless of the process that users are completing or the product they are using.

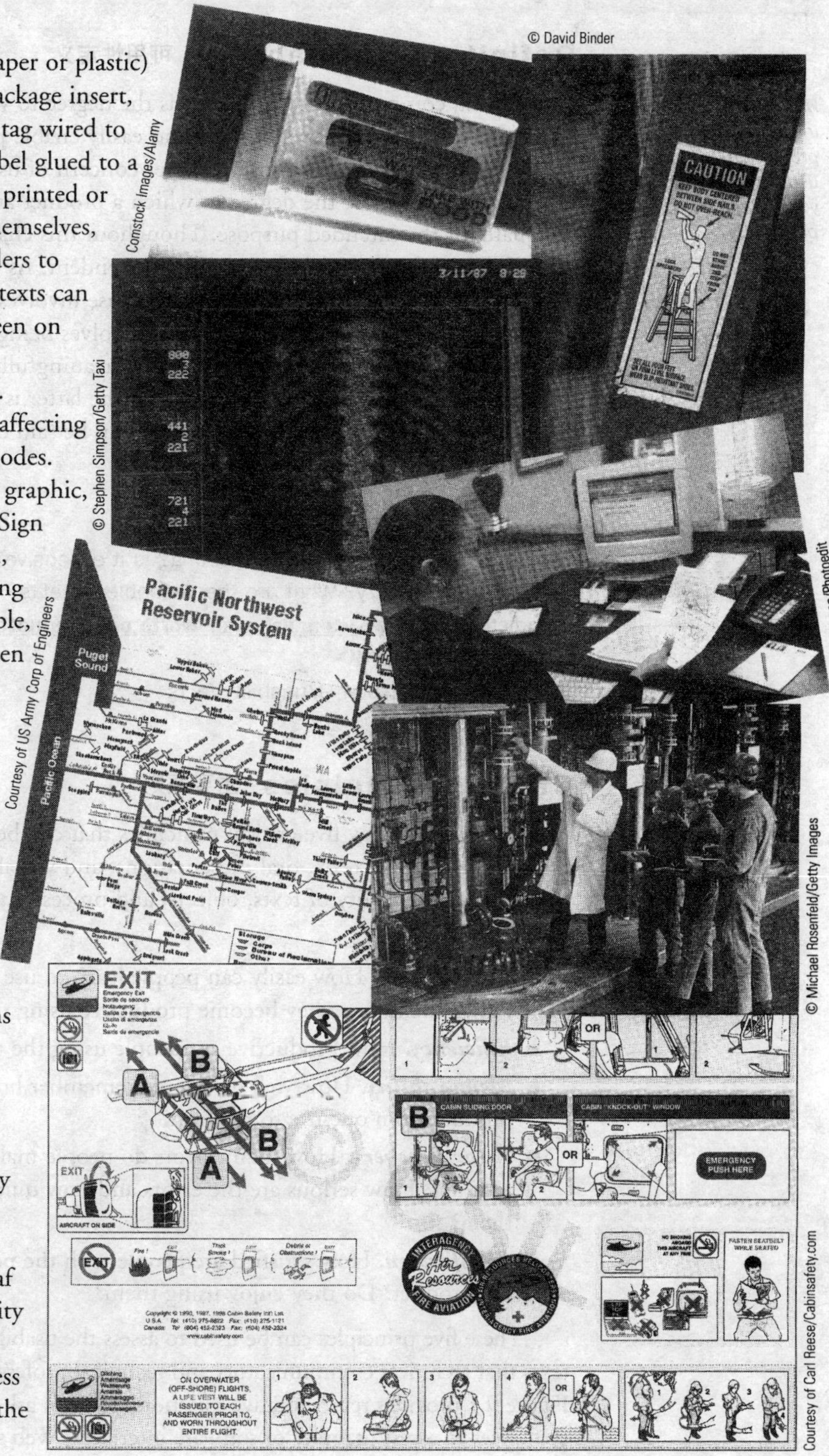

© David Binder
Comstock Images/Alamy
© Stephen Simpson/Getty Taxi
© Tony Freeman/Photoedit
Courtesy of US Army Corp of Engineers
© Michael Rosenfeld/Getty Images
Courtesy of Carl Reese/Cabinsafety.com

Definition of Usability 可用性定义

How is usability defined in your discipline or profession? Why is usability important in your discipline or profession?

In technical communication, *usability* is the degree to which texts, regardless of their materiality or mode, effectively and easily enable people to accomplish their goals. Usability is one aspect of the larger concern of usefulness. Usefulness also encompasses *utility*, or the degree to which a product and related texts are adequate for the intended purpose. Thoughout this chapter, you will see that usability, usefulness, and utility are interdependent. As researcher Barbara Mirel suggests about software interfaces, "Ease of use involves being able to work the program efficiently and easily; usefulness involves being able to use the program to do one's work in context effectively and meaningfully. Stripping usefulness from ease of use and focusing primarily on the latter is an incomplete recipe for usability or user-centeredness."[1] The same can be said of all types of communication.

WWW

WEBLINK

What's the truth behind usability testing? Is it expensive? Time consuming? Stifling? Unnecessary? What are the definable benefits? To differentiate fact from fiction, go to **www.english.wadsworth.com/burnett6e** for links.

CLICK ON WEBLINK

CLICK on Chapter 9/usability facts

Critical Principles 重要原则

Usability is guided by five critical principles that can be applied to many types of print and electronic texts, oral presentations, and visuals. These principles apply equally to the usability of texts, objects, and processes with which people interact.[2]

- ***Learnability.*** How easily can people learn to use the text and the product? How quickly can they become productive using them?
- ***Efficiency.*** How productive are people using the text and the product?
- ***Memorability.*** How well do people remember how to use the text and the product from one use to the next?
- ***Error Recovery.*** How many errors do people make using the text and the product? How serious are the errors and how quickly can users correct them?
- ***Satisfaction.*** How satisfied are people with the performance of the text and the product? Do they enjoy using them?

These five principles can be used to assess the usability of different types of texts that technical communicators and technical professionals typically develop. Figure 9.1 provides representative questions you can ask when you use these principles to assess usability of software interfaces, Web sites, and print information.

FIGURE 9.1 Representative Questions for Applying Usability Principles to Different Genres

Usability Principle	Interfaces and Web Sites	Print Information
Learnability	■ How quickly can users begin using the software to accomplish tasks? ■ Must users sift through a manual to find information about using the software, or is the interface intuitive?	■ Do textual cues help readers determine the key terms they need to learn? ■ Does the sequence of information simplify the task of learning it?
Efficiency	■ How are menu items on a software interface organized? ■ Are menus and links on a Web site labeled in a way that enables users to readily determine what content is available? ■ How many "clicks" are required on a Web site for users to access the information and services they need?	■ How quickly can readers find information using an index or table of contents? ■ Do headings help readers use the text? ■ What elements of the design (e.g., tabs, screened sidebars, index) help readers use the text?
Memorability	■ Can users remember the calculation for completing a complex task in Excel? PowerPoint? PhotoShop? Flash? ■ Can users easily remember keystroke shortcuts rather than using menus?	■ Are safety warnings clustered at the beginning of the manual or placed with the appropriate steps? ■ Are instructions written so that readers can remember steps?
Error Recovery	■ If users make a mistake, how easily can they fix it? ■ If users click to the wrong place on a Web site, how easily can they find their way back?	■ If readers lose their place in the text, how easily can they find it again? ■ Does the format assist readers in avoiding errors while performing a task?
Satisfaction	■ What will prompt users to return to a Web site? ■ Do users report that their needs are effectively met by a Web site or a software interface?	■ What will prompt readers to return to a text? ■ Do readers report that their needs are effectively met by a text?

Interpreting the effectiveness of each principle is highly situational; it is influenced by the genre and media, by the type and complexity of the text, and by the users' prior knowledge, experience, needs, and expectations. Consider the complexity of assessing learnability. For example, most people learn to use an automatic teller machine (ATM) fairly quickly and then learn to use other ATMs even more quickly because the task is simple, the instructions are short, the sequence of steps is usually intuitive, and the process is very similar from one situation to the next. What determines learnability in this situation? A simple measure could be that a person could make a withdrawal from virtually any ATM, whether in the United States or in another country.

Select any one of the other usability principles and explain how it might be interpreted in various situations, both simple and complex and with both print and electronic documents.

However, people typically take much longer to learn more complex tasks such as manipulating digital images. When faced with a new software for manipulating digital images, they may be faster than the first time they ever tried this type of software, but they probably won't be speedy. The task is complex, the instructions are usually long, the sequence of steps is not necessarily intuitive, and the process is usually idiosyncratic from one situation to the next. What determines learnability in this situation? Unlike using an ATM, using software for manipulating digital images is a complex process, so measuring its learnability is more complex.

Characterizing Usability Testing

可用性测试特点

Iterative is an adjective that means "repetitious."

- *In computer programming,* iterative *describes a sequence of instructions that can be performed multiple times. One pass is called an* iteration. *If the sequence is executed repeatedly, it is called a* loop.
- *In software development,* iterative *describes heuristic planning and development processes; an application is developed in small sections called* iterations. *Each iteration is reviewed and critiqued by the software team and potential end-users.*
- *In usability testing,* iterative *describes the cycle of testing, rewriting, and retesting.*

Now that you have a basic understanding of usability principles and the complexity of measuring them, this section focuses on defining usability testing, identifying the types of such testing, and considering the importance of *iterative* testing.

Definition of Usability Testing 可用性测试定义

As you've learned, usability is the degree to which texts (regardless of their materiality or mode) effectively and easily enable people to accomplish their goals. *Usability testing* is a structured process that gathers information about specific use from people similar to the intended users. This user-centered approach to testing allows people involved in all aspects of design and development to assess usability by observing people interacting with products and texts. Usability testing provides a realistic context (whether in natural workplace settings or in testing labs) for measuring learnability, efficiency, memorability, error recovery, and user satisfaction.

Purposes. Usability testing has both immediate and long-term purposes. The immediate purpose is to identify problems prior to the release of a text so the problems can be fixed. A long-term purpose is to maintain a historical record of test results and benchmarks that can be referenced during development. This is particularly helpful for future editions of documents, for the development of additional materials, or for new versions of Web sites or interfaces.

In usability testing, test administrators elicit feedback from subject matter experts, design and development professionals, and either actual users or testers who represent various user groups. With effective planning, implementation, and evaluation, usability testing provides specific and useful information about how well texts meet usability principles. Choices of testing procedures and selection of test participants provide information about the ways in which users think, believe, feel, and perform:

- ***Cognition.*** How are users thinking about the text?
- ***Perception.*** How do users understand the text? Envision results of use?
- ***Affect.*** What are users' attitudes toward the text and the process they're engaged in?
- ***Performance and behavior.*** What do users actually do with the text (and, of course, with the product)? How do they try to solve problems? What do they do when faced with a problem?[3]

Quality Standards. Usability testing is one method of ensuring high-quality texts. When a text is not usable, various kinds of minor, moderate, or severe problems result. Minor problems probably irritate users, but they do not actually delay the completion of the task. Moderate usability problems actually hinder completion of the task, but users usually can develop workarounds. However, severe usability problems prevent the completion of the task or "result in catastrophic loss of data or time."[4]

Many types of communication benefit from careful testing: Web sites, software interfaces, online help and user manuals, form letters, advertising copy, product descriptions, spec sheets, and standard sections of proposals (such as the boilerplate sections about an organization). Usability testing should not be limited to the language sections of communication; other components should be tested as well, including visuals and the overall design. Your goal is to determine the effectiveness of communication quality for the intended audience.

The International Organization for Standardization (ISO) defines usability as "the extent to which a product can be used by specified users to achieve specified goals with effectiveness, efficiency and satisfaction in a specified context of use."[5] ISO 9241, *Guidance on Usability*, is one of several ISO standards that are central to quality and usability. For a link to sites dealing with ISO and usability, go to **www.english.wadsworth.com/burnett6e**.
CLICK ON WEBLINK
CLICK on Chapter 9/ISO and usability

WEBLINK

Limitations 局 限

Testing results are only as good as the tests; they can be accurate but not necessarily representative. Usability tests, whether conducted in usability labs or in work sites, can't be conducted on every potential user and in every likely situation, so when you're designing a test, you need to consider these limitations:

Test validity is the extent to which tests measure what they claim to measure.[6] *Test reliability is the extent to which results on tests are repeatable and yield consistent scores.*[7] *Valid tests are always reliable, but reliable tests are not necessarily valid. In what ways might weak reliability or weak validity of usability tests distort the results and lessen their usefulness?*

- ***Test participants.*** The usefulness of test results depends in part on choosing test participants who reflect the needs and attitudes of the actual end users.
- ***Test situation.*** Testing doesn't guarantee a communication's usefulness. In order to be generalizable beyond the specific situation, tests need to be carefully designed to reflect a variety of situations in which the communication will be used.
- ***Test techniques.*** Test techniques must be appropriate at various stages of text development. Different stages require different procedures. For example, user testing does not replace evaluations such as expert or technical reviews; it supplements them. Your goal should be to design appropriate testing for each stage of development.
- ***Testing procedures.*** Testing procedures can also affect results. However, with effective planning, implementation, and evaluation, testing can provide more specific and useful information than other forms of feedback (such as postpublication satisfaction surveys).

Benefits 益处

Everyone involved in the design and development of technical communication — writers, designers, technical experts, managers, designers, editors, prepress technicians, print/production managers — agrees that testing takes time. The

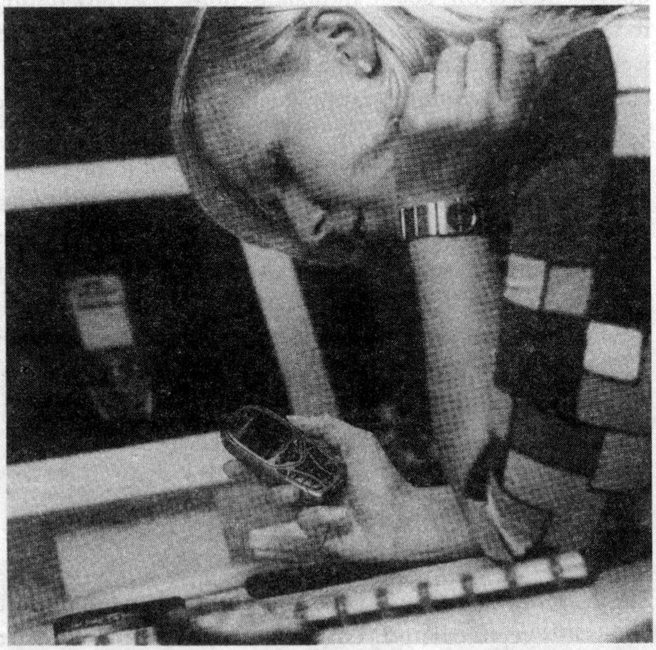

Courtesy of Siemens

Testing in Siemens' ICM Usability Lab.[8] One of the benefits of testing is eliminating expensive design changes at late stages of development. This is one of the reasons that many companies have a usability lab. The test participant in this photo is in the Siemens' ICM Usability Lab, testing a cell phone to determine how easy it is to operate. Other typical users test the menus and keys on cell phones and cordless phone in all stages of development to determine their ergonomic comfort. In various scenarios, users in the lab might use the phones themselves, print directions, or access online help.

benefits, though, are undeniable, because a well-planned usability testing program can provide invaluable information for revising and editing communication. Successful testing looks for unrecognized problems so that they can be eliminated; testing communication for flaws you've already identified wastes time and energy.

Does usability really matter? To read some success stories about the benefits of usability, go to **www.english.wadsworth.com/burnett6e** for links.
CLICK ON WEBLINK
CLICK on Chapter 9/usability benefits

WEBLINK

Types of Usability Testing
可用性测试种类

Organizations must make testing part of their process development and production schedules, or it simply will not get done. As the value of testing becomes more widely recognized, more organizations are employing some kind of testing. In the long run, testing during development and revision is much more cost effective than dealing with the results of poor communication. Testing throughout the development process increases the chances that serious usability problems can be avoided. Waiting until the project is completed to do some kind of testing usually means that no time will exist to incorporate necessary changes.

What important information about usability might you miss if you just asked users to recall the path they took in moving through a series of steps to activate online banking? To sort materials into recycling bins? To store hazardous products according to OSHA guidelines?

Three broad categories of testing — text-based, expert-based, and user-based testing — are distinguished by the ways the information is collected and by the nature of the feedback. Each type of test provides a different kind of feedback that can be used to improve communication quality. When you have access to information from several kinds of testing, you can suggest changes to improve the functionality as well as the technical and textual accuracy of communication. Perhaps more important, you can make communication more accessible, comprehensible, and usable for your intended audience.

When you decide to conduct a usability test, you can choose from quite a number of tests. The links at **www.english.wadsworth.com/burnett6e** provide specific information about tests you can administer, ranging from card sorting and focus groups to surveys and user profiles, from think-aloud protocols to observations of task performance.
CLICK ON WEBLINK
CLICK on Chapter 9/test choices

WEBLINK

Most kinds of testing can be *structured* (that is, planned to include specific questions and tasks) or *unstructured* (that is, asking for feedback without specific questions or tasks). And most kinds of testing can take place in an actual workplace or in a usability lab.

Text-Based Testing 文本测试

People doing text-base testing examine a range of local-level language, visual, and design features and then draw conclusions about changes that are necessary to improve the text's accessibility and comprehensibility. Text-based testing can incorporate a variety of guidelines and checklists, readability tests, and computer programs to assess structural and stylistic features (for example, types of sentences or active versus passive voice). It can also incorporate analyses of the visuals and the design, including comparisons between two (or more) design alternatives. Figure 9.2 identifies the general functions, benefits, and limitations of four common types of text-based testing.

Several simple text-based tests for consistency can be performed at any time in the development process on selected pages or individual documents using word-processing software such as Microsoft Word®. After checking the spelling and grammar in a text, Microsoft Word displays two types of readability test scores of your text: Flesch reading ease and grade-level ratings.

> *Imagine a technically accurate text that is assessed as having a Flesch-Kincaid score of 8.0, but the lab technicians (all with two-year or four-year college degrees) consistently make errors in implementing the new process. What factors in the text might contribute to the problem even though the reading level says "eighth-grade"?*

- ***The Flesch Reading Ease*** score claims to indicate how easy the text is to read. It rates chunks of text on a 100-point scale; the higher the score, the easier the text is presumed to be. Standard documents aim for a score of approximately 60 to 70. Lower scores indicate that the text might be more difficult.
- ***The Flesch-Kincaid Grade Level*** score rates text on a U.S. grade-school level. For example, a score of 8.0 means that an eighth-grader should be able to understand the document. Standard documents aim for a score of approximately 7.0 to 8.0. However, the purpose(s) and audience(s) must be considered in determining the grade level.

Unfortunately, readability tests are not a useful measure of the difficulty that actual users will have reading the information. Why? These readability scores are based on various ratios between word length and sentence length. While these scores do little to reflect the actual difficulty of the text because they omit consideration of critical factors such as content complexity, use of explanatory examples, use of visuals, and document design, these scores can be useful to determine the relative difficulty and the internal consistency of text. For example, if you're testing pages for a Web site and some pages score 80 in the Flesch test and others score 30, the range of scores indicates inconsistency in the writing across the site. Consistency is an issue that should be resolved before the site is tested with actual users.

Text-based tests are useful for identifying specific errors and for establishing the presence or absence of common textual, visual, and design features. Quick and inexpensive, text-based testing reminds writers and designers about things they need to check. However, such tests do have drawbacks:

FIGURE 9.2 **Text-Based Testing**

Test Types	Phases in Development: Early	Middle	Late	Post Release	Functions	Benefits	Limitations
Document Design Review	✔	✔			Assesses consistency, correctness, and conventions of design	Provides data for revision; can be formal or informal	Reviewers need to know generic and disciplinary conventions of design
Comparison Test	✔	✔	✔	✔	Compares design alternatives for the overall text	Provides data for decision making; can be formal or informal, quantitative or qualitative	Best results are achieved when substantively different alternatives are used
Visual Review		✔	✔	✔	Assesses consistency, correctness, and conventions of visuals	Provides data for revision; can be formal or informal	Reviewers need to know generic and disciplinary conventions of visuals
Editorial Review		✔	✔	✔	Assesses consistency, correctness, and conventions of language	Provides data for revision; can be formal or informal	Reviewers need to know generic and disciplinary conventions of language

- They provide generalized information without criteria for assessing how effectively a feature has been used.
- They ignore contextual factors.
- They do not assess the technical accuracy of a text.
- They do not indicate how actual users will respond to a text.

Can you think of any circumstances in which text-based testing alone would be sufficient?

Despite the obvious limitations, text-based testing can help assess a whole range of factors related to language, visuals, and design, such as adherence to language conventions, consistent terminology, sentence structure, documentation, verbal and visual coherence, adherence to visual conventions, and consistent design features. Since writers and designers have a difficult time seeing their own errors, this kind of testing can be very helpful.

Why isn't technical accuracy sufficient for a text?

Expert-Based Testing 专家测试

Expert-based testing includes several kinds of reviews: technical reviews by subject-matter experts, substantive editorial reviews, and design reviews. Expert-based testing is particularly useful for assessing technical accuracy and also for selecting supporting evidence and for identifying the level of detail for the intended audience. Recent workplace research supports the practice of using several kinds of experts in testing. Figure 9.3 identifies the general functions, benefits, and limitations of two common types of expert-based testing.

What kinds of texts do you think should be reviewed and tested by experts in several areas? What areas might benefit from expert testing in addition to those in identified in Figure 9.3?

"Expert" does not just mean technical subject-matter expert (SME). For example, consider the expert testing conducted for a user manual accompanying impendance spectroscopy software for a multinational market. The manual benefited from review by three kinds of experts: experts in engineering, in information design, and in nonnative readers of English.[9]

FIGURE 9.3 **Expert-Based Testing**

Test Types	Phases in Development: Early	Middle	Late	Post Release	Functions	Benefits	Limitations
Expert Review	✔	✔	✔	✔	Reviews various components such as design accessibility, international audiences, and legality	Provides expert feedback to developers about factors such as design, readability, legal compliance, and safety	Provides expert perspective without necessarily understanding what users need
Technical Review	✔	✔	✔	✔	Reviews text or presentation for accuracy as well as adherence to professional standards	Provides detailed feedback about accuracy of content and compliance with professional standards	Provides peer perspective without necessarily understanding what users need

Many large companies and agencies have formal review boards that read every publication that goes out of the company, both to ensure technical accuracy as well as to ensure that writers are not unintentionally revealing proprietary information (that is, guarded or secret information such as production processes). Such committees are also sometimes charged with ensuring that texts adhere to the organization's policies and practices regarding publication, which might include anything from checking the correct bibliographic format to assuring that the texts are coherent.

Formal review is a process that is mandated by some organizations. It is a sequence or cycle that texts go through to be assessed for consistency and appeal in format and design. Documents may move back and forth between writer, editor, designer, and SME and then back two or three times, or perhaps a dozen or more times. Similarly, a text may cycle back and forth between experts, for example, the SME and a graphic designer. In many organizations, texts cycle through a review-revise-review sequence several times, with different reviewers at different levels in the organization who identify problems in textual and technical accuracy.

Informal expert-based testing doesn't follow such a rigid process. Rather, informal expert-based testing generally means stopping by the office of a colleague and saying, "Sandy, I'd appreciate it if you had the time to read through this to check *X*." You fill in the *X*, asking for a review of technical content, logic of your argument, organization of information, and so on. As you develop a significant text or presentation, you may see that it receives dozens of these informal reviews by various kinds of experts.

Although experts can examine both specific and overall features of a text, they cannot predict how actual users will respond, largely because they know so much more than the intended users. However, feedback from experts is important because they can identify areas that need improvement in accuracy, completeness, coherence, consistency, and appeal for the verbal and visual aspects of a text. Revising and editing are much easier when you have expert feedback.

Experts know an immense amount about their area of specialization, certainly much more than average users. Why can't they assume the role of users and identify problems in a text?

User-Based Testing 使用者测试

Because text-based testing and expert-based testing aren't always sufficient predictors of usability, user-based testing elicits information directly from users. Revisions based on user feedback is so important that the U.S. government urges federal departments and agencies to user-test their documents. Figure 9.4 identifies the general functions, benefits, and limitations of five common types of user-based testing.

Information collected from users as they read and use a text is called *concurrent testing.* Information collected from users after they have finished using a text is called *retrospective testing.* Generally, writers have their choice of two kinds of concurrent testing.

Concurrent Testing. One of the most effective kinds of concurrent testing involves creating brief, realistic scenarios to which users can respond. Scenarios are

FIGURE 9.4 **User-Based Testing**

Test Types [All can be either *concurrent* or *retrospective*.]	Phases in Development: Early	Middle	Late	Post Release	Functions	Benefits	Limitations
Exploratory Test	✔				Assesses user assumptions, needs, skills, goals, concepts	Provides user feedback about conceptual design	Deals with abstractions; may require high level of user/tester contact
Assessment Test	✔	✔			Assesses implementation of conceptual model	Provides data about lower-level skills in time to modify design and content; focuses on user performance; easy to implement	May require high level of user/tester contact
Validation Test		✔	✔		Assesses usability; evaluates the ways components in the product or process work together	Provides data about the text for revision; provides data to benchmark future documents	Requires retesting of the changes at the last minute
Beta Test			✔		Provides limited review of initial published version of document	Provides feedback from actual users about a product in limited release	Customer already has the product; may influence their future attitude toward the company and product
User Feedback				✔	Provides postpublication review	Provides feedback that may help solve problems in later versions; provides feedback to strengthen future documents; adds information about customer base	Customer already has the product; difficult, costly, and inconvenient to fix problems; involves resources in customer service that might be spent in product development or marketing

what usability researcher Ginny Redish calls an "intersection of user analysis, task analysis, [and] context (environment) analysis" that capture a story of who, what, why, and how.[10] For example, imagine that an online airline reservation system is testing whether a new site design is accurate, fast, and hassle-free for users. Based on profiles of typical users, notes from observing other users, and conversations with individual users about situations they encounter, the test designer creates this scenario:

> Amelia James, a 26-year-old engineer who lives in Jackson, Mississippi, is considering a job offer in Houston. The company has asked her to come to Houston for an on-site interview next week. While the company will pay for her travel expenses, she has been asked to provide an airline itinerary, arriving Wednesday evening or very early Thursday morning and leaving Friday evening. Amelia prefers nonstop flights. She has less than 15 minutes before her next meeting to find the information and e-mail it to the company in Houston so the Human Resources Department can purchase the ticket she prefers.

Or imagine that a professional association offers its members the choice of receiving its quarterly publication in print or electronic format. The association wants to assess the accuracy and ease of completing an online form for switching to the online journal. The test designer creates a scenario based on file information about members, observation notes from previous testing, and conversations with individual members:

> You're busy and have little storage space in your office, so you've decided to shift from a print to an electronic journal for one of your primary professional organizations. You want to be able to receive upcoming publications electronically as well as access back issues electronically. You also want to be able to forward citations about interesting articles with your comments to colleagues and to bookmark articles you want to refer to again. You want the site to keep track of what you've already accessed. Complete the form provided by the association.

What do you see as the benefits and disadvantages of conducting tests in a natural workplace setting or in a usability testing lab?

Concurrent testing often involves watching users' behaviors as they perform a task (in a scenario or not). Whether in a natural workplace setting or in a usability testing lab, as you observe the users, you can identify places where they have difficulty interpreting or completing the information. For example, you can observe the amount of time or apparent ease or difficulty they have in locating information or performing individual tasks or sequences of tasks. You can keep notes on any number of factors, from the number and type of errors they make to their attitudes while using the document.

Another kind of concurrent testing asks users to read and think aloud — that is, not only to read aloud but also to say aloud all their comments, reactions, and opinions. Users' comments are tape-recorded as they read a document, browse a Web site, or use a software interface. By reviewing the tape, you can identify specific places where information is confusing or tasks are difficult for users.

Why is user testing often considered the most important kind of usability testing?

If you conduct user-based testing with several individuals, you will begin to see patterns of problems signaling areas in the text that need revising and editing or features of design and navigation that need improvement. As few as five to eight test participants gives you usable data for revision. Concurrent testing takes time, requires trained testers, and involves costs that are not incurred in text-based and expert-based testing. But the advantage is that writers, designers, and developers receive critical feedback directly from actual users.

During retrospective testing, why would some test participants make up what they think they probably did while completing a task rather than saying, "I don't remember"?

Retrospective Testing. Retrospective testing includes such methods as questionnaires, interviews, focus groups, and audience feedback cards. Although retrospective testing does provide information from actual users, it should be used cautiously because readers' memories are not necessarily accurate, and the information they provide is often vague. Despite the challenges of retrospective testing, it provides invaluable information. Using this feedback, you can revise and edit communication so that it is more accessible, comprehensible, and usable for the intended audience.

Conducting Usability Testing
进行可用性测试

In order for testing to ensure usability, you must carefully plan tests and incorporate them at various stages of the project. This section suggests preliminary steps for conducting testing. These generic steps will need to be modified to fit specific situations.

Creating a Usability Testing Plan 创建可用性测试计划

Before starting the testing process, define the broad goals and scope of your testing plan and determine what types of usability tests will best meet your goals, when they should be conducted, and how the results will be reported and used. Consider the following issues as you plan your testing.

1. ***Goals.*** Establish the goals for your testing. What do you want to find out? Ways to reduce time on task? To increase accuracy? To reduce calls to the helpline?
2. ***Criticality.*** Assess the importance of the text you plan to test and decide what kind of testing feedback you need. For example, Web sites and user manuals require text-based, expert-based, and user-based testing. However, this degree of testing would be excessive for a document such as a monthly progress report.
3. ***Constraints.*** Identify the constraints that you have to work with. They typically include available expertise (someone to conduct and interpret the tests), available test participants, time, and budget.

4. ***Schedule.*** Build the time for testing into the project schedule, and provide for that testing in the project's budget. Establish a schedule that, if at all possible, includes testing of different kinds as an ongoing part of the project.
5. ***Involvement.*** Explain the purpose and procedures of usability testing to all key personnel on the project so that they understand the goals and cooperate with the testing.
6. ***Timing.*** Test products and texts at various points in the development cycle, including the initial stages. Feedback on early design is essential for test results to become part of the design process.
7. ***Goodness of fit.*** Test procedures should elicit data that is appropriate and relevant to your specific goals. You may, for instance, need to test separately for information retrieval and for reading.
8. ***Ease of use.*** Test procedures must be easy for test participants to understand and for testers to facilitate.
9. ***Usable form.*** Manage the production of test data so that usable results are achieved.
10. ***Updating.*** Determine how the test results will be used as part of the development and revision process.[11]

Which of these issues will be most challenging for you? Which will be the easiest?

Many organizations expect a testing plan to be presented and approved as part of a project. Which of these issues would you choose to address in a testing plan in your discipline or field?

Are you ready to develop a test plan? To learn more about usability tools and strategies that you'll find useful, go to **www.english.wadsworth.com/burnett6e** for several links.

CLICK ON WEBLINK

CLICK on Chapter 9/usability tools

WWW

WEBLINK

A well-planned program of testing for a complex document, Web site, or software interface generally incorporates text-based, expert-based, and user-based testing at various points in the project cycle. When user-based testing is part of the design and development process, decisions about usability are based on observed use and problems rather than drawn from untested speculation. In other words, instead of working from guesses (even educated guesses) about how a product works with actual users (e.g., "When the users perform a particular task under certain circumstances, the result is probably going to be this."), user-based testing helps product developers get answers to practical questions about the ways in which the product will function ("What happens when the users do this?"). User-based testing can answer questions at various stages during iterative development while changes can be made relatively easily.

Testing processes vary considerably, depending on the kind of test you're conducting; the following steps are typical, although their specific form differs from situation to situation:

Give examples of how the complexity and time requirements of these steps will change in different situations.

- Analyze the users and tasks for which you are preparing communication.
- Locate representative test participants.
- Develop strategies for inquiry.
- Identify and prepare a test location and test materials.
- Explain the test procedures to participants.
- Conduct the tests.
- Report test results so the information can be used to improve design.

Analyzing Users and Tasks 分析使用者和任务

When you design documents, Web sites, and software interfaces, you often focus attention on content, design preferences, and perceptions of the task or activity that the communication is meant to facilitate. This focus may mean you don't adequately account for the needs of actual users, the demands of their particular situations, and the tasks and limitations of the users in those situations.

Three major components affect the effectiveness of communication: the people, the activity, and the context. Testing helps you focus on users and their tasks so you can better deal with important usability issues. For example, when you develop a Web site, you probably have in mind a target audience of people who are most likely to use your site. Since you can't know about everyone who will visit your site, focus your analysis on your perception of your intended audience or representatives of actual users.

User Analysis. Many users have significantly different skills, attitudes, expectations, and experiences than the writers and designers. What do you need to know about your users, and how do you find out? Usability experts Joann Hackos and Janice Redish, in *User and Task Analysis for Interface Design,* recommend that writers and designers investigate the ways that users think about what they do ("jobs, tasks, tools, mental models") and "how they differ individually (personal, physical, and cultural characteristics, as well as motivation)."[12] When analyzing your users, consider the user characteristics listed in Figure 9.5.

The questions in Figure 9.5 are representative, not inclusive. What additional questions can you add?

Try to answer as many of the questions in Figure 9.5 as possible about your intended audiences. Use the information to write brief user profiles that you can use to guide your design and development. To address the many different needs and situations for which you develop communication, you need to recognize that usability is determined by how well the text works for users who want to accomplish specific tasks.

FIGURE 9.5 **Characteristics for User Analysis[13]**

Learning styles	■ Do Web site users read help files and manuals, or do they prefer to experiment when they use software? ■ Do Web site users use menus, site maps, or search functions when they encounter a new site?
Physical differences	■ Do users have visual, hearing, or motor disabilities, color blindness, or other characteristics that will affect their perception, interpretation, and use of the information?
Language and culture	■ How do users from different cultures respond to different metaphors, concepts, or organizational structures? ■ Does your information need to be provided in several languages?
Reading preferences and abilities	■ Do users read material on computer screens? Scan it? Print it out? ■ Do they prefer large print? Illustrations?
Motivation	■ How motivated are users to use your information? Motivated users might be more tolerant of design flaws than users who are less motivated.
Attitudes toward the type of communication you're preparing	■ Is the communication positive or negative? ■ How will target audiences react to the communication you're preparing?
Environment in which the communication is used	■ Will your audiences use your communication at work, at home, at school, or in a public location?
Users' job titles and job responsibilities	■ Do your audiences include managers? Professionals? Craftspeople? Students? ■ Do they often use the type of communication you're preparing?
Extent, purpose, and comfort using the type of communication	■ How do your audiences perceive their level of expertise? Do they consider themselves to be novices? Experts?
Types of tasks performed using the communication	■ What tasks will your audiences use your communication to accomplish?
Levels of knowledge provided in the communication	■ What do users already know about the information? About the task?
Types of training users have received in using the type of communication	■ Have users been trained to use similar communication? Will training be provided? How much additional help or documentation will you need to provide?
Users' mental models of communication	■ How do the audiences conceptualize the tasks that your communication is designed to facilitate? ■ What metaphors do they comprehend? Use?
Users' vocabulary	■ What terms do users recognize for various tasks and products?
Tools available for using the communication	■ What technology — for example, modem speeds, screen sizes, browsers, etc. — is available to the users?

Task Analysis. Once you have completed a preliminary user analysis, select representative users who fit the profile of your target audiences and begin assessing the tasks in which they are involved. Whether you are writing a technical manual or designing a Web site, understanding the tasks people will accomplish with your communication is a critical part of assessing and improving usability. Several strategies are available for gathering information about workplace tasks:

1. Interview users about their tasks and, if possible, observe them working. Ask them to show you what they typically do and what they do most frequently.
2. Prepare a list of important and frequent tasks people do with the type of communication you're developing. Note the important tasks that your communication should support.
3. Focus on the most important tasks in detail. Several aspects of tasks are particularly important:
   - ***Task Steps.*** What individual actions are required to complete the task? Do some users use shortcuts? Conflate steps? What variations in steps and methods are possible?
   - ***Resources.*** What tools do users need to complete the tasks (documents, computers, databases, search tools)? What information do they need? What processes do they use?
   - ***Constraints.*** What limits, such as time or knowledge, affect the task?
   - ***Task Environment.*** Where is the task performed — an office, retail store, factory? Does the communication need to be portable? What aspects of the environment, for example, noise or interruptions, affect task performance?
   - ***Problems.*** What problems are common? How can they be avoided? If problems occur, what information can best be given to help the users resolve the problem?
   - ***Frustrations.*** What aspects of the task or task environment irritate users? What aspects of the type of communication you're preparing confuses users?

Once you understand the audience for your communication and the tasks in which they're involved, you'll be better able to prepare tests and identify test subjects.

Implementing the Test Plan 执行测试计划

Once your plan has been completed and you have carefully analyzed your users and their tasks, you're ready to implement the plan. This involves selecting test participants, developing and then piloting your test questions or scenarios, preparing the setting and materials, introducing the procedures to the test participants, and conducting the tests themselves.

Locate Representative Test Participants. Locate and schedule participants for your test. If you have completed user and task analyses, your user profile should identify test participants who are representative of the intended users. Successful user-based testing doesn't require the participation of large numbers of people. In fact, according to usability expert Jakob Nielsen, you can identify 80 percent of usability problems by testing your site with five to eight people.[14] Make sure, though, that your test participants have various levels of experience with the type of communication you are developing.

Why should you not have all novice users or all expert users?

Develop Strategies and Pilot Test for Inquiry. Develop a list of questions, scenarios, and key points that you want to explore during testing. For example, you may ask users to participate in a think-aloud protocol in which they respond orally to questions such as these, about a Web site:

- Describe the first items you notice on the page.
- Identify which elements on a page are actionable/clickable.
- Explain what you expect to find behind this link.
- Given the situation of *X*, show what steps you'd take to resolve it.
- Please describe your experience when trying to complete *X* task.

Before testing with participants, "test the test" with a trial or pilot run of the test procedures with other people in your class, department, or company. Pilot tests can help you identify any adjustments that you need to make to the test before testing with participants.

Conducting pilot tests adds time, effort, and expense to a project. What do you lose when you skip them?

Identify and Prepare a Test Location and Materials. Find an appropriate place to conduct tests that is free from serious distractions or interruptions (no one works in complete silence, so a little background noise will not interfere with your test) and keep the setting of the evaluation informal and comfortable. Make sure the space you choose is large enough to accommodate both test participants and test administrators without making anyone uncomfortable.

Regardless of where the test is held, prepare and inspect the room the day prior to the test. Organize all the required supplies, including copies of documents you're testing; pencils, pens, and forms for recording test activities; computers and software if applicable; tables, chairs, and sufficient lighting. Prior to your test procedure, make sure that everything is working properly.

Explain the Test Procedures to Participants. You should consider the value of writing an introductory script summarizing the test purposes and procedures that can be explained by a test administrator or read individually by the participants. A script ensures that each participant hears or reads the same introductory information about what a usability test is, how it works, and what can be done to help you get the best information.

When you are administering a usability test, are you more comfortable using a script, a full outline, notes, or your own good memory? What are advantages and disadvantages of each?

© Christina Micek

Observation Room in IBM Lotus Usability Testing Lab.[15] This corporate usability testing lab provides a room for the test participants and one for the text administrators to observe the participants.The 42-inch monitor in the observation room shows two inputs: each user's computer screen and each user's face. The large monitor enables test administrators to see exactly what the user is clicking on. The audio speakers are strategically placed so test administrators can hear what the user is saying.

Test administrators should put participants at ease, so before testing starts, tell participants the following information:

- Please be honest in your responses. I didn't design the [document, Web site, interface, manual . . .] you are testing, so your comments won't hurt my feelings.
- The test is meant to evaluate the text's performance, not yours. We expect you to encounter some problems, but if the text were perfect, we wouldn't need to test it.
- Do things just as you would if you were at home or at work. (Participants may try too hard to complete tasks to please the test administrator. For example, make sure they don't spend more time reading instructions than they normally would.)

Remind participants that they are helping you by testing the text, helping you to identify places that need to be revised in some way — reworded, defined, more fully explained, or illustrated. And remember to thank them.

Conduct the Tests. While the duration of user-based tests depends on the complexity of the communication you're testing, individual tests generally range from about 20 to 90 minutes. Test administrators should avoid asking questions too quickly and should give test participants sufficient time to frame their responses. User feedback is usually more useful when the test is run like a conversation rather than an interview. However, test administrators should focus on the user's perspective and refrain from giving their opinions about the features of the communication being tested.

Why are writers and designers typically bad choices to act as test administrators for their own work?

During the tests, record test results by taking notes, by audio or video taping, or both. Note-taking and taping both have benefits and limitations. If you choose to take notes, you can determine in advance how you will record information and you can focus on specific aspects of the testing. On the other hand, note-taking requires you to divide your attention between observing the participants' activities and writing down their reactions and comments as well as your own observtions. Recording frees you to focus on the user, but yields a considerable amount of "unfiltered" data from which you'll need to take notes later.

What are you likely to choose as ways to record information during testing? Why?

Test administrators who keep these additional tips in mind will generally obtain more useful data:

Arrange practice testing sessions with classmates or colleagues to try out these suggestions as you test drafts of your own documents.

- Ask participants for clarifications when necessary, but avoid leading questions. If you're not sure about a participant's response, paraphrase what you think the user is saying and ask if your interpretation is correct. For instance, you might ask, "Just to clarify, I think I hear you saying that following the directions on page 10 was difficult because you're not told what results to expect. Is that accurate?"
- If participants become confused or frustrated, request that they move on to the next task or question. Determine whether the participant can complete the task in a reasonable amount of time under typical conditions. Make sure to remind participants that their performance is not "wrong."
- When participants identify problems, document them clearly. Ask participants what they would recommend to eliminate the problem. Also, record information about aspects of the communication that users find particularly effective or satisfying.
- When most participants notice the same deficiency or encounter the same problem repeatedly, note the pattern and eliminate the question or task from the test. Once the presence of a problem is clear, you don't need to continue testing that aspect of the communication.
- Pay attention to participants' actions, facial expressions, and body language. What users do during a test is as important as what they say. Nonverbal communication also conveys significant information. You may be able to discern when participants are confused, frustrated, satisfied, or confident.

During the test itself, be flexible and depart from your planned questions when necessary. If users testing a text or Web site bring up issues that you didn't anticipate, encourage them to talk about what they notice.

Reporting Test Results 报告测试结果

When you follow a testing plan that includes text-based, expert-based, and user-based testing, you will collect quite a bit of raw data to review, organize, and report. Your first task will be to review your data from each test to identify key quotes, recurring comments, and interesting findings. Then determine which findings are most critical.

Organize critical findings, using categories that will be helpful in determining revision priorities and goals. For example, you might organize your findings by the assessment criteria presented in Chapter 1 of this text: accessibility, comprehensibility, and usability. Or you might focus on types of usability areas such as learnability, efficiency, memorability, error recovery, and user satisfaction.

You may also need to determine ways to quantify some results. Decisions about quantification should be decided prior to administering the test, because the way you decide to evaluate the tests may affect the type of test tasks and questions you include. Consider these possibilities:

- ***Time*** — how long test participants take to complete tasks
- ***Error rate*** — how many errors occur during various tasks
- ***Number of similar comments*** — how often different test participants note the same usability issues

User satisfaction is more difficult to quantify. However, you might ask questions about user satisfaction with various aspects of the communication using a Likert scale.

Once key findings are identified and prioritized, prepare a test report. Clearly identify your test procedures, participants, and findings. Also provide analyses of your findings that help you and others make judgments about what changes should be made to the communication you tested. Your goal for the written report is to prepare a useful and readable document for the designers and often for clients, not just a compilation of data without conclusions.

Well-written testing reports are easy and interesting to read. Figure 9.6 presents an excerpt from a testing report that describes usability tests conducted by the National Cancer Institute (NCI) on two Web-based booklets that they created for patients. Notice that the report provides readers with background information about goals, materials, test participants, and methodology before presenting results and recommendations. By conducting tests with a variety of users, including patients and clinicians, the developers were able to identify and report on specific usability problems with the booklets.

FIGURE 9.6 **Excerpt from National Cancer Institute Web Testing Report**[16]

Goals of the Usability Tests

We wanted to find out more about issues that may make an online booklet more usable:

- Will users have more success using a "detailed" table of contents (a set of links showing primary and secondary headings) or a "minimal" table of contents (a set of links showing only primary headings)?
- What makes a heading informative enough to help users find the information they are looking for?
- Do anchor links (links at the top of a page that take users to information further down that page) help users?
- Will users scroll through long pages of text? Can they easily find what they are looking for by scrolling?
- How much of a booklet do users want to print at one time?
- How much explanatory text is needed to go with icons that indicate other ways of getting a booklet? Icons include "print," "pdf," and "order" (for a paper copy).

Clear identification of testing goals, phrased as questions

What Was Tested

We tested two online booklets: *Chemotherapy and You* and *Facing Forward: Life After Cancer Treatment*. Primary audiences for the booklets include patients, their family, and friends. The secondary audience is the health care professionals who provide the booklets to the patients.

Both online booklets are written at the eighth-grade reading level.

Chemotherapy and You has information on what to expect during chemotherapy and what patients can do to take care of themselves before and after treatment. *Facing Forward: Life After Cancer Treatment* addresses issues faced by patients who have completed treatment.

Specification of online documents being tested: titles, primary and secondary audiences, content

Who Participated in the Usability Tests

Fourteen participants tested the booklets:

- 9 clinical nurses
- 1 clinical assistant
- 2 cancer patients
- 2 family members of cancer patients

Identification of the test participants: number, role, general sense of prior knowledge

Most clinicians were very Web savvy. The patients and their family members were not as Web savvy.

Methodology Used

Each participant used the two online booklets for about an hour spending one half-hour on each booklet. During this time they:

- Answered questions on who they think the booklets are for, what they think the booklets are about, and what they would do with them
- Used each online booklet to search for specific information.
- Answered questions about their impressions of the online booklets
- Answered questions specifically about the format of the icons in the booklets, the format they prefer, and reasons for their preference.

Process used to test each online document

Figures 9.7 and 9.8 show two of the recommendations included in the report — what the NCI report calls "Lessons Learned." Each separate "lesson" includes the same categories of information: a recommendation, an explanation of that recommendation, a suggestion about how to implement it, and a visual example and text summary of the problem. This deductive organization of each subsection makes understanding the argument easy: the point is made in the recommendation; the rest of each subsection provides support. The evidence is credible, in large part because readers are presented with an annotated screen capture that illustrates the problem. As a result of the organization and the evidence, the recommendations are easy to accept.

FIGURE 9.7 **Excerpt from National Cancer Institute Web Site Redesign: Classification Problem**[17]

Summary of recommendation #4a to increase usability of the navigation

4. Organize information in a way that users understand, and then write descriptive headings.

Explanation of reason for recommendation, based on testing results

Comment: When chunking information, consider the logical placement of information from the users' perspective. For example, in *Facing Forward* while 'Practical Matters After Cancer Treatment' might have seemed like a reasonable place to have information on support organizations for cancer patients, participants in our usability tests did not expect it there. An overwhelming number of participants thought they would find support organizations under 'Additional Resources.'

Suggested way to accomplish recommendation

Once the information is chunked appropriately, write headings that are descriptive of the information. On the Web, page headings become links out of context on a previous page – like the table of contents of a printed booklet. Therefore, headings should clearly explain to users what page they are about to link to.

Example 4a

Illustration of the navigation problem of the site itself.

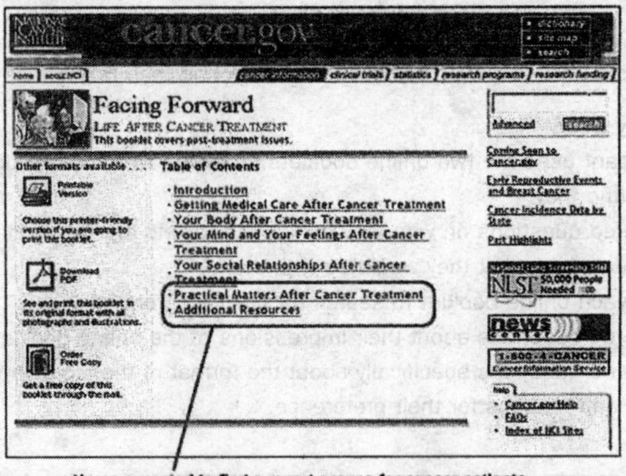

Users expected to find support groups for cancer patients under "Additional Resources." It is under "Practical Matters After Cancer Treatment."

FIGURE 9.8 **Excerpt from National Cancer Institute Web Site Redesign: Vocabulary Problem[18]**

6. Use terms that are clear and readily understandable by all audiences. Avoid jargon.

Comment: The patients and family members who participated in the testing were not familiar with the term 'complementary therapy,' a key link to critical health information. Only one patient, who had been in treatment for several years, knew what it means. (Complementary therapies are alternate therapies, such as massage therapy, yoga, etc.)

Summary of recommendation #6 to increase usability

Explanation of reason for recommendation, based on testing results: lack of familiarity with a technical term

To find out the best words to use for uncommon terms and phrases, you can use surveys, interviews and other data collection techniques.

For more information, look at http://www.usability.gov/methods/data_collection.html

Suggested way to accomplish recommendation

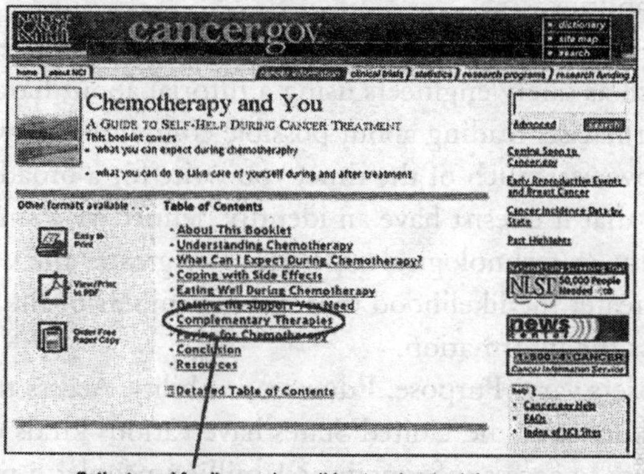

Illustration of the vocabulary problem of the site itself.

Patients and family members did not understand the term "Complementary Therapies." Only clinicians were familiar with the term.

Ensuring Accessibility

确保可访性

As part of improving usability, designers of communication, whether print or electronic documents, oral presentations, or visuals of various kinds, should also consider *accessibility,* an important aspect of usability that focuses on providing access to information and services, especially to people who have disabilities. Despite the growth of the Internet and advancements in computer hardware and software, barriers to information and to technologies used to communicate exist for many people. Technical communicators and technical professionals should promote access to information and services for all people. In thinking about audiences for all types of documents, presentations, and visuals, consider differences in users' vision, hearing, dexterity, cognition, and other learning and perception areas as well as limitations in their economic, educational, and physical environments.

Do you know someone in the United States who has a disability that affects communication?

- *Nearly 3 million people in the United States have speech impairments.*
- *Approximately 3 million people in the United States are color blind.*
- *Over 8 million people in the United States have visual impairments.*
- *Approximately 22 million people in the United States are deaf or hard of hearing.*
- *More than 40 million people in the United States are affected by dyslexia.*[19]

Mobility

- difficulty reaching equipment
- difficulty manipulating physical objects or parts

Vision

- color blindness
- low vision
- total blindness

Hearing

- selective hearing loss
- total deafness

Cognition

- memory disabilities
- perception disabilities (e.g., dyslexia)
- problem-solving disabilities
- conceptualization disabilities

Barriers to communication are created when designers don't consider the full range of users' abilities.

Sometimes you design and write for very specific audiences with whom you are familiar, such as safety engineers using a tutorial about hazardous waste disposal or pharmacists reading about possible complications with a new medication. However, much of the time, you write for a broad audience, one that is so diversified that it doesn't have an identity defined by a singular purpose, education, ability, or technological expertise. The greater the variability in the audience, the greater the likelihood that some members of the audience will not be able to access the information.

How can users vary? Purpose. Education. Ability. Access to technology. How much of the audience in the United States have various kinds of impairments that affect their ability to access information? 1 million people? 5 million? 20 million? Check the marginal annotation for demographic data.

WWW

WEBLINK

Many agencies, businesses, and organizations provide accessible information for various audiences. For a link to examples, go to **www.english.wadsworth.com/burnett6e.**

CLICK ON WEBLINK

CLICK on Chapter 9/accessible information

Principles of Accessibility 可访性原则

In an effort to address the differences and reduce barriers to communication, a group of architects, product designers, and environmental design researchers has identified seven principles for evaluating existing designs, guiding the design process, and educating both designers and consumers about the characteristics of accessibility, in products themselves and in the environments in which they're used. These researchers and advocates have collaboratively established universal design principles to guide a wide range of design disciplines, including communication. Some of these principles overlap the general principles of usability, although not all the principles are applicable in all instances:

- ***Equitable use.*** The design is useful and marketable to people with diverse abilities.
- ***Flexibility in use.*** The design accommodates a wide range of individual preferences and abilities.
- ***Simple and intuitive use.*** The design is easy to understand, regardless of the user's experience, knowledge, language skills, or current concentration level.
- ***Perceptible information.*** The design communicates necessary information effectively to users, regardless of ambient conditions or the user's sensory abilities.
- ***Tolerance for error.*** The design minimizes hazards and the adverse consequences of accidental or unintended actions.
- ***Low physical effort.*** The design can be used efficiently and comfortably and with a minimum of fatigue.
- ***Size and space for approach and use.*** Appropriate size and space are provided for approach, reach, manipulation, and use, regardless of user's body size, posture, or mobility.[20]

In what ways do universal design principles overlap with usability principles?

Identify a text or a piece of software that you have used recently that violates one or more of these universal design principles. How might the application of one or more of the principles make the particular text or software more accessible?

To learn more about universal design principles, go to **www.english.wadsworth.com/burnett6e** for interesting links.
CLICK ON WEBLINK
CLICK on Chapter 9/universal design

WEBLINK

Accessibility and Electronic Communication 可访性与电子交流

With people's increasing reliance on computers and the Internet for information and services, hardware, software, Web sites, and Web-based applications pose challenges for designers because of the diversity of the audiences. For example, to design Web sites that are usable by and accessible to the largest number of potential users, designers need to understand accessibility concepts in a number of areas including hardware, software, and design principles.

Eliminating biased or stigmatizing language is always important. Some organizations offer guidelines for unbiased language. To learn ways to avoid using biased language, go to **www.english.wadsworth.com/burnett6e** for a link.
CLICK ON WEBLINK
CLICK on Chapter 9/unbiased language

WEBLINK

FIGURE 9.9 Technology Affects Accessibility[21]

Disability	Technology Aids Access
Mobility	Special-purpose hardware and software — such as on-screen keyboards, eyegaze keyboards, and sip-and-puff switches systems — provide alternate ways of creating keystrokes for people with severely limited dexterity.
	Voice recognition is used both by people with some physical disabilities or temporary injuries to hands and forearms as well as by users interested in greater convenience. It's also an input method in some voice browsers.
	Extended keyboard and mouse capabilities provide extended keyboard, mouse, and sound access. For example, the "sticky key" function solves the problem of having to press two or more keys at once (like performing CRTL-ALT-DEL). One key at a time does the job.
	Alternative keyboards and alternative mice allow people with limited or no ability to use their hands to perform keyboard activities.
	Word prediction software predicts the word a person is typing and the next word based on word frequency and context. This software, which may include spell checking, speech synthesis, and hot keys for frequently used words, is useful for slow typists, probe or pen users, and for people with visual disabilities or dyslexia.
Vision	Scanning reading systems allow printed information to be scanned into a system and read to a person using a speech synthesizer.
	Screen readers, used by people who are blind or have learning disabilities, interpret what is displayed on a screen and direct it either to speech synthesis for audio output or to a refreshable braille reader for tactile output.
	Screen magnifiers, used primarily by individuals with low vision, magnify a portion of the screen for easier viewing. Some screen magnifiers offer two views of the screen: one magnified and one default size for navigation.
	Dynamic or refreshable braille involves a mechanical display that raises and lowers dots to allow any braille words to be displayed. Some braille printers allow simple graphics to be drawn.
Hearing	Visual notification — rather than sound notification — allows people who are deaf or hard of hearing to receive a warning about a computer error.
	Real-time chat capabilities are possible with assistive technology that helps people who are deaf or hard of hearing to participate in real-time online chats.
Cognition	WYNN software reads, spells, and defines electronic text aloud so that people with dyslexia or other reading challenges can perform day-to-day work more easily. People can simultaneously view the text and hear it read aloud, thus taking advantage of both aural and visual input.

While accessibility can be restricted because of physical or cognitive barriers, technology provides a remarkable variety of tools to help overcome such barriers. Figure 9.9 summarizes technology that helps address problems with mobility, vision, hearing, and cognition. While technology is powerful and effective, it may be expensive, incompatible with existing hardware and software, too complex to use easily, infrequently accompanied by easy-to-use and thoroughly tested instructions, and insufficiently supported by knowledgeable technicians and usable online help.

Why are accessibility principles so important to Web-based products? Technical communicators are increasingly involved in the design of Web sites and Web-based applications, as you'll read in the ethics sidebar below; thus, they must be aware of all aspects of usability, including accessibility. In addition, recent regulations pertaining to disability and information technologies require that certain Web sites, software, and other communication products meet accessibility standards. Most important, meeting the needs of people who use information technologies is ethically responsible as well as practical and profitable.

Designing accessible, usable online help for blind and low-vision users of text-based readers is important and challenging. This article provides very helpful suggestions that are clearly explained and illustrated. For a link to the article, go to <u>www.english.wadsworth.com/burnett6e</u>.
CLICK ON WEBLINK
CLICK on Chapter 9/low vision

WWW
WEBLINK

ETHICS 职业道德规范知识吧 SIDEBAR

"What You Say!" "你说什么!"

"All Your Base Are Belong to Us!" is an enigmatic phrase that has become a phenomenon on the Web,[22] which is littered with sites that tell its story. It comes from the strange Japanese-to-English translation of the introduction to Sega Genesis' 1989 arcade game *Zero Wing*, part of the story of a hapless flight crew facing off against a villainous enemy called "Cats." In 2101, war was beginning:

Captain: What happen?
Mechanic: Somebody set up us the bomb.
Operator: We get signal.
Captain: What!

What arguments could you make to colleagues who say these things:

- *"I had three years of Spanish in high school, so I can probably translate this product description; it's not very long."*
- *"Let's just use a machine translation."*
- *"It's an American product. Let's keep it in English."*
- *"I think Gemma in Public Relations has a degree in French literature from the Sorbonne. Let's ask her to translate these instructions about biohazardous waste disposal into French for the Haitian facilities workers."*
- *"Translation is simply too expensive; let them read it in English."*

Operator:	Main screen turn on.
Captain:	It's You!
Cats:	How are you gentlemen! All your base are belong to us. You are on the way to destruction.
Captain:	What you say!
Cats:	You have no chance to survive make your time. HA HA HA HA . . .
Captain:	Take off every 'zig'! You know what you doing. Move 'zig'. For great justice.[23]

Would you know how to take off your 'zig'?

Of course, poor translations from English to other languages occur as well. For instance, Coca-Cola first introduced its brand-name drink in China with a translated name that means "bite the wax tadpole." Coca-Cola corrected the unfortunate mistake, renaming the drink with a word that roughly translates to English as "happiness in the mouth." Liz Elting of Transperfect Translations notes that, "One of the biggest failures of a product was for the Chevy Nova in Latin American countries. 'No va' in Spanish means 'no go,' not a good name brand for a car."[24]

The results of bad translations may be funny, and they can be costly from a marketing perspective, but imagine poorly translated information on package insert with prescription medicine; the unusable results could be disastrous.

And what happens if no translation is provided at all? According to Andrea Perera of the *Philadelphia Inquirer,* "Nearly 30 percent of people surveyed in three major metropolitan areas in [2003] guessed at the proper dosage of their drugs because they weren't sure what their prescription said. More than half of the Spanish-speaking participants said they found it 'impossible' to fully understand their prescriptions because of language difficulties."[25] Pharmacies throughout the United States are seeking ways to rectify the problem by translating prescription directions into various languages.

When technical translations are poor or nonexistent, products become unusable and even dangerous. What should you do if you need to have a text translated?

- Don't rely on computer-generated translations, which can be particularly poor.
- Do hire a reputable translator with a track record who is fluent in both the original language and the target language of the translation.
- Make sure the translator is conversant with the subject matter. The translator's understanding of technical terms in areas such as medicine, law, and engineering is critical as well.
- Don't depend on literal, word-for-word translation to convey information. Good translations reflect cultural contexts and norms as well as correct lexical and grammatical aspects of text.
- Don't skimp on translation costs. The real costs in terms of usability will be higher in the long run.

Understandable text — in any language — is a usability issue.

Accessibility and Government Regulations 可访性与政府规章

"Accessibility" often refers to the Americans with Disabilities Act. In the case of technical communication, this means Section 508 of the statute, which requires that the electronic and information technology of federal agencies, vendors, and contractors be accessible to people with disabilities, including employees and members of the public.

What example of compliance with accessibility do you see on your campus or workplace, both in the physical environment and in the electronic environment?

As a result of this far-reaching federal act, government agencies have been reducing these barriers so that their Web sites are accessible to broad audiences. Many of them have statements that announce their efforts, such as the one in Figure 9.10, which provides recourse to users who believe that the site is not accessible to them.

Creating accessible Web sites is boring? Expensive? Too difficult? Unnecessary? Too many people have the wrong idea about what Web accessibility means. To differentiate fact from fiction, go to www.english.wadsworth.com/burnett6e for a link.

CLICK ON WEBLINK

CLICK on Chapter 9/accessibility myths

WEBLINK

FIGURE 9.10 **Public Statement of Accessibility**[26]

Home ▪ Search ▪ Subject ▪ Organization ▪ Project ▪ Facilities ▪ Resources ▪ People

NASA Web Accessibility Statement

The Web page you just visited has been reviewed to be accessible to individuals with disabilities in accordance with provisions of Section 508 of the Workforce Investment Act and the Rehabilitation Act. If you experience problems accessing this information please contact the Web site curator directly. If your initial request is not acknowledged within five business days, contact the Discrimination Complaints Program Manager at 216-433-2323, or write to the Office of Equal Opportunity Programs, NASA Glenn Research Center, Mail stop 500-311, Cleveland OH 44135.

ACCESSIBILITY AND ATTITUDE
可访性与态度

Accessibility in the workplace has to do with building access as well as with screen resolution and font size. But it also has to do with attitude and the way you communicate that attitude.

When you prepare communication for others, one of the most important responsibilities you have is to represent the needs and concerns of the people in your audience. Another is to recognize how language can either exclude and stigmatize people or include and empower them.

Read the following scenarios and consider how language can be as much a barrier to full participation as other factors in the workplace environment. As you read them and formulate a position, decide how you would behave in each situation.

SCENARIO 1

You use a wheelchair to get around. Your friend is visiting you in your home and invites you to go out to her favorite restaurant for lunch. You accept the invitation but say, "I assume the restaurant is accessible."

The friend then decides to call to make a reservation, using your speakerphone so you can listen in. The friend begins by saying, "I want to make a reservation for lunch but I also need to find out if your establishment has handicapped facilities since my friend, who is a victim of polio, is wheelchair-bound."

The manager of the restaurant responds, "Oh yes, we comply with all of the handicapped requirements. We have handicapped parking, a new wooden handicapped ramp at the back door and a newly remodeled restroom with grab bars. It has a handicap sink with a sloped mirror. We are proud to serve our friends with special needs."

© Jean Dobbs

Your reaction

You are disappointed that your friend decided to make the call in your behalf, especially now that you know how the conversation went. You resent the demeaning tone of the conversation on both ends of the phone.

Both your friend and the manager of the restaurant used the term "handicapped." You know the connotations of the word "handicap," which has its origin from beggars who put their caps in their hands on street corners. You take offense at the term, especially when it is used in a condescending manner to describe you. You do not like your friend's reference to you as a "victim" of polio. You are also not "bound" to your wheelchair; it is simply a device you use to get from place to place.

As for the restaurant manager, you question why everything, including parking, restrooms, sinks and mirrors need to be described as "handicapped." What is so special about being given access to a building and a restroom? You also do not understand why the ramp is at the back door. Why should you have to have a separate, stigmatizing experience to enter the building, and why did they choose to install a wooden ramp? You also question why they selected a special sink with a sloped mirror. Special sinks are unnecessary and expensive and sloped mirrors do not work well for standing people. An open counter with a mirror that extends down to the top of the counter works well for everyone, regardless of a person's height or standing or seating position. You believe that the choice of a "special fixture with a sloped mirror" reflects an attitude of the owner/manager, who apparently thinks of accessibility accommodations as providing extras, rather than serving everyone on an equal basis.

You do not feel "handicapped" by old or poorly remodeled buildings nearly as much as by people's attitudes.

SCENARIO 2

You use a wheelchair to get around. Your friend is visiting you in your home and invites you to go out to her favorite restaurant for lunch. You accept the invitation but say, "I assume the restaurant is accessible."

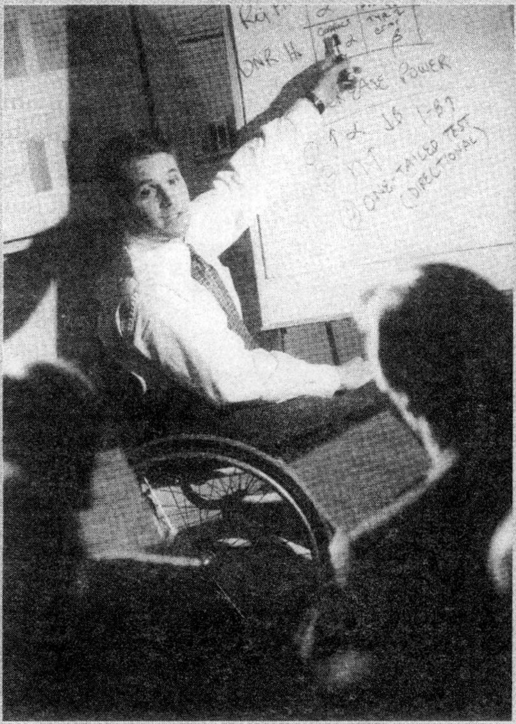

Anton Vengo/Superstock

The friend asks you if you think it is a good idea to call the restaurant to find out if reservations are needed and to make sure the restaurant is accessible. You agree that it is a good idea. Your friend asks you if you would like to make the call. You say that you would like to make the call.

When the owner/manager answers, you begin by asking if there is a wait. You also ask if the restaurant is accessible. The manager responds, "Our restaurant is fully accessible. Do you have any specific questions for me regarding access?" You answer, "I use a wheelchair. Will I have any difficulty getting in, getting seated, or using the restroom?" The manager says "No, I don't believe so, but if you do experience any problems with our building, our service, or our menu items, I welcome your suggestions on how we can make improvements."

Your reaction

You appreciate your friend's invitation to lunch and the concern about the restaurant being accessible. You appreciate your friend asking you if you would like to make the call, instead of the friend assuming that the call needs to be done for you. You appreciate the restaurant owner/manager's candid responses and the fact that you were given the opportunity to make suggestions for improvements to the building, services, and menu.

Most of all, you appreciate being treated with respect by both your friend and the restaurant owner/manager without any patronizing terms being used in the conversation.

The barriers people face can be as specific as the lack of access to the front door of a building or the content of a Web site or as general as attitudes expressed through communication. When you imagine yourself in the position of others in the workplace, you can begin to assess the ways that barriers interfere with people's autonomy and participation in workplace tasks and activities. In your communications with and for others, identify and eliminate as many barriers as possible.

Dr. Arvid E. Osterberg is a professor of architecture at Iowa State University where he teaches and conducts research in the areas of safety, accessibility, historic preservation, and design.

He also conducts building assessments and does consulting on safety and accessibility issues. He is coauthor (with Donna J. Kain) of *Access for Everyone: A Guide to Accessibility with References* to ADAAG.

Individual and Collaborative Assignments

个人作业和小组作业

1. **Evaluate a software application.** Write a review of a software application you've recently used. Evaluate the usability of the software. Prepare this review for publication in a local Society for Technical Communication (STC) newsletter so that other technical communicators and professionals who might use this software will have access to your assessment.
2. **Plan usability testing.** Select a print or Web document that you are working on that would benefit from usability testing. Prepare a usability test plan, drawing on the questions in Figure 9.5 to help you focus on the critical issues. Write the test plan as a memo to your instructor or to the client for the project.
3. **Conduct usability testing.** Select a print or Web document that you are working on that would benefit from usability testing. Prepare a testing report that includes these three parts:
   (a) Your best shot before usability testing — that is, what you consider the very best you can do in preparing the document.
   (b) The usability testing results. You must include at least one kind each of text-based, expert-based, and user-based testing. Identify the tests you selected and justification for the selection, the test results, and your analysis/interpretation of the results.
   (c) The revision of your best-shot document based on the testing results and your analysis/explanation of the changes.
4. **Assess and redesign a Web site.** Go to http://uaweb.arizona.edu/resources/makeovers/demo.shtml to study two versions of the same Web site, one inaccessible and the second one revised to be compliant with section 508.
   (a) Carefully read the features that made the old site inaccessible. Then review the revision.
   (b) Select a site to analyze that you believe is inaccessible for a portion of the intended audience. List the problems (as in the example above) and write specific recommendations for revision.
5. Do all Web sites need to be accessible to people with vision impairments? Yes, if it's a federal Web site or a site provided under contract to a federal agency. Should other sites be accessible? Yes, if they want to reach the broadest audience. To learn more about access guidelines developed by the Web Accessibility Initiative of the World Wide Web Consortium, go to these Web sites:

   http://usability.gov/accessibility/index.html#understanding
   http://usability.gov/accessibility/508.html

(Alternatively, go to **www.english.wadsworth.com/burnett6e** and then Chapter 9/accessibility for direct links.) After you have reviewed the information, prepare a presentation that could be used in a workplace workshop introducing accessibility.

Chapter 9 Endnotes

1 Mirel, B. (2002.) Advancing a vision of usability. In B. Mirel & R. Spilka (Eds.), *Reshaping technical communication: New directions and challenges for the 21st century* (pp. 167–189). Mahwah, NJ: Lawrence Erlbaum.

2 Adapted from Nielsen, J. (1993) *Usability 101* [electronic version]. Boston: Academic Press. Retrieved December 10, 2003, from http://www.useit.com/alertbox/20030825.html

3 Adapted from Nielsen, J. (1993) *Usability 101* [electronic version]. Boston: Academic Press. Retrieved December 10, 2003, from http://www.useit.com/alertbox/20030825.html

4 Artim, J. M. (n.d.). *Usability problem severity ratings.* Retrieved December 10, 2003, from http://www.primaryview.org/CommonDefinitions/Severity.html

5 *Usability Partners. (n.d.). ISO standards.* Retrieved December 18, 2003, from http://www.usabilitypartners.se/usability/standards.shtml

6 Brown, J. D. (2000). What is construct validity? *Shiken: JALT Testing & Evaluation SIG Newsletter, 4*(2): 7–10. Retrieved January 2, 2004, from http://www.jalt.org/test/bro_8.htm

7 Neill, J., Campbell, H., & Dalby, S. (2003, August 4). *Essentials of a good psychological test.* Retrieved January 2, 2004, from http://www.wilderdom.com/personality/L3-2EssentialsGoodPsychologicalTest.html

8 Siemens. (n.d.). *Testing in Siemens' ICM usability lab.* Retrieved January 2, 2004, from http://www.siemens-mobile.com/cds/frontdoor/0,2241,hq_en_0_3911_rArNrNrNrN_img%253A1124297,00.html

9 For further information, see Molitor, K. (1995). *How participants' expertise influenced expert testing of a technical user manual.* Unpublished master's thesis, Iowa State University, Ames, Iowa.

10 Redish, G. (2001). *Storytelling: The power of scenarios.* Retrieved January 3, 2004, from http://www.redish.net/content/handouts.html

11 Schumacher, G., & Waller, R. (1985) Testing design alternatives: A comparison of procedures. In T. Duffy & R. Waller (Eds.), *Designing usable texts* (pp. 377–403). Orlando, FL: Academic Press.

12 Hackos, J. T., & Redish, J. C. (1998). *User and task analysis for interface design* (p. 35). New York: Wiley.

13 Hackos, J. T., & Redish, J. C. (1998). *User and task analysis for interface design* (p. 35). New York: Wiley.

14 Nielsen, J. (1998). *Cost of user testing a website.* Retrieved October 10, 2003, from http://www.useit.com/alertbox/980503.html

15 IBM. (n.d.). *Usability.* Retrieved December 10, 2003, from http://www-10.lotus.com/ldd/use.nsf/308c971706adfdef8525640500696fa8/b89473efab094bbe852565e50070168f?OpenDocument

16 National Cancer Institute, Office of Communications. (n.d.). *Designing educational booklets for the web.* Retrieved December 16, 2003, from http://usability.gov/lessons/chemo.html

17 National Cancer Institute, Office of Communications. (n.d.). *Designing educational booklets for the web.* Retrieved December 16, 2003, from http://usability.gov/lessons/chemo.html

18 National Cancer Institute, Office of Communications. (n.d.). *Designing educational booklets for the web.* Retrieved December 16, 2003, from http://usability.gov/lessons/chemo.html

19 Meyertons, J. (n.d.). *Accessibility of online materials: Assistive technologies.* Retrieved December 10, 2003, from http://www.willamette.edu/~jmeyerto/Accessibility/workshops/technologies.htm

20 Connell, B. R., Jones, M., Mace, R., Mueller, J., Mullick, A., Ostroff, E., Sanford, J., Steinfeld, E., Story, M., & Vanderheiden, G. (1997). *Principles of universal design.* Version 2.0. Raleigh NC: North Carolina State University. Copyright © 1997 NC State University. The Center for Universal Design. Retrieved December 10, 2003, from http://www.design.ncsu.edu:8120/cud/univ_design/princ_overview.htm
For additional information, also see *General concepts, universal design principles and guidelines* from the Trace Research & Development Center, College of Engineering, University of Wisconsin-Madison, http://www.trace.wisc.edu/world/gen_ud.html

21 Meyertons, J., & Bowers, N. (2000, October 27). *Accessibility of Online Materials: Assistive Technologies.* Portland State University. Retrieved on December 10, 2003, from http://www.access.pdx.edu/workshops/technologies.html

22 Benner, J. (2001, February 23). When gamer humor attacks. *Wired News.* Retrieved January 6, 2004, from http://www.wired.com/news/culture/0,1284,42009,00.html

23 Story of All Your Base. (n.d.). *All your base are belong to us.* Retrieved January 6, 2004, from http://www.planettribes.com/allyourbase/story.shtml#game; also reprinted in Pearrow, M. (2002). *The wireless web usability handbook* (p. 100). Hingham, MA: Charles River Media.

24 Transperfect Translations, Press Room. (2003, January 6). *Bad translations make for a good laugh but are bad for business.* Retrieved January 6, 2004, from http://www.transperfect.com/tp/eng/badxlate.html

25 Perera, A. (2003, October 7). Directions for prescriptions in English a problem for some. *In the News.* Retrieved January 6, 2004, from http://www.transperfect.com/tp/eng/phillyinq100703.html

26 NASA Glenn Research Center. (n.d.). *NASA web accessibility statement.* Retrieved December 10, 2003, from http://www.grc.nasa.gov/Doc/access.html